Spotlight Canada

NEW EDITION

J. Bradley Cruxton
and
W. Douglas Wilson

Oxford University Press
Toronto

Oxford University Press, 70 Wynford Drive, Don Mills, Ontario, M3C 1J9
Toronto   Oxford   New York   Delhi   Bombay   Calcutta   Madras
Karachi   Petaling   Jaya   Singapore   Hong Kong   Tokyo   Nairobi
Dar es Salaam   Cape Town   Melbourne   Auckland

and associated companies in
Berlin   Ibadan

Oxford is a trademark of Oxford University Press

Canadian Cataloguing in Publication Data

Cruxton, J. Bradley
   Spotlight Canada

New ed.
Includes index.
ISBN 0-19-540590-0

1. Canada – History – 20th Century. I. Wilson,
W. Douglas. II. Title.

FC600.C78   1988   971.06   C88-093378-X
F1034.2.C78   1988

Cover photo: Masterfile/Bob Anderson – Sunrise, Parliament Hill,
                Ottawa, Ontario
Illustrators: Pam Kinney, Halina Below
Assembly: Halina Below
Project Editor: Geraldine Kikuta
Editor: Maryjean Lancefield
Photo Researcher: Jennifer McColl
Compositor: Colborne, Cox and Burns • Typographers
Printed and bound in Canada by D.W. Friesen & Sons Ltd.

    4   5   6   7   8   9   FP   92   91

Acknowledgements

We would like to acknowledge our long-standing and stimulating relationship with the editorial and production staff at Oxford University Press
(Canada). Since 1977, we have enjoyed the creative assistance and friendship of our editors who have helped us bring books, like *Spotlight*, to life:
Geraldine Kikuta, Maryjean Lancefield, Tilly Crawley, and Richard Teleky.
We would like to thank these dedicated and hard-working individuals for
their encouragement, insight, and professional expertise.

Dedication

For Dianne and Mary,
for your encouragement and constant support.

Contents

Canada and the World

Regional Development

Multiculturalism

Technology

Canadian-American Relations

Women

People and Lifestyles

Economics

National Identity

Canada and Britain

Politics

English-French Relation

Law

War and Peacekeeping

Labour

Government

These symbols are used throughout the book to identify major
themes in Canadian history.

1
Government: It's all around us

EARLY IN THE TWENTY-FIRST CENTURY

Imagine you have been living on a space station orbiting the earth. Now you are returning to earth on a shuttle craft called the *Cosmos*. The captain and eleven passengers are on board the craft.

Suddenly the *Cosmos* starts to lose power. The computer points to a malfunction in the rocket thrust mechanism. The captain has to climb outside the craft to fix the problem. Although he completes the repairs successfully, he accidentally breaks contact with the shuttle and drifts helplessly into space.

This is a real disaster. The captain has been lost. You are still thirty days away from earth. Everyone is wondering how the *Cosmos* will return safely. One passenger thinks she can navigate the shuttle successfully.

The passengers range in age from twelve to nineteen, and weigh from 38 to 61 kg. On board the *Cosmos* you discover the following:

- 30 days supply of fuel
- 15 days supply of food
- 21 days supply of water
- vitamin supplements and first-aid supplies
- laser weapons in a locked cabinet

Have a discussion about the problems you face.

1 What will you decide about the food and water supplies?

2 List at least three decisions you have to make on the first day after the disaster.

3 How will you select a new leader?

4 What kind of person would you want as your leader?

5 Make a list of three to five rules that will allow the passengers to live in peace and harmony for thirty days. Who will make these rules?

6 Could you survive the rest of the voyage without rules? Explain your answer.

As you examine these questions, think about the problems that face any group of people trying to work together. All organizations, groups, and nations must service the same basic needs. They must establish rules, make decisions, and choose leaders. In other words, they must set up a system of government. The people on board the *Cosmos* need some form of government to make rules and to satisfy their basic needs if they are to survive.

Governments provide ways for people to live together in an organized and co-operative manner. They also try to protect people in the society from danger. The government does this by making laws. A law is a legal rule that is enforced by the police and the courts. If a person breaks the law, s/he will be punished. The degree of the punishment is determined by the government and is based on the severity of the crime.

What would happen if we had no government? Perhaps if you lived alone and produced everything you needed to survive, you would not need governments and laws. You could do whatever you wanted because your actions would not affect anyone else. Since we do not live in isolation, organization and rules are essential. You need rules to know what you are allowed to do without harming or impeding others. These rules also protect you from being harmed or inconvenienced by others.

What is government? There are many answers to that question as government comprises many different facets and is involved in many areas of our lives. Here are a few ideas of what people think about government.

Government is the people in Ottawa running the country

GOVERNMENT CENSORS THE MOVIES

GOVERNMENT IS MY PENSION CHEQUE

Government gives traffic tickets

GOVERNMENT COLLECTS OUR GARBAGE

Government repairs our roads

GOVERNMENT PROTECTS OUR ENVIRONMENT

GOVERNMENTS OF CANADA

Governments are formed to meet our needs, to protect us, and to help us live in safety and harmony. We have many different needs and, therefore, many kinds of government activities. We also have different levels of government to meet our different needs.

Some of our needs are for fire protection, garbage collection, and road maintenance. These services benefit our local community. Our local or municipal government looks after these services.

Public transit is one of the services provided by municipal governments.

Some things are needed by the people of the province. We need highways to connect towns and cities, we need hospitals and schools, we need common-sense rules for protecting our natural resources. These needs are met by the provincial government.

Education is provided by provincial governments.

The federal government is responsible for postal service.

Some things affect all people in Canada. These matters are the responsibility of the federal government. Our federal government is located in our nation's capital, Ottawa. The federal government looks after monetary matters, defence, the postal system, and Canadian affairs with foreign countries.

Canada has a federal government system. The power is divided between the federal government and the provincial government. The two governments are independent of each other. The provincial government does not receive its authority from the federal government, although it must follow the laws of the federal government.

Canada is a democracy. In a democracy, individual people have a voice in their government through their elected representatives. All Canadian citizens over the age of eighteen may vote for the representative of their choice federally, provincially, and locally. These representatives discuss issues and make decisions on behalf of all Canadians.

Democracies or representative governments work the same way at all three levels of government. A candidate is elected to represent everyone in a geographical area. The candidate is usually a resident of that area. These areas are known by different names: a riding, constituency, ward, or township.

Voters cast their ballots for the candidate that they think will best represent their wishes. But what happens if the candidate you vote for does not win? Does this mean that you aren't represented in the government? No. The winning candidate must represent all the people, regardless of whether they voted for her or him. You are always represented in your government.

However, this does not mean that your representative will vote the way you would like on every issue. Elected people have viewpoints and ideas of their own. But they must always be prepared to listen to the ideas and thoughts of the people they represent.

SOME POWERS OF THE FEDERAL GOVERNMENT

Section 91 of the British North America Act

- regulation of trade and commerce
- unemployment insurance
- raising money through taxes
- borrowing money for government spending
- postal services
- keeping statistics about Canada
- armed forces and national defence
- shipping and navigation
- seacoast and inland fisheries
- international and interprovincial ferries
- currency and coinage
- banking and the issuing of paper money
- savings banks and trust companies
- weights and measures
- interest rates
- bankruptcy
- copyright
- Native people and land claims
- criminal law
- penitentiaries
- all other matters not controlled by the provinces

SOME POWERS OF THE PROVINCIAL GOVERNMENTS

Section 92 of the British North America Act

- direct taxation for provincial purposes
- borrowing money for provincial purposes
- provincial prisons
- hospitals and mental institutions
- charities
- supervision of local governments

- licences for shops and taverns
- licensing of companies operating in the province
- administration of justice and the courts
- punishing people for breaking the laws of the province
- development and management of natural resources and energy resources
- all matters of a local or private nature in the province

Section 93 of the British North America Act

- education

SOME POWERS OF LOCAL GOVERNMENTS

- libraries
- local roads
- police protection
- public utilities commissions
- local school business
- fire protection
- recreation facilities
- garbage collection
- public transit
- sewage disposal
- local museums
- local planning

DEVELOPING SKILLS:
USING AN ORGANIZER

Sometimes you start to collect too much information on a topic and you need to put it all in order. An easy way to do this is with a chart or organizer. An organizer is a visual summary of information; it is usually limited to one page. An organizer helps you to focus on one topic. It also aids you in learning and remembering because it is visual and concise. Timelines, cause and effect charts, comparison charts, and decision-making/issue-analysis charts are all examples of organizers you will learn to use in history.

Let's start with a simple organizer that requires a bit of research. Suppose you want to find out who represents you at all three levels of government. You'll also need to know how to get in touch with them. You can develop an organizer that focusses on the question "Who represents me in government?"

Focus: Who Represents Me in Government?

In The Federal Government		In The Provincial Government		In The Local Government	
Name of the riding where I live.		Name of the riding where I live.		Name of the city, town, village, or borough.	
Name of my member of Parliament (MP) and her/his political party.		Name of my member of Provincial Parliament (MPP) and her/his political party.		Name of the mayor or reeve, and the name of at least one councillor or controller, and the name of one trustee of the Board of Education.	
Address and phone number of my member of Parliament (use your phone directory to help you).		Address and phone number of my member of Provincial Parliament.		Phone number of the mayor or reeve. Phone number of councillor or controller. Phone number of a school trustee.	

DIGGING DEEPER

1   Find out which level of government – federal, provincial, or municipal – looks after the following government activities.

- automobile licences
- metric system
- keeping streets clean
- motorcycle helmet legislation
- CBC
- regulating the drinking age
- restaurant and food inspection
- RCMP
- importing oil from Saudi Arabia
- local parks and recreation facilities
- importing goods
- immigration policy
- censorship of movies and video tapes
- libraries
- sending an ambassador to foreign countries

2   Read the problems that these citizens face. With the help of the blue pages in your telephone directory, figure out who they should call for help.

a) Bob Russell has lost his poodle, Cuddles.

b) Sarah and Bill Harrison are complaining about the smell and taste of their drinking water.

c) Andrew Kim wants to sponsor his nephew coming to Canada from Hong Kong.

d) Mary-Sue Gallivan wants to investigate a career in the armed forces.

e) Anatoly Jarozsek needs a patent for an insulated lunch pail that he has invented.

f) Maria Sanchez wants to get her pilot's licence.

g) N-P Window Washers Inc. wants to take a client to small claims court for not paying a bill.

h) Joseph Singh wants to get a fishing licence so he can take part in the Great Salmon Derby.

i) Dr. LaRoque wants to divide a house she owns into apartments.

j) Elizabeth Cardor wants the potholes repaired on her street.

3   The government not only provides services for people, it can also make people do things. Make a list of things that governments have the powers to make us do (e.g. pay income tax). When you have completed the list, have a mini-debate on the issue: The government has too much control over our lives.

2
The Federal System
of Government

The first job of a federal government is to make laws and regulations. In Canada, this function is carried out by Parliament. Parliament is comprised of two separate houses. The lower house, which is called the House of Commons, is composed of our elected representatives. The upper house, or the Senate, is composed of appointed representatives called senators. This part of the government is called the legislature.

Making the laws is just the beginning. Someone must carry out and enforce the laws. In Canada, the governor general, prime minister, and the members of the Cabinet are responsible for carrying out the laws. To help them, many civil servants, such as administrators, secretaries, police officers, scientists, and economists, are hired. This part of government is called the executive.

A third branch of government decides what the laws mean and whether a person has broken the law. Judges in the courts settle disputes between individuals and the government. This part of government is called the judiciary.

Look at the diagram of the branches of the federal government to see how each branch of the government fits together.

THE EXECUTIVE BRANCH OF THE GOVERNMENT

The Queen and the Governor General

Canada was created in 1867 by a law passed in the British Parliament. This law, the British North America Act (BNA Act), placed executive power in the hands of the monarch. The monarch of Great Britain is the Canadian head of state.

The Government of Canada

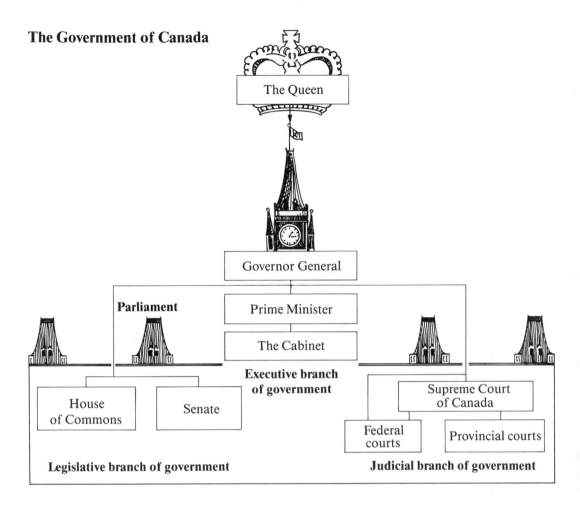

Since the monarch, now Queen Elizabeth II, lives in England and only visits Canada occasionally, she is represented in Canada by the governor general. Today the governor general's role is mainly formal and symbolic. S/he must ensure that the government carries on its business. If the prime minister died suddenly, the governor general would appoint a replacement. S/he would meet immediately with the deputy prime minister and Cabinet. They would suggest the name of a temporary leader. The governor general would ask the person to form a new government.

The governor general's signature is required on all bills before they become law. The governor general can refuse to sign a bill, however, this is rarely done. The governor general usually removes herself or himself from political controversy and partisan political disputes.

The rest of the time the governor general performs ceremonial and social duties. These include touring all parts of Canada, entertaining foreign leaders, opening and closing of Parliament, and making speeches.

Governor General Jeanne Sauvé accepting the Nansen Peace Medal from the UN in the name of the Canadian people

Until 1952, the governor general of Canada was always from England. Since then the Canadian prime minister recommends a Canadian for the position. Canadians who have held this honoured position are Vincent Massey (1952–1959), Georges Vanier (1959–1967), Roland Michener (1967–1974), Jules Leger (1974–1979), Edward Schreyer (1979–1984), and the first woman governor general, Jeanne Sauve (1984–). You will notice that it is a tradition to alternate the honour between French- and English-Canadians.

The Queen in Canada

Queen Elizabeth II is queen of Canada and head of the Canadian government. She reminds us of Canada's close ties with Britain over hundreds of years. Her ancestors, such as Elizabeth I (1558–1603), were strong rulers with enormous powers. However, the power of the monarch has gradually decreased. Power has shifted to the people's representatives who sit in the House of Commons. Today we have a constitutional monarchy. This means that the powers of the monarch are limited by the Constitution and laws of the land. The monarch has little political power in Canada or Britain. However, the monarch provides colour, pageantry, and tradition.

Queen Elizabeth II

The Prime Minister in Canada

The real political power rests in the hands of the prime minister. How do we choose our prime minister? The people of Canada do not vote directly for the prime minister. The prime minister of Canada is the leader of the political party that wins the most seats in the House of Commons. The prime minister is a member of Parliament elected by voters in one of the 295 electoral districts or ridings.

A job advertisement in Canada's newspapers requesting applications for the position of prime minister might look like this.

Position available: Prime minister of Canada

Duties to include:
- choosing members of the Cabinet
- providing leadership in the Cabinet and the House of Commons
- appointing Supreme Court judges
- appointing senators

- appointing ambassadors to foreign countries
- developing programs, projects, and policies for the country
- keeping the political party popular with the voters
- representing Canada at international conferences
- providing effective government for all Canadians

Qualifications:

The successful candidate must be a woman or man who is:
- a Canadian citizen over eighteen years of age
- leader of the political party with the most seats in the House of Commons

Other characteristics:

The successful man or woman should be:
- fluent in both official languages
- well educated
- experienced in government
- energetic
- possess a great deal of charisma
- an excellent public speaker
- well known and popular in all parts of the country
- knowledgeable about world affairs and world economics
- aware of the problems in all regions of Canada
- supported by a strong political party
- willing to work long hours
- experienced at problem solving
- able to delegate authority and work well with people
- able to persuade Canadians to work together in harmony
- skilful at using the media, especially television

Term of employment:

- up to five years or as long as the candidate has the support of the majority of the House of Commons

- eligible for reelection with the support of the candidate's political party

Remuneration:
- annual salary of $122,900 plus tax-free allowance of $19,100
- entertainment allowance
- a large private mansion at 24 Sussex Drive overlooking the Ottawa River
- summer home in the Gatineau Hills outside Ottawa
- private government jet for travelling across Canada and abroad
- chauffeur and limousine
- 24-hour security for candidate and her/his family
- opportunities for worldwide travel
- opportunities to work with international leaders

Applications will be received by the voters of Canada every time there is a federal election.

Executive of the federal and provincial governments

Federal Government	Provincial Government
CROWN (queen or king)	CROWN (queen or king)
GOVERNOR GENERAL • appointed by queen or king on recommendation of the prime minister	LIEUTENANT GOVERNOR • appointed by governor general on advice of prime minister
PRIME MINISTER • leader of political party with the most seats in the House of Commons	PREMIER OF PROVINCE • leader of the political party with the most seats
CABINET • members of Parliament chosen by prime minister from his/her political party	CABINET • members of provincial Parliament chosen by the premier from his/her political party

Seal of Canada

The Cabinet

Canada is a nation of great regional diversity and as such has many different interests and goals. This makes governing Canada a massive task. The prime minister could not possibly do it alone. So, one of the prime minister's first responsibilities is to choose advisors. The prime minister picks members of Parliament (MPs) to assist with governing the nation. Collectively, they are called the Cabinet.

Each member is given a different portfolio. A portfolio is the term used to describe the position and duties of a Cabinet minister. For example, the minister of Defence is responsible for the national defence of Canada. This includes the armed forces, the building and purchasing of defence equipment, and Canada's involvement in defence alliances such as NATO and NORAD.

Choosing a Cabinet is a true juggling act. It's not just a matter of picking the most competent people for the jobs. The prime minister must ensure that all regions of Canada are represented in the Cabinet. The minister of Fisheries usually comes from Atlantic Canada or British Columbia. The agriculture portfolio is often given to someone from western Canada. Women must also be well represented in Cabinet. Popular and able members also expect to be included. The multicultural aspect of Canada means the Cabinet should include people sharing various languages, religions, and ethnic backgrounds.

Sometimes the prime minister wants an MP to be an advisor in the Cabinet, but does not have a portfolio for that person. Then the person is made a minister without portfolio. S/he is free to move from one special assignment to another.

Some government departments are:

- Agriculture
- Citizenship and Immigration
- External Affairs
- Trade and Commerce
- Indian Affairs and Northern Development
- Energy, Mines, and Resources
- Finance
- Justice
- Transportation
- Fisheries
- Health and Welfare
- Labour
- Fitness and Amateur Sport
- International Trade

All members of the Cabinet are called "minister" and have the title "The Honourable" before their name for life. The prime minister's title is "The Right Honourable." Current and former prime ministers, governors general, and chief justices are the only people who may use this title.

What does a Cabinet minister do?

- oversees the running of her/his department.
- explains the policies and answers questions about the department in Parliament and to the media.
- discusses general government policy with the prime minister and other Cabinet ministers.
- presents and guides new laws that affect her/his department through Parliament.
- interprets and defends government policy to the public.
- advises the prime minister.

Cabinet meetings are always held *in camera*. This Latin term means behind closed doors. The Cabinet meetings may not be discussed outside the meeting. All ministers are expected to publicly support government decisions and policy. If this is not possible, the minister is expected to resign from Cabinet.

On 13 October 1976, Defence Minister James Richardson resigned from Prime Minister Pierre Trudeau's cabinet. Here is part of his letter to Trudeau.

Dear Prime Minister

It has become increasingly apparent that you and I do not share the same vision of Canada, the land we both love. On Thursday evening, October 7, I told you that I wished to resign from the Cabinet and I explained, in our more than hour-long conversation, my valid reasons for wishing to do so. . . .

Because my reason for resigning is one of principle, and because the issue on which I am resigning is vital to the future of Canada, I am, once again, after carefully considering your objections, presenting you with my resignation from the Cabinet. . . .

I believe that it is important that Canadians everywhere be made aware of the far-reaching implications for Canada contained in some of the proposals concerning the Constitution that will be considered at the forthcoming Conference of First Ministers. For that reason it is urgent that I obtain freedom to speak openly and publicly without the constraints imposed by my position in the Cabinet.

Each MP of the governing party is also bound to support the government's policies. This is known as party loyalty. If a MP does not support his government, s/he will often be asked to resign.

Flora MacDonald

Profile of a Cabinet Minister

Flora MacDonald was born in 1926 in Sydney, Nova Scotia. In 1972, she was elected to the House of Commons as the Progressive Conservative (PC) member representing Kingston and the Islands. Four years later, MacDonald ran unsuccessfully for the leadership of her party. It was apparent that the PC party, and perhaps Canada as a whole, was not ready for a woman as a leader. In 1979, Prime Minister Joe Clark, who had defeated MacDonald for the leadership, named MacDonald as the first woman minister of External Affairs. In this capacity, she approved and aided Ken Taylor's daring venture helping six Americans escape from Iran. When Brian Mulroney became prime minister in 1984, he made MacDonald the minister of Communications.

Women in the Cabinet

Prime Minister Brian Mulroney has appointed more women to the Cabinet than any other Canadian prime minister. Pat Carney is responsible for International Trade. In this position, she has been in the forefront of a historic free trade deal with the United States. Barbara McDougall held the important portfolio of minister of State for Finance. She has faced tough opposition and criticism in the wake of the collapse of western banks. However, her political allies and opponents have come to recognize her as a skilled politician. At the moment, Ms. McDougall is the minister of State (Privatization and Regulatory Affairs). Other woman ministers are: Monique Vezina, State (Transport); Monique Landry, External Relations. Some women who were in the Cabinet include Suzanne Blais-Grenier, Environment; and Andree Champagne, Youth.

THE LEGISLATIVE BRANCH OF GOVERNMENT

Members of Parliament

Canada is divided into 295 electoral districts called ridings or constituencies. Each riding sends one representative to the House of Commons in Ottawa. This person is known as a member of Parliament (MP).

Members of Parliament have many duties to perform. In their riding, they have a constituency office to help the people deal with a wide range of problems. Often people need assistance to understand the government bureaucracy.

MPs must stay in touch with their ridings and be aware of the problems and issues faced by their constituents. Good MPs are always receptive of the views presented by the people they represent.

In Ottawa, MPs are expected to attend Question Period and any special sessions of Parliament. MPs are also responsible for making speeches in the House of Commons, especially on issues of major concern to their constituents. MPs vote on all bills that are presented to the House of Commons. They also work on parliamentary committees studying proposed laws.

MPs must not forget their responsibilities to their political party. They must attend weekly caucus meetings. The caucus consists of all elected members of the party. In caucus meetings, MPs have a chance to form the policies and discuss the strategy their party will follow. MPs are also expected to make speeches, give interviews to the media, and raise funds for their political party.

THE SENATE

The second body of the Parliament is the Senate. Unlike the House of Commons, its members, called senators, are appointed. The appointments are made by the governor general, however, s/he appoints people recommended by the prime minister. There are 104 members in the Senate. They represent the various regions of Canada. Twenty-four senators are appointed from the Maritimes (ten from Nova Scotia, ten from New Brunswick, and four from PEI). Newfoundland has six senators. Quebec and Ontario each have twenty-four senators, each western province has six senators, and the Yukon and the NWT each have one senator.

The qualifications for the Senate are:

- a Canadian citizen over thirty years of age and under seventy-five years of age
- must not miss two consecutive sessions of Parliament
- must have real estate worth $4 000 net
- must have total net assets of at least $4 000
- must reside in the province or territory for which they are appointed.

Although the Senate can create its own bills, this is rarely done. Usually the senators debate and vote upon bills sent to them from the House of Commons. They must pass, defeat, or amend a Commons' bill. Usually they make minor amendments to clarify the legislation. In fact, the Senate has not vetoed a bill in forty years. On constitutional amendments, their veto only extends for 180 days.

Periodically there is a movement toward Senate reform. This

has occurred because many senators obtained their seats through patronage. Perhaps the most famous round of patronage appointments in recent times occurred in 1984, when Trudeau made numerous Senate appointments just before he left office.

In 1978, the Liberals were interested in making the Senate more representative of the distinct regions of Canada. However, the idea received little support. Another proposal was that the senators be provincial delegates. However, this idea was criticized as it would have weakened federal authority and strengthened the provinces.

What will happen to the Senate? No one or group has been able to devise reforms acceptable to all involved. Senate reform will be quite difficult as a constitutional amendment, approved by Parliament and at least seven provinces that have 50 percent of Canada's population, is necessary to alter the Senate.

MAKING A FEDERAL LAW

The legislative branch of the government makes all laws. Every law must pass through the following steps.

The Cabinet

Imagine that a recent television documentary has revealed that many lakes and trees in Canada are dying because of acid rain. Pressure from all sides is mounting. Environmentalists, sports enthusiasts, and cottagers are urging the government to make industry reduce sulphur emissions from their plants. The opposition parties have been criticizing the government for not making this change sooner. Public opinion polls show that 70 percent of Canadians favour stronger controls.

The prime minister and the Cabinet decide to make the change. The proposed law is known as a bill.

House of Commons

The bill must be given three readings in the House of Commons.
First reading: The bill is introduced in the House.
Second reading: The advantages and disadvantages of the bill are debated and a vote is taken.
Third reading: The members of the House accept or reject the bill. If the bill is accepted, it goes to the Senate.

The Senate

The bill must go through exactly the same steps in the Senate that it did in the House.

First reading: The bill is introduced and there is no debate.

Second reading: The bill is discussed, debated, and a vote is taken. A Senate committee examines the bill phrase-by-phrase.

Third reading: With a vote on the whole bill, the Senate accepts or rejects the bill. If the Senate has made any changes in the bill, it must be sent back to the House of Commons for approval.

Royal Assent

The governor general, as the representative of the monarch, signs the bill. It is now a law and an Act of Parliament. Its provisions are binding on all Canadians.

A WORKING DAY IN THE HOUSE OF COMMONS

What is it really like in the House of Commons? A typical day in the House begins at 2:00 p.m. when the Speaker of the House enters the House of Commons. The Speaker is a member of Parliament who has been chosen to act as a referee. It is her/his responsibility to make sure the rules and regulations of parliamentary debate are followed. The Speaker holds a honoured position.

The Speaker sits on a raised platform at one end of the long chamber. Around the Speaker's chair sit several pages. A page is a young person who is responsible for delivering messages and running errands for members of Parliament.

The Sergeant-at-Arms, who is in charge of security, lays the mace on a large table in front of the Speaker. The mace is a gold-plated war club and it symbolizes the Speaker's authority over the House.

Members of the government sit to the Speaker's right and opposition MPs sit to the Speaker's left. The first few rows of desks on the government side, near the centre, are occupied by the prime minister and the Cabinet. The other seats on the government side are filled by backbenchers. A backbencher is a government MP who is not a Cabinet member.

The leader of the Opposition and the shadow cabinet sit opposite the prime minister and the Cabinet. The shadow cabinet is composed of opposition MPs who follow a specific minister's port-

House of Commons, Ottawa

folio. They make sure the minister is doing her/his job satisfactorily. The Official Opposition is the second-largest party in the House of Commons. The leaders of the smaller opposition parties sit in the front row, but farther away from the Speaker. The role of the opposition is to criticize, improve government legislation and, if possible, to defeat the government.

At a long table in the middle of the House are clerks who keep official records of decisions made by the House. In the space between the government and the opposition sit reporters who record word-for-word all the speeches. These speeches are printed in a daily publication called Hansard. All speeches are simultaneously translated into French and English. The proceedings of the House of Commons are televised.

Members of the press and the public can observe the proceedings by sitting in galleries above the floor of the House of Commons.

After the Speaker reads the daily prayer, Question Period begins. At this time, members, mostly from opposition parties, question the government and its ministers on government policies. Question Period lasts about forty-five minutes and is usually incredibly lively. This period is an important part of keeping the government open and honest. The balance of the day is taken up with debate and discussion of bills.

LOCAL GOVERNMENTS

Regardless of how various municipal governments are organized, they have similar duties and powers.

Rural	**Urban**
(townships and counties)	(cities)
Reeve – elected by people of the township	Mayor – elected by people of the city
Councillors – elected by people to represent parts of the township	Councillors – elected by people in different wards

In many parts of Ontario, there is a second tier of local government. Groups of townships form a county council. The reeve of each township sits on the county council.

In ten urban areas of Ontario, the second tier of government is known as regional government. Large cities, like Metropolitan Toronto, have a number of city governments as well as an overall government for the whole metropolitan area.

In order to control its areas of jurisdiction, (You learned about local governments responsibilities in chapter 1.) local governments pass by-laws. By-laws are local laws. They have the force of national and provincial laws. However, the legality of by-laws can be reviewed by provincial courts.

DIGGING DEEPER

1 Have a class discussion about the nature of Canada and the nature of the job of prime minister. Look at the imaginary job advertisement for the prime minister. Are there any qualifications and characteristics that should be deleted from the list? Why? Are there any that should be added to the list? Why? Rank the five most important characteristics and qualifications. Justify your ranking.

2 Sir John A. Macdonald began the tradition of making the Cabinet representative of the regions of Canada. Find out the names of the Cabinet ministers today. What portfolio does each minister hold? From which province does each minister come? Are all provinces represented in the Cabinet today? How many women are in the Cabinet?

3 Assume you have just finished reading a newspaper article called the "Queen in Canada." It suggests Canada should cut its ties with the monarchy in Britain. Write a letter to your newspaper editor stating your viewpoint. Do you think that the British monarch should be Canada's head of state? Provide reasons for your opinion.

4 Refer to the issue-analysis organizer (pages 26-27) that deals with the Canadian Senate. Work in small groups to discuss each of the points raised in the organizer. Try to think of additional points that you could add to the three positions. As a group, answer the questions: What should be done to the Canadian Senate? Why?

5 Choose an issue that is presently being discussed in your community.

Invite someone from your local government (planning or finance departments, mayor, or councillor) to discuss the issue. Also, listen to the views of the people in your neighbourhood or committees who are both for and against the project. Review what your local newspaper(s) are saying. Use an issue-analysis/ decision-making organizer to help clarify the issue. Your organizer should:

- focus
- organize information
- locate information
- synthesize and draw conclusions
- communicate conclusions

Decide what is fact and opinion, analyse the issue and present a plan of action to the appropriate local authority.

DEVELOPING SKILLS: USING AN ISSUE-ANALYSIS ORGANIZER

At various times in Canada's history the role of the Senate has been questioned. Many people think the Senate has outlived its usefulness. It has been called outdated and undemocratic. There has been a call for Senate reform, however, no one is quite sure what changes should be made to the Senate. You can analyse this controversial issue by using an issue-analysis organizer.

1 Focus
What should be done with the Senate?

2 Organize information
The criteria related to membership in the Senate.

3 Locate information
Locate as much information as possible on the three alternatives for the Senate. Read what people with differing opinions have written or, if possible, invite local politicians or activists into your class to speak on the issue.

4 Synthesize and draw conclusions
Individually or in groups, weigh the various alternatives. What is your conclusion on the Senate?

5 Communicate
Again either in groups or individually communicate, either orally or in writing, your conclusion concerning the Senate to an interested group of students, teachers, or parents.

2 Organize information

The criteria related to membership in the Senate

	Abolish the Senate	Keep the Senate as it is	Reform the Senate
Historical Reason	The democratically elected House of Commons should be the only body to make laws and carry out the wishes of the Canadian people.	The Senate serves as a useful check on the House of Commons. Sir John A. Macdonald wanted the Senate to take a sober second look at all legislation. The Senate was to keep the House of Commons on its toes.	The Fathers of Confederation would probably support the idea of updating and reforming the Senate after more than 100 years of its existence.
Present-day functions	Most senators do very little work. The Senate rarely makes changes to the laws and, therefore, does not have any meaningful use or function.	On occasion, the Senate has done some extremely useful work. For example, the senatorial work on mass media and poverty has been useful to all Canadians.	There is a great deal of talent in the Senate. Senators should be given greater responsibilities to investigate and report on issues of vital national concern. It would be cost effective to have senators investigate public problems instead of royal commissions or task forces (because senators are already paid and a permanent staff is available).
Cost	The cost of maintaining the Senate and the senators' salaries is too high.	As it now stands, the cost of the Senate is a worthwhile government expense.	The Senate is worth keeping, but to justify the cost the workload and the responsibilities should be increased.

	Abolish the Senate	Keep the Senate as it is	Reform the Senate
Age	The Senate is for aged politicians. Most senators are not appointed until they are in their fifties. At that time they don't have innovative ideas and are not energetic enough to fulfil their duties.	Senators are required by a 1965 law to retire at the age of seventy-five. At this age people can still make valuable contributions to society. It is age discrimination to suggest that most people stop being useful members of society when they get older.	Reduce the age of compulsory retirement to sixty-five or make ten years the maximum term of service in the Senate.
Selection	The Senate is undemocratic because senators are appointed not elected. Although the senators must live in the province that they represent, they do not necessarily share the same viewpoints as the government or the people of the province.	One of the original purposes of the Senate was to protect the interests of the provinces. Smaller provinces have better representation in the Senate than in the House of Commons.	Let the provinces elect senators. This would give provincial interests even more protection than they have now.
Experience	Many senators are appointed because of political connections with the party in power. Very few are chosen solely because of their knowledge or talent.	Senators bring many years of knowledge and expertise to their jobs because of their political, business, legal, and administrative experience.	The Senate should be selected from occupations outside the world of politics. In that way, the experience and knowledge of people from all walks of life can be tapped.

3
Political Parties and Elections

You have probably read about an election in the newspaper or seen political advertisements on the television. By the time the election gets to those stages a lot of work has already been done by many people.

Governments in Canada are elected in much the same way as your students' council or your class executive. People, called candidates, put forward their names for election. During the campaign, meetings are held, speeches are made, and newspapers and television screens are filled with political announcements. Each candidate tries to convince the voters that s/he is the best person to represent them. Finally, on election day, the people vote for the candidate of their choice. By voting, Canadians have an opportunity to say how they want things run and what kinds of leaders they want.

Getting Ready

In Canada, the law states that an election must be held at least every five years. However, the prime minister can decide to call an election earlier. Why would an election be called early? In 1984, John Turner was elected leader of the Liberal party, however he didn't have a seat in the House of Commons. As Turner was now prime minister, yet hadn't been elected, he called an election.

As soon as the election is called, the Chief Electoral Officer swings into action. The Electoral Office organizes all the details that make an election run smoothly.

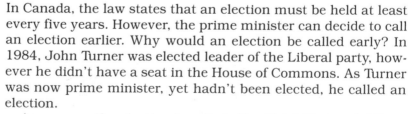

One of the main functions of the Chief Electoral Officer is to prepare a list of eligible voters. An eligible voter is a Canadian citizen over eighteen years of age. Enumerators are hired to go door-to-door to make up the voters' list. In rural areas, the list is often made from personal knowledge of people in the area or a neighbour's knowledge. If you are not enumerated, you have until the day before the election to get your name on the voters' list.

The Electoral Office employs fifty people on a full-time basis, but by election day employs close to one hundred thousand. The hours of voting are very long, so that everyone will have a chance to vote. If you suspect you won't be able to vote on election day, you can vote in advance.

Soon after the election is called all major political parties, and some fringe parties, are busy nominating candidates in Canada's 295 ridings. Any Canadian can run for office, after fulfilling some legal requirements, though, independents are very rarely elected to office.

The Campaign

Every federal election is approximately sixty days long. During this time, the candidates make speeches and public appearances. The candidates, or their supporters, try to visit every one in the riding. They give out pamphlets outlining their views on national and local issues. Candidates make election promises, erect lawn signs, and put up posters that urge voters to cast their ballots for them.

Chaviva Hošek campaigning in the 1987 provincial election

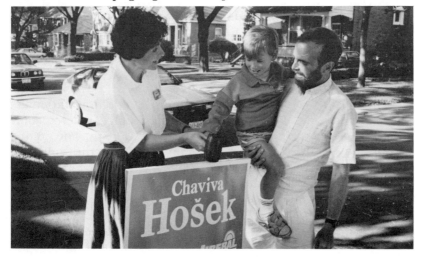

On a national level, the political parties spend millions of dollars for television, radio, and newspaper advertisements. Frequently, the leaders of the parties will hold a nationally televised debate. During the debate, the leaders state the views of their respective parties on issues of national importance.

More and more, in this electronic age, political parties, their leaders, and their candidates are judged on their performances during the debate and on nightly news clips about their day. Some people have complained that voters are not seeing the "real" leader, and are being forced to judge the leadership of their country based on personality and not substance.

Election Day

On election day, voters go to polling stations. A polling station is a place, often a school gym or a community centre, where people vote. The polls are open from 9:00 a.m. to 8:00 p.m. The polling station may be divided into various polls, called a multiple poll. When a voter arrives, s/he is given a ballot. The ballot contains the names of the candidates in alphabetical order and the party they represent. The voter goes to a polling booth, a screened area, where the voter can mark her/his ballot in private. If the voter does not mark the ballot properly it will not be counted later. Then the ballot is refolded and the deputy returning officer (poll official) drops it into the ballot box.

Ballot marked incorrectly

Ballot marked correctly

The polling stations are run by electoral officials. There are deputy returning officers and poll clerks, who are responsible for a polling station, and scrutineers, people assigned by the candidates to ensure the vote count is accurate and honest.

At campaign headquarters the workers are doing their best to "get out the vote." They want to be sure that every possible supporter has the opportunity to vote. Voters are phoned and reminded to vote. Rides are arranged for people who would have difficulty getting to the polling station.

The Result

The ballots are not counted until after all the polls are closed. Many Canadians watch the results come in on television. They want to know who won in their own riding, and also which political party has won the most seats in the House of Commons.

When one party wins more seats than any other party or the other parties combined, it is a majority government. In the 1984 federal election, Brian Mulroney and the Progressive Conservatives won the largest electoral majority in Canada's history. With 211 seats, the Progressive Conservatives had a strong majority. As long as there is caucus solidarity, they can pass all their bills. A majority government has a strong advantage in the House of Commons.

Suppose, however, that no political party wins a majority in the House of Commons. That was the situation in 1979.
The Progressive Conservative party still forms the government since they elected more members to the Commons than any

1979 federal election	
Government	**Opposition**
136 Progressive Conservative MPs	114 Liberal MPs
	26 New Democratic Party MPs
	6 Social Credit MPs
Total: 136 MPs	146 MPs

1984 federal election	
Government	**Opposition**
211 Progressive Conservative MPs	40 Liberal MPs
	30 New Democratic Party MPs
	1 Independent MP
Total: 211 MPs	71 MPs

other party. However, when the seats of all the opposition parties are combined, the opposition parties hold more seats than the Conservatives. This is a minority government. A minority government has elected members to fewer than half of the seats in the Commons.

A minority government must always listen to the opposition parties. At any time the opposition parties may outvote and defeat the government. When this happens it is called a vote of non-confidence. If a government has lost the confidence of the House, an election is usually held.

This is exactly what happened to Prime Minister Joe Clark on 13 December 1979. John Crosbie, then minister of Finance, presented the Conservative budget to the House of Commons. The opposition parties did not like it, and held a vote of non-confidence. Clark and his Conservatives were defeated.

Non-confidence vote against the Progressive Conservatives			
	Voting for the government	Voting against the government	Abstaining
Conservatives	133		3
Liberals		112	2
NDP		27	
Social Credit			5
Total:	133	139	10

When Clark's government resigned, they were honouring the principle of responsible government. Responsible government is an unwritten rule in Canada's Constitution. It means the government may only remain in office as long as it has the support of the majority of the legislature.

Some key dates in Canadian electoral history

1874   Dominion Elections Act introduces the secret ballot. Before that time voting was done in public. People could be bullied or bribed into voting for certain candidates.

1885   Most Canadians over the age of twenty-one can vote except Native people, people from the Orient and other parts of Asia, prisoners, lunatics, federal government employees and, of course, women.

1918   Women gained the right vote in federal elections and, in 1919, women became eligible to run for election to the House of Commons.

1948   Citizens of Asian descent received the right to vote.

1960   Native people living on reservations were given the right to vote.

1974   Election Expenses Act is passed. It limits election expenses of political parties and candidates.

Many Canadians had a long, hard struggle for suffrage (right to vote). And yet, surprisingly, in every election there are people who do not plan to vote. Why don't people bother to vote? Many people feel one small vote will not count. Others don't know which candidate to vote for. How would you convince someone that it is a right and a responsibility to vote?

Liberal Party

POLITICAL PARTIES

There are three main political parties – the Liberals, the Progressive Conservatives, and the New Democratic Party in Canada. There are, however, other political parties in Canada. Many are only represented at the provincial level. For example, the Union Nationale and the Parti Quebecois in Quebec.

Every political party develops a platform. A platform is a package of ideas or policies that the party believes in. The party hopes voters will agree with their platform and vote for them. Many voters find that platforms make it easier to decide which party they want to support.

The main goal of politics is to gain power. To win an election, a party must please as many voters as possible. Sometimes people think one party sounds just like the next one. The differences in the parties is not in what they stand for, but in how they want to reach their goals. For example, all three main parties stand for full employment. But each has different ideas about how to achieve that goal.

In fact, there is a wide range of viewpoints on political matters. One way to illustrate this is to put differing political viewpoints on an imaginary line called the political spectrum. In the middle is where people with moderate political opinions find themselves. This is the centre of the political spectrum. On either side of the centre are positions we call left- and right-wing. The chart shows some of the characteristics of these positions on the political spectrum.

Political Spectrum

	Left	Centre	Right
Change	We want to change conditions as quickly as possible.	There may be things that are unjust in our society, however, changes do not happen overnight. We must attack the problems but realize it may take years to bring about change.	Conditions are fine as they are now. We do not want any changes at all.
Role of Government	The government has a role to care for the less fortunate.	Believe in searching for ways to settle problems that are acceptable to the greatest number of people.	The government should not interfere in the lives of individuals.
Government Ownership	The government should own key industries and resources (transportation, natural resources).	Accepts moderate government management and intervention in the economy.	Business and industry should be kept in the hands of individuals.
Individual Rights	Rights of the individual have high priority.	Believe in law and order, but rights of the individual come first.	Law and order have high priority.

DIGGING DEEPER

1   Try to build a platform for a school election that will appeal to a large number of students. Remember to include planks in your platform that will appeal to males and females, junior and senior students, athletes, non-athletes, people with differing musical tastes, and high-achieving students. Present your platform to an interested group in the school.

2   Write to the national headquarters of the major federal parties to obtain the most recent policy statements. Compare the positions of the parties on the same issue. Summarize the positions in a comparison organizer on a variety of issues such as the one shown here.

	Liberals	Progressive Conservatives	New Democratic Party
Environment Acid Rain			
Toxic waste Disposal			
Economy Employment Support for industries			
Women's issues Affirmative action Equal pay for work of equal value			
Taxation Corporate Individual			
Other issues Free trade Capital punishment Foreign ownership			

After studying the party policies, decide where each of the three main parties is on the political spectrum.

3   Indicate where you stand on the political spectrum. Be ready to provide definite proof.

4 Write a short paragraph to tell where an adult who you know very well should be placed on the political spectrum. Explain your reasons for making this judgement.

5 Divide the class into three groups representing the major political parties in Canada and hold an election. Each party should choose a candidate to run for office. As a class, select a problem as the election issue. Decide what your party's position will be on this problem. Make buttons, posters, and pamphlets to promote your candidate and the party. Each candidate should make a short speech outlining her/his position on the issue and making promises to the voters. Prepare ballots, a voters' list, and a ballot box. Set up a polling station in your classroom. Hold your election using the same procedures as in a federal election.

4
Law in our Lives:
Criminal Law

Imagine a hockey game with no rules. How long would spectators enjoy watching a game with no organization? How long would players put up with a game where there were no rules to guarantee fairness?

Imagine a society with no laws about stealing. None of your possessions would be safe. People could take whatever they fancied. Stores would go bankrupt as thieves emptied their shelves.

A world without laws would soon be in a terrible mess. Laws are the rules for living in human groups. Laws protect our rights in society. They also help ensure that we fulfil our responsibilities as members of society. In Canada, there are thousands of laws and by-laws to help protect us all.

We may not always agree with the laws of our society. However, if we accept the rule of law, all laws must be obeyed by everyone, regardless of whether we consider them fair or not. Laws make us equal and no one has more rights under the law than anyone else.

We may not always know all the laws. But "ignorance of the law is no excuse." If you break a law you must pay the penalty. It doesn't matter if you didn't know you were breaking the law.

What do you know about Canadian law? Do you know how the law is enforced by the government and the police? Do you know your rights and responsibilities? Do you know that there are two types of law – criminal and civil – in Canada?

CRIMINAL LAW

Criminal law deals with crimes such as murder and theft. Its purpose is to protect society from wrongdoers. A person who commits a criminal offence can be taken to court. If the person is found guilty, s/he may be fined, imprisoned, or otherwise punished. The Criminal Code of Canada lists offences and sets out appropriate penalties for them.

For an action to be considered a crime in Canada, it must meet the following three conditions:

1 It must be forbidden by the Criminal Code of Canada.
2 The accused must have intended to commit the offence, or have been able to see that such an action could result in breaking a law.
3 The accused must be of sound mind (able to understand the difference between right and wrong).

In Canada, before the accused can be found guilty, the Crown (the government) must prove that all three conditions existed.

Case Study: An European Adventure

Jennifer, a young Canadian woman, is returning from a month-long tour of Europe. On her travels, she met another young Canadian, Tracey, and they are flying home together. As they are getting off the plane in Toronto, Tracey asks Jennifer to help her with her luggage. Since Jennifer has only her backpack and Tracey has a lot of luggage, Jennifer agrees.

Tracey goes through Canada Customs first. When Jennifer goes through customs, the officer finds something suspicious at the bottom of Tracey's bag. The bag is turned over to the RCMP for a closer look. Their examination shows the bag has a false bottom that conceals a small fortune in diamonds. Jennifer looks frantically for Tracey, but can't see her anywhere.

Does Jennifer's action constitute a crime?

CLASSIFICATION OF CRIMINAL OFFENCES

The Criminal Code divides crimes into two classes: summary and indictable offences. The simple distinction is that summary

Federal and Provincial Courts

Supreme Court of Canada	Federal Court of Canada
• final appeal court for Canada • appeals come from provincial courts and Federal Court • gives advisory opinions to the federal government	• deals with original cases and appeals involving the Crown (government)

Supreme Court of Ontario

Court of Appeal	Supreme Court of Ontario
• hears requests to change or overturn decisions made by other courts • these requests are known as appeals	• has jurisdiction over serious criminal matters • deals with more serious civil actions including contract and property disputes, damages for personal injury, and divorce

Provincial Court Criminal Division	Provincial Offences Court	Small Claims Court
• deals with people charged with minor criminal offences	• deals with minor offences contained in provincial laws for example, the Highway Traffic Act, the Fish and Game Act, and other laws on matters such as pollution and consumer products	• an easy and efficient way to settle small claims worth less than $1000 ($3000 or less in Toronto) • court costs may be kept to a minimum

Provincial Court Family Division	Surrogate Court
• deals with family matters such as child custody and family support • also deals with young offenders	• deals primarily with the wills and estates of deceased persons

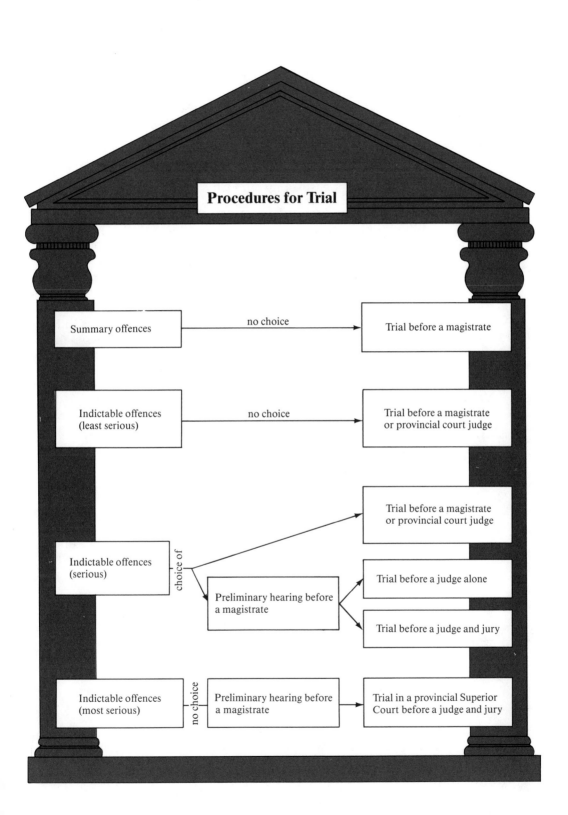

Procedures for Trial

Summary offences	no choice	Trial before a magistrate
Indictable offences (least serious)	no choice	Trial before a magistrate or provincial court judge
Indictable offences (serious)	choice of	Trial before a magistrate or provincial court judge
	Preliminary hearing before a magistrate	Trial before a judge alone
		Trial before a judge and jury
Indictable offences (most serious)	no choice — Preliminary hearing before a magistrate	Trial in a provincial Superior Court before a judge and jury

offences are less serious and have lower maximum penalties. Summary offences are tried before a magistrate.

Some examples of summary offences are:
- traffic violations such as speeding tickets
- causing a disturbance
- breaking municipal noise by-laws
- cruelty to animals
- selling or possessing slugs for coin- or token-operated machines

Indictable offences are more serious than summary offences. Indictable offences are placed in three different categories, and the Criminal Code has procedures for dealing with each one.

The least serious indictable offences, such as theft under $1000, are tried before magistrates or provincial court judges. For serious indictable offences, such as armed robbery, the accused has the choice of being tried before a magistrate, a judge, or a judge and jury. The most serious indictable offences, such as murder, must be tried before a judge and jury in a provincial superior court. This occurs after a preliminary hearing before a magistrate. The Canadian Charter of Rights and Freedoms protects people who get into trouble with the law and the police.

WHAT HAPPENS DURING A TRIAL?

The most interesting and exciting way to discover what happens during a trial is to visit a courtroom as an observer. See if you can arrange a class visit to a provincial court. If it is impossible to visit a courtroom, you can follow Gordon Mowbray's trial.

Before your visit to the courtroom, or before you read about Mowbray's trial, you should prepare a set of questions. They might include:

1   What do each of the following people do at a trial?
   a) judge   e) witnesses
   b) jury   f) foreperson for the jury
   c) crown prosecutor   g) the accused
   d) defence lawyer
2   Which lawyer speaks first? Why?
3   Explain the following terms:
   a) cross-examine   c) verdict
   b) hearsay   d) contempt of court.
4   What kind of evidence is allowed? What kind is not allowed?
5   Is the use of a jury a good way to decide whether or not a person is guilty?
6   Why do you think trials are public?

7   How does this trial differ from trials you've seen on television or in the movies?

Gordon Mowbray's Trial

You are attending the trial of the *R. v. Mowbray.* "R" is the Latin short form for Regina, which means queen. The Latin for king is Rex, therefore, the name of the trial would be the same if a king was on the throne. Mowbray is the defendant, the person against whom legal action is being taken.

This system of justice is sometimes called an adversary system. The Crown prosecutor presents evidence to find the accused person guilty. The adversaries, the accused and her/his lawyer, present evidence to prove the accused person is innocent.

Gordon Mowbray has been charged with arson. Apparently, he wilfully set fire to a neighbouring farmhouse. The house burned to the ground and the owner, Harriet Wright, and her daughter were seriously burned. Before Mowbray's trial begins, a number of preliminary legal procedures will have happened.

First, Mowbray was brought before a magistrate. At the preliminary hearing, the magistrate decided there was sufficient evidence to bring Mowbray to trial. Mowbray decided to be tried by a judge and jury. Many months will elapse before the case actually comes to trial.

Before the trial date, Mowbray's lawyer, Elizabeth Sullivan, and the Crown attorney, Zahid Singh, will prepare their cases. They will also choose the jury. A jury is a group of twelve local people, picked at random, to hear evidence during a trial. The selection of a jury is a time-consuming and difficult process. Both lawyers question the potential jurors. They have the right to accept or reject the jurors. They might reject someone because of suspected prejudice or bias toward the accused. Only a few professions are exempt from jury duty. They are doctors, lawyers, clergy, members of the Armed Forces, and anyone working in the court system.

Now the trial is ready to begin. The judge informs the jurors to listen to all the evidence and decide whether the accused person is guilty or innocent. The judge also instructs the jurors not to discuss the case with anyone.

Trials are quite formal in Canada. Mowbray's lawyer has told him to dress neatly. Ms Sullivan also warned Mowbray that verbal outbursts, eating food, chewing gum, drinking coffee, and smoking in the courtroom might lead the judge to cite him for contempt of court. Contempt of court means disobedience or disrespect for court laws.

First, the Crown attorney presents a summary of the case. The evidence against Mowbray is presented and witnesses are called. Each witness is sworn to tell the truth. A witness who lies on the stand will be charged with perjury. It is a very serious offence, and the person could be sent to jail.

Frequently the best evidence is an eyewitness account. In this case, the eyewitness is the farmer. She testifies that she was at the barn when she saw Mowbray pour gasoline on the front porch and set fire to it. She was badly burned while saving her son.

Two witnesses identified Mowbray as the man they saw running away from the burning house at the approximate time of the fire. However, they didn't see him light the fire. This is circumstantial evidence. This is events or facts that make certain conclusions evident. Another neighbour testified that he had seen many old rags and gasoline cans in Mowbray's garage.

Another witness said that she heard, from a neighbour, that Mowbray had wanted his neighbour to sell her land to a developer. The developer would only buy if both farmers sold their land. Apparently, Mowbray had threatened Harriet Wright if she did not agree to sell her land. This is hearsay evidence. This is evidence based on testimony of another person, not firsthand knowledge. The judge would not accept this evidence as the witness did not actually hear Mowbray make these threats.

After each witness has testified, the defence may cross-examine the witness. Cross-examination tests the reliability of the witnesses and the truth of their evidence. After all its witnesses have been heard, the Crown rests its case.

Now, it's Ms. Sullivan's turn to call witnesses on Mowbray's behalf. The Crown is entitled to cross-examine these witnesses.

Mowbray has been sitting beside Ms. Sullivan throughout the trial. He has the right to be present at his trial, but is not required to give evidence. However, Ms. Sullivan puts him on the witness stand. Mowbray's defence is that he was intoxicated and had no idea what he was doing. He desperately needed the money and Harriet would not sell. He had hoped to terrorize her into selling.

All the witnesses have been called, the lawyers make their closing statements. They try and convince the jury to agree with their view of the facts. The judge instructs the jury in the legal meaning of the charge against the accused. The judge tells the jury they must reach a decision called a verdict.

The jury retires to a private room. The foreperson leads the discussion. They discuss the evidence they've heard and try to reach an unanimous decision. All twelve members of the jury must agree on the guilt or the innocence of the accused. This can take a long time and require several votes. Sometimes the jury cannot agree upon a verdict. This is called a hung jury. When this happens, the jury is dismissed and a new trial is ordered.

The jurors at Mowbray's trial have reached a verdict. They file back into the courtroom. If they've found Mowbray not guilty, he is free to leave. However, if he is found guilty, the judge will have to decide on an appropriate punishment. The foreperson informs the court that the jury has found Mowbray guilty.

The judge must impose a sentence upon Mowbray, but only within the limits of the law. The Criminal Code is quite specific. It suggests limits within which the judge must choose the penalty. The punishment should accomplish three objectives. First, it must act as a deterrent. It must persuade Mowbray not to commit any further crimes for fear of the punishment. Secondly, the punishment should try to rehabilitate Mowbray. Today, prisoners are provided with psychiatric, medical, and religious help while in prison. They are taught trades so they will have a better chance of finding employment when they are released. Sometimes, instead of prison, the criminal does community service work. Thirdly, the punishment may have to segregate dangerous criminals from the rest of society. This is for the protection of all people and as an example to others not to turn to crime.

1   What do you think Mowbray's punishment should be?

CONSIDER YOUR ACTIONS

The consequences of a criminal record are quite serious. Besides having your liberties taken away, you will probably have difficulty finding or holding a job upon your release from prison. Employers are leery of hiring people who have broken the law. Some jobs, such as a bank teller or security guard, require employees to be bonded. A bond is a guarantee of trustworthiness. A person with a criminal record cannot be bonded. Also, a released convict could have difficulty obtaining a business or liquor licence if s/he wanted to start a business.

Prisoners cannot vote and people convicted of illegal or corrupt electoral practices may lose their right to be a candidate for public office.

If a person is arrested again, after release from prison, the bail is usually much higher. A judge could give a harsher punishment to someone with a previous criminal record.

Although you can still obtain a Canadian passport if you have a criminal record, it might be difficult to enter a foreign country. A foreign citizen may have trouble getting landed immigrant status in Canada. A criminal record may also hinder an application for citizenship.

DEVELOPING SKILLS:
DEBATING

What is a debate? A debate is a discussion where reasons are presented for and against an idea. You probably debate more often than you think. You are debating when you try and decide whether or not to buy a new bike. You are debating when you and a friend discuss who you think will win the Stanley Cup.

There are other types of debates too. There are debates on television among politicians. They are more formal as there are rules and a format. In the 1984 federal election Brian Mulroney, John Turner, and Ed Broadbent had a three-way debate on national television. Can you think of any benefits to watching a television debate rather than reading about the debate the next day in the newspaper?

In the House of Commons in Ottawa, members of Parliament debate various issues that affect the nation. A MP must be recognized by the Speaker of the House before s/he can speak. Just like the television debate, there are rules that must be followed.

There are formal debating rules, but they are rarely followed. Frequently the rules are modified. In many debates there are two teams. Each team consists of three people. The object is to see which team has more skill in speaking and reasoning. The teams will debate a statement, for example, "Prisoners should have no chance for parole." One team takes the "pro" side of the issue. They are in favour of the statement, therefore, they argue that prisoners should *not* be paroled. The other team takes the "con" side. They are against the statement, so they would argue for parole.

Before you debate, you'll need to prepare. Here are some steps to follow.

1   Research your topic thoroughly. Make sure you separate fact from opinion.

2   Organize your information so you can easily present your argument.

3   Practise your delivery at home or with the other members of your team. Have your teammates suggest ways to improve your presentation.

4   With your teammates, develop a "game plan" so that everyone knows the procedure.

5   Try to anticipate the arguments your opponents will use. Have some counter arguments prepared to use against them.

6   Remember every team member must prepare and participate equally.

During the debate, there are some pointers to remember.

1   Argue with reason, not with emotion. Never lose your temper. Don't exaggerate.

2   Make your strongest points first. Do not get bogged down in a lot of minor details. Don't let your opponents sidetrack you from your argument.

3   Present a "reasoned argument." To do this, support your opinions with facts. Use statements by experts on your topic.

Hold a debate

"Many people who support capital punishment believe it is a deterrent to others who would consider crimes such as murder."

The class should be divided into two groups. One group should take the position that there should be capital punishment for murder. The other group should argue that there should *not* be capital punishment.

When your group is finished preparing, choose three people to speak for your side. Choose one student to act as a moderator. After the debate is finished, the class should vote to decide which side has won the debate. You're voting based on the debaters' skills not whether you agree with their position.

DIGGING DEEPER

1   In groups, role play an arrest scene for your class. Have the other students decide whether it was a legal arrest or not. You must be able to justify your opinions.

2   Have a class discussion about what happens when the rights of an individual conflict with the rights of society in the following cases:

  a) smoking in a public place;
  b) drinking and driving;
  c) censorship;
  d) noisy party that disturbs the neighbourhood.

3   How much freedom does a judge have when deciding on a penalty? Why do you think the Criminal Code imposes limits on the judge?

4   Consider the kinds of punishments that the courts use. In each case the punished people lose something they value.

  a) For various punishments identify what you think the person is losing.
  b) Which loss do you think is the most severe? Why?
  c) Judges often impose more than one punishment when passing a sentence. Why?

5   Statistics show parole encourages prisoners to reform. About 75 percent of paroled prisoners manage to stay out of trouble. Only about 25 percent of paroled prisoners commit other crimes and are returned to prison. Some Canadians believe that criminals should not be released until they have served their full sentence. It is argued that one of the main reasons for incarceration is to protect society from criminals. What is your opinion on parole?

6   Select a law that in your opinion needs changing. Collect data to support the change you wish to make. Share your findings with the class. After you've discussed the change with your class, draft a letter to the appropriate government official outlining your recommended changes.

Major Offences by Offenders in Federal Prisons, 1980–1981

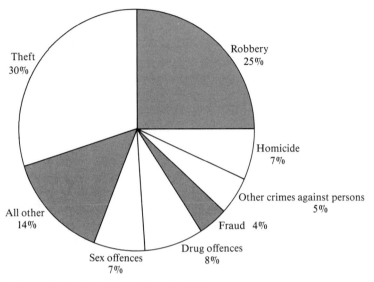

Robbery
25%

Theft
30%

Homicide
7%

Other crimes against persons
5%

All other
14%

Fraud 4%

Drug offences
8%

Sex offences
7%

Source: Correctional Services Canada, 1981.

5
The Law and You: Civil Law

Civil law deals with disputes and disagreements between people. Its purpose is to make sure people live up to their agreements and do not violate another individual's rights. When someone takes another person to court over such matters it is called a civil suit. The person suing is known as the plaintiff. The person being sued is the defendant. The court acts as the referee. The court can order the winner to pay damages to the loser, but it has no power to punish anyone. Let's look at some aspects of civil law.

CONTRACTS

More people get into trouble over contracts than any other kind of civil law. A contract is a bargain between two or more parties. Every time you exchange money for a service, you are performing a contract. You, the purchaser, and the seller are called the parties to the contract.

Contracts can be verbal. Both parties make a spoken agreement. A college student offers to shovel your driveway after a mid-winter blizzard and agrees upon twenty dollars for the work. When she has finished shovelling, you give her the money. This is a simple verbal contract. You can't decide to pay her less once you have agreed upon the price without breaking the contract.

Contracts can be implied. If you go out for dinner with some friends, it is taken for granted that when you have finished your meal you will pay your bill. It is an implied contract between the diner and the restaurant.

Contracts can be written. Maria and Janet went to their travel agent to book a holiday in the sun. The price included their flight, accommodation in a luxury hotel on the beach, and some meals. Maria and Janet signed a contract agreeing to pay for this vacation.

When they arrived nothing was what they had been promised. The hotel was full, so they were given alternate accommodation in a rundown hotel five kilometres from the beach. The meals were unfit to eat and the swimming pool was closed for repairs. The holiday was a disaster!

When Maria and Janet arrived home, they complained to their travel agent. He said there wasn't much he could do. He pointed to the fine print on the contract. It said the company reserved the right to substitute alternate accommodation if necessary.

The moral of the story is *caveat emptor*, a Latin saying that means "Let the buyer beware."

But all is not lost. Maria and Janet decide to take the travel agency to court. Small claims court can make awards, usually up to $1000. The procedure is simple, so neither Maria and Janet nor the travel agency will need a lawyer. Both sides discuss the details of the case with the judge. Typical cases handled in small claims court involve broken contracts, bad debts, squabbles over wages, and the recovery of personal property.

Minors and Contracts

Minors are not legally considered adults. In some provinces minors are people under the age of eighteen, while in other provinces the legal age is nineteen or twenty-one. Minors are treated differently in contract law to give them protection. They cannot make legal contracts.

Case study

Bob and Leo are fifteen-year-old friends. They enjoy watching martial arts films and want to learn kung fu. One day they are walking downtown and they see a martial arts studio. It's offering a special two-for-one deal. Two people can get fifteen weeks of kung fu instruction for the price of one person. Bob and Leo are quite excited and decide to check it out.

A high-pressure salesperson talks them into signing a contract. It sounds like a good deal, but when Bob and Leo are walking home they begin to get a little worried. They've signed up for three hundred dollars worth of lessons, and neither of them has a job.

People engage in contracts when they have their cars serviced.

Issue   1   Are Bob and Leo legally bound to their contract?
      2   Are their parents legally responsible for their sons' contract?

Decision 1   No
      2   No

Reason   People under the age of eighteen are not legally bound to any contract they sign. Their parents or guardians cannot be held responsible for contracts signed by minors, except in the case of necessities. A martial arts course wouldn't be considered necessary.

Renters and Leases

The Landlord and Tenant Act ensures the rights of the tenant (renter) and the landlord (owner of the building). The rental unit can be an apartment, house, mobile home, or town house. The act explains the rights and responsibilities that landlords and tenants owe each other and it protects both parties in case of a disagreement. The contract between a landlord and a tenant is a lease. A lease does not need to be written, but it is a good idea. The lease states the conditions of renting such as the amount of rent, the length of tenancy, and who pays for heat, hydro, and water.

Offer to Lease

I/WE

of the   of   (as Lessee)

having inspected the premises, hereby agree to and with

                                                                                                                                (as Lessor)

through   Agent for Lessor

to lease premises consisting of

for a term of

from   to

at an annual rental of

payable in equal monthly instalments of   in advance on the   day of each

month during the said term. Submitted herewith is the Lessee's cheque for

payable to the said Agent as a deposit to be held in trust pending completion or other termination

of the agreement resulting from the acceptance of this offer, and to be credited on account of rental

payable on the   day(s) of   . Vacant possession of the

premises shall be delivered to the Lessee on the   day of   , 19   .

Prior thereto, the Lessor and the Lessee shall execute and deliver a lease of the said premises in the

Lessor's form subject to such amendments as may be mutually agreed between the parties and their

respective solicitors. Provided and it is hereby agreed that such lease shall contain the following

provisions as to:

 (i) Repairs *(Indicate nature and extent of respective obligations to repair)*

This is a standard lease used between landlords and tenants.

A tenant has the right to:

- a place in good state of repair (the heat and plumbing must work)
- privacy (the landlord can only enter after receiving the tenant's permission, in an emergency, or after twenty-four hours written notice)
- ninety days written notice of a rent increase.

The landlord has the right to:

- expect the tenant to pay the rent in full and on time
- have the property kept clean and be informed of needed repairs
- not have damage done to the property
- in the case of apartment buildings, the rights of other tenants must be respected.

Landlords can no longer evict tenants without following an involved legal process. Tenants can only be forced to leave by a court order. A landlord can try to evict a tenant for:

- failure to pay rent
- disturbing other tenants
- using the property for illegal purposes
- causing damage
- overcrowding.

Before court action is started, the landlord must give the tenant written notice. The notice must state the reason(s) for eviction and give twenty days for the tenants to leave.

Case study
Sylvie and Carol are university students. They decided to share an apartment. Sylvie and Carol signed a lease as joint tenants. Their lease was to run for one year, and they were each to give the landlord $265 per month. However, after four months, Carol moved back to her parents' home. It was much cheaper and she didn't have to do her own laundry and cook her own meals.

Sylvie didn't have enough money to pay for Carol's share of the rent. Carol refused to pay Sylvie any money. Mr. Hoy, the landlord, claimed that Sylvie was responsible for Carol's share of the rent. Sylvie argued that Mr. Hoy knew that half the rent was coming from Carol.

Issue   Is Sylvie responsible for half or all of the rent?
Decision   Sylvie is legally responsible for the full rent.
Reason   The lease says that Sylvie and Carol were joint tenants. The law says this makes no difference to the landlord. If one tenant does not pay her/his full share, the other is responsible to pay the full amount.

Sylvie could sue Carol in small claims court to recover the money.

DISCRIMINATION IN THE WORKPLACE

Most provinces in Canada have laws to make sure that no person is discriminated against in the workplace. The Ontario Human Rights Code states "no person shall be refused employment because of race, creed, colour, age, sex, marital status, nationality, ancestry, or place of origin."

Some employers breach the code by asking for information about an applicant's race. Some employment agencies might breach the code by not referring women or French Canadians to prospective employers.

If a person feels discrimination might have occurred, s/he may file a complaint at the nearest office of the Human Rights Commission. The complaint will be investigated and, if necessary, a Board of Inquiry may be set up. At the inquiry, the commission's lawyers will argue on behalf of the victim. The person or company accused may also bring a lawyer. Evidence is heard and witnesses may be called.

Women are now exploring careers in forestry.

Case study

Anne Adams had just finished taking an auto mechanics course at a community college. She saw a job in a newspaper that said:

JUNIOR AUTO MECHANIC
Required for east end garage.
Must be a good worker with
community college background
Apply: MMM Garage

Anne went to apply for the job, but she was told it had already been filled. However, one week later the advertisement was still running in the newspaper. Three weeks later, Anne went by the garage and noticed that a man had been hired. Anne filed a complaint with the Human Rights Commission.

The owner of the garage told the commission the job was too physically demanding for a woman. Anne worked in a garage in her hometown during the summers and never had any difficulty performing any task. Her teacher at the community college said Anne was the best student in the course.

Issue Is being a male a genuine requirement for the job?
Decision No. Anne was discriminated against.
Reason During the investigation, evidence and witnesses demonstrated that Anne could fill all the job requirements.

Another branch of civil law deals with victims who go to court to recover damages from a wrongdoing. Sometimes the wrongdoing comes from intentional actions. Other times it comes from carelessness or negligence. Consider these cases and see whether damages should be recovered or not.

Case study

The plaintiff, a fourteen-year-old student named Lise Tremblay, was seriously injured while doing a gymnastic manoeuvre during gym class. Lise was an aspiring gymnast and hoped to participate in the next Olympic games. Lise was one of several students allowed to practise their gymnastic routines in a room adjacent to the gymnasium. There were no teachers to supervise the practice session. However, students were asked to act as spotters for each other and told not to attempt any manoeuvre they could not complete easily.

At the end of a very successful routine, Lise tried a very complicated dismount from the parallel bars. Her spotters could not prevent her from landing on her back. Lise suffered severe spinal injuries and became a quadriplegic.

Issue Were the school authorities responsible for supervising Lise and the other students during the practice session? If so, did they provide adequate supervision?
Decision The defendants, the school authorities, were found guilty of not providing adequate supervision for Lise. At the trial, the plaintiff was awarded $2.5 million.
Reason The standard of care required was that of a careful parent. The judge indicated that students doing gymnastic routines alone was dangerous. The teacher should have seen that injuries were a distinct possibility. A cautious parent would not have allowed a child to participate in this activity unsupervised.

Case study

The fifteen-year-old plaintiff, Kyle O'Banion, was a student with limited athletic ability. The defendant was his physical education teacher, Mr. Smylie, who had twenty-one years' teaching experience.

Mr. Smylie had noticed that Kyle was shy, had few friends, and did not socialize well with his classmates. One day, Kyle was placed in a group with three other boys and instructed to practise for the United Way three-legged race. All the boys were given instruction on how to do this safely. Kyle followed the instructions but, nevertheless, fell and broke his leg.

Issue   Was Mr. Smylie negligent in having Kyle participate in an activity where he might get hurt?

Decision   No, Mr. Smylie was not guilty.

Reason   The duty of a physical education teacher is to act in the manner of a kind and judicious parent. The judge said it was reasonable for a fifteen-year-old boy to participate in a three-legged race as part of a supervised physical education class.

WHY LAWS CHANGE

Attitudes and values change over the years and so do our laws. Laws that were perfectly acceptable to our great-grandparents are not necessarily acceptable to us today. For example, in the late-nineteenth century, young children, ten to twelve years old, were often sent to work in factories and coal mines. Today, that is totally unacceptable and we have laws to make sure it doesn't happen. Changes in laws come only when society is ready to accept them.

Sometimes society needs a bit of help to accept changes in laws. Canadian women went through a struggle to gain the right to vote and hold public office. At the turn of the century,

1   Women were not allowed to vote.

2   Women could not be elected to federal or provincial offices in government.

3   A man had a great deal of control over his wife and children. It was assumed that the views of married women were adequately represented through their husbands' votes.

4   It was felt that a woman's greatest contribution to society was to keep house for her husband and to bear his children.

By 1900 ideas about women were slowly beginning to change. Women, in many countries, began to organize themselves to obtain the vote. These women, called suffragists, wanted to win the same rights and opportunities that men enjoyed. They used arguments, humour, petitions, and demonstrations to attain their goal.

Many Canadian suffragists got their start working in the Women's Christian Temperance Union (WCTU). It was an organization of women whose aim was to combat the problems created by alcohol. In their crusade against liquor, many women began to realize that unless they had the right to vote no government would listen to them. It was not surprising then that many leaders of the WCTU became active in the movement for women's suffrage.

Nellie McClung, prominent Canadian suffragist

Nellie McClung was one of Canada's great social reformers. She led the fight with the Manitoba government to let women have the right to vote. "Certainly," she said, "women belong in the home, but not twenty-four hours a day! They should have exactly the same freedoms as men." McClung confronted the premier of Manitoba with the words – "We are not here to ask for a gift or a favour but for a right – not for mercy or for justice!"

When World War I started in Europe in 1914, it helped to prove that Nellie McClung was right. With so many men away fighting the war, there was a serious shortage of workers in many vital industries. Women were called upon to do jobs formerly performed only by men. Women made bombs and shells in munitions factories, drove streetcars, and worked in banks, offices, and stores. They did the same jobs as men and did just as well as men. They proved that women were every bit as capable as men. Therefore, women should have exactly the same freedoms as men.

In early 1916, a new Liberal government came to power in Manitoba. The Liberals had promised to give Manitoba women the right to vote if they were elected. On 27 January 1916, the bill was passed and the law was changed. Manitoba was the first province to grant women the right to vote. About two months later, a similar bill was passed in Saskatchewan, and a few weeks later, in Alberta.

In 1917, the Canadian government passed the Wartime Elections Act. It gave the vote to wives, widows, mothers, sisters, and daughters of Canadian soldiers serving overseas. It was only a matter of time until women were given the vote. On 24 May 1918, woman's suffrage was finally won in Canada!

Another fighter for women's rights was Agnes MacPhail. She was the first woman elected to the House of Commons in 1921. She was reelected four times. In 1921, Nellie McClung was elected to the Alberta Legislature.

DIGGING DEEPER

1 In each of the following situations, who is in the wrong? Explain your reasoning.
   a) Chantal is surprised when she comes into her apartment after work and finds her landlady just leaving. The landlady says she was just checking to see if all the windows were closed as it looks like rain. Chantal is quite angry and tells her landlady not to go into her apartment again without permission.
   b) Bob celebrates his promotion by throwing a wild, noisy party. His neighbours complain and call the police to quiet the crowd. The next morning, Bob's landlord brings him a written eviction notice that states Bob has seven days to get out of his apartment.

2 The law says that a buyer has the responsibility to check out what s/he is purchasing. Imagine buying a used car without first taking it out for a test drive or having a mechanic check it out. The law says that it is your own fault if you find out later that the car is a "lemon." Discuss the fairness of the idea of *caveat emptor*.

3 Have a class debate on the issue: People between the ages of sixteen and eighteen should have the right to sign their own contracts if they hold a permanent job.

4 Phone the nearest Legal Aid office to find out more about legal aid. Who is eligible? How does the system work? Invite a Legal Aid lawyer to speak to your class.

5 The Ontario Human Rights Code forbids discrimination in the workplace based on race, creed, colour, age, sex, marital status, nationality, ancestry, or place of origin. It says nothing about handicapped people. Do some research to discover what rights handicapped people have in the workplace.

6 In groups, make laws for your history class. Be prepared to explain why your laws are necessary. Select one of the laws and hold a class discussion on its merits and faults.

6
Rights and Responsibilities of Citizenship

Many Canadians take their rights for granted. We have the right to speak out and criticize our government. We have the right to practise any religion or none at all. We are free to travel outside Canada whenever we wish. We have the right to move, live, and work in any province in Canada. However, in some countries of the world citizens do not have these rights.

All these privileges are rights we have as Canadian citizens. These rights, and many others, are guaranteed in the Charter of Rights and Freedoms. The Charter is an important part of the Constitution Act of 1982.

Before our Constitution was repatriated in 1982, these rights were considered part of Common Law. Although we had a Bill of Rights (1960), it was only an Act of Parliament and could be changed by a parliamentary vote. Now, our freedoms are entrenched in the Constitution.

Our most important rights and freedoms are guaranteed under the Charter. They are:

1 **Fundamental freedoms**
   a) freedom of conscience and religion;
   b) freedom of thought, belief, opinion and expression, including
      i) freedom of the press,
      ii) freedom of peaceful assembly,
      iii) freedom of association.

2 **Democratic rights**
   a) the right to vote;
   b) the right to run for election.

3 **Mobility rights**
   a) the right to enter, remain in, and leave Canada;
   b) the right to live in, move to, and work in any province.

4 **Legal rights**
   a) the right to life, liberty, and security;
   b) protection against unreasonable search and seizure or arbitrary detention or imprisonment;
   c) the right to be informed quickly about the charges, if arrested;
   d) the right to hire a lawyer
   e) the right to trial within a reasonable time
   f) the right to be presumed innocent until proven guilty according to law in a fair and public hearing;
   g) the right not to be subjected to cruel and unusual treatment or punishment.

5 **Equality rights**
   a) protection from discrimination on the basis of race, national or ethnic origin, colour, religion, age, sex, or mental or physical disability.

6 **Official languages**
   a) the right to use English and French in the government and courts of Canada and the province of New Brunswick.

7 **Minority language education rights**
   a) the right to education in English or French where there are sufficient numbers of students.

8 **Aboriginal rights**
   a) recognition of the existing aboriginal and treaty rights of the Native people (Inuit, Indian, and Metis).

OBLIGATIONS AND OPPORTUNITIES OF CITIZENSHIP

Rights impose obligations. If you have the right to freely express your ideas, then you have the obligation to let others freely express their ideas.

A group of high school students made a list of the basic rights they thought they should have. Here is their list. We have the right to:

- choose our own friends
- go out with and marry the person of our choice
- say what we please
- go where we like
- read and see what we wish
- be educated
- be safe from being mugged or beaten up
- enjoy our privacy
- be able to keep our personal property
- keep our cultural heritage
- live in an unpolluted environment
- practice our own religion
- be treated with respect by the police
- be treated with respect by our parents and teachers
- vote in an election at a certain age.

What obligations are imposed upon the students by these rights?

Obligation: Get Involved

Elections give you a chance to participate in the governing of your country. Your vote helps in the choice of the government. It is a very important right. Yet, in some elections, there is a very low turnout of voters. Federal and provincial elections sometimes only draw about 60 percent of the voters. In municipal elections, the turnout may drop as low as one-third. An election victory, in some cases, is decided by only a few votes, so every vote *does* count.

The table shows the percentage of people on the voters' list who actually voted in the 1980 and 1984 federal elections.

Some Canadians have suggested that the franchise (the vote) should be taken away from citizens who do not vote in each election. In Australia, a different solution to low voter turnout has been tried. The eligible voters who do not vote in each election are fined. Should everyone in Canada be required to vote? Why?

Ideal voters are informed voters. They examine closely the

Percentage of voters casting ballots 1984 and 1988 federal elections		
	1984	1988
Ontario	76	75
Quebec	76	75
Nova Scotia	75	75
New Brunswick	77	76
Manitoba	73	75
British Columbia	78	79
Prince Edward Island	85	85
Saskatchewan	78	78
Alberta	69	75
Newfoundland	65	67
Yukon	78	78
Northwest Territories	68	71
Canadian average	75	76

different parties and candidates. They know the issues and make a careful decision on how to vote.

One way to become a well-informed voter is to get involved in a political party. You can participate more fully in an election by contributing your time and labour. To encourage Canadians to take part in the election process beyond voting, the Income Tax Act allows a generous tax credit for contributions to political parties.

You may even consider becoming a candidate. In order to run for federal office, you must:
- be eighteen years old by election day
- be a Canadian citizen
- give a $200 deposit (which is returned if you win more than 15 percent of the votes cast in your riding).

The money qualification is intended to make sure candidates are serious. Although some candidates have no hope of winning they are still willing to run. Some are looking for a chance to express their ideas or raise certain issues in the campaign. Some candidates simply want to poke fun at elections and are viewed as nuisance candidates.

It costs a lot of money to run an election campaign. Candidates must rent a campaign office and install phones and other office equipment. They must also spend large sums of money on advertising. Posters, lawn signs, and pamphlets need to be printed. They are a crucial part of the campaign as they introduce the candidates to the voters and keep their names visible throughout the campaign.

Since 1974 there has been a limit on how much each candidate and each political party can spend on their campaigns. This limit was introduced to ensure that wealthy candidates did not have an unfair advantage over other candidates. Also, candidates who are elected or receive 15 percent of the votes have their $200 returned and are reimbursed 50 percent of acceptable election expenses.

1   Which of the three main political parties encouraged the most female candidates?

2   Which party had the most women elected?

3   How many women were elected to the House of Commons in 1984? How many men?

4   Alberta, Saskatchewan, and Manitoba had thirty-three female candidates in the 1984 federal election. Keeping in mind what you know about the women's suffrage movement in Canada, why does this number surprise you?

5   Discuss how more women could be elected to the federal government. What are some ways political parties could encourage female candidates?

Opportunity: Write Your Member of Parliament

Citizens have the right to make their views known to their elected representatives. Members of Parliament welcome the ideas and opinions of their constituents. MPs can do a better job when they know their constituents' views. If you write to your federal MP in care of the House of Commons in Ottawa, it's not necessary to put a stamp on your envelope.

The law on capital punishment has caused great debate among Canadians. In 1976 the death penalty was abolished. However, many Canadians are in favour of bringing back the death penalty. It is felt that violent crime, like murder, is increasing and the only way to curb this increase is by the return of the death penalty.

In 1987, the House of Commons held a free debate on capital punishment. A free debate allows MPs to vote according to their conscience and not party policy. In the months leading up to the

Number of Female Candidates, MPs, and their Party Affiliation – Federal Elections 1988

	PC	Lib.	NDP	SC	Comm.	Libert.	Rhino	RP	GP	CRWP	Com'lth	Ind.	Total
Ontario	11	17	35		6	10	3		4	1	4	16	107
(elected)	(5)	(7)											(12)
Quebec	16	11	17	1	7	1	9		6		6	12	86
(elected)	(11)	(2)											(13)
Nova Scotia		3	4										7
(elected)		(2)											(2)
New Brunswick			3										3
Manitoba		2	1				1					3	7
(elected)	(1)												(1)
British Columbia	6	6	9		6	1	1	4	4	1		5	43
(elected)	(2)		(4)										(6)
PEI			4										4
(elected)		(1)											(1)
Saskatchewan	1	3	1							2			7
Alberta		8	7		1	1		4	1		1	6	29
(elected)	(2)							(1)					(3)
Newfoundland		1	2										3
Yukon			1										1
(elected)			(1)										(1)
NWT		1											1
(elected)		(1)											(1)
Total	34	51	83	1	20	13	14	8	15	4	11	42	296
(elected)	(21)	(13)	(5)					(1)					(40)

RP = Reform Party; GP = Green Party; CRWP = Confederation of Regions Western Party; Com'wlth = Party for the Commonwealth of Canada

( ) = elected

debate thousands of citizens wrote to their MPs and to newspapers expressing their views.

People supporting the return of the death penalty gave these arguments:

Capital punishment is a deterrent. Potential killers will think twice if they know they will lose their own lives if they are caught.

A police chief wrote:

The penalty must fit the crime, and if you have a crime of murder is a twenty-five-year jail term enough? I don't think it is. I think if you have taken a life, the death penalty is the only answer.

The cost of keeping criminals in jails is a tremendous cost to the taxpayers of Canada. It is estimated that it takes a least a half a million dollars to keep a convicted killer in jail for fifty years.

People opposing the return of the death penalty wrote letters showing a different side of the argument.

It is ridiculous to think the death penalty is a deterrent for any murderer. Most killers do not plan the crime beforehand. Most murders occur in the heat of an argument or fight. People who are exploding with anger do not stop to think about the death penalty. They act instead.

A leading civil rights lawyer wrote:

When you analyze the statistics in countries that still have the death penalty, you find that the murder rate is no lower than it is in Canada. It appears that capital punishment does not effectively reduce the number of violent crimes that are committed.

The state should not bring back the death penalty for the simple reason that mistakes are often made. We could put to death an innocent person. Look at the Donald Marshall case in Nova Scotia.

A member of Amnesty International, a human rights group, wrote:

Life is sacred. It should always be respected. The best way to foster this truth is for society to set an example by its own actions. As long as a convicted murderer is kept alive there is still a chance that a human life can be rehabilitated and s/he can become a useful citizen again.

In June 1987 political analysts predicted the parliamentary vote on capital punishment would be very close. It could go either way. Newspaper polls indicated that 60 percent of Canadians were in favour of capital punishment. But Canada's MPs surprised the analysts and the pollsters and voted against the return of capital punishment.

After the vote, political commentators said that one of the decisive factors influencing the vote was the well-organized letter-writing blitz by opponents of the death penalty. These people used their influence and power to convince enough MPs to defeat the motion.

Opportunity: Join a Pressure Group

We have examined how an individual can influence the decision-making process. If individuals join forces they have even more power.

Suppose a group of neighbours is concerned about plans to open a dump site in their area. They decide to support the mayoralty candidate who has emphatically stated her opposition to dump sites near residential areas. Their support ensures that she wins the election.

Pressure groups can do a number of things to express their opinions and influence government decision making. They can lobby people in government. Lobbying is making personal contacts with government officials and making the ideas and goals of your interest group known to them. A lobbyist hopes to exert enough influence or pressure so that legislation will be favourable to their cause. Where does the word "lobby" come from? Groups of business people used to wait in the lobby of the British House of Commons. They hoped to get government contracts as the members of Parliament passed through the lobby.

The best lobbyists are people who already have contacts in Ottawa and the provincial capitals. Lobbyists are often former government officials or former politicians. They know who is making the decisions and have access to them. A pressure group can hire a lobbyist to keep their interests constantly in front of the decision makers.

Another way to apply pressure is to use the media to get public attention for your cause. Greenpeace has used the media quite effectively. Through the media, worldwide attention has been focussed on the seal hunt that takes place off Canada's east coast. Millions of people saw the killing of the cute baby harp seals and refused to purchase products made from the seal pelts. By 1984 the market for pelts had been reduced drastically.

For many people on Canada's east coast and Arctic communities, the seal hunt is a way of life, and often their only source of income. In Resolute, NWT, population of 170, the community's

Greenpeace worker spraying baby harp seal with paint. This makes the pelt worthless to sealers.

income from the sale of fur pelts dropped from $55 000 in 1982 to $1800 in 1983.

In August 1984, Native leaders from Canada, the United States, and Greenland met to make a counter-attack. They decided to join forces with the fur industry and form their own pressure group. They are lobbying the government and the media to inform them of their view of the seal-hunting issue.

Opportunity: Speak to a Parliamentary Committee

On issues of great importance and far-reaching impact, the government establishes special parliamentary committees. Members of the committee, or task force, travel across the country hearing the views of average Canadians. From these views, members of the task force make recommendations to the government. Appearing before a parliamentary committee provides Canadians with an opportunity to influence government policy and the laws of the land.

In 1983 a parliamentary committee was set up to report on visible minorities in Canadian society. It was composed of seven MPs representing the three main political parties. The committee was asked to study ways of promoting racial harmony and tolerance among Canadians.

Why was this parliamentary task force established? During the early 1980s many Canadians were becoming increasingly concerned about race relations. There are, after all, about 2 million Canadians who belong to visible minorities. These groups include Native people as well as citizens with origins in Africa, Asia, and the Caribbean. Newspapers were frequently carrying reports of racial insults and attacks directed at visible minorities. The government was alarmed enough to appoint a task force.

For seven months the committee heard briefs from citizens at public hearings. In March 1984 the report, entitled *Equality Now*, was presented to Parliament. Here are some individual opinions contained in the report.

> Many of my countrymen do not approach life in Canada from the standpoint of service. They are not observant of how the majority behaves, and they are not sensitive to the values and customs of the majority. ...In India it is not the custom to say "excuse me." Yet such a small thing can cause a misunderstanding. In India if you want to get through a crowded place, you just push through without any kind of "excuse me." If you do that in Toronto, especially if you are an East Indian, you only add fuel to the racism. There are hundreds of other small things like these.
>
> Kam Singh

But what we get in the Canadian media is a fantasy. Worse than that, it's an outright lie – especially in advertising. The women and men in the commercials are all WASPs. It's so stereotyped and artificial that you don't even see a white person *with red hair* – only blondes and brunettes. The whole advertising industry, both clients and agencies, live in a sterile, out-of-touch fantasy world that has very little connection with the human reality of the Canadian public. Viewers here get a bigger dose of reality by watching American commercials than they do from the daily diet of lily-white, totally predictable commercials from Canadian advertisers.

I'm a fighter and a survivor, and that's what I want to contribute to young Canadians who are non-whites. The first step is to bring economic pressure on the advertisers to change their policies. As far as I can see, there is only way to do that – hit them in the pocketbook.

Lynda Armstrong

We have identified language training as the key factor in preparing our Chinese immigrants for employment – for decent jobs with decent pay. And employment, in turn, is the key factor in enabling them to participate in Canadian society and to make a contribution to the community. Many of the other kinds of troubles that immigrants encounter – family tension, medical ailments, psychological breakdown, criminal behaviour – these stem from the lack of good employment.

Angela Kan

Opportunity: Hold Demonstrations and Protests

Sometimes demonstrations and protests are the only ways to make the government listen. Peaceful demonstrations and large meetings not only bring your cause to the attention of the legislators, but to every Canadian. This increases the pressure on the MPs to take action on your issue.

When Pierre Trudeau was working to "bring home" Canada's Constitution, the original proposals contained no mention of aboriginal or treaty rights. Native groups wanted to safeguard their rights by writing them into the Constitution.

In 1980, Native people decided they had to take direct action. They decided to hold a demonstration in Ottawa to make their point of view known.

A group of Native people left Vancouver on two transcontinental trains. The trains travelled on different routes in order to pick up as many passengers as possible. In Winnipeg the two trains came together to form the Constitution Express.

All along the route the Native people received a lot of support and publicity. By the time the Constitution Express arrived in Ottawa and the Native people had staged a demonstration on Parliament Hill, most Canadians were well aware of their group and its goals. A clause that recognized "existing" aboriginal and treaty rights was eventually inserted in the Constitution.

AN ISSUE TO CONSIDER

In Sudbury, Ontario, there are 50 000 Francophones, about one-third of the population. Only two of the four hospitals are bilingual. Maternity services are available in only one English hospital and a specialized heart program in the other. Therefore, a French-speaking couple must have their baby delivered in the English hospital. A Francophone patient needing risky heart

Native Canadians protesting for aboriginal rights

treatment must cope at the English hospital. Should the rights of 500 000 Franco-Ontarians (and Anglophones inside Quebec) be protected? Use the issue-analysis organizer to reach and communicate a conclusion.

DEVELOPING SKILLS:
HOW TO READ A NEWSPAPER

If you're like most Canadians, you try to keep up with the news by watching it on television. The problem with TV is that, in most cases, there are severe time limitations on every story. The journalist has sixty seconds to get the main idea of the story across to the viewers. That's just not enough time to examine the issue in any depth. So what you get from television is not much more than a front-page headline service.

To be a very informed citizen, you have to get the whole story. You have to get behind the TV headlines for a complete account, and sometimes analysis, of the news from a well-edited, well-written newspaper. Regular reading of the newspaper will help you to be well-informed about current international, national, and local events.

FOCUS **Should the rights of Francophones outside Quebec and Anglophones inside Quebec be protected by federal and provincial laws?**

Alternatives		Yes, their rights should be protected by law.	No, their rights should not be protected by law.
Organize information	Legislation: What does the law say about the issue? • Charter of Rights and Freedoms • Courts • Education • Government services Public Opinion: What would each of these groups say about the issue? • Francophones outside Quebec and Anglophones inside Quebec • Anglophones outside Quebec and Francophones inside Quebec • Recent immigrants to Canada who are not French- or English-speaking		
Conclusions	What conclusion did you reach? Why?		
Communication	To whom will you communicate your class decision? How can you communicate your conclusions?		

There are a few things you should know about the setup of a newspaper. The size of the headline will tell you how important the story is. For example, when the stock market plummeted in late 1987, most newspapers proclaimed this in very large, bold type. The less important the story, the smaller the headline.

The main story of the day is usually the one with the largest headline. But newspaper editors attract your attention to the story by placing it above the fold in the newspaper. So, when you walk by a newspaper box or stand, you'll see the major story.

A good newspaper story provides you with four basic ingredients to give you a thorough understanding of the news: information, background, analysis, and interpretation.

Information   First, you need basic, straight facts. A news story should just report the news. It should give you both sides of the issue and not slant the news.

Reporters write a story in a special way – the inverted pyramid style. Reporters start with the climax, or the end, of the story first. This is done to get the readers' attention. The most important details come next, followed by the details that are less important. Knowing how a news story is written will help you sift through the facts.

Background   A well-reported story will tell you *who, what, where, when, how*. The best news stories will tell you *why*. The "why" is often missing, and it is often the key ingredient.

Reporters who tell you "why" are giving you background information. This will help you understand the story and evaluate it, and other related events, for yourself.

Analysis   Leading newspapers also offer analysis of the news. This goes beyond the facts. Newspapers hire columnists, who are usually experts in a particular field, to explain and offer insight into various current events.

Interpretation   In a reliable newspaper, interpretation isn't mixed with the news. It is usually reserved for the editorial page. Interpretation goes beyond the news and beyond analysis. It tells you not just what will probably happen but what should happen. Editorial opinions are interesting to read, but are often quite biassed. Don't let editorial writers do your thinking for you. Read about the issue, wrestle with different approaches to the issue, and come to your own conclusion about the impact of the issue upon your life or nation.

Put your newspaper skills to work
Tonight, pick an important story on the television news that interests you. Dig into the same story in a newspaper. Follow it and continue to follow it closely in print. You should develop a

much better understanding of the event.

Write a short paragraph comparing the treatment of the story on the television news with the story in a newspaper.

DIGGING DEEPER

1   Rank these rights, from the Charter of Rights and Freedoms, in order of importance to you. Give reasons for your choices.

- aboriginal rights
- assembly
- association
- conscience
- equality
- language
- legal rights
- minority language
- mobility
- press
- run for public office
- thought
- vote

2   You may wish to broaden your research by conducting a survey to find out which rights Canadians value most. In 1977, the *Toronto Star* asked "Which of the four human rights do you consider to be the most important – freedom of religion, freedom of speech, freedom from want, or freedom of fear?" Here are the results:

Speech	47 percent
Fear	21 percent
Want	13 percent
Religion	11 percent
No opinion	8 percent

The *Toronto Star* also recorded the results by age groups to see whether different age groups valued different freedoms. If you would like to see these results write to the newspaper and ask them to send you the results printed in the 23 July 1977 edition.

3   Divide into groups and compose a "Students' Bill of Rights" or a "Child's Bill of Rights."

4   a) Who sponsored the report *Equality Now*?

b) Why do parliamentary committees usually travel across Canada instead of holding their hearings in Ottawa?

c) The cover of *Equality Now* is black and white. How do the colours relate to the title?

d) How do parliamentary committees and hearings involve individuals and groups in the decision-making process?

e) Some people criticize governments for setting up parliamentary committees. They believe the committee just makes it look like the government is taking action. Explain why these critics feel the way they do. Find out what has happened to the report *Equality Now*. Have any of their eighty recommendations been implemented? What, if any, action has been taken by the federal government?

5   a) Was the Constitution Express and the demonstration by the Native people an effective way to influence the decision makers? Why?

b) What preparations would be necessary if you intended to stage a public protest?

6   Research other arguments in favour of or against capital punishment. Choose sides and debate the issue. See if you can stage the debate before another class that has not studied the issue. When the debate is finished, have your audience vote on the issue. How different is the vote than the one taken by MPs in June 1987?

7   What is a good citizen? Brainstorm the criteria of good citizenship. Establish the characteristics that the class considers essential. Then choose Canadians, historical and contemporary, who meet these criteria.

Invite the "Citizen of the Year" from your local community to address your class.

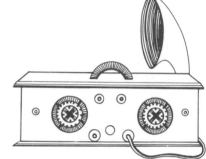

7
The Twentieth Century Dawns

In the evening hours of 22 January 1901, a tired old lady died. She was Victoria, queen of England and empress of India. For sixty-three years, Victoria had ruled nearly one-quarter of the globe. A quarter of the human race were her subjects, including 5.3 million Canadians. Her Empire stretched around the world, carrying with it British laws, customs, and language.

Queen Victoria had always tried to keep things as they were. Though her husband, Albert, had been dead for thirty-nine years, the queen left his room exactly as it had been. Albert's clothes were laid out as if he were alive. Victoria even ordered that hot water for shaving be brought to his room every morning. Now Victoria herself was dead, and with her death came the end of an age.

Among the subjects who watched her funeral procession, very few people could remember a time when she was not their queen. But now that Victoria was dead, people sensed that nothing could ever be the same again. Her eldest son "Bertie" became King Edward VII. Edward was a new king in a new century.

WHAT WAS IT LIKE TO LIVE IN CANADA IN 1901?

Horses played a significant role in everyone's life. When a baby was born a horse-drawn carriage brought the doctor to the house.

Yonge Street, Toronto, 1900

Similarly, the undertaker's sleek black horses pulled the ornate hearse to the cemetery at the end of a person's life. Horses were always in the picture. Farmers used them to pull their ploughs and town dwellers kept them for transport. Every business – the bakery, the dairy, the coal company – had to have horses to pull its delivery wagons. Horse-drawn streetcars were still in use in many Canadian towns and cities. Montreal and Toronto, however, were beginning to make the switch to the electric railway. The sight of horse-drawn fire engines racing through the streets was an exciting thing to behold. There were traffic jams in larger cities and people were run over, though there was nothing to match the traffic accidents of today. A more common cause of excitement was when a horse ran away and had to be stopped by a police officer or a brave passerby.

By the turn of the century the bicycle craze swept Canada. One in every twelve persons owned "a wheel." The police force in many cities found the bicycle useful for patrolling city streets. Bicycles were cheaper to purchase and operate than horses,

Fire engine, 1912

which had to be fed and housed. For many ordinary city residents a bicycle solved the problem of transit within the city. People could now live farther from their place of work and get to their job more easily. Yet bicycles were more than transportation, they were romance. Couples honeymooned on them. On summer Sundays the roads were dusty from cyclists heading into the countryside for picnics. A new sense of freedom and mobility had been given to those willing to take up the sport.

The automobile was just being introduced into society. Henry Ford had founded the Detroit Automobile Company in 1899, nine years after Daimler started his company in Germany. King Edward VII was an enthusiastic supporter of "horseless carriages" and helped to make them popular. In Ontario the first motorist was John Moodie of Hamilton, who imported a $1000 Winton from the United States in 1898. However, it was not until the 1920s that the automobile was no longer considered a rich person's toy. Not until the development of the assembly line did the price of a car move within the grasp of nearly everyone. Certainly no one at the turn of the century foresaw the problems of accidents, parking, and congestion which the new invention would bring.

It was not until 1903 that the American brothers, Orville and Wilbur Wright, successfully flew the first airplane. That flight, on the beach of Kitty Hawk, North Carolina, lasted just twelve seconds. But the Wright brothers proved that a machine that was heavier than air could fly. The air age had begun.

Meanwhile in Canada Alexander Graham Bell, the inventor of the telephone, also worked on the problem of flight. At Baddeck, Nova Scotia, he formed a group known as the Aerial Experiment Association (AEA). In 1908 Casey Baldwin, a member of the AEA, flew a plane they had built, *Red Wing*, a distance of 97 m. By the summer of 1909 Douglas McCurdy was making flights of 32 km over the water at Baddeck in the *Silver Dart*. The *Silver Dart* was the finest and most easily flown aircraft of its day. McCurdy and Baldwin tried hard to convince the Canadian government of the military value of an air force. However, when the *Silver Dart* crash-landed during the flight trials, military officials rejected the idea of using airplanes in warfare. Thirty years later the Canadian government asked McCurdy to become the director of government aircraft production during World War II.

Around the turn of the century the telephone was being used increasingly. Household needs could now be ordered by telephone and delivered to the home. Small storekeepers could hire youngsters with bicycles to deliver packages throughout the city. Party lines were the rule in those days. All calls had to be channelled through the telephone exchange. Operators sitting at boards connected the parties. The telephone had a great social impact because it provided new opportunities of employment for women as operators.

In 1901, at Signal Hill in St. John's, Newfoundland, Guglielmo Marconi received the first radio signal sent across the Atlantic Ocean. The following year, with the backing of the Canadian government, Marconi built a wireless station at Glace Bay, Nova Scotia. From here he set up official transatlantic wireless communication. However, another twenty years elapsed before radio broadcasting began as a means of mass entertainment. In the first years of the twentieth century, people were more dependent on home-made entertainment such as the piano, banjo, and amateur theatrical productions. The phonograph or gramophone was coming in, but the thick, flat discs sounded scratchy and tinny. Not until the invention of electrical recording in the 1920s did the sound of the records become more musically exact, and not until the 1950s was it possible to play the whole of a major composition on one record.

The first movie theatres were opened in the early years of the century and soon sprang up all over. The movies were known as

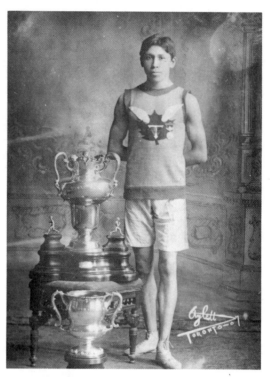

Tom Longboat, 1907

silent movies because dialogue was shown on the screen as cap-
tions. A pianist or a small orchestra accompanied the film and
provided important sound effects. It was twenty years before
talking films arrived. Canada's own Mary Pickford made her first
film in 1909, and Charlie Chaplin made his in 1911.

Another common form of entertainment was professional
sport. Baseball was the most popular in the United States, where
the World Series began in 1903. In Canada at this time tremendous attention was focussed on Tom Longboat. This young boy
was born on the Six Nations Reserve near Brantford, Ontario. By
1906, at the age of nineteen, Tom could outrun a horse around a
19-km course. The next year he raced the tough, hilly course of
the Boston Marathon. Against 125 opponents, Longboat set a
record of 2 hours, 24 minutes, 24 seconds in the marathon, bat-
tling snow, rain, and slush. This record was not surpassed until
the course of the Boston Marathon was changed to make it easier.
Each time Tom Longboat ran, crowds flocked to see him. At Madi-
son Square Gardens he took part in the "race of the century." He
raced against a professional runner, Alfie Shrubb. At the 39-km
mark Longboat passed Shrubb and went on to win the race.

Longboat was proclaimed the world's best long-distance runner. Tom later enlisted in the Canadian army and fought overseas in World War I. He died in 1949 at the Six Nations Reserve.

In the early 1900s other changes were taking place in industry, science, and every aspect of life. Bathrooms and modern conveniences became more common. Electric washing machines took some of the drudgery out of washday. Other gadgets included sewing machines, electric hearing aids, and vacuum cleaners. Canadians, who could afford them, purchased these gadgets from the Eaton's catalogue. The catalogue was considered by several generations to be the most popular book in Canada. Rural families particularly depended on the catalogue for everything from fence posts to fashionable hats. For Canadian children and adults Eaton's catalogue became a "wish book" that they could gaze at for hours and dream about the things they hoped to buy someday.

IMMIGRATION AND URBANIZATION

Between 1901 and 1911 Canada experienced the greatest wave of immigration in its history up to that time. Almost 2 million people immigrated from Europe, Britain, and the United States.

British immigrant family, 1908

They were looking for new homes and better opportunities. Not only did the number of people grow rapidly, but the make-up of the population changed a lot. By 1912 almost one-fifth of the population was not of British or French origin. The great influx of settlers meant that the population of western Canada grew rapidly.

Towns sprang up, roads were built, and railway lines branched out. Regina, Saskatoon, Calgary, and Edmonton mushroomed in size almost overnight. Grain elevators, which stored the harvested wheat, quickly began to dot the plains. On every side were endless fields of grain. Prosperity had arrived! The West was booming.

As the population of the West grew, two new provinces were created. In 1905 Alberta and Saskatchewan became the newest members of Confederation. In thirty-eight years, Confederation had grown from the joining of four provinces in eastern Canada to the union of nine provinces coast to coast.

At the turn of the century Canada was becoming more and more urbanized. In 1903–1904 the greatest railway boom in Canadian history began. One in three wage earners in eastern Canada worked for a railway or a company making railway supplies. Thousands of people found jobs surveying the routes, clearing and grading the land, and laying the ties and the track. Between 1904 and 1914, 18 200 km of new lines were added in Canada.

Railway building became the greatest single factor in the industrialization of Canada at this time. Gigantic quantities of steel, timber, dynamite, spikes, tools, and bridge-building materials were needed. Orders poured in for new freight cars and locomotives. Hundreds of grain elevators, docks, and warehouses had to be built as well. Every little town had its station, and in Montreal and Toronto the huge Windsor and Union stations were constructed for the increasing throngs of railway passengers. Grand hotels such as the Chateau Laurier in Ottawa, the Empress Hotel in Victoria, and the Chateau Frontenac in Quebec City were erected to provide luxury living for travellers.

Urbanization led to a serious problem of overcrowding in many Canadian cities. This was further complicated by the rapid increase in the number of immigrants coming to Canada. In one year alone, 96 000 immigrants arrived, and many of them settled in Montreal, Toronto, or Winnipeg. Often the housing accommodations were pitifully inadequate for all these people. Immigrants were forced to live in slums and work in basement or attic factories. Urban poverty and related problems of high unemployment and poor housing became very serious.

EQUALITY AND INEQUALITY

Perhaps the thing that would strike you most if you were to step back into the Canada of 1901 would be the inequality between man and man and between man and woman. People were divided by their work and by their wealth. In those days the rich really were rich, and taxes were so low that they were left with almost all of their money to spend. Most of it went on clothes, houses, horses, and carriages. Sir Henry Pellatt was a prime example of the wealth in Toronto. Pellatt is reported to have made $17 000 000 in the Toronto Electric Light Company and mining stocks. In 1910 he sank $2 000 000 into the building of Casa Loma, a palatial home in Toronto. Casa Loma contained thirty bathrooms, three bowling alleys, fifty-two telephones, and the world's finest indoor rifle range. The stables had mahogany stalls and Persian rugs, and Pellatt once had a custom set of false teeth made for his favourite horse.

However, the average Canadian at the turn of the century still lit a kerosene or gas lamp and cooked on a wood stove. Women shopped every day, scrubbed clothes on a washboard, put up pickles and fruit preserves, and beat their rugs with a wire whip.

At the bottom of the economic ladder were the immigrants. They were often forced to live in terrible conditions, crowded into basement rooms where sanitation was poor and ventilation was worse.

There was also the inequality between man and woman. For a respectable woman to enter a tavern, a pool room, or even a bowling alley was unthinkable. To go alone to a concert or the theatre was frowned upon. Women in Canada had just begun to fight to get as good an education as men. Women in professions, such as medicine, were still a rarity. Women tended to work in stores and factories, and girls from poorer families became domestic servants. Girls from wealthy or middle-class families had to choose between nursing and teaching as a possible career. The early twentieth century was still very much a man's world, run by men for men. Women in Canada could not vote or stand for political office. In New Zealand and Australia women had recently won the right to vote (1893 and 1902 respectively).

But some Canadian women were working very hard to improve their situation in society. In 1876 Dr. Emily Stowe had formed the Toronto Women's Literary Club. This name was deceiving. The purpose of this club was to teach women their rights and to help them secure these rights. It persuaded the University of Toronto to admit women in 1886. The Club also struggled for laws to improve the wages and working conditions for women as well.

Women telephone operators, 1910

Other important organizations for women included the Women's Christian Temperance Union (WCTU) whose aims were to combat the problems created by alcohol in society. Nellie McClung, Canada's great woman social reformer, got her start in the WCTU. McClung argued that women should have exactly the same freedom as men, and she led in the fight for women's rights. With such dedicated workers the twentieth century would obviously bring about great changes in the role and status of women.

DEVELOPING SKILLS:
NOTE MAKING 1

Many times you will need to take notes on what you read, hear, or see. You take notes when someone calls on the phone and leaves a message, when you are going shopping and need a list, when you are invited to a friend's house and are given directions, when your teacher is lecturing, and when you are reading from a text and need to record some information.

Every history student should learn how to keep a good set of notes. Your notes should be clear, concise, and complete. Writing notes will help you to remember what you have learned. Good notes will assist you to study for tests and examinations. Notes are certainly easier to remember than many pages of a textbook.

Writing notes from a text requires several skills. First, it demands comprehension. You have to be able to understand and pick out the main idea of the passage. You are doing this when you decide on a heading for a paragraph in a textbook. Secondly, note making requires the skill of categorizing. When you categorize you pick out statements that are very important to the main topic from statements that are less important to the main topic or argument. You are also categorizing when you decide which events are causes and which are effects.

Note making requires the skills of summarizing and organizing. You have to select your material and put it together in a logical way. Many words have to be reduced into a few. The main idea has to be kept and expressed in such a way that in six months you can still understand what you have written.

Note-making skills that you learn now will be very valuable to you in the future. Most adults have to do some paperwork at some point in their lives. They need to be able to summarize reports or to make written reports from minutes of a meeting. They need to be able to pick out the important parts of a discussion and record them in such a way that they can recall these points when necessary. In an office, in a store or business, in a profession, note-making skills are essential.

Here is a chance to practice some of the skills you will need for note making.

a) Read the section "What was it like to live in Canada in 1901?" from pages 76 to 81. In two sentences write a general summary of what this passage is about.

b) Read the first paragraph (that begins "Horses played a significant role. . . .") on page 76. Give the paragraph a heading. Under your heading list seven examples of how horses were used in Canada at the turn of the century. Here you are using the skills of comprehension.

c) Read the second paragraph (that begins "By the turn of the century. . . .") on page 77. What changes did the widespread use of the bicycle have on the way Canadians lived?

A heading for this paragraph might be "Why the bicycle craze swept Canada." Pick out three statements from the following list that you consider more important to the main idea of the paragraph. Which three statements do you consider least important to the main idea of the paragraph?

1 Bicycles were cheaper to buy and operate than horses.
2 Couples could honeymoon on bicycles.
3 People could live farther from their jobs.
4 Bicycles provided freedom and mobility.
5 People could take picnics in the countryside.

6 Police officers could patrol city streets.

Under your heading, write the three most important statements. You are using the skill of categorizing.

Read the paragraph (that begins "The automobile was just being introduced. . . .") on page 78. What is it about? Give the paragraph a heading. This paragraph contains over 140 words. In no more than 30 words, summarize the paragraph. Use words and phrases instead of sentences. You are using the skill of organizing and summarizing. Compare your summary with those done by other students in your class. Which ones are the best? Why?

Mastering the skills of comprehending, categorizing, organizing, and summarizing will help you to make useful notes from a text.

DIGGING DEEPER

1 The railway boom assisted all aspects of the economy in Canada. Draw two columns in your notebook. In the left-hand column make a list of all the materials that would be required for the railway boom. (Remember that railways are more than trains and track.) In the right-hand column make a list of the industries that would benefit from making these materials for the railway boom.

8
The Golden Age of Laurier

In 1896 Wilfrid Laurier entered the House of Commons in Ottawa to the sound of cheering and applause. He made his way to the seat Sir John A. Macdonald had occupied for nineteen years. Now Laurier, the leader of the Liberal party, was the new prime minister of Canada. The next fifteen years were known as the "Golden Age of Laurier."

Laurier had once said that the nineteenth century belonged to the United States, but that the twentieth century would certainly belong to Canada. As the twentieth century dawned, it looked as if Laurier might be right. The worldwide economic depression of the early 1890s began to clear and prosperity started to return to Canada. Once again factories began to hum, people had jobs, and there were markets for Canadian products. Good times returned, and for the next fifteen years things went well for Canada. It certainly was a "Golden Age" for most Canadians, and for the Liberal party.

Laurier was Canada's first French-Canadian prime minister. He brought to this high political office his great gifts as a person and as a politician. He was born near the village of St. Lin in the province of Quebec on 20 November 1841. Laurier's family had deep roots in Canada. His first Canadian ancestor helped to found Montreal in 1642. Members of Wilfrid Laurier's family had settled the land and explored the continent. His ancestors had lived through the conquest of Quebec by the English in 1760. Like all French Canadians they must have watched nervously as English troops, with their foreign language and religion, marched into Quebec. After the conquest, many French-Canadian families, like Laurier's, moved into rural areas in order to protect and maintain their French-Canadian way of life.

Sir Wilfrid Laurier campaigning.

Wilfrid Laurier's character was shaped by his rather unusual background. When he was eleven, his father did a surprising thing. He decided to send young Wilfrid to school in the English-speaking settlement at New Glasgow, an hour's drive by calèche from St. Lin. There the boy studied English and became fluently bilingual. He lived with the Murray family who were Scottish Protestants. In his free hours Wilfrid used to clerk in John Murray's store and practised speaking English with the customers. In this way Laurier learned a great deal about the ways and religion of English-speaking Protestants. He also learned to be tolerant of people different from himself. In later years, as prime minister of a largely English-speaking Canada, this knowledge was extremely useful. Often Laurier told students that they owed it to themselves to be able to read and speak both languages of Canada. He added that he was grateful to his own father for giving him the chance to do so.

In 1861 Laurier chose to study law at McGill University in Montreal. Wilfrid did well in his courses at McGill and graduated in 1864. He was invited to give the valedictory address. He spoke to a large audience about the role of the lawyer in the nation. In his speech he touched on a concern that was to dominate his life. "Two races share today the soil of Canada," he said. These people had not always been friends. "But I hasten to say it, and I say it to our glory, that race hatreds are finished on our Canadian soil. There is no longer any family here but the human family. It matters not the language people speak, or the altars at which they kneel."

Following graduation, Laurier opened a law practice at Artha-baskaville, Quebec, a small town on the south shore of the St. Lawrence River. Here he pleased the townspeople with his honesty, his courage, and his sense of fair play. Eventually they chose him to represent them in the provincial legislature at Quebec City in 1871. Three years later he was elected to the federal government in Ottawa, and in 1887 he became the leader of the Liberal party. In Parliament Laurier impressed everyone as an excellent speechmaker. Macdonald admired his political opponent and recognized him as one of Canada's most promising politicians.

Probably Laurier's greatest gift to Canada was his ability to see both English and French points of view. His main aim was to keep both language groups together and to make sure each treated the other fairly. Laurier's sense of fair play helped him to work out compromises that would be acceptable to both English and French Canadians.

State dinner at Government House, 1912

Laurier used all his skills of compromise to solve the Manitoba Schools Question. When the Red River Settlement became the province of Manitoba in 1870, most of the people living there were French-speaking and Roman Catholic. They had been promised that they could have Roman Catholic schools maintained by money raised from public taxes. Over the next twenty years, large numbers of English-speaking Protestants, many from Ontario, had moved into Manitoba. The French Canadians in Manitoba gradually became a minority. By 1890, most of the members of the Manitoba legislature were English-speaking Protestants. They passed an act to set up a single school system that would not be connected with any church. All citizens of the province, whatever their religion, would pay for the school system through their taxes. The government would no longer support separate, Roman Catholic schools. Roman Catholics themselves would have to pay for separate schools if they wanted to have them.

In 1896 the Roman Catholic school supporters complained to the federal government in Ottawa. Laurier tried to find an answer that would satisfy both sides. He said that Manitoba had the right to decide its own education and schools. This pleased the majority in Manitoba and Protestants in the rest of Canada. But he also persuaded the Manitoba government to allow religious instruction to be given in the last half-hour of the school day. Also, in schools where there were more than ten children speaking French or another European language, a teacher of that other language must be hired. This part of the compromise satisfied the French Roman Catholic people in Manitoba and Quebec. It also pleased the other minority groups who were moving into Manitoba from Europe.

In 1897, Laurier and his wife Zoë journeyed to London, England. They went to take part in the celebration of Queen Victoria's Diamond Jubilee. Queen Victoria had ruled for sixty years, and a great celebration was planned to honour the event. Dignitaries from all parts of the British Empire had come to honour the queen. The greatest parade that London had ever seen moved through the streets toward St. Paul's Cathedral. Some of the loudest cheers were reserved for Sir Wilfrid Laurier and the North-West Mounted Police. The day before the parade, the queen had knighted Laurier.

Before he returned to Canada, Laurier wanted to visit France. It was the country of his forebearers, and he had never been there. In two brilliant speeches in Paris, Laurier won over the French as he had the British. He said, "French Canadians have not forgotten France . . . Here in France people are surprised at

Queen Victoria's Diamond Jubilee procession

the attachment French Canadians feel for the Queen of England.
We are faithful to the great nation which gave us life [France], and
we are faithful to the great nation which has given us liberty
[Britain]."

Sir Wilfrid Laurier returned in triumph to Canada. Canadians
had never received more respect from other nations of the world.
Now the prime minister had to turn to tasks at home.

DEVELOPING SKILLS:
NOTE MAKING 2

In the preceeding chapter you learned the basics of good note
making. However, good note-making skills are only developed
with practice. Let's look closely at three paragraphs in this chapter, and with the assistance of these questions draw out the most
important ideas and information for your notes. With practice,
you will be able to write good notes from a text without any help
at all. Then you will have mastered the skill of good note making.
1 On page 89, read the paragraph that begins "Probably
Laurier's greatest gift. . . ." and the two following paragraphs.

Write a general summary of the paragraphs in one or two sentences.

2   Reread each paragraph. What is each one about? Write a one sentence answer for each paragraph. Give each paragraph a subheading.

3   According to the first paragraph, what was Laurier's main goal? How did he try to reach this goal?

4   According to the second paragraph, what were the causes of the Manitoba Schools Question? What happened in Manitoba between 1870 and 1890? What did the majority of people in 1890 want? What did the Manitoba government decide to do?

5   According to the third paragraph, what were the three parts of Laurier's solution to the Manitoba Schools Question? Beside each of the three parts, name the group(s) that would be pleased with the action taken.

6   Write a summary of the whole passage by answering this question. What does the Manitoba Schools Question tell us about Laurier?

DIGGING DEEPER

1   What qualities and characteristics did Laurier possess that prepared him for the position of prime minister?

2   Compare the characteristics and background of Prime Minister Laurier and another French-Canadian prime minister (Louis St. Laurent or Pierre Trudeau).

3   What were the advantages for Canada of belonging to the British Empire?

4   The following words have been used by Wilfrid Laurier's friends and enemies to describe him. Use a dictionary to make sure you understand the meaning of all the words. Make two lists, one for those descriptions that are complimentary and another for those words that are not:

appeasing	humane	stubborn
charming	liberal	tolerant
clear-sighted	nefarious	traitorous to
compromising	pro-British	French Canada
elegant	reasonable	
eloquent	responsive	

Which words would you use to describe Wilfrid Laurier? As you continue reading, you may wish to revise your list, or add words of your own.

9
Canada: Between Britain and the United States

Though the years around the turn of the century were a golden age, some problems arose in Canada's relations with both Britain and the United States.

Difficulties first came with Britain. The great issue of Laurier's day was imperialism. Imperialism was a policy of having colonies and building an empire. Colonies provided a source of raw materials, a market for manufactured goods, a great deal of prestige, glory, and military strength for the mother country. In the latter days of Queen Victoria's reign, imperialism triumphed in Britain. There was a tremendous feeling of pride that Britain had extended its rule over many countries and colonies. What was Canada's place to be within the British Empire? In England and in English Canada, the imperialist movement was very strong and popular. As prime minister, Laurier had to walk a tightrope. Most French Canadians were anti-imperialists and felt little sense of pride or responsibility in belonging to the British Empire. Laurier had to frame policies that would be popular in both English and French Canada.

The Boer War

In 1899 war broke out in South Africa, where the discovery of gold and diamonds had attracted many British settlers. Trouble developed between the British and the Boers, who were the descendants of the early Dutch colonists. While the war did not

directly concern Canada, the British government asked Canada to send soldiers as "proof of the unity of the Empire." Many Canadians were anxious to take part. English Canada said "Yes" to the imperialist request, and French Canada said "No." Quebec politicians such as Henri Bourassa argued that Canada should not get involved in any of Britain's imperialist wars. Bourassa was a French-Canadian nationalist who wanted people to think of themselves as Canadians, rather than as members of the British Empire.

Laurier tried to provide a compromise solution that would satisfy both the English and the French. The compromise worked out by Laurier was that Canada would not send an official army to South Africa. Canada would equip and transport 1000 volunteers, but they would be part of the British forces once they arrived in Africa. In the end Canada sent about 7300 volunteers to South Africa and spent $2.8 million in their support.

Laurier's compromise did not fully satisfy anyone. Imperialists felt that Canada had let Britain down while many French-Canadian nationalists felt Laurier had done too much. In spite of the differences in attitude to Laurier's compromise solution, his government was returned to power in the election of 1900.

The Alaska Boundary Dispute 1903

Canada and the United States came into conflict over the border between Alaska and Canada. When the United States purchased Alaska from Russia in 1867, the deal included the "panhandle." This was a strip of coastline extending south from Alaska as far as Prince of Wales Island. The wording of the old treaty was fuzzy, but no one cared very much until the discovery of gold in the Yukon. During the Gold Rush, in 1898, thousands of prospectors flooded into the Klondike. Suddenly, the ownership of the land through which they passed became very important. Gold seekers needed outfits and supplies. Both Canadian and American merchants saw a chance to get rich.

The Americans maintained the ports of Skagway, Dyea, and Juneau belonged to them. The Canadians argued that those ports belonged to Canada. Whoever owned these ports could charge customs taxes on all goods going into the area and all the gold going out.

The Canadians argued that the boundary should be measured from the mountains nearest the ocean. This would give Canada direct access to the Pacific Ocean by way of several deep inlets. Gold could be brought out of the Yukon and supplies brought in without passing through American ports. The Americans were

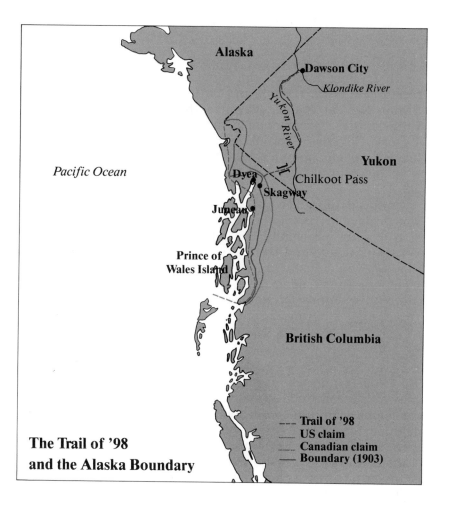

determined to keep as much land as they could. President Theodore Roosevelt threatened to send troops to Alaska to protect the American claim.

Eventually it was decided to submit the boundary dispute to a court of six judges. Three judges were appointed by the United States, and Roosevelt made sure these three men thought that the American claim was right. Three judges were chosen by Britain. Two of the judges appointed by the British government were Canadians; the third was Lord Alverstone, an Englishman.

After a full month of discussion the tribunal decided 4 to 2 against Canada. Lord Alverstone had sided with the Americans. Britain was facing growing problems with Germany in Europe and, therefore, was not willing to risk losing its friendship with the United States at this time.

When the decision was announced, Canadians were outraged. There was hostility toward the United States because Canadians thought they had been bullied by their much more powerful

southern neighbour. At the same time Canadians felt bitter resentment toward Britain and Lord Alverstone. It appeared that Britain had let Canada down in this confrontation with the United States. The reaction in Vancouver was so hostile that the *Victoria Colonist* reported on 23 October 1903 that some hot-headed citizens had pledged "they will not sing 'God save the King' again until England has justified itself in the eyes of Canada."

One good thing did come out of the Alaska boundary dispute. It was decided in 1909 to set up the International Joint Commission to settle peacefully any future disputes that might arise between Canada and the United States. This permanent commission would deal with all matters concerned with boundary waters or rivers along the Canadian-American border. In the future this commission would solve many controversies between these two North American neighbours in a friendly manner.

The Naval Crisis

By 1909 Britain was facing a crisis. The possibility of a war between Britain and Germany was very real. Without help from its colonies, Britain would soon fall behind in a race with Germany to have the largest navy in the world. The British emphasized that they were now facing a major emergency. They wanted Canada and the other Dominions to contribute funds to build ships for the British navy.

This became a crisis for Canada. It was just as serious an issue between English and French Canada as the Boer War had been. Should Canada add to the British navy, or develop its own navy? Every aspect of the problem threatened to separate French and English Canadians.

Again Laurier offered a compromise – the Naval Service Bill. Canada would have a navy of its own under the control of the Canadian government. In the time of an emergency the Canadian navy could be placed under British control with the consent of Canada's Parliament. Service in the navy would be voluntary. Five cruisers and six destroyers would be built immediately. Canadian naval bases would be established at Esquimalt, British Columbia and Halifax, Nova Scotia.

A storm of protest in Canada greeted Laurier's Naval Service Bill. On the one hand, Bourassa and some French-Canadian nationalists complained that this policy would mean that Canadians could be sent anywhere at any time to fight Britain's imperialist wars. On the other hand, the Conservatives, led by Robert Borden, attacked the bill. They thought Canada should make an outright contribution to the British navy. They accused Laurier of setting up a "tin-pot Canadian navy" when an immediate contribution to the British navy was urgently needed. Laurier admitted that when Britain is at war, Canada is also at war. However, he made it clear that Canada would decide the extent of its participation in future wars.

Reciprocity

The last great issue that faced the Laurier government was reciprocity. Reciprocity means that an arrangement exists between two countries who have agreed to trade certain products without tariffs or taxes on them. In December 1910 a large group of western farmers demonstrated on Parliament Hill in Ottawa. They complained of high prices caused by high tariffs on farm products and materials. The farmers demanded the lowering of taxes or tariffs on certain goods traded between Canada and the United States.

The farmers in western Canada had a legitimate complaint. They had to pay high freight rates to the eastern railway companies to ship their grain and supplies. They were charged high interest rates on money they borrowed from banks. When they visited friends or relatives across the border in the western American states, they were annoyed to discover that farm machinery cost half as much as it did back home in Canada. High costs were blamed on Ontario and Quebec manufacturers who grew rich because of the tariffs that kept out foreign competition.

Laurier was prepared to try to do something about the farmers' complaints. He managed to work out a reciprocity agreement with the Americans. Canadian products of farms, fisheries, forests, and mines were to be allowed into the United States free of tariffs. Taxes on American items coming into Canada, such as farm implements, automobiles, building materials, and canned goods would be lowered. It was the kind of tariff deal that every Canadian government since Confederation had been trying to make with the United States. When news of the proposed agreement became known the leader of the Conservative party, Robert Borden, became so discouraged that he wanted to resign. It seemed impossible that the Laurier Liberals could be defeated in the next election. But Borden was persuaded to stay on and fight it out.

Then the tide turned. Laurier's right-hand man, Clifford Sifton, was opposed to reciprocity. He joined seventeen other wealthy Liberals in fighting the idea. Business people, manufacturers, and bankers of both political parties were afraid that

A NEW FIELD FOR CONQUEST.

cheaper American goods in Canada would put them out of business. Canadian railway builders such as Canadian Pacific Railways' president William van Horne, who for years had been constructing east-west lines in Canada, feared the railway would be ruined if trade suddenly became north-south. Canadian nationalists felt that most Canadian natural resources should be kept at home and not shipped across the border. Anti-American feelings were still strong in Canada from the decision made over the Alaska boundary dispute.

President Taft of the United States forecast that Canada was at the parting of the ways with Britain. Another prominent American politician, Champ Clark, declared that he was all for reciprocity. Clark remarked, "I hope to see the day when the American flag will float over every square mile of the British North American possessions, clear to the North Pole."

That was enough ammunition for the Conservatives. They waved the British flag in every campaign speech during the election of 1911. They preached an anti-American policy. They warned that if reciprocity passed, it would mean a political as well as economic takeover of Canada by the United States. Borden campaigned with the slogan "No truck or trade with the Yankees."

UNCLE SAM—"I CAN ALMOST HEAR THEM SINGING 'THE STAR SPANGLED BANNER' IN OTTAWA, BE GOSH."

In the election of 1911, Laurier's Naval Bill was also an important issue. Anti-imperialists like Bourassa joined forces with the Conservatives and supporters of imperialism to defeat Wilfrid Laurier. The Laurier government probably would have survived the crisis of the Naval Bill had it not been for the added complication of the issue of reciprocity with the United States.

The headlines of 22 September 1911 told the election results: "The government goes down to defeat" *(The Globe)*, "Conservatives sweep country, reciprocity killed" *(The Mail and Empire)*.

Two issues were central in the Liberals' defeat: the Naval Service Bill and introducing free trade with the United States. French-speaking Canadians did not want to become involved in British imperialist disputes. English-speaking Canadians did not want to be taken over by American economic interests. However, a great many Canadians may have been ready for a change of government, and were willing to find any reason to vote against the Liberal government that had been in power almost fifteen years. Neither Laurier's great personal charm nor his program could save the Liberals from defeat in 1911, and Sir Wilfrid was never again to be prime minister of Canada. He died on 17 February 1919.

DEVELOPING SKILLS:
ANALYSING POLITICAL CARTOONS

Modern political cartoons began around the time of Confederation, and they became regular features in Canadian newspapers by the 1890s. What the cartoonists lacked in artistic ability they made up for in their ability to accurately satirize Canadian politics and politicians. One of Canada's most noted cartoonists was J.W. Bengough. He made his mark with his caricatures of Sir John A. Macdonald in his weekly magazine *Grip*. Political cartoonists often use caricature to make a statement about significant issues or events.

At the turn of the century, political cartoons played a prominent role in the lives of Canadians. People depended upon the cartoon to put issues into perspective.

Today, Duncan Macpherson of the *Toronto Star* is one of Canada's foremost political cartoonists. Not only has Macpherson made cartoons much more artistic, but he has forged a new editorial role for many cartoonists. In the past, cartoonists simply illustrated one of the editorials. However, Macpherson insisted on the right to pick his own subject matter, and make his own comment on it. Now many other Canadian cartoonists have this privilege.

When you look at political cartoons, ask yourself these questions. They will help you to interpret and understand the cartoonist's message.

1   Does the cartoon have a title? If so, what does it mean?
2   What current event prompted the cartoon?
3   Who are the characters in the cartoon? What are they saying? What is their mood?
4   Where and when does the cartoon take place?
5   Are there symbols or other objects in the cartoon? What do they stand for?
6   What comparisons, if any, are being made?
7   Who or what is the cartoonist satirizing?
8   What is the message of the cartoon?
9   What is the cartoonist's view of the people or events? Does the caricature give you an idea of the cartoonist's opinion?
10   Does the cartoonist get the message across? Why or why not?
11   Does the cartoonist's viewpoint differ from yours? Explain.

Interpret a political cartoon

Look carefully at the political cartoons on pages 98 and 99. Use the questions to analyse what the cartoonist is saying.

DEVELOPING SKILLS:
INTERPRETING PRIMARY SOURCES

Have you ever wondered why people acted as they did in the past? What were they thinking? What was their motivation? One way to answer these questions is by reading primary sources. A primary source is a document – letters, diaries, pamphlets, commentaries – written at the time of the event.

Imagine you are a historian studying the election of 1911. You are wondering if the media influenced the outcome of the election. In your research, you come across an old copy of the *Kingston Daily Standard* from 20 September 1911 – the day before the election. You notice the following article on reciprocity. To discover what people were thinking in the past you must use the skill of critically reading and analysing a primary source. Read the article and answer the questions.

Workingmen, Your jobs are in danger. This is what Reciprocity means to you.

It will at once rob our east-and-west railways of much of their business. The local industries will be hit. The port of Kingston will be badly crippled. This means that railway hands and dock hands will be discharged, and will compete in our labour market. We will have no more work to share: but many more workers to share it, competition will beat wages down.

Then our dock labourers will be out of work; for our shipping will go to American ports. Again, labour on the market will cut wages.

Certain local industries will be crippled or smashed. American firms will stop building branches in Canada. Less work, again; and more workers. Our factories will run on short time, and wages will fall.

Then Taft and the grain growers say that Reciprocity will lead to "Free trade in everything." That means the closing of all protected industries. It probably means the closing of your industry.

Away goes your own job.

Vote against Reciprocity, keep the price of labour up and the "cost of living" down.

1 To whom was the *Kingston Daily Standard* appealing and why?
2 What arguments did it put forward to try to prove its case?
3 How convincing were these arguments and why?

4   Why was this appeal effective? Suggest some modern newspaper articles that appeal to peoples' emotions.

Here is another primary source document to read and interpret. In Montreal, in 1912, Henri Bourassa published a pamphlet entitled "Why the Navy Act Should Be Repealed [cancelled].

Let the Navy Act be repealed.

Above all, let our system of transportation, by land and by water, be completed without a minute's loss. While we are talking 'battleships,' populations, drawn to western Canada by alluring advertisements, are clamouring for the means of selling and shipping their wheat. If our politicians lose their time in trying to save the British fleet and the motherland in spite of the British people, they may suddenly awaken from their magnificent dreams of Imperialism, and be confronted with serious troubles in Canada by their neglect to secure Canada's economic safety and national unity.

Let Canada first be looked after. . . . If in order to do other people's work, we neglect our own, neither the British nor the Australians will come and help us in setting our house in order.

1   What arguments does Henri Bourassa put forward for cancelling the Navy Act?
2   What help does he think Canada should give to the British Empire and why?
3   Rewrite the last paragraph in your own words.
4   Why would a French-Canadian nationalist be likely to feel this way about Britain?

Note making is helpful for a paragraph or a chapter, but to review and comprehend an entire unit a summary chart is helpful. One method of organizing a summary chart is the use of a matrix. The matrix should cover two pages of your notebook. The themes should be written in columns across the top. Down the side, in the left-hand column, the time period should be indicated. Your matrix should look similar to this one.

Be sure to update your matrix at the end of each unit. You'll be thankful you've done this as a matrix is an excellent way to summarize information. It is especially helpful when reviewing for tests and exams. As your matrix expands, it will provide you with a visual picture of the events that have dominated Canadian history.

Contemporary Canada: Life in the twentieth century

Time period	French-English relations	Canadian-American relations	International relations	Citizenship, government, and law	Social issues	Economic/ technological issues	Regional issues
1900–1913							

SOME IMPORTANT THEMES IN UNIT TWO

The Laurier Era
1896–1911

Economics
- Increasing prosperity and growth
- Settlement of the West
- The wheat boom
- New railway construction
- Reciprocity

French-English Relations
- Early settlement of Canada by the French
- The Conquest 1759–60
- Manitoba Schools Question
- Differences over imperialism, Boer War, and Naval Service Act
- Bourassa and French-Canadian nationalism

Multiculturalism
- People from other countries move to Canada

Labour
- Increasing number of jobs caused by urbanization (one in three people in eastern Canada involved in railway boom)

Regional Development
- Gold develops the Yukon
- Alberta and Saskatchewan become provinces

Canada and Britain
- Death of Queen Victoria
- Victoria's Diamond Jubilee
- Imperialism
- Boer War
- Bitterness over Alaska boundary decision
- Naval crisis

Canada and the United States
- Alaska boundary dispute
- International Joint Commission
- Reciprocity
- Election of 1911

Canada and the World
- Canada becomes an exporting nation
- Foreign policy largely determined by British Empire

Women
- Inequality between man and woman
- Women organize for change

People and Lifestyles
- Living in Canada in 1901
- Differences between rich and poor
- Living in the city
- Robert Borden, Alexander Graham Bell, Nellie McClung

Politics
- Laurier's leadership as prime minister
- Government supports railway building
- Laurier's compromises

National Identity
- Canadians – still British?
- Anti-American feelings

Technology
- Inventions

War and Peacekeeping
- Boer War

DIGGING DEEPER

1 a) What were the causes of the Boer War?

  b) How did English Canadians and French Canadians react to the British request for Canadian assistance in South Africa? Why?

  c) Make a list of the possible solutions open to the Laurier government. What might have been the potential outcome of each solution?

  d) Explain and evaluate the eventual compromise worked out by Prime Minister Laurier.

2 In 1903, F.H. Turnock, a Canadian journalist, discussed the anti-British feeling caused by the Alaska boundary dispute:

> The callousness, the selfishness, and the bad faith with which Canadians consider Britain has treated Canada in this matter will long rankle in the breasts of Canadians. It is bound to affect Canada's destiny. What the ultimate outcome may be, it is perhaps too early yet to predict. But it will sensibly loosen the tie which binds Canada to Great Britain. It will quench the spirit of Imperialism which has for some time been growing in Canada. Canadians now realize how little their services in the cause of the [British] Empire have been appreciated.

Account for and describe the anti-British feeling triggered by the Alaska boundary dispute.

3 Role play: Reciprocity. Various members of the class should role play the following characters.

   i) president of the CPR
  ii) a Saskatchewan wheat farmer;
 iii) a fisherman in Prince Edward Island;
  iv) an Ontario manufacturer of farm implements;
   v) a housewife;
  vi) an owner of a meat canning factory in Quebec;
 vii) a worker on the docks of British Columbia;
viii) a worker in a Canadian steel company;
  ix) a pro-British imperialist;
   x) a wealthy Conservative businessman;
  xi) a French-Canadian Liberal.

Prepare arguments for or against reciprocity depending on your role. Then stage a public meeting in the class to debate the issue "Is reciprocity a good policy for Canada in 1911?" A vote can be taken in the class in order to reach a consensus.

4 How would you have voted in the election of 21 September 1911?

10
Murder at Sarajevo

Sarajevo was a sleepy little city in Austria-Hungary. On Sunday morning, 28 June 1914, its citizens were getting ready to welcome Archduke Franz Ferdinand and his wife Sophia. The archduke was an important visitor because he would someday be their ruler, the emperor of Austria-Hungary. That day the archduke was in uniform – a light-blue tunic, black trousers, and a hat topped with large green ostrich feathers. Sophia was wearing a high-collared white dress and a white hat.

As a four-car motorcade drove the royal couple toward the town hall at 10:00 a.m., someone threw a bomb. The bomb exploded against the hood of the limousine without hurting the archduke. The tour continued. At the town hall the archduke complained angrily to the mayor, "I come here on a visit and get bombs thrown at me. It is outrageous!" Both the mayor and the chief of police assured the archduke there would be no more danger. The visitors' cars moved on to the governor's palace. Several minutes later, a nineteen-year-old, Gavrilo Princip, stepped up to the car and fired two shots from a pistol at point-blank range. The first shot hit the archduke in the throat; the second hit Sophia in the stomach. Franz Ferdinand, blood pouring from his mouth, saw that his wife was wounded. "Sophia," he cried, "don't die! Keep alive for our children." However, both died on the way to the hospital.

Meanwhile, Gavrilo Princip swallowed poison. The poison failed to work. Within minutes Princip and five others were rounded up by the police. They were members of a Serbian terrorist group known as the Black Hand. Their plan had been to murder the archduke and then to commit suicide. However, their plan was foiled. Three of the terrorists were hanged and three others, including Princip, died in prison.

Archduke Franz Ferdinand and Sophia

That day a friend of the assassins sent a message to the Serbian capital. It read, "Excellent sale of both horses." Members of the Black Hand in Serbia knew exactly what this code meant. What they could not know was the terrible effect those two shots would have on world history.

The shots fired that day were the immediate cause of World War I. However, in explaining an historical event as complex as a world war, there are many background causes to be investigated. No single cause ever adequately explains why a historical event happened. There are always a number of causes to explain something as complicated as a world war. To understand World War I, some of the causes must be traced back to the late nineteenth century.

THE BACKGROUND OF WORLD WAR I

The countries that went to war in 1914 were Britain, France, and Russia on one side, and Germany and Austria-Hungary on the other. France and Germany had been enemies for centuries. Each had tried to find other countries to be its friends or allies in case of future wars. Just as two or three children sometimes band together for safety or protection against a bully on their street, so countries also band together for protection against threatening enemies. The process of banding together is called forming alliances. France had allied itself with Russia and Britain in what was known as the Triple Entente. Germany, on the other hand, made the Triple Alliance consisting of itself, Austria-Hungary,

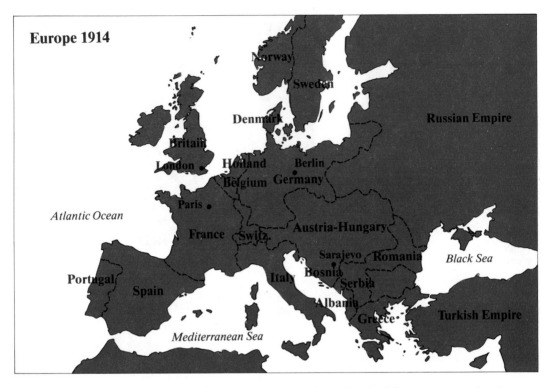

Europe 1914

Norway
Sweden
Denmark
Russian Empire
Britain
London
Holland
Berlin
Belgium
Germany
Atlantic Ocean
Paris
France
Switz.
Austria-Hungary
Black Sea
Portugal
Spain
Italy
Sarajevo
Bosnia
Serbia
Romania
Albania
Greece
Turkish Empire
Mediterranean Sea

and Italy. These countries of the Triple Alliance were also known as the Central Powers. When the war did start, Italy left the Central Powers to join the Triple Entente.

Thus at the time of the assassination of Archduke Franz Ferdinand, Europe was already divided into two hostile camps. The alliances were dangerous because they increased fear and suspicion among rival nations. With alliances, a war between two countries would likely involve many more!

Nationalism

Nationalism is a feeling of deep loyalty to one's nation. In Europe of the nineteenth century it was a powerful force helping people of the same culture to come together to form strong nations. But by the early twentieth century, extreme nationalism was one of the forces causing problems. People under its spell seemed willing to take any action to help their own nation, regardless of the effect on others. They were even ready to start wars to promote the interests of their homeland.

A strong feeling of nationalism existed in the small country of Serbia in the early 1900s. Serbia was a nation bordering on the Austrian province of Bosnia. Many people of Serbian descent

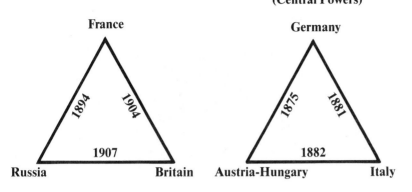

TRIPLE ENTENTE

France

1894 1904

1907

Russia   Britain

TRIPLE ALLIANCE
(Central Powers)

Germany

1875 1881

1882

Austria-Hungary   Italy

lived in Bosnia and bitterly disliked being under Austrian control. Some Serbs and Bosnians, who thought that Bosnia should be a part of Serbia, formed the terrorist organization known as the Black Hand. Their motto was "Union [with Serbia] or Death." Gavrilo Princip belonged to the Black Hand which claimed responsibility for the assassination of the Archduke Ferdinand. The Austrians were also expressing feelings of nationalism when they strongly opposed the attempts of any group to break away from their empire.

Thus nationalism was causing suspicion and jealousy in the world in the early 1900s.

Imperialism

During the late nineteenth and early twentieth centuries, the nations of Europe became more industrialized. As a result the spirit of imperialism became increasingly important. This is a policy of controlling lands far from home as colonies and building an empire. Colonies are a source of raw materials and a market for manufactured goods. They also give the home country glory and military strength.

By the early twentieth century, France owned large areas in northwest Africa and the Far East. Russia controlled a vast empire across northern Europe and Asia. The largest empire was owned by Britain. Its empire included Canada, Australia, New Zealand, India, Burma, Malaya, South Africa as well as parts of Africa, the East and West Indies, and islands in the Pacific. The

Kaiser Wilhelm II

United States had gained power in the Pacific by taking the Hawaiian and Philippine Islands. Germany also wanted its share of colonies and world markets. But by the time Germany began to build an empire, all that remained were some territories in Africa and the Pacific that were not particularly valuable.

Imperialism led to frequent quarrels among the great powers of Europe in all parts of the world. Arguments over colonies and trade constantly threatened peace.

Militarism

Closely related to nationalism and imperialism was the rise of militarism. Militarism is the belief in the power of armies and navies to decide issues. Leaders of the armed forces insisted that the only way to guarantee peace was by preparing for war. If a nation was strong, they argued, no enemy would dare to attack it. If a war did start, the militarized nation would be able to defend itself. This kind of thinking led to an arms race. Each country produced steel battleships, high-powered cannons, and explosives. Each tried to have a bigger and more deadly war machine than its rival. The size of armies and navies determined who would be the largest and most powerful nation in Europe. Britain was particularly upset by the fact that Germany was building a huge navy. Britain was an island. Britain depended on its giant navy to "rule the waves" to guarantee its safety. By building a powerful navy, Germany challenged Britain's supremacy at sea.

Thus, as the nations of Europe became more militarized, they became increasingly suspicious and alarmed by each others' military power.

When Princip fired those two fateful shots on the morning of 28 June 1914, Europe was already divided into two well-armed hostile camps. In the next few weeks a chain reaction of events gradually entangled the Central Powers and the Triple Entente (or the Allies, for short) in a major war. The Austro-Hungarian government blamed the Serbian government for the deaths of the archduke and Sophia. Austria-Hungary saw the assassination as an opportunity to crush Serbian nationalism once and for all. With Germany's support, it sent Serbia an ultimatum. An ultimatum is a demand by one government that another government accept its terms or face the threat of war. In the ultimatum the main terms that Austria-Hungary insisted on were that Serbia should

1 put down all forms of nationalist hatred against Austria-Hungary;

The British battleship, the HMS Dreadnought

2   punish all those involved in the assassination plot;
3   allow Austro-Hungarian officials to enter Serbia to help crush all terrorist movements such as the Black Hand.

The Serbs were given forty-eight hours to reply to the ultimatum. The Serbs agreed to all the conditions except one. They refused to allow Austro-Hungarian officials into their country. Austria-Hungary took this as a complete refusal of its ultimatum, and declared war on Serbia on 26 July 1914. Russia, considering itself a friend and "big brother" of the Serbs, started to mobilize its armies (get them ready for war). France, as Russia's ally, also mobilized its forces for war. Germany now felt threatened by the actions of its two neighbours, France and Russia. Germany ordered them to stop mobilizing. When they refused, Germany declared war on Russia on 1 August 1914, and on France on 2 August 1914. The German plan of attack on France was to invade through the small, neutral nation of Belgium. Up to this point Britain was not at war. However, Britain had signed a treaty guaranteeing to protect the neutrality of Belgium. When Belgium was invaded, Britain decided to act and declared war on Germany. In London, England, that evening, Sir Edward Grey, British foreign secretary, told a friend, "the lamps are going out all over Europe. We shall not see them lit again in our lifetime." By midnight on 4 August 1914, all the countries of the two alliances, except Italy, were at war. The world war had begun!

WAR!

In Canada the giant headline on the front page of the *Toronto Star* announced the news simply: WAR! When Britain entered war with Germany, Canada and the other countries of the British Empire were automatically at war too. The reason for this was that the colonies were still not independent. They could neither declare war nor make peace. All across Canada, in cities, towns, and villages, there was widespread support of Canada's involvement in the war. In 1914 Canada had close ties with Britain and the monarchy. It was natural that Canadians would want to aid Britain in its hour of need. Most politicians agreed.

Laurier was on record as having said, "There is in Canada but one mind and one heart . . . . When Britain is at war, Canada is at war also." Even Henri Bourassa, the nationalist spokesman for French Quebec, agreed that it was Canada's duty "to contribute within the bounds of her strength . . . to the triumph and to the endurance of the combined efforts of France and England." In Montreal both French and English Canadians linked arms in the street and sang "La Marseillaise," the French national anthem,

Canadian Army Service Corps at Camp Niagara

and the patriotic song "Rule Britannia." Across Canada there was a strong conviction that the Allies must be supported.

The beginning of the war was welcomed with enthusiasm in Canada. Sir Sam Hughes, minister of Militia and Defence, ordered an immense camp constructed at Valcartier, near Quebec City. When the call went out for volunteers, recruiting offices across the country were flooded with men willing to fight for a private's pay of $1 a day. Wealthy and patriotic men donated machine guns and trucks. Everyone believed the war would be short, glorious, and full of adventure. Within the first two months, over 30 000 soldiers had been recruited and were on their way across the Atlantic Ocean. Most thought that the war would be over by Christmas. Who could have known it would take more than four years and the involvement of another 400 000 Canadians before peace would return to the world?

The Events of the War

The war that began in August 1914 eventually became a world conflict. At first it involved seven countries, but by its end thirty countries were involved, including the United States. It was a world war in the sense that fighting was not limited to Europe. Battles were also fought in African jungles, Asia, and the Pacific and Atlantic Oceans. In Europe there were four major fronts or lines of battle which are indicated on the following map.

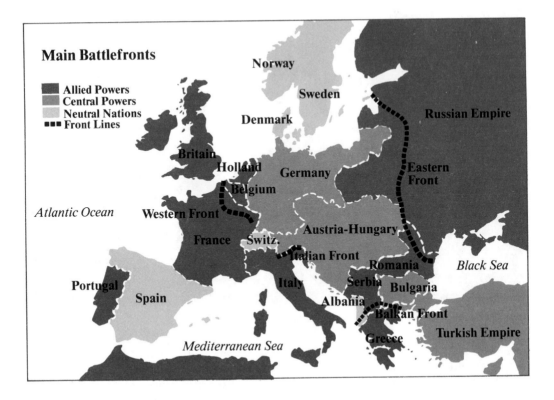

Main Battlefronts

- ■ Allied Powers
- ■ Central Powers
- ■ Neutral Nations
- ■■■ Front Lines

Norway

Sweden

Denmark

Russian Empire

Britain

Holland

Belgium

Germany

Eastern Front

Western Front

Atlantic Ocean

France   Switz.

Austria-Hungary

Italian Front

Romania

Black Sea

Portugal

Spain

Italy

Serbia

Bulgaria

Albania

Balkan Front

Greece

Turkish Empire

Mediterranean Sea

1   Locate the four main fronts of the war.
2   Identify the countries that joined with the members of the Central Powers.
3   Identify the countries fighting with Britain and France.
4   Identify the European countries that had decided to remain neutral.

Canadian forces made their greatest and most significant contribution to the war effort along the Western Front.

DEVELOPING SKILLS:
HOW TO USE A LIBRARY FOR RESEARCH

You are about to start on a bicycle trip and you discover something is wrong with your bike. What do you do? Cancel your trip? Pull out your hair? No. Head to the local library. You can borrow a bicycle-repair manual that gives step-by-step instructions on how to fix your bike.

This year you've decided you will improve your tennis game, but you can't afford lessons. What do you do? Go to your library for a few books on improving your tennis form.

You can discover all kinds of things at your library resource centre. You've been reading about World War I, and your teacher has asked you to research more about the war. What do you do? Go to your school resource centre and research your topic.

If you are unfamiliar with your resource centre, here are some steps to follow to make your visit more productive.

1 Learn to use the card catalogue. Check the card catalogue before you do anything else. It is the nucleus of any library. The catalogue lists every book in your resource centre by author, title, and subject.

Suppose your group has decided to research the types of airplanes used during World War I. There are several possible subjects to look under in the card catalogue. You could look under "airplanes," "World War I," or "weapons." It might be helpful to look under all three or other related subjects. You will probably be surprised by the amount of information you discover.

Hint: Always have a pencil and paper with you when using the card catalogue. Jot down the call numbers of the books so you can locate them on the shelves.

2 Learn how to find the books. You will notice a number in the corner of the card. This is the call number, and it tells you where the book is located in the resource centre. You will find a lot of other books on the same subject in this area of the library.

3 Some of the best-informed people are librarians. Introduce yourself, state your problem and, you will be amazed at how much reference help the librarian can give you.

Hint: Do not waste the librarian's time by asking questions that you can answer yourself. Only ask questions that you really need help with.

4 A useful tool is the Readers' Guide to Periodical Literature. This guide indexes all the articles in major magazines. It provides the most up-to-date, expert information on any subject that interests you.

To do a first-rate job, find out which magazines are in your resource centre. Consult the Readers' Guide, and try and track down the latest article on your topic. When you use this guide effectively, you are showing the mark of a good researcher.

Some additional hints: If you are working on a research project that requires several visits to the library, keep a small notebook to record the call numbers of the books you will be using. This will save you valuable time as you won't have to consult the card catalogue on each visit.

Some of the best books in the library are reference books that cannot be borrowed. Learn what topics these books cover and how to use them. These books are wonderful sources of human knowledge.

DIGGING DEEPER

1 The diagram in the text (page 109) shows how the Triple Entente and the Triple Alliance were formed.
   a) Which alliance was made first?
   b) Which two nations formed the first agreement? In what year?
   c) When was the Triple Alliance completed?
   d) Which European nation was the last to join an alliance?

2 Why did the system of alliances make countries feel safer? At the same time, how did alliances make a major war more likely?

3 When the Triple Entente was formed, Germany complained that it was being surrounded. Examine the map of Europe on page 108. How justified was Germany's complaint that it was being encircled?

4 In 1914 Europe was divided into two armed and hostile camps that alarmed each other. Were the alliances the cause or the effect of the buildup of armies and navies? Is there any parallel in the world situation today? Can the arms race today be slowed down or stopped? If so, how? If not, is war inevitable?

5 When officials of Austria-Hungary proposed to enter Serbia to track down the archduke's assassins, Serbia insisted this would violate its national sovereignty. National sovereignty is a nation's right to run its own affairs. Does this seem like a reasonable position to you? Explain your answer.

11
Horror on the Western Front

THE WAR ON LAND

During August 1914 German forces swept through Belgium and into northeastern France. The Germans wanted to capture Paris before the British and Russians could fully mobilize their armies. Within a few short weeks they had advanced almost to the outskirts of Paris. The Allies moved faster than the Germans expected. Using every available vehicle – including the taxicabs of Paris – the French rushed troops to the front. With British help, the German advance was stopped. Gradually the Allies managed to drive the Germans back. By October 1914 both sides decided to strengthen and secure their positions by digging in before winter. They dug rows of deep trenches. These were protected by machine guns and barbed wire. The lines of trenches soon stretched several hundred kilometres from the English Channel to the border of Switzerland. These parallel trenches twisted and turned across the countryside, separated in some places by only 25 m. The corridor between the enemy trenches was called a no-man's land. This strip of land was armed with buried land mines and covered with barbed-wire entanglements. Any soldier who ventured into this area was an easy target for enemy fire. Sometimes those who died in no-man's-land could not even be buried because it was not safe to go to bring back their bodies. Often the wounded in no-man's-land could not be brought back to safety. The soldiers in the trenches could do nothing but listen to the cries of agony of their dying comrades.

Trench warfare

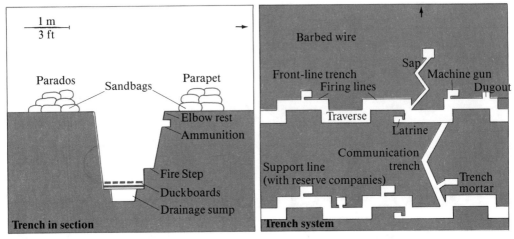

The front-line trenches were dug until water began to seep in. Usually they were about two or more metres deep. The diagram above illustrates how the firing lines were linked by traverses. This zigzag layout helped prevent enemy fire from sweeping along the whole length of the trench. From the front-line trenches, communication trenches were dug back to a line of support trenches. Here at the rear were command posts and reserve companies of soldiers. Sometimes small trenches, known as saps, probed out into no-man's-land to serve as lookout posts.

In wet weather the trenches became slippery and waterlogged. Even though wooden floorboards (duckboards) were placed in the bottom of the trenches, the troops often stood in water up to their knees. The soldiers slept where and when they could, often standing up or slumped against the sandbags. At other times they crawled into crude underground dugouts carved in the walls of the trenches.

The early days there, for the first winter, oh boy, I want to tell you, primitive living alright. They were packed into a lot of dugouts, six or seven or eight men all pushed in together as tight as they could go, and wet right straight through. We never took off our shoes or our clothes, we just slept in them. But we'd take any sandbags that were halfway dry and pull them over our feet and tie them one on top of the other, four or five on each leg. Your body heat and that of the other men would more or less heat the place, provided it wasn't too drafty. And in the morn-

ing when you woke up, why the outside sandbag would
be soaking wet...

Because the soldiers were constantly cold, wet, and dirty, sickness and disease spread rapidly. Two of the most common
illnesses were trench foot and trench mouth. The former was
rotting of the flesh between and around the toes. The latter was a
painful infection of the gums. Everyone had body lice living in
their mud-caked uniforms. Rats as big as alley cats ran through
the trenches feeding on the garbage and human waste. No wonder some people suffered nervous breakdowns under the stress.
These were the shell-shock cases who were sometimes physically unharmed, but whose minds and will to fight were destroyed.

Canadian troops washing up in a shell hole

Meals were monotonous, with little variety. Most times they consisted of "bully" beef (tinned corned beef), bread or hard biscuits, and hot tea. Occasionally there was stew, which was mostly vegetables and not much meat. The soldiers looked forward to packages from friends and families at home in Canada. Then they received treats of chocolate, fruit cakes, and tins of jam.

Nighttime was the worst time in the front trenches. Everyone was tense and watchful of any signs of enemy attack. It was at night that raiding parties would creep across no-man's-land. They would cut through the barbed wire with wire cutters and make a surprise attack on enemy trenches with their bayonets.

Companies of soldiers patrolled the front lines and the support and reserve lines in rotation. Troops in the support lines brought up food and ammunition through the communication trenches. They also dug new trenches and repaired old ones that had been damaged by shell fire. After a month or so in the trenches the units would be allowed to go to the rear for the chance to sleep in a dry place, to rest, to eat a decent meal, and above all, to bathe and clean up.

The soldiers in the trenches must often have wondered what they were doing there. On Christmas Eve 1915, Canadian and German soldiers joined in singing "Silent Night" across the shell-torn no-man's-land. Another soldier put his feelings this way:

> It seemed to be that they [the Germans] didn't want to be there any more than we did. But it seemed to be that somebody else was manipulating the strings behind the line, and we were just put there to work out a game. It wasn't really hatred. Only sometimes you did hate, when you see your chums and your friends get shot. It would be pretty hard on you that way, and you could say you'd hate for a while, but not necessarily hate that you wanted to kill. But you had to kill or be killed, if you wanted to survive. . . . Sometimes at that time there, I felt, well, it's so unnecessary. A bunch of men, say a hundred and fifty yards or a hundred yards away – you could talk to them and you could hear them talking, hear them working, and here you was, you got to make an attack. And you had to kill them or get killed. And you would sometimes wonder what it was all about.

THE WAR ON THE WESTERN FRONT

The first division of 20 000 Canadian troops took up places alongside their allies on the front lines in mid-April 1915. In the

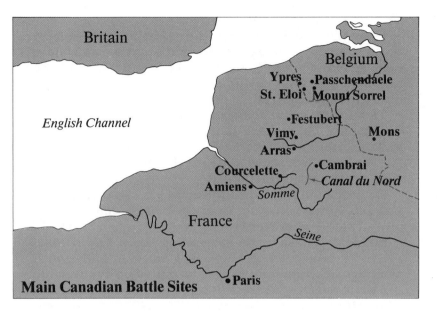

Britain

English Channel

Belgium

Ypres •Passchendaele
St. Eloi Mount Sorrel

•Festubert
Vimy.
Arras•   Mons

•Cambrai
Courcelette.   Canal du Nord
Amiens• Somme

France
                        Seine

Main Canadian Battle Sites •Paris

months and years that followed, they were joined by another
400 000 fellow Canadians. Some of Canada's greatest moments
in the Great War are associated with battles along the Western
Front. Canada's contribution will never be forgotten at Ypres,
Festubert, the St. Eloi craters, Mount Sorrel, the Somme, Course-
lette, Vimy Ridge, the Scarpe, Passchendaele, Amiens, Arras, the
Canal du Nord, and Cambrai. Here are a few of the major battles
in which Canadians were involved.

Ypres

The Canadian First Division was assigned to the front lines near
the ancient city of Ypres in Belgium. Their task was to hold about
3.5 km of the line in the face of heavy German attack. They had
only been in action for a few weeks when the Germans unleashed
the first deadly poison gas. Made of chlorine, it was released from
canisters when the breeze was blowing toward the Allied
trenches. The chlorine gas burned eyes and throats and destroyed the lungs. Those who breathed the gas choked, gagged,
gasped, coughed, and died. During the attack French-African
troops positioned beside the Canadians broke ranks and fled
from the poisonous gas. The Germans then came pouring
through the hole in the line. The Canadians, with makeshift gas
masks, managed to hold their position and eventually closed the
gap in the line.

The Gas Attack at Ypres

I saw the whole picture of the gas attack as probably no one else did. I have never been in a battle – and I have been in many – where the men were suffering in such numbers that their crying and groaning could be heard all over the battlefield.

There were some who ran away, French, British and Canadians. These were individuals. They were young and they were terrified.

They had never seen gas before. None of us had – it was the first gas attack in history.

But not a single unit skipped out – some individuals, yes, but formations, no. In every battle someone runs away. I saw it wherever I was.

Suddenly we saw the gas rolling up in a brownish-yellowish bank. It was between 1 and 3 m high and it wouldn't rise higher unless it was puffed up by the wind.

I went over to where the line had been broken and where there was confusion. No Canadian troops were running.

The gas was dreadful and suffering was immediate. The only thing we could do was soak our handkerchiefs in urine and hold them over our noses.

Thousands were lying around gasping and crying. They were being drowned by the gas. They didn't know how to protect themselves.

But we held our position.

The Canadians suffered dreadful casualties at Ypres. More than 5200 Canadians died, and one in five was listed as killed in action, gassed, missing, or wounded.

Later in the war even more deadly poison gases were used. Worst of all was mustard gas. This burned the skin and the respiratory tract, and caused blindness. Eventually more effective gas masks were invented that held filters through which the air could be purified.

Battle of the Somme

The first day of the battle along the Somme River in France – 1 July 1916 – was the most disastrous the British army had ever suffered. The Canadian corps fought as part of the British forces under the command of General Douglas Haig. These pictures, taken at the Somme attack, record what happened in the first few minutes. At exactly 7:30 a.m. the British officer leapt to the top of the trench, and with a wave of his cane ordered his troops to go forward. The soldiers went over the top.

One man was hit as soon as his head appeared over the trench, and he fell back into the mud. The soldiers stumbled through the barbed wire of no-man's-land heading for the German trenches. The soldiers faced a hail of German machine-gun fire. The British and Canadian attackers were mown down by the thousands. A British sergeant recorded, "Our dead were heaped on top of each other . . . in places three and four deep." Only a few Allied soldiers ever reached the enemy trenches. By nightfall British and Canadian casualties totalled 57 470, the heaviest ever in warfare for one day's fighting. Ninety percent of the Royal Newfoundland Regiment were killed or wounded that day. In spite of the heavy loss of men in the first day of the attack, hardly any ground had been captured.

Despite the death toll, General Haig insisted that the attack go on. For 141 days the Battle of the Somme continued. The Canadians fought so heroically at the Somme that they were marked out as storm troops, and during the rest of the war they were often brought in to lead an attack. British Prime Minister Lloyd George later wrote in his *War Memoirs*, "Whenever the Germans found the Canadian corps coming into their line, they prepared for the worst."

When the Battle of the Somme ended five months after it began, both armies were exhausted. Casualties for both sides had reached 1.25 million, of whom 24 000 were Canadians. The British had advanced no more than 11 km through shell-torn rubble. People at home were horrified and disillusioned by this massacre. Many blamed General Haig; others blamed the politicians who had started the war. To many soldiers the real enemy was not the Germans or the Austrians, but the war itself.

At the Somme, tanks were used for the first time in warfare. A British invention, tanks were huge armed "land ships" weighing over 25t which lumbered along at less than 5 km/hr. Their first appearance at the Somme was a bad shock for the German forces. Though they often got stuck in the mud, tanks were able to break through the barbed wire of no-man's-land. Although the British High Command did not at first appreciate the potential value of the tank, this new weapon eventually helped to win the war.

Vimy Ridge

Today a white stone Canadian war memorial stands high on Vimy Ridge. Here on Easter Monday 1917, Canada won its greatest victory. German forces had dug in on the height of land at

Vimy. From this vantage point they could control all the surrounding areas. Several unsuccessful attempts had been made by both British and French to push out the Germans. Finally, after months of preparations and weeks of heavy preparatory bombardment, 100 000 Canadians launched their attack. For the first time, all four Canadian divisions fought together. In a blinding sleet storm, they forced their way up the hill. In a few hours, the Canadians had captured the ridge. That day more ground, more guns, and more prisoners were taken than in any other Allied offensive on the Western Front in the first two-and-a-half years of the war. It was a magnificent victory!

Four Canadians won the Victoria Cross (the most prestigious award given by Britain to its heroes) at Vimy. Major-General Currie, who led the First Division, was granted a knighthood from King George V. Tragically, 11 000 Canadian lives were lost. However, since it was the first time the Canadians had fought as a national unit, the victory was a great morale booster and a source of enormous pride. Some people said that at that moment – its first clear-cut national military success – Canada became a nation.

Passchendaele

One of the most bitter disasters for Canadians occurred at Passchendaele in the fall of 1917. Here the Canadians were ordered to advance into a sea of mud. This Belgian land had once been beneath the North Sea, and when the shelling destroyed drainage ditches, the land became waterlogged. Soldiers sometimes wept with the sheer frustration of trying to advance through the mud. Narrow duckboards were placed as pathways over the mire, but thousands of soldiers and horses who slipped into the mud were sucked in and drowned. Locomotives sank to their boilers and tanks quickly bogged down. A British official, seeing the battlefield for the first time, cried out, "Good God! Did we really send men to fight in that?" Almost 16 000 Canadian lives were sacrificed in this insane enterprise. The offensive gained 7 km of mud which the Germans soon won back again.

The Last Hundred Days

By the spring of 1918, Germany's leaders realized a crisis had come. Food supplies were running short, but German submarine attacks on food ships had failed to force Britain to surrender. Now the United States had entered the war. Austria-Hungary and Turkey, Germany's allies, were on the point of collapse. The only hope for Germany seemed to be a mighty offensive on the Western Front before the United States Army could arrive in Europe in large numbers. In one last desperate gamble the German generals launched a devastating attack all along the Western Front.

Thousands of Germans poured into France and were stopped only 80 km from Paris. This swift advance exhausted the German troops. On 8 August 1918, the battle-proven Canadians and Allies launched a counter-attack. Fresh American troops had arrived and were a great encouragement for the Allies. Now there was no stopping them! Supported by 500 tanks, the Allies swept north and east toward Germany. The Germans fought well, but they fell back steadily. Eventually France was liberated, and then Belgium. By November the Allies reached the frontiers of Germany. On 11 November 1918, at a pre-dawn ceremony, the Germans formally surrendered. Hostilities were to cease at 11:00 a.m. on that morning. For some Canadian troops the war ended on the streets of the Belgian town of Mons with General Currie taking the salute on horseback. The Belgians flew flags that had been hidden for four years while their country was occupied by Germans. Grateful Belgians shouted, *"Vive les braves Canadiens!"*

DIGGING DEEPER

1   Use the following words correctly in a sentence to illustrate their meaning:

no-man's-land   crater
over the top   duckboards
barbed wire   sap

2   Choose a single battle either the Somme, Passchendaele, or Vimy Ridge. Do some research and write a detailed account of it.
3   You are a front-line soldier. Write a diary describing the conditions in the trenches.
4   Soldiers were frequently expected to fight in intolerable conditions. At Passchendaele it was almost impossible to carry on trench warfare in the mud of the battlefield. Many believed that the battle should have been stopped because of the conditions and the high number of casualties. Yet the commander ordered the fighting to continue. Would soldiers ever be justified in refusing to carry out the orders to fight? Why? Do you think military

leaders were to blame for the high number of casualties? Why?
5 Research the life of Sir Arthur Currie, Canada's greatest soldier of World War I, or Sir Sam Hughes, the minister of Militia.

12
War in the Air,
War at Sea

THE WAR IN THE AIR

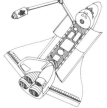

When war broke out in 1914, the airplane was a new and unproven invention. The Wright brothers had made their first successful flight only eleven years before. Few military leaders had any confidence in the airplane as a weapon of war. Colonel Sam Hughes is reported to have said, "The airplane is an invention of the Devil and will never play any part in such a serious business as the defence of a nation."

Recruiting office, Halton, Ontario

Canada had no air force of its own, but 25 000 joined the British Royal Flying Corps. The earliest planes were usually single-seaters. Their maximum speed was between 95 and 125 km per hour and they could stay airborn for only an hour without refuelling. At first unarmed airplanes were used just to scout enemy troop movements behind the lines and to observe enemy strength and position. Some pilots carried pistols, rifles, and shotguns, while others threw bricks or links of rusty chain at the propellers of enemy planes!

The Germans started the war with several advantages in Europe. They had the most aircraft (400 compared with 156 French and 113 British). They had a superior plane called the Fokker, a monoplane with one set of wings. It was armed with a machine gun whose firing mechanism was timed so that bullets did not hit its own propeller blades. The Germans also had gas-filled balloons called Zeppelin dirigibles or airships. These were used on observation missions and bombing raids. Eventually both sides used airships. By 1917, the Allies developed the Sopwith-Camel, an excellent fighter plane. Their fighting technique was to engage in aerial "dogfights" or duels, manoeuvering their light planes to dive on the enemy from the rear.

The pilots were usually very young, daring, and brave. The percentage of pilots killed was higher than in any other branch of the military. In late 1916 it was said that the average life of a pilot was three weeks. There were no parachutes to save those unlucky enough to be shot down. The great air aces – Germany's Manfred von Richthofen, Britain's Alfred Ball, and Canada's Billy Bishop – were a special breed of soldiers. An ace was a fighter who had shot down at least five enemy planes. Von Richthofen, known as the Red Baron, had downed eighty planes. Von Richthofen had icy nerves, lightning reflexes, and dead-eye aim. After each victory he ordered the date and the type of aircraft he had shot down engraved on a silver cup, until eventually the Berlin engraver ran out of space.

Few people know it was a Canadian air ace who finally shot down Germany's Red Baron. On 21 April 1918, von Richthofen, flying about the Somme Valley, spotted an Allied plane far below. He put his Fokker into a steep dive and moved in on his eighty-first victim. His target was an inexperienced Canadian flier, Wilfred ("Wop") May. May was helpless because his gun jammed. Fortunately, behind the German ace was another Canadian pilot, Captain Roy Brown, from Carleton Place, Ontario. Brown, in his Sopwith-Camel, opened fire on von Richthofen. The Red Baron fell into a deadly spin. The dreaded German ace was dead at the

Billy Bishop, World War I flying ace

age of twenty-six. Roy Brown was given the seat from the Red Baron's plane as a trophy. Today the seat is on display at the Royal Military Institute in Toronto, and you can put your finger through the bullet hole in the seat.

Billy Bishop

Canadians thrilled to the victories of a reckless young pilot, W.A. "Billy" Bishop. As a boy in Owen Sound, Ontario, Billy Bishop practised shooting at moving targets with his rifle in the woods. Now his expert marksmanship made him one of the greatest fighter pilots of the British Commonwealth. On his first day behind the front lines, he shot down a German plane. On his last day he destroyed five enemy planes. In one five-day period, Bishop destroyed thirteen planes. His total enemy kills were seventy-two.

Billy often prowled the skies alone. On one occasion he attacked a German air base near Cambrai, France. Two enemy planes rose to chase him, and Bishop shot down both of them. Two more enemy planes came up to attack the single raider. One fell from the deadly fire from Bishop's gun, and the other was driven off, out of ammunition. Billy Bishop returned safely to his home field.

By the end of the war, Billy Bishop was awarded the Victoria Cross by Britain and the highest honours of France. He was among the top three Allied air aces. He went on to become Director of Recruiting for the Royal Canadian Air Force in 1940. He died in Florida in 1956.

As a group, Canadian fighter pilots brought down 438 enemy aircraft during World War I. Four of the top seven leading aces of the Royal Air Force were Canadians. It was a truly remarkable record!

Soldiers testing equipment on armoured car

THE WAR AT SEA

In early May 1915, the British luxury liner *Lusitania* was crossing the Atlantic Ocean on a calm sea. The unarmed ship carried almost 2000 passengers. Suddenly a torpedo streaked through the waves toward the hull of the *Lusitania*. Moments later there was an explosion, panic, chaos, and death. At sea there was a new terror. A sinister and deadly weapon had been added to naval warfare – the submarine. More than half the passengers on board the *Lusitania* that day were Americans. Eleven hundred and ninety-eight people were drowned. The United States, still neutral at this stage of the war, did not want to get involved with European wars. But the sinking of the helpless *Lusitania* shocked the American people and swung public opinion in the United States against Germany. Eventually it helped to bring about the entry of the United States into war against Germany.

Britain was an island and, therefore, command of the seas was of supreme importance to it. The country depended on its navy to keep the sea lanes open for supplies of food and raw materials. British naval policy had to make sure that supply ships got safely to British ports. At the same time the navy tried to blockade the German coast, or control everything going in or out, so that food and war supplies could not get into Germany by sea. The German naval policy was to try to blockade Britain by means of submarines. All waters around Britain were declared a war zone. Allied merchant ships heading to British ports were to be sunk on sight by German submarines. This is what had happened to the *Lusitania* in 1915.

Both Britain and Germany began the war with strong fleets of battleships. Only once, at Jutland, off the coast of Denmark, did these two great fleets face each other. In May 1916, 149 British warships met 99 German warships head on. It was one of the most dramatic nights of the war. Within a few hours Britain had suffered greater losses both in ships and sailors. The German navy claimed a victory! The Germans, however, recognized the superior size of the British fleet and headed for port. After Jutland the Germans risked no more major sea battles. Their fleet remained in port. German shipyards stopped producing surface ships and started producing more submarines.

Germany's most deadly weapon was the submarine or U-boat *(Unterseebooten)*. Submarines carried a crew of thirty-five and twelve torpedoes. Torpedoes were very expensive, but could be fired underwater at a moving target. The early submarines could stay submerged for two-and-a-half hours. However, they preferred to come to the surface and sink their enemies by gunfire.

Canadian soldiers returning from victory at Vimy Ridge

By late 1916 German submarines were sinking an average of 160 ships per month. Germany was predicting an early defeat for Britain.

By 1917 the war on the Western Front still had not been won. Germany now decided that some more drastic action had to be taken to defeat the Allies. The German navy introduced a policy of "unrestricted submarine warfare." This meant that German U-boats would sink any Allied or neutral ship approaching Britain. The results of this policy were almost disastrous for Britain. In the first four months the policy was in operation, Germany sank:

February 1917	212 ships
March 1917	297 ships
April 1917	335 ships
May 1917	230 ships
Total	1074 ships

An enormous amount of much-needed cargo, as well as human lives, was being lost. An answer had to be found for the U-boat menace or Britain would be starved into surrender.

One answer was the convoy system. Instead of cargo ships sailing alone from Canada and the United States to Britain, they sailed in fleets escorted by armed destroyers. Destroyers kept constant watch like sheepdogs guarding a flock of sheep. Convoys of the necessary supplies began to get through to Britain again.

Two other methods were used to combat the threat of the U-boats. The first was the use of underwater mines which exploded on contact with submarines. The other was to employ "Q-ships." Q-ships were actually battleships disguised as unarmed, harmless merchant vessels. When a U-boat surfaced to attack, Q-ships would suddenly open fire from hidden guns. Many deadly U-boats were sent to the bottom of the ocean in this way.

Though the U-boats did tremendous damage to British and Allied shipping, the policy of "unrestricted submarine warfare" backfired on Germany. The sinking of American ships by U-boats brought the United States into the war against Germany. The entrance of the Americans in 1917 helped to turn the tide in favour of an Allied victory.

Canada's main contribution to the war at sea lay in the provision of sailors and ships for the Royal Navy. Canadian shipyards built more than 60 antisubmarine ships and more than 500 smaller antisubmarine motor launches. Several thousand Canadians served in the British Royal Navy, in the Royal Naval Canadian Volunteer Reserve, and in the Royal Naval Air Service

DIGGING DEEPER

1 a) Describe the various roles played by the air force in World War I.

   b) Outline the problems which might be encountered by pilots in wartime flying.

2 a) In what ways was the submarine a revolutionary new weapon?

   b) Explain the defensive measures that were taken against the submarine.

3 a) Explain why Germany felt it was necessary to sink the *Lusitania*.

   b) Describe the reaction of Britain and the USA to the sinking of the *Lusitania*.

   c) Was the sinking of the *Lusitania* a justifiable act in a time of war? Explain.

4 a) In small groups, choose one of the following topics on
World War I.
    i) trench warfare   iv) airplanes
    ii) poison gas   v) submarines
    iii) tanks   vi) role of women

  b) Research your topic. Use your textbook as a starting point
for information, but visit your school and local library to do
further research.

  c) Present your group's research to the rest of the class. You
can do this in a variety of ways: oral presentations, maps,
displays, and models.

DEVELOPING SKILLS:
USING THE BASIC INQUIRY MODEL

Sometimes you are presented with a historical problem that
requires you to organize your material in a very systematic manner. A helpful tool is the Basic Inquiry Model. It helps you to
recognize, understand, and analyse issues and events. The
major steps outlined in the model can be followed to find answers
in other subjects too.

Suppose you are trying to figure out why the assassination of
Archduke Ferdinand set off a chain of events that culminated in a
world war. Why were so many nations dragged into a full-scale
war over what should have been just a squabble between
Austria–Hungary and Serbia? Were there other factors that contributed to a world war?

The following Basic Inquiry Model leads you through the steps
toward finding an answer to these questions.

The Basic Inquiry Model

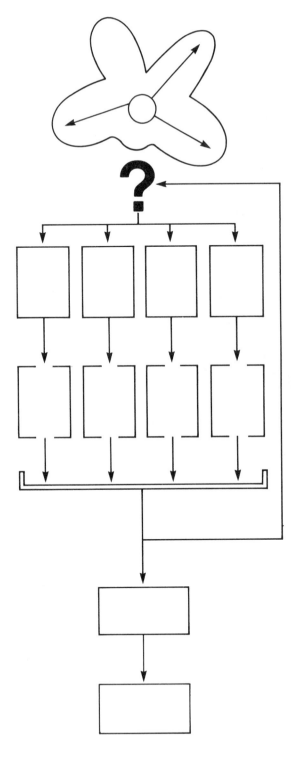

The Starting Point
This is the first step in the inquiry process. At this stage, you bring information together from a number of experiences.

Asking the Question
Think of a question based on the information gathered in the starting point.

Looking at the Alternatives
Not all questions have one answer. What are the different answers or alternatives to your question?

Collecting your Data
Now, collect information about each alternative. This will help you to decide which alternative is the best.

Finding an Answer
Look at all the information you have collected. Which alternative seems to have the most or best information to answer the question? Sometimes the best answer might combine two or more alternatives. Your final answer is called the conclusion.

Assessing your Conclusion
This is your chance to make sure that your conclusion fully answers the question.

Expressing your Conclusion
This is where you present your conclusion. There are many different ways to do this. You can write a paragraph about it, draw a cartoon, or do a role-playing activity. This can be done in groups or by yourself.

Evaluating your Conclusion
Do you have any new ideas about your alternatives and conclusion? What would you do differently next time? Evaluation is important. It will help you to do an even better job next time.

From the Ontario Ministry of Education, *Research Study Skills Document*, Toronto, 1979.

An Example of an Inquiry Activity in History

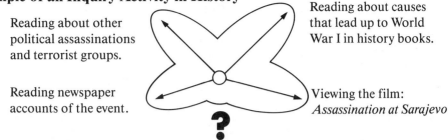

Reading about other political assassinations and terrorist groups.

Reading about causes that lead up to World War I in history books.

Reading newspaper accounts of the event.

Viewing the film: *Assassination at Sarajevo*

Asking the Question

Why did the assassination of Archduke Ferdinand and Sophia escalate into a war involving many nations?

Looking at the Alternatives

MILITARISM	NATIONALISM	IMPERIALISM	ALLIANCES

Collecting your Data
Factors to consider

		The positive and negative factors for each of the alternatives can be gathered from the text, other history books, newspapers and magazines, films, slides, charts, maps, graphs, tables, etc.	

Finding an Answer
After research and discussion, come to a group decision about why the incident escalated into a world war.

Assessing your Conclusion
Have you answered the original question: why did this incident escalate into a world war?

Expressing your Conclusion
Present your conclusion to your classmates. You should explain the reasons for your conclusion.

Evaluating your Conclusion
After you have heard the conclusions of other students, evaluate your own conclusion in the light of new information or insights you have gained.

13
War on the Home Front

World War I was different from every other war that had ever gone before it. It was total war, which meant that it involved civilians almost as much as soldiers. This war had an effect on everybody. And when at last it was over, life could never be the same again.

Canadians at home got behind their troops overseas in many different ways. There was a feeling that no sacrifice should be spared to ensure a victory in Europe. Many people planted "victory gardens" in order to produce as much food as possible. Canadians were sending large amounts of food to feed the fighting forces as well as the civilian populations of other Allied countries. At home people were trying to waste nothing and to reduce their own food consumption.

ADVICE TO THE HOUSEWIFE
1 Use nut-butter or margarine.
2 Remake leftover bread into new bread, cake, or pudding.
3 Instead of one beefless day, why not try for six to make up for people less patriotic?
4 Eat as little cake and pastry as you can.
5 Use oats, corn, barley, and rye instead of wheat.
6 Use ham and pork bones in other dishes.
7 Chew your food thoroughly – you will be satisfied with less.

8   All kinds of cold cereal can be saved, and when not enough to roll into balls to fry, they can be used in batter cakes and corn breads.

9   Cut each slice of bread as required.

10 Mix your own cleanser (use white sand, washing soda, soap, and chalk).

11 Fifty million dollars is thrown away in garbage cans annually.

12 Do not display the joint of meat on the table. It is an inducement to eat more than you need.

13 Do not eat both butter *and* jam with bread.

Students in Saskatchewan and other wheat-producing areas were often dismissed early to replace the farm workers who were overseas. Groups of women of all ages met regularly to knit socks for the soldiers and to roll bandages. Every community held card games, dances, and variety shows. The profits from these evenings were used to send cigarettes, candy, soap, writing paper, and pencils to the troops.

Scouts boosting the sale of Victory Bonds in Saskatchewan, 1918

Women holding a bazaar to aid the war effort.

During 1918 the war cost Canada over $1 million a day! Workers helped to pay the enormous costs of the war by buying Victory Bonds. Private and commercial investors loaned over $1 billion to the government. This would be paid back with interest when the war was over. Children could also play a part by buying Thrift Stamps. Each stamp cost 25 cents and was stuck on a card. When a child had bought $4.00 worth of stamps, s/he received a War Savings Stamp. A War Savings Stamp bought before the end of 1918 could be cashed in for $5.00 in 1924.

It was at this time that the Canadian government introduced the practice of an income tax. This was supposed to be a "temporary measure" to help finance the war. But as we know, the income tax has never been abolished.

Agricultural and industrial production reached dramatic new heights during World War I. Especially important for the war effort was the production of munitions. Plants manufacturing airplanes, shells, and ships sprang up across the country. By 1918, 300 000 men and women were employed in Canada in these factories and almost one-third of the shells fired by the armies of the British Empire were being made in Canada.

Women munitions workers

The munitions industry brought the war dramatically close to home for the citizens of Halifax. Halifax was the Canadian port from which all North American convoys left. On the morning of 6 December 1917 a terrible explosion rocked the city of Halifax. The *Mont Blanc*, a French munitions ship carrying a cargo of time-bomb explosives, collided with the Belgian vessel *Imo* in the harbour. The blast levelled large sections of Halifax, killed 2000, and was heard all over the province. It was even felt in Sydney, over 320 km away. It was one of the worst disasters in Canadian history. All that was ever found of the *Mont Blanc* was a cannon and part of an anchor that landed over 3 km away.

THE ROLE OF WOMEN

World War I brought about great changes in the lives of Canadian women. The war deprived many thousands of women of their husbands, sons, fathers, and brothers. But the war also demanded a much greater involvement by women outside the home. With the general shortage of labour in Canada, the number of women who were employed in industry rose dramatically. In many cases women started to work in occupations that would have been considered unsuitable for women before 1914. Examine these pictures and documents on the role of women and answer these questions:

1   What do these pictures and documents tell you about women's activities during the war at home and overseas?
2   What problems might women encounter doing these jobs?
3   What changes might occur in the lives of women as a result of these new responsibilities outside the home?

I had a very hard job. It had to be that you run a machine of weights into the shell, and the weight had to be just exact. Quite a few of them didn't have the patience.

It was interesting work but very hard on your nerves. There was a machine went on fire. This friend from Beaverton was on the machine that blew up, and I run to her and we had to go down on our hands and knees and crawl out of the place. So we had a little experience of what it was to be right in a war.

We decided to become farmerettes when we read in the paper that there was a big crop and they needed people to come, and there were no men. So this friend and I said that we would go. We volunteered. Masses of young people went out and brought that all in.

I wanted to help do my share, and I joined the Red Cross and helped roll bandages and knit socks. My first ones were big enough to fit an elephant, and after that, I became very proficient – *so* proficient that I knit a pair of socks a day without any trouble.

You see, *everybody* felt they had to do something. You just couldn't sit there. There was such a thing as just doing nothing but going to afternoon teas and dances and parties, which we had done. That was *out!*

There was a phrase, 'Doing your bit.' Well, that was pretty well the keynote feeling all through that First World War. Everybody was extremely patriotic, and everybody wanted to 'do a bit'.

That was the stock phrase. I don't know who started that. It came out in some speech or other, and everybody took it up. You must 'do your bit.' And we all felt the same way. If there's anything we could do to help, we must do it.

Women, of course, all took to knitting. Every woman was knitting socks and so on for the troops overseas. I remember a cartoon showing women knitting socks. The caption was:

Your parcel of socks received. Some fit!

I wear one for a helmet and one for a mitt.

I'll see you after I've done my bit,

In the meantime, where did you learn to knit?

Well, there was some pretty weird knitting done, I suppose, but also some very competent knitting.

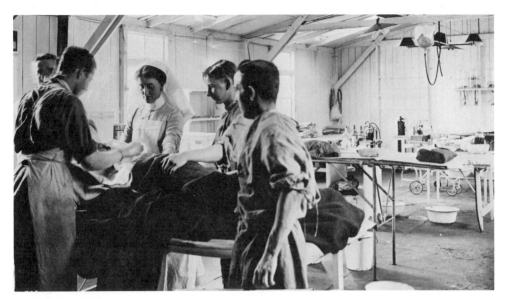

Wartime hospital

It was during World War I that an important step forward was taken in Canada for women's rights. At the beginning of the twentieth century, women in many countries had begun to organize themselves to gain the vote for women. Members of this movement were called suffragettes in Britain, and suffragists in Canada. Their purpose, however, was the same: to win rights and opportunities that men enjoyed. Getting the vote was just the first step.

Nellie McClung was a suffragist and one of Canada's great social reformers. She wrote, "Certainly women belong in the home, but not twenty-four hours a day. They should have exactly the same freedom as men." When World War I broke out, it helped to prove that Nellie McClung was right. Women were called upon to do the jobs formerly performed only by men. The war brought women together in volunteer organizations and employment, and once together, they began to talk and dream of political equality with men.

Suffragists campaigned enthusiastically for women's suffrage. Their leaders included Dorothy Davis in British Columbia, Margaret Gordon in Ontario, Emily Murphy and Alice Jamieson in Alberta, and the dynamic Nellie McClung in Manitoba. The first breakthrough for women's suffrage came in Manitoba when, in 1916, women were given the right to vote in that province. Within a few months Saskatchewan, Alberta, British Columbia, and Ontario followed.

Elsie Inman

The main goal of woman's suffrage, of course, was to gain the right to vote in federal elections. In the election of December 1917, the government granted the vote to the mothers, sisters, and wives of soldiers in the Armed Forces, and Canadian nurses serving in the forces. By the time the war had ended, the right to vote in federal elections had been extended to all women in Canada over the age of twenty-one. However, the franchise was not extended to Native women or most Native men. The Dominion Elections Act (1920) also gave women the right to run for election to Parliament.

Canadian Women Win the Vote

British Columbia	5 April 1917
Alberta	19 April 1916
Saskatchewan	14 March 1916
Manitoba	28 January 1916
Ontario	12 April 1917
Quebec	25 April 1940
New Brunswick	17 April 1919
Nova Scotia	26 April 1918
Prince Edward Island	3 May 1922
Newfoundland	13 April 1925

Not everyone thought it was a good idea to give women the vote. Some men in Prince Edward Island would not allow their wives to vote. Senator Elsie Inman recalls one such incident.

Most of the women were afraid of their husbands. The majority of husbands refused to let them vote. Well, I remember one woman who was scared to vote because her husband might see her at the poll. She was anxious to vote and I said, "Would he know you if you were dressed up in other clothes?" Well, she didn't think he would, so I went home and she was about my size. We wore veils in those days, so I took my clothes and coat and put the veil on her and took her to vote.

CONSCRIPTION

The beginning of the war was welcomed with great enthusiasm in all parts of Canada. Britain was at war and, therefore, Canada was at war. Canadians, especially those who were born in Britain, rushed out to volunteer for service. The country was flooded with patriotic appeals. Volunteers marched behind brass bands to the enlistment offices. Men in civilian clothes were sometimes given white feathers as a symbol of cowardice by girls in the street. This unfortunate incident happened once to a winner of the Victoria Cross who had been sent home to recover from an injury. By the end of 1916, as the war dragged on and the death toll mounted, the number of volunteers began to dwindle. Obviously the war was not going to be short and glorious as Canadians had first thought.

Early in 1917 Prime Minister Robert Borden left to attend an Imperial Conference in England and to visit the Canadian soldiers at the front. Borden was shocked by the information he received in Britain. Britain was on the brink of disaster because of the German U-boat menace. Casualties were mounting daily on the Western Front. British military officials urged Borden to send even more Canadian troops to Europe. Meanwhile in Canada volunteer enlistments were not keping up with the number of men killed or wounded.

Enlistment/Casualty Rate for 1917

Month	Enlistments	Casualties
January	9 194	4 396
March	6 640	6 161
May	6 407	13 457
July	3 882	7 906
September	3 588	10 990
November	4 019	30 741

Borden returned home and asked Parliament to pass a conscription bill. Conscription means compulsory enlistment in the Armed Forces for all able-bodied men in Canada.

The mention of conscription brought a storm of protest in some parts of Canada, especially in French Canada. Many English-speaking Canadians believed that the reason why the number of volunteers had fallen was simply that the province of Quebec was not doing its part. Newspapers in English Canada had pointed out that Ontario had provided 63 percent of the volunteers in proportion to its population, Manitoba and Saskatchewan 81 percent, Alberta 92 percent, British Columbia 104 percent, Maritime provinces 38 percent, while Quebec had only provided 20 percent in proportion to its population.

French Canadians simply did not share the enthusiasm that English-speaking Canadians felt for Britain's war. Nor did they feel any real tie to their country of origin, France. The French Canadians had been conquered by British forces in 1760, and deserted by France. Since that time many French Canadians felt they were being treated like second-class citizens in Canada. Louis Riel, they believed, had been hanged by the English-dominated government in Ottawa. Riel had led a rebellion of Métis and Indians against the increasing white settlement in the West. More recently, Ontario's Department of Education had limited the teaching of French in Ontario schools by a bill known as Regulation 17. French Canadians felt they were not being treated as equal partners in Confederation.

Sir Sam Hughes, Minister of Militia, also annoyed the people of Quebec. Hughes made the mistake of appointing a Protestant clergyman to supervise recruiting in Roman Catholic Quebec. He insisted on using English to train French-Canadian volunteers who often did not know the language. Very few French-speaking officers received any important army posts. Only one French-speaking regiment – the 22nd, the famous "Vandoos" – had been

Convalescing soldiers

sent to the Western Front to fight. At Courcelette the 22nd regiment served with outstanding distinction. However, it did seem to many French Canadians as though Hughes and his policies were doing nothing to encourage greater French-Canadian participation in the war. Eventually, in 1916, Hughes was dismissed by Borden, but not before he had done long-term damage in Quebec.

Borden knew that conscription was a dangerous idea. It could divide the French and English in Canada. Still he realized that the shortage of troops was so severe that he had no other choice. The Military Service Bill was passed in the summer of 1917. Military service became compulsory for all males between the ages of twenty and forty-five. Men in vital wartime production jobs, the sick, or conscientious objectors were exempt from fighting. Conscientious objectors were those people who refused to fight on the grounds that war went against their moral and religious beliefs.

Those in Quebec who strongly opposed conscription were led by Henri Bourassa and were known as nationalists. Bourassa was the brilliant editor of the Montreal newspaper *Le Devoir* and one of the most powerful speakers in Canadian history. Bourassa was a Canadian who believed that Canada should be independent from Britain. Just because Britain was at war, he argued, there was no reason for Canada to go to war. Bourassa summarized his opposition to conscription in a pamphlet published on 4 July 1917.

We are opposed to further enlistments for the war in Europe, whether by conscription or otherwise, for the following reasons:

1   Canada has already made a military display, in men and money, proportionately superior to that of any nation engaged in the war;
2   any further weakening of the manpower of the country would seriously handicap agricultural production and other essential industries;
3   an increase in the war budget of Canada spells national bankruptcy;
4   it threatens the economic life of the nation and, eventually, its political independence;
5   conscription means national disunion and strife, and would thereby hurt the cause of the Allies to a much greater extent than the addition of a few thousand soldiers to their fighting forces could bring them help and comfort.

Anti-conscription parade, Montreal, May 1917

More moderate French-Canadian opinion was represented by Sir Wilfrid Laurier, the leader of the Liberal party. Laurier had struggled all his life to keep Canada united. He could not support conscription because he realized it was an issue that could tear the country apart. Laurier was heartbroken when twenty-two Liberals from Ontario, the West, and Atlantic Canada voted with the government for conscription. Only the Liberals in Quebec and a handful of English-speaking Liberals stood with Laurier against conscription.

With a general election coming in December 1917, the government passed two further bills. They were both meant to strengthen Borden's position on conscription. The Military Voters Act provided for the taking of the soldiers' votes overseas. More important was the Wartime Elections Act. It gave the vote to female relatives of soldiers. These women could be expected to vote for conscription and a government that promised to support their loved ones overseas. This act also took the right to vote away from immigrants from enemy countries who had become Canadian citizens since 1902. Since many of these immigrants had fled from Europe to get away from compulsory military service, Borden's party feared they might vote against conscription.

The Conservatives were now joined by the Liberals who had deserted Laurier. Conservatives and Liberals who believed in conscription formed a Union government. The election of 1917 was particularly bitter. Voters were asked by the Union government "Who would the Germans vote for?" The Liberals were accused of letting down the soldiers at the front. The election results saw Borden and the Union government returned with an overwhelming majority in English-speaking Canada, and with only three seats in Quebec.

1917 Election Results

Number of Seats in House of Commons		
	Liberal	Union (Conservatives plus some Liberals)
PEI	2	2
NS	4	12
NB	4	7
Quebec	62	3
Ontario	8	74
Manitoba	1	14
Saskatchewan	0	16
Alberta	1	11
BC	0	13
Yukon	0	1
	82	153

The split in Canada that Laurier had feared for so long had finally occurred. There were riots in Montreal and Quebec City against the conscription act. Troops had to be sent in with rifles and machine guns to restore order. Farmers from both English Canada and Quebec marched to Ottawa in protest in May 1918. They were objecting that their sons – who were needed on the farms – were not being excused from military service. Many immigrants were bitter that their votes had been taken away. When war ended in November 1918, Canada was an unhappy and divided nation.

Did conscription work? The call up for conscripts did not begin until the new year, 1918. Thousands of men, both French and English Canadians, claimed exemption from service. A man could be excused from military service if he had an essential occupation like farmer, was a member of the clergy, or because of physical handicap. By the time the war ended in November 1918, only about 45 000 conscripts had reached the battlefield.

Was conscription a success in Canada? Most historians would

agree that conscription was a failure. National unity had been destroyed. English Canadians were lined up against French Canadians, Protestants against Roman Catholics, majority against minority. There was widespread disagreement about conscription between farmers and city dwellers, and between civilians and soldiers. National unity was a high price to pay for 45 000 soldiers.

Casualties of World War I			
The Allies (British figures include Canada)	Military deaths	Wounded	Civilian dead
France	1 357 800	4 266 000	40 000
British Empire	908 371	2 090 212	30 633
Russia	1 700 000	4 950 000	2 000 000
Italy	462 391	953 886	not available
United States	50 385	205 690	not available
The Central Powers			
Germany	1 808 545	4 247 143	760 000
Austria-Hungary	922 500	3 620 000	300 000
Turkey	325 000	400 000	2 150 000
Direct Costs of War		
U.S.	$22 625 253 000	includes all
Britain	35 334 012 000	expenditures in
Canada	1 665 576 000	carrying on
France	24 265 583 000	hostilities
Russia	22 593 950 000	
Germany	37 775 000 000	
Austria-Hungary	20 622 960 000	
Turkey	1 430 000 000	
Property Losses		
Belgium	$ 7 000 000 000	estimates
France	10 000 000 000	land and
Russia	1 250 000 000	sea
Italy	2 710 000 000	
British Empire	1 750 000 000	
Germany	1 750 000 000	

Robert Borden

1 Which country had the largest number of military dead as a result of the war? Which country had the most wounded?
2 Which of the Central Powers lost the greatest number of soldiers? Suggest possible reasons for this.
3 Which of the Allies suffered the smallest losses? Suggest reasons for this.
4 Which country on the Allied side lost most civilians? Suggest reasons for this.
5 Why would Canadian casualties be included with the figures for the British Empire?

THE COST OF THE WAR TO CANADA

The first item on the balance sheet for the war was written in red to symbolize the blood of those Canadians who died. A total of 60 661 Canadians lost their lives, and another 173 000 were wounded or gassed. Many thousands of this latter group lived on for years in veterans' hospitals. For these people the suffering of war never ended. They were victims who had lost their limbs, their minds, or whose lungs had been destroyed by gas attacks.

The second disastrous effect of the war on Canadian life was the deepening French-English differences over conscription. The

gulf between Quebec and the rest of the country steadily wid-
ened. The hurt, pain, and distrust lingered on into the peace time
after the war.

On the other hand, Canada emerged from World War I as a
more independent nation than it had been when it entered the
war. Canada's war effort had helped it to earn a position of prestige among other countries of the world. The outstanding contribution of Canada's soldiers won respect and a separate seat for
Canada at the peace conference following the war. Previously,
Great Britain would have signed the peace treaty on behalf of all
the British Empire. Now Canada signed the treaty as a separate
nation. There was no doubt that Canada had achieved the status
of an independent nation.

The war had produced a great economic boom in industry in
Canada. Steel and munitions production and manufacturing had
grown fantastically. During the war almost everyone who could
work had a job. Then the demand for wartime goods suddenly
stopped. Large numbers of employees were laid off. The problem
was further complicated by hundreds of thousands of soldiers
coming back into the Canadian labour force. Many returning
heroes were disillusioned to find that there were no jobs for them
in Canada.

Returning veterans were surprised by a number of other
changes. One was the dramatic change in the role of women. The
war had given women the chance to use their abilities. Women as
wage earners had won much greater freedom for themselves.
They had obtained the right to vote as full and equal citizens of
Canada.

Another change that surprised the returning soldiers was that
in most parts of Canada their favourite bars and saloons had
disappeared. This was due to Prohibition. Closely connected
with the campaign for women's suffrage had been the campaign
against the evils of drinking alcohol. Many women who had
fought for the right to vote had also joined the Women's Christian
Temperance Union. This organization was committed to stamp-
ing out the use of all intoxicating liquor. Women like Nellie
McClung spoke out strongly against the use of alcohol. Drinkers
were urged to sign the pledge to "abstain from the use of all
intoxicating liquor." Supported by farm, church, lodge, and merchant associations, the women persuaded provincial governments to introduce Prohibition. It was argued that it was patriotic
to use grain to feed soldiers and civilians rather than to make
alcohol. One by one the provinces prohibited the sale of alcohol,
with the exception of Quebec. The fact that Quebec was the only
province that did not have Prohibition was just another factor

isolating that province and separating Quebec from the rest of Canada.

By the time the war was over, if a person wanted a drink, it was necessary to have a doctor's prescription or to visit a bootlegger.

As the decade drew to a close, three of the most important Canadian leaders were leaving the spotlight of politics. On 19 February 1919 the great statesman, Sir Wilfrid Laurier, ended his long and illustrious career. After suffering two strokes, he died of a fatal third stroke. With Laurier gone, Henri Bourassa became less involved in the political scene. Sir Robert Borden, exhausted from leadership during wartime, resigned as leader of the Conservative party in 1920. Three new leaders in Canada were about to emerge – William Lyon Mackenzie King, Arthur Meighen, and J.S. Woodsworth.

DEVELOPING SKILLS:
RECOGNIZING SEXISM

World War I was a turning point for women. The war effort allowed them to become involved in many activities that had been considered traditionally male, such as working in munitions factories. The war also brought the franchise. Canadian women could now vote. However, when the war ended, most women returned to working in their homes. The traditional view of women as wives and mothers remained. It was not until the sixties that the place of women in society and the discrimination they faced was seriously discussed.

The traditional roles of women were perpetuated by a powerful new medium – television. In the 1950s, programs like "Leave it to Beaver" and "Father Knows Best" showed men as the breadwinners and decision makers of the family and the women as wives, mothers, and housekeepers.

The role of women slowly began to change in the real world. More women were working outside the home, choosing non-traditional careers, and deciding to work and raise a family at the same time. However, television programming took awhile to catch up with the new roles of women in society.

By the 1980s , viewers could watch shows such as "Kate and Allie" that showed two divorced women sharing accommodation and raising their children alone. Or they could watch "Cagney and Lacey," a show about two women police officers. One is single and is happy being single, and the other is married yet continues to work.

In Canada, women play a prominent role in broadcasting. Women report local news and host many public information programs.

1   In groups, brainstorm to discover television shows from the 1950s, 1960s, 1970s, and 1980s. Make a timeline that shows the evolution of television programming from its early days until the present.

2   Do some investigation to identify women involved in Canadian broadcasting. What kind of background do broadcasters need? Is there still discrimination against female broadcasters?

3   What areas of television are still dominated by men? Can you suggest reasons for this.

DEVELOPING SKILLS:
RECOGNIZING BIAS AND FRAME OF REFERENCE

Frequently in Canadian history, French and English Canada have looked at issues from two different sides. Many people from Quebec have always felt like outsiders in Confederation. They became part of the British Empire only because of military defeat. Their frame of reference has been formed by their background and their experiences. In the same way, English-Canadian frames of reference have been formed by their background and experiences. These frames of reference create a bias.

Two reporters writing about Sir Sam Hughes, Borden's minister of Militia may have very different frames of reference. A person of British descent, who is Protestant and lives in Ontario might see Hughes as a hero. A French-Canadian Roman Catholic living in Quebec may believe that Hughes is a crook and a threat to French-Canadian survival.

Read the two fictional newspaper accounts of the dismissal of Hughes as minister of Militia in 1916. Then, answer the questions that follow.

Montreal Matin
November 1916
**HUGHES FIRED FROM
THE CABINET**
At long last, Prime Minister Borden has done the honourable thing! He has thrown Sir Sam Hughes, his incompetent minister of Militia, out of the Cabinet. Now, Hughes will be unable to do any more damage to Canadian unity. Hughes, more than any other person, has divided and torn this country apart with his policies.

Hughes has managed to antagonize everyone in Quebec. Those French Canadians who have volunteered for the English war have been insulted. The recruitment posters, training and instruction manuals are in English only. More importantly, promotions have only been given to the English-speaking officers. How can Hughes and other Canadians expect French Canadians to join in the war effort when they are treated so poorly?

As minister of Militia, Hughes has disgraced the nation by rewarding his friends and cronies with munitions contracts. These shady deals have allowed his friends to make millions at the taxpayer's expense.

Why should we spill one more drop of precious French-Canadian blood in Europe. Canada only wants Quebec in Confederation when we are willing to sacrifice for the British Empire. Britain started this war. Let Britain finish it!

Toronto Times
November 1916
SIR SAM STEPS DOWN!
Sad news was announced in Ottawa today. Sir Sam Hughes is no longer the minister of Militia. The prime minister, bending to howls of criticism from Quebec, has dismissed this able, competent minister. Hughes has done more for the war effort than any other Canadian. He has recruited thousands of volunteers and raised thousands of dollars.

Canada entered the war with only 3000 in the armed forces. By the end of 1915, thanks to Sir Sam's tireless energy and inspired leadership, more than 200 000 of our noble sons have taken their places on the battlefield.

Without Sir Sam's efforts how will Canada maintain its contribution to the war cause? Many English Canadians are angered by the reluctance of French Canadians to volunteer for overseas service. English Canadians are willing to defend the British Empire. The Empire that has done so much for Canada.

Sir Sam Hughes, through the force of his personality, has persuaded reluctant industrialists to invest heavily in the production of much needed war materials. We should be thankful that, through the contracts negotiated by the minister, tons of vital munitions are making their way to our soldiers at the front.

1   Briefly state the bias of the *Toronto Times* and *Montreal Matin* articles.

2   Find two facts that both articles discuss but disagree on.

3   Find two negative words or phrases in the *Toronto Times* story that describe the French-Canadian contribution to the war effort. What two words or phrases in the *Montreal Matin* article describe English Canadians or Hughes in negative terms?

4   Search for two words or phrases in the *Toronto Times* that describe Hughes in a positive light. In the *Montreal Matin* find two words or phrases that justify the French-Canadian contribution to the war.

5   Look at the fact that Hughes has awarded his munitions contract to his friends. Suggest reasons why the two newspaper accounts treat this fact differently. Which source do you trust? Why?

6   Explain how the *Toronto Times*'s frame of reference might account for their bias in reporting the firing of Hughes.

7   How might the *Montreal Matin's* frame of reference influence their reporting of the same story?

DIGGING DEEPER

1   Explain why these statements are true or false.
   a) British-born Canadians volunteered more promptly than Canadian-born citizens.
   b) Only French-Canadians opposed conscription.
   c) The conscription issue caused a serious split in Canada.

2   Why did a spirit of excitement and confidence exist in Canada at the outbreak of the war in 1914?

3   What attitude did Borden and Laurier take in 1914 toward the war? What were their reasons for feeling this way?

4   Explain why Canadians were considered to be part of the British army. What does this suggest about the relationship between Britain and Canada?

5   Which provinces might be expected to support the war most strongly? Suggest reasons why this would be so. Of the first 36 267 Canadian troops to go overseas, 10 800 were born in Canada. More than 23 000 were born in the British Isles. How do you account for the large number of British-born people in the first group going overseas? Among Canadian-born volunteers, what sort of person would be most enthusiastic about enlisting to fight in Europe?

6 Stage a mock parliament to debate the conscription issue, 1917.

Participants: Sir Robert Borden
                Sir Wilfrid Laurier
                English-speaking Conservatives
                Liberals who refuse to support Laurier
                French-speaking Conservatives and Liberals

7 In 1917, Borden took away the right to vote from Canadian immigrants from Germany, Austria, and other countries with whom we were at war. Find out what other measures were taken against these people. Were such actions justified? The individual rights that were taken away are called "civil liberties." List some examples in which peoples' civil liberties are taken away today. Is it ever right to take away an individual's civil rights? How can we prevent our civil liberties from being eroded? For more information, you could contact the Canadian Civil Liberties Association, 229 Yonge St., Suite 403, Toronto, Ontario, M5B 1N9.

8 During World War I the Canadian government found that colourful posters were an effective way of reaching a widely scattered public. Examine the selection of posters.

    1 List four different purposes for which posters were used by the government.

    2 What sorts of reasons do the posters suggest for supporting the war effort?

    3 To which emotions do the posters appeal?

    4 How successful do you think these posters would be? Why?

    5 What methods would the government use today to achieve the same purpose?

Divide the class into four groups. On large sheets of paper, design and produce posters which will be used to

- recruit soldiers;
- encourage the purchase of war bonds;
- help reduce food consumption;
- recruit children to work in the war effort.

14
The Peace
Settlement

THE TREATY OF VERSAILLES

Almost five years after the murder at Sarajevo, government leaders met at Versailles, near Paris, to sign the peace treaty. Thirty-two victorious countries were represented, including Canada. Canada was not content just to be part of the British delegation. Borden had demanded and received the right for Canada to be represented as a separate nation at the meetings and at the official signing of the treaty. He argued that Canada deserved an independent voice in the peace talks because of its support for the war effort. Most of the important decisions, however, were made by the leaders of the three strongest winning powers. They were Georges Clemenceau, premier of France, David Lloyd George, prime minister of Great Britain, and Woodrow Wilson, president of the United States.

These three world leaders, or the 'Big Three' as they were known, had very different views on what should be done with defeated Germany. Clemenceau wanted to crush Germany once and for all. Twice in his lifetime he had seen Germans invade his homeland. Much of the war had been fought on French territory. Clemenceau wanted to punish Germany and see that it was left too weak ever to attack France again.

On the other hand, President Wilson wanted a fair peace. He argued that the defeated nations should be treated justly so that they would not want a war of revenge in the future. Wilson's view was natural since the United States had suffered less than any nation involved in the war. He also thought that this was a good opportunity to make a better world for the future. Wilson suggested "Fourteen Points" that included complete disarmament and free trade among nations. He also suggested that a League of

PEACE

Official Peace Despatch

WASHINGTON, Nov. 11.—"The news that has been signed." This brief announcement made was made by the State Department at 2:45 o'clock this afternoon. "It was signed at five o'clock a.m., Paris time, and hostilities will cease at 11 o'clock this morning, Paris time."

Praise God from whom all blessings flow!
Praise Him all creatures here below!
Praise Him above, ye heavenly host!
Praise Father, Son and Holy Ghost.

Our Warehouse Closed All Day Monday In Honor of Our Victorious Armies and Allies

The T. EATON C°. *Limited*
REGINA.   CANADA

Sign at Windsor Station, Montreal encourages Canadians to remember the soldiers who fought overseas.

Nations be established. Wilson wanted each nation to send representatives to a permanent world parliament that could settle future disputes among countries.

Prime Minister Lloyd George held a middle position. His country had lost many lives in the war and Lloyd George promised his people that he would make Germany pay. He helped to work out many of the compromises that made the peace treaty possible. Here are major terms of the Treaty of Versailles:

Article 42
Germany is forbidden to build any military fortifications on the left bank of the Rhine River. It may not build any fortifications on the right bank for a distance of 50 km.

Article 45
To pay for the destruction of the coal mines in the north of France, Germany turns over to France its coal mines in the Saar Basin for fifteen years.

Article 51
The territories of Alsace and Lorraine taken from France in 1871 are restored to it.

Article 80
Germany must accept the complete independence of Austria.

Article 81
Germany must accept the complete independence of Czechoslovakia.

Article 87
Germany must accept the complete independence of Poland.

Article 89
Poland will allow persons, goods, vessels, carriages, wagons, and mails to pass freely between East Prussia and the rest of Germany over Polish territory. (This was necessary because Poland was given a strip of German territory in order to provide it with access to the sea at the city of Danzig. This was called the "Polish Corridor." It separated East Prussia from the rest of Germany).

Article 119
Germany must give up all its rights and titles to its overseas possessions (colonies in Africa and the Far East).

Article 160
After 31 March 1920, the German army must not exceed 100 000 soldiers. The army shall be used only to maintain order within Germany and to control the frontiers.

Article 181
German naval forces must not exceed six battleships, six light cruisers, twelve destroyers, and twelve torpedo boats. Germans are forbidden to have any submarines.

Article 198
The armed forces of Germany must not include any military air force.

Article 231
Germany must accept the responsibility for causing all the loss and damage that the Allies and their citizens have suffered. (This is known as the "War Guilt Clause.")

Article 232
The Allied governments require Germany to pay for all wartime damages to the civilian population and the property of Allied powers. (These payments are known as reparations.)

Article 233
The amount of the above damage will be determined by an Allied Commission.

Article 428
A guarantee is needed to make sure the treaty will be carried out by Germany. Therefore, the German territory west of the Rhine River will be occupied by Allied troops for fifteen years.

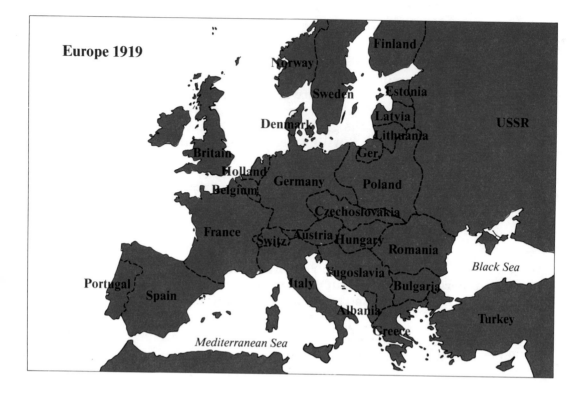

Europe 1919

1 In a chart, summarize the terms of the Treaty of Versailles. Use these headings in your chart:

   i) military terms;
   ii) territorial terms in Europe;
   iii) territorial terms outside Europe;
   iv) economic terms;
   v) other terms.

2 Compare the attitudes of the "Big Three" toward defeated Germany. Examine the terms and decide whose views had more influence on the treaty. Why?

3 Which of the following terms of the Treaty of Versailles do you consider fair treatment for Germany? Why?

   a) The Allies took away all Germany's colonies.
   b) Germany's army was limited to 100 000 soldiers.
   c) Germany was held responsible for causing World War I.
   d) Germany was required to pay $33 000 000 000 as reparations for the war damage.
   e) Germany would not be allowed to place troops in the Rhineland for fifteen years.

4 Explain what the Polish Corridor was and what happened to the German city of Danzig.

5 What possible objections might Germany raise to the terms of the Treaty of Versailles?

6   It has been said that the Treaty of Versailles contained within it the seeds of another war. What do you think this statement means? Do you think this statement is correct? Why?

Other Peace Treaties

Peace treaties with the other Central Powers also brought about major territorial changes in Europe. Four new independent nations were created out of the old Austro-Hungarian Empire. These were Czechoslovakia, Poland, Hungary, and Yugoslavia. Austria itself was reduced to a small nation. The peacemakers justified changing the boundaries of nations by the principle of self-determination. This means that people of similar language and nationality have the right to rule themselves.

The Russian empire was also broken up as a result of World War I. Finland, Estonia, Latvia, and Lithuania were given independence as new nations. Russia also lost large regions to Poland, Czechoslovakia, and Romania. It may seem strange that one of the Allies – Russia – lost so much territory after the war. This happened because Russia had come under communist rule in 1917. A revolution had overthrown the Russian czar and Russia became the first communist state. Communist theory believes in a classless society where all goods, services, and means of production (factories, farms, etc.) are owned by all the people. People should share equally all the things they need to live. The new Russian government had withdrawn from the war at that time and made peace with Germany. Russia was so busy establishing a new government at home that it did not have the time and energy to continue fighting with Germany. The delegates to the peace conference hoped that these new nations in the centre of Europe would keep communism from spreading westwards from Russia.

DEVELOPING SKILLS:
OBTAINING INFORMATION FROM MAPS

You cannot begin to understand World War I without having an idea of the countries involved and their proximity to each other. While you may have a mental image of the geographical area where you live, you are not likely to be sure of the location and boundaries of European countries. There are many different kinds of maps and maps can contain a wealth of information. Maps and atlases are indispensable sources of information.

When studying the First World War, you can find maps that will show the strategic location of countries, the sites of famous battles, and the routes of advancing and retreating armies. Maps will help you to figure out why the location of countries make them friends or enemies. From these maps, you can even hypothesize what might cause future wars!

Compare the 1914 map of Europe with the 1919 map of Europe (see pages 108 and 162). Remember that in a comparison you determine the similarities and differences between the two maps.

Look at the maps and answer the following questions.

Comprehension
1   What does each map show? At what period of time?

Interpretation
2   Compare the size of Germany before and after the war. Locate two countries that received territory that formerly belonged to Germany.
3   What happened to Austria–Hungary in 1919? Name the newly independent nations that were created in Europe?
4   Name and locate four new countries that were created from former Russian territory. To what other countries did Russia lose territory?

Hypothesizing
5   Locate the Polish Corridor on the map. How might the creation of the Polish Corridor lead to problems among nations in the future?
6   Name and locate the new independent states created after World War I. How might the creation of a number of small, weak nations in Europe lead to future territorial disputes?

DIGGING DEEPER

1   Many small independent countries were created by the peace treaties. People have said this was an unwise decision. Can you suggest any possible problems that might develop as a result of their size and location?
2   What do you think are the lessons to be learned from the study of World War I? Has the world gained anything from the lessons of the war? Give your reasons.
3   Refer back to the matrix you started at the end of the second unit (page 103). You are now ready to add information for the time period 1914–1918. Trace the development of the same themes through World War I.

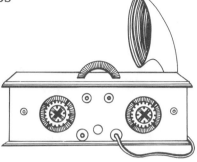

15
Moving into the Twenties

Al Capone rode around Chicago in an armour-plated limousine, accompanied by a bodyguard who sat with a machine gun on his lap. A flashy dresser, he always wore a priceless diamond ring and carried $50 000 cash in his wallet. He received fan mail from all parts of the world. Some letters asked for the gangster's help in "rubbing out" irritating neighbours. No one had a more unpleasant reputation in the 1920s than this American gangster. Capone was almost as well known to Canadians as to Americans.

Born to immigrant parents in Brooklyn, New York in 1899, Capone was drawn into violent street gangs as a boy. Later he moved to Chicago and quickly became the head of a crime syndicate that made and sold illegal liquor during Prohibition. This is the name given to the years when the American government prohibited the making and selling of all liquor – whisky, beer, and even wine. As a result, some people produced illegal liquor, known as bootleg booze. So vast were the profits from bootleg liquor that even police, politicians, and judges were drawn into Capone's network of crime. He crushed all rival gangs by ruthless tortures and threats and was said to have been involved in more than four hundred murders. Capone was known as "Public Enemy Number One," but no charges of murder were ever brought against him. Eventually he was jailed for tax evasion and sent to Alcatraz prison for eleven years. After his release from prison, Capone lived on a Pennsylvania farm until his death in 1947.

When he was at the height of his power as a leader of organized crime, Capone was only twenty-nine years old. The newspaper headlines and stories of his criminal activities fascinated Canadians and Americans. Al Capone seemed to represent the wild, lawless 1920s.

Al Capone (left)

No wonder people called this decade the "Roaring Twenties." It was a time of glamour and prosperity, and yet at the same time an era of immense crime and corruption. This was the age of "hot" jazz and the dance called the Charleston. Women finally dared to wear short skirts, lipstick, and rouge. New forms of entertainment became available for almost everyone – movies, radio, dance halls, and cars. During the 1920s it looked as if people were making up for the misery of war by enjoying themselves as much as possible.

The Prohibition era in Canada started in 1916 and 1917 during World War I. Many Canadians agreed that it was unpatriotic to enjoy oneself at home while soldiers were suffering hardships at the front. As a result, the manufacture and sale of alcohol became illegal.

Total Prohibition never really took place. People could always find a drink if they had the money. Speakeasies, which were elegant private clubs, sprang up. Patrons were approved through a peephole in the front door, and then entered fashionable surroundings where they could drink to their heart's content. They bought inferior, homemade spirits from bootleggers. It was still possible to buy alcohol legally from a drug store if it was to be used for medicinal purposes. Some druggists did a roaring business by filling prescriptions of alcohol for a tonic.

The United States was also officially "dry" during this period, and some Canadians made fortunes smuggling Canadian liquor south of the border. By every means possible, "rumrunners" smuggled their cargo across the line. Under the cover of dense woods, Quebeckers using horse-drawn sleighs and snowshoes smuggled booze into Maine, New Hampshire, and Vermont. From ports along the shores of Lake Ontario and Lake Erie fast boats ran cargoes of rum to the American shores. Estimates suggest that almost $1 million of liquor crossed from Windsor to Detroit each month. On the Atlantic coast, schooners from Halifax, Charlottetown, St. John, and other maritime ports took cases of liquor to Americans in chartered boats at meeting points along the American seaboard. A small fleet of World War I planes was used by "rumrunners" to fly illicit cargo to obscure landing fields in the United States near the Canadian border.

Beyond a doubt Prohibition brought some real benefits to society. The crime rate dropped, and arrests for drunkenness decreased dramatically. Workers took their pay cheques home instead of to the tavern. Industrial efficiency improved because fewer work days were missed. However, it became obvious during the 1920s that Prohibition was impossible to enforce. Underworld characters were making fortunes in illegal liquor.

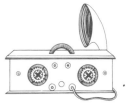

Raid on a bootlegging operation

Provincial governments realized that they were losing millions of dollars in potential tax revenue. It became clear that Prohibition was unpopular with many citizens. Pressure was brought to bear on governments for a more moderate liquor policy. People argued that legalizing liquor under strict government controls would be easier to enforce than total Prohibition. Gradually individual provinces dropped Prohibition throughout the 1920s, though Prince Edward Island held out until 1948. In the United States Prohibition was finally repealed in 1933.

Were the "Roaring Twenties" as carefree and exciting as many television programs and movies lead us to believe? Did everyone have money and spend it freely, or were there Canadians who did not share in the prosperity? What were the important changes in the 1920s that affected the lives of all people?

THE ECONOMY ON THE UPSWING

As World War I ended in November 1918, wartime industries – such as munitions factories – closed down. Women, who had played such an important role in the wartime factories, now found they were under pressure to return to household duties so that men could have jobs. Thousands of soldiers were returning home to Canada and looking for work. But jobs were hard to find and many war veterans were unemployed and bitter. Many veterans looked at their medals and wondered why there were no jobs for them in the country they had fought to defend. They also resented the fact that business people at home had become enormously rich by producing goods for the war. Business people had made huge profits while the soldiers had been risking their lives in Europe. Now veterans felt that the country owed them something – at least a job and a chance to make an honest living.

People who did have jobs in Canada in 1919 were not much better off than the unemployed veterans. The problem was the rapid rise of inflation. This meant that prices of basic things like food and clothing had increased greatly, while wages had not. The cost of living had gone up between 75 percent and 80 percent from 1914 to 1919, but wages had risen by only 18 percent during the same period. Housing was scarce and costly. Building had failed to keep pace with need, and rents were very high.

However, in the 1920s life got better for most Canadians. By the middle of the decade, the economy was on the upswing. At last, prosperity arrived for a generation who had waited so long.

The prairie provinces enjoyed huge wheat crops from 1925 to 1928. Wartorn Europe was hungry for Canadian wheat, and the world price of wheat moved steadily upward. In 1924 Ottawa

War veterans protesting lack of work

lowered the tax on imported farm machinery. More and more farmers began to buy trucks and mechanical harvesters, and replace their horses with tractors. Railway branch lines were extended and settlers now moved into the region around Peace River in northern Alberta. The development of early-maturing strains of wheat meant that wheat could be grown in more northerly regions. More and more farmers organized themselves into wheat pools and co-operatives. Their goal was to loan money to other farmers at lower interest rates than eastern Canadian bankers charged. Farmers hoped that the co-operatives would be able to find customers for their grain, cattle, and dairy products. In this way they could skip the "middlemen" by marketing their own products. By 1928, Canada had a record wheat crop and a major share of the world market. Though every available grain elevator was bursting at the seams, prices of wheat remained at an all-time high through the first half of 1929.

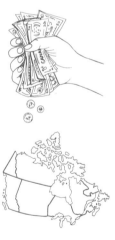

In the 1920s the production of newsprint became Canada's largest industry after agriculture. From Nova Scotia to British Columbia there were vast forests of softwoods such as spruce, pine, and poplar, which are used to make newsprint. Most of the American sources of pulpwood had been used. Giant American newspapers, such as *The New York Times*, provided a ready market for Canadian pulpwood. By 1929 exports of Canadian pulpwood equalled the total exports of the rest of the world.

Not everyone in Canada thought this was a good situation.

Canada's forests were being destroyed. So much newsprint was shipped across the border that the Canadian government finally had to urge Canadian producers to save some of the supply for our own newspapers. A new problem was developing caused by the fact that our nation's exports were primarily raw materials. Thousands of Canadians were following these raw materials to the United States and finding jobs in American industries.

Quebec and Ontario saw a dramatic increase in the production of hydro-electric power in the 1920s. Niagara Falls had been first used for power in 1895. Rivers such as the Saguenay and the St. Maurice were developed as resources for water power in the 1920s. Industries were beginning to use methods of production that required hydro-electric power instead of coal. In this same period, people were demanding electricity for their homes in order to use the new electrical appliances coming onto the market. Canada's output of hydro-electric power became the second largest in the world.

At the same time people called the 1920s the "Oil Age." As more and more Canadians took to the road in automobiles, the demand for gasoline and lubricating oils soared. Also, the increasing use of oil and gas for heating and cooking led to an all-out search for new sources of this "black gold." Excitement grew in Alberta about the potential development of oil and natural gas of the Turner Valley south of Calgary.

In October 1924, oil speculators struck it rich. A drilling in the Turner Valley (known as Royalite #4) came in. The well exploded into flames and burned out of control for several weeks. Eventually the well was tamed and became a great moneymaker. It produced a million barrels of oil and large quantities of natural gas. After that the confidence and optimism of the Alberta oil speculators grew. They continued to pour their investment dollars into exploration and development of their oil resources.

Exciting new mining discoveries were made in the 1920s in the Canadian Shield. Large deposits of copper were found near Noranda along the Ontario–Quebec border. By 1929 Canada was producing almost 80 percent of the world's supply of nickel at Sudbury. In northern Manitoba, the city of Flin Flon was built after the discovery of copper and zinc in large quantities. Kimberley, in British Columbia, developed the world's largest lead and zinc mines. Many of these rich mining deposits were developed with American capital (money).

At the beginning of the twentieth century, the biggest foreign investors in Canada were the British. Bankers from Britain had invested largely in Canadian government bonds and railroads. Very little British capital went into industrial enterprises because

Branch Plants in Canada

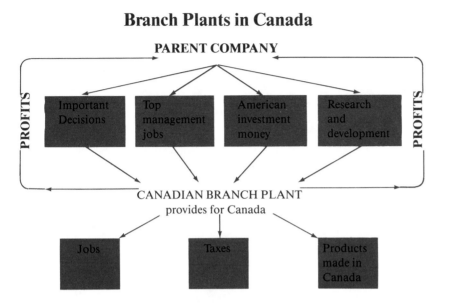

PARENT COMPANY

PROFITS

| Important Decisions | Top management jobs | American investment money | Research and development |

PROFITS

CANADIAN BRANCH PLANT
provides for Canada

| Jobs | Taxes | Products made in Canada |

of the greater uncertainty of making a profit. The outbreak of a world war in 1914 slowed down British investment in Canada. The British had practically the same amount invested in Canada in 1920 as in 1914.

As British investment in Canada fell off, American investment increased. Americans preferred to put money into the rapidly expanding areas of the Canadian economy – mining, pulp and paper, and hydro-electric power. Another difference between American and British investors was in the amount of control they took. British investors usually left Canadian business people alone to run their businesses in their own way. Americans, on the other hand, usually introduced the branch plant system. American investors saw advantages and profits that could be made by opening branch plants for the Canadian market. These branch industries were copies of the American parent company. The branch plant produced the same product as the parent company in the United States. Because the manufactured products could be marked "Made in Canada," the parent company avoided high tariff (tax) barriers. In return for the foreign capital and the jobs it provided, Canadians had to accept the increasing "Americanization" of the economy. Many important decisions concerning Canadian branches were made in the United States. Top management jobs frequently were held by Americans. Profits earned by the Canadian branch plant were often drained away from Canada and found their way back to the United States.

Foreign capital invested in Canada 1900-1930

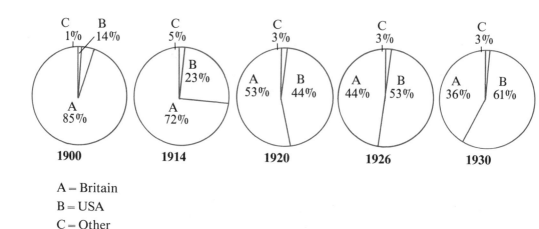

C 1%   B 14%
A 85%
1900

C 5%
B 23%
A 72%
1914

C 3%
A 53%   B 44%
1920

C 3%
A 44%   B 53%
1926

C 3%
A 36%   B 61%
1930

A = Britain
B = USA
C = Other

Canadian opinions about American investment differed widely. Some people thought that American investment should be feared. They saw the possibility of a complete economic takeover of Canada by the United States. Others argued that it was a good thing. American capital would help develop Canada into a powerful nation.

One of the important results of the industrial boom of the 1920s was that more and more Canadians gradually started to believe in their own country again. People grew more optimistic about Canada. Riches seemed to be within the reach of anyone. They could see others around them who had struck it rich.

Probably the most powerful business tycoon of the time was Sir Herbert Holt. Holt arrived in Canada from Ireland as a nineteen-year-old during the depression of 1875. One of his first jobs was working as an assistant engineer on railroad construction. Eventually Holt built up a multimillion-dollar empire which included railroads, banks, mines, hotels, utilities, and the Famous Players theatres. He was the president of twenty-seven major business enterprises. Montrealers in the late 1920s complained. "We get up in the morning and switch on one of Holt's lights, cook breakfast on Holt's gas, smoke one of Holt's cigarettes, read the morning news printed on Holt's paper, ride to work on one of Holt's streetcars, sit in an office heated by Holt's coal, then at night go to a film in one of Holt's theatres." Holt had no hobbies and few close friends. Although he was the richest man in Canada, few people really knew him well. When he died in 1941 at the age of eighty-five, his coffin was followed by eight cars

Tycoon and family

filled with flowers. However, few mourners bothered to attend his funeral.

Financial success stories inspired ordinary citizens to believe that they too could dream of riches and prosperity. Two dollar bets on horses, investing in stocks and bonds, and hockey pools were all seen as ways for the ordinary working man and woman to get rich quick. The 1920s was a take-a-chance time in Canada.

DIGGING DEEPER

1   Explain how the war helped to bring about Prohibition in Canada. What other factors contributed to the spread of the Prohibition movement?

2   Suggest some arguments that might be used by supporters of Prohibition.
Suggest arguments that could be put forward by those opposed to Prohibition.
Who has the stronger arguments? Why?

3   Describe the ways in which Canadians profited from Prohibition in the United States after the war. Locate on a map of Canada those areas where it would be easy to run liquor into the United States.

4   Do you think the Prohibition "experiment" worked? Why or why not? What lessons do you think we can learn from the experiment?

5   Someone remarked about the Prohibition experiment that "the cure was worse than the disease." What does this mean?

6   Give reasons why Americans invested in Canada in the 1920s.

7   Correctly use the following terms, related to the branch-plant economy, in a sentence.

   branch plant

   tariff barrier

   parent company

8   Today Canadian economic nationalists oppose American investment in this country. Do some research to find out what they consider are the harmful effects of a branch-plant economy.

9   The defenders of the US investment in Canada claim that American capital is vital to the Canadian economy. Do some research to find out the advantages of American investment in this country.

16
Inventions Bring Change

Radio was the great invention of the 1920s. It was now possible to broadcast voices, news, and music through the airwaves by using radio signals. It was the invention of the radio that helped shrink the vastness of Canada's size. People living in isolated rural parts of the country were brought in touch with the cities of the nation. It became possible for a farmer living far from the city to twist the dials on his battery set and listen to a hockey game from Montreal or a music program from New York. Radio provided cheap entertainment in people's homes.

Radiola
Super Hetrodyne
(Second Harmonic)

Music from Across the Continent without the Aid of Aerials or Wires

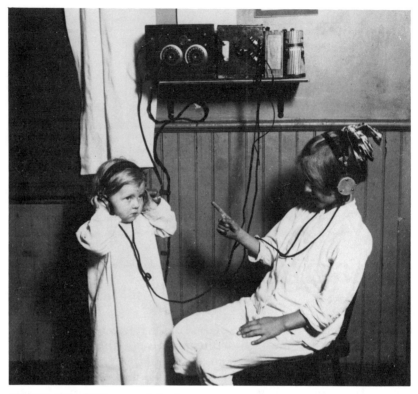

Children listening to a crystal set

The earliest home sets had no tubes but used a crystal (a thin piece of quartz). Listeners tuned in a signal by moving a fine wire "whisker" over the surface of the crystal. Sounds from crystal sets were never very loud, so earphones were often needed. Several pairs of earphones were provided when neighbours came to visit and "listen in." A person could take a crystal set on a picnic, hang the antenna on a tree, and sit back and listen through the headphones. In the 1950s, when transistorized portable radios with earphones were introduced, people thought they were a great invention. They had forgotten the crystal sets of the 1920s which predated the transistorized radios by thirty years.

Before long, much more improved and expensive radio sets were sold. These were built in elaborate wooden cabinets. Tubes replaced the crystal and whisker, and speakers replaced earphones. The radios operated by large batteries that had to be recharged frequently. In 1925, a brilliant young Toronto inventor, Edward "Ted" S. Rogers, discovered a way of plugging the radio directly into household electrical current. His invention was the world's first battery-less radio, which sold for approximately $150. In February 1927 Ted Rogers set up his own radio station in Toronto. His station's call letters – CFRB – continue today to stand for his invention (R for Rogers and B for Battery-less).

The Automobile

One of the most obvious signs of the prosperity of the 1920s was the growth of the automobile industry. Henry Ford dreamed of making an inexpensive car that almost anyone could afford to buy. But if this was to be done, the cost of making cars had to be lowered. Ford decided to apply to car manufacturing a method of mass production that was beginning to be used in some other industries. This method made use of an assembly line, a division of labour, and standardized parts.

How did the mass production of automobiles work? Ford set up a line or belt running from one end of the building to another. At the beginning of the line were the frames of the cars. At first the line did not move and workers walked along it adding parts to the automobiles. Later the line itself moved like a conveyor belt. As the line moved, new parts were added to the frame by workers who remained in one place. By the time a car reached the end of this line, it had been assembled and was ready to be driven. Each worker on the assembly line had a separate job to do. Some added parts, while others secured the parts in place and tightened them. This is called division of labour. Ford used standard parts for his cars, which meant that wheels, engines, and bodies were exactly alike for each car. As a result Ford was able to produce the famous, practical "Model T" at a price that average North Americans could afford. The "Tin Lizzy", as the Model T was affectionately called, had a hideous design. But in 1924 it could be purchased for around $395.

The automobile has probably done more than any other machine to change our way of living. It put North Americans on wheels. It brought all parts of the country together. On Sunday, a family with a car could call on relatives 15 or 20 km away, and still be home for supper and evening chores. New industries sprang to life because of the car: gasoline, rubber, glass, and paint. New jobs were created in service stations, parking lots, and repair shops. Traffic police and streetlights appeared on street corners. The family car made it possible to have a summer cottage and to travel longer distances for summer vacations. Along the major roads, tourist cabins, and hotels popped up to house the increasing number of travellers. More and more trucks were used for hauling freight and food from factories and farms.

Governments began to spend increasing amounts of money on highways. Main roads were paved and even country roads were given a surface of gravel. A crank and a tow rope were standard equipment. The crank was needed to get the engine started. A tow rope was required because motorists never knew when they

Motorists trying to free their car from the mud

might get stuck in mud or snow. More than one pleasant Sunday drive was spoiled when the family car became mired in a muddy road. As in the days of the old stage coach, everyone climbed out of the car and tried to free it by using nearby fence poles as levers.

Most people did not attempt to drive in the winter at all. They put their car up on blocks because the engines tended to seize up with the cold. Few municipalities had invested in any snow removal equipment. The car made it possible for people to live farther from their place of work. People sought open and green spaces for their houses, so suburbs started to sprawl on the outskirts of many cities. It became increasingly difficult to sell a house without a garage and a driveway.

However, the automobile has created problems too. No one knew that this great invention would pollute the air, cause incredible traffic jams, and bring death to thousands of people each year. Criminals also made use of the automobile. In 1919 the Vancouver police were reporting at least six robberies a night in which the thieves made their getaway in a car. Police departments were soon forced to buy automobiles themselves.

Motor Vehicle Registration in Canada	
1903	220
1911	22 000
1921	465 000
1931	1 201 000

DIGGING DEEPER

1   Imagine that you are living on a homestead in Alberta during the early 1920s. Your farm is a long way from urban centres. Your nearest neighbours are located a few kilometres away. What difference would a radio make to your family's life?

2   Make a list of ten jobs that came into being with the invention of the automobile.

3   Draw a chart of the benefits and problems that have resulted from the invention of the automobile.

4   How has the car contributed to the quality of Canadian life? Would we be suffering from urban sprawl today if the car had not been invented?

5   Cars create large amounts of pollutants. Yet antipollution devices use more fuel and give fewer kilometres per litre. Suggest ways of combatting this double problem.

17
Politics of
the 1920s

As the 1920s began two new politicians moved into the spotlight as leaders of Canadian political parties. Both the Liberals and Conservatives had new leaders. The Liberals chose William Lyon Mackenzie King to succeed Sir Wilfrid Laurier, and the Conservatives selected Arthur Meighen to replace Sir Robert Borden.

In July 1920 Arthur Meighen was sworn in as prime minister of Canada. Born and educated in Ontario, Meighen went to Manitoba as a young man to practise law. He became widely known as a successful trial lawyer, and in 1908 was elected to Parliament. Meighen had many of the qualities of a successful politician. He was a brilliant debater, using razor-sharp words to shred the ideas and arguments of his political opponents. But for all of his talents, Meighen was never able to win the affection of the Canadian voters. His reserved manner and his gaunt appearance earned him the reputation of being a "figure of ice." While Meighen was respected, he was never loved.

The Canada that Meighen inherited was restless and torn apart by regional interests. French Canada was still seething over the conscription crisis of 1917. Maritimers were demanding more jobs, increased recognition, and better treatment. Prairie farmers, suffering from a postwar slump, opposed tariffs. They claimed these only increased their costs of operation. Farmers also demanded that railways be taken over by the government and freight rates reduced. Organized labour saw Meighen as a friend of big business and an enemy of the worker. With so many groups opposed to him, Meighen and the Conservatives lost the federal election in 1921.

Arthur Meighen, Canada's ninth prime minister

The man who became prime minister in 1921 was destined to be the most successful political leader of his age. He was the grandson of William Lyon Mackenzie, the leader of the Rebellion of 1837. For almost thirty years, until his death in 1950, William Lyon Mackenzie King dominated the political life of Canada. King was the longest-serving prime minister.

On the surface King seemed to possess few qualities that would attract large numbers of voters. He was not attractive. He was a pudgy little man, dumpy in appearance. He was cautious and careful, and extremely shrewd. King was in many ways a lonely and unhappy man who was friendless except for his pet dog and a couple of associates with whom he corresponded freely. His beloved mother, who died in 1917, was the most important person in his life, and King never fully recovered from her death. His desire to make contact with her led to an interest in spiritualism. Like many other Canadians of the day, he tried through mediums and seances to contact the dead. There were times when King believed he had received political advice from important figures of the past, including Laurier.

King's political genius lay in his realization that without national unity, there was no hope for Canada. King knew that he would have to form policies that would be acceptable to various groups and sections of the nation. He had the uncanny knack of being able to do this. His secret was that he listened to what

various regions of Canada wanted, and waited for a long time before reaching a decision. Then he worked out compromises and bargains among the diverse interests in the country. King was often able to maintain unity among Canadians.

In 1926 the relations between Britain and its colonies were redefined. A meeting of all the members of the British Empire was held that year. At the Imperial Conference, King demanded to know the powers of the dominions, and the nature of their relationships to each other and to Britain. It was decided that Canada and the other dominions were a self-governing, independent, "commonwealth of nations." Members of this commonwealth were equal in status and united by a common allegiance to the king or queen. The Commonwealth was a voluntary family of nations scattered throughout the world.

By the Statute of Westminster, in 1931, Canada had become fully independent in all but two minor legal details. Appeals could still be carried from the Supreme Court of Canada to the Judicial Committee of the Privy Council in Britain. Also, it was still necessary for Canada to ask the British Parliament to amend the Canadian constitution (BNA Act). However, it was understood that both of these legal arrangements would be ended when Canadians agreed on powers to be held by the provincial and federal governments. Except for these two minor details, Canada had achieved full independence.

William Lyon Mackenzie King and his parents

Emily Murphy, the first woman magistrate in the British Empire

WOMEN

Women in Canada had won the right to vote in federal elections by 1918, but still did not enjoy all the privileges men had.

An event took place that pointed out this lack of equality. Emily Murphy was the first woman judge appointed to a court to hear cases involving women. A lawyer in her courtroom challenged her right to judge any case because she was a woman. He said that no woman was a "person" in the eyes of the law. Emily Murphy was supported by the Supreme Court of Alberta which said that a woman had every right to be a judge. This should have settled the matter, but it did not.

During the 1920s, women's groups asked Prime Minister Meighen to appoint a woman to the Senate. The British North America Act outlined the qualifications required for an appointment to the Senate. It said that qualified "persons" could be appointed to the Senate. Again, the old question of "persons" showed its ugly head. Was a woman a "person" in the eyes of the law?

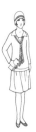

In August 1927, Emily Murphy and four of her friends decided to petition the prime minister. The group of women included Nellie McClung, Louise McKinney, Henrietta Edwards, Irene Parlby, and Judge Murphy. They asked, "Does the word 'persons' in Section 24 of the British North America Act include female 'persons'?" In April 1928, the Supreme Court of Canada decided that women were not 'persons' qualified for appointment to the Senate in Canada.

Judge Murphy and her supporters, nicknamed the "Famous Five," were discouraged, but not defeated. They decided to appeal their case to the Privy Council in Britain. The Privy Council was the highest court of appeal in the British Empire.

After three months of consideration and four days of debate, the judges of the Privy Council announced their decision. They declared that the word 'persons' referred to men and women. Women were indeed qualified to sit in the Senate of Canada. Emily Murphy won her fight.

Many of her friends thought that Emily Murphy deserved to be the first woman appointed to the Senate. However, it was two more years before the first woman was named to a Senate seat. When it did happen it was not Emily Murphy, but Cairine Wilson, who received this honour. Senator Wilson of Montreal had worked as an organizer and president of the National Federation of Liberal Women.

DIGGING DEEPER

1 Name the provisions of the Statute of Westminster that prevented Canada from becoming fully independent in 1931. Suggest possible reasons why Canada did not ask for full independence.

2 Do some research on the Commonwealth today. Begin by marking the members of the Commonwealth on a world map. Investigate a Commonwealth nation. Explore such issues as the role of the queen in the Commonwealth; the possibilities of a central Parliament for the Commonwealth; and the multicultural aspect of the Commonwealth.

Present your topic to the class and hold a discussion comparing your country with other Commonwealth nations.

3 Research "Women of the Commonwealth." Possible subjects include: Queen Elizabeth, Margaret Thatcher, and Mother Teresa of Calcutta. Can you think of any other famous women in the Commonwealth?

4   Research the background of the "Famous Five." Each of the other four women was chosen by Emily Murphy to join her in signing the petition requesting the Supreme Court to declare that women are "persons." Try to decide why Murphy chose each one.
5   Write a dialogue in which a modern feminist explains to Emily Murphy and Nellie McClung the problems facing women in Canada today. Include information on what gains Canadian women have made since the time of Murphy and McClung. What would the suffragists' reactions be to the changes in the position of Canadian women?
6   Name some modern Canadian women who should be appointed to the Senate. Give reasons for your choices.

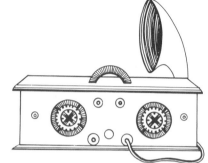

18
Fads, Fashions, and Entertainment

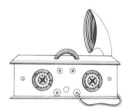

Fads swept the country during the "Roaring Twenties." No one can explain how fads "catch on," but suddenly many people get interested in something and take it up with great enthusiasm. Before you know it, everyone is doing it. Usually the craze does not last long and fads are dropped as quickly as they are taken up.

From the gambling parlours of China came one of the first fads of the twenties. It was the ancient Chinese game of mah-jong. The game is a combination of dice and dominoes. It is played with tiles made from the shinbones of calves. The game caught on quickly in North America, and in 1923, 1.5 million sets were being imported. In homes across the land people were shouting "pung!" and "chow!" and other Oriental words connected with the game. Mah-jong parties became the rage and people even imported Chinese robes, furniture, and decorative objects to make their parties perfect. But by 1927 the novelty had worn off. The mah-jong set that had cost $25 in 1923 could be purchased then for $1.69. It was time for a new fad.

The novelty that replaced mah-jong was the crossword puzzle. Two young American publishers, Simon and Schuster, brought out a book of crossword puzzles with a pencil attached. Suddenly everyone was crazy about crosswords! Dictionary sales soared. Some railways even provided dictionaries to help travellers solve crossword puzzles.

Every kind of long race or contest became the rage of the twenties. Non-stop talking, kissing, eating, drinking, flagpole sitting, and rocking-chair marathons were some of the contests in which people tried to establish records. Of all the marathons, dancing was the most popular. Dancers sometimes competed for prizes of

Flappers, 1928

thousands of dollars. Couples dragged themselves around the dance floor with blistered feet and backs aching with fatigue. One man dropped dead on the dance floor after eighty-seven hours of continuous dancing. Some contestants kept themselves awake with smelling salts and ice packs and a few desperate dancers slipped sleeping pills into the drinks of their rivals. Mary "Hercules" Promitis of Pittsburgh took a tip from bare-knuckle prize-fighters and soaked her feet in vinegar and brine for three weeks before a 1928 marathon. Her feet were so pickled that she felt no pain at all!

Fads also filled the world of fashion. For young women the flapper look was the new rage. A flapper was a rather wild young girl who dressed outrageously in order to attract attention. In winter she wore galoshes with buckles unfastened to create the greatest possible flap. Hemlines rose above the knees, silk stockings were rolled down, and the flat-chested look became popular. Long hair was cut off and set in a short – "bobbed" – boyish style. Fashions for a young man were often as outrageous. He sported baggy pants or knickers, a bright snappy hat, and a bow tie. His hair was greased down and often parted in the middle to imitate the popular movie idols of the day.

For flappers only one kind of music would do, and that was jazz. Jazz moved north from New Orleans and was made popular by such musicians as Duke Ellington and Louis Armstrong. Out of the black culture also emerged the dance of the decade – the Charleston. Its fast and wild pace quickly caught on with the

Dancing the Charleston

high-spirited younger generation. Members of the Boston City Council tried to have the dance banned, but the Charleston was here to stay, and it became the emblem of the roaring jazz age.

Stunt flyers and air travel were also part of this high-stepping decade. Canadian aces, who returned from the First World War, bought up war surplus biplanes and barnstormed across the country. For "two bucks a flip" they would take up the more adventuresome for an airplane ride. These aces would perform daring stunts over country fairs. As onlookers below gasped in horror, they would dive and loop-the-loop, and even hang from the wings of their flimsy craft. Eventually the public and government began to see the possibilities of air travel. Bush pilots helped to open up the northern frontiers of Canada by flying prospectors and supplies into mineral-rich areas of the Canadian Shield. In 1927, the post office hired other pilots to fly mail into remote communities within Canada. In the same year a young American airmail pilot, Charles A. Lindbergh, completed the first non-stop transatlantic flight from New York to Paris. This important event signalled the possibility of long-distance air travel. Suddenly the world seemed smaller!

Slang of the Twenties

EXPRESSION	MEANING
all wet	wrong, mistaken
baloney	nonsense
bee's knees	compliment meaning a wonderful person or thing
big cheese	very important person
bump off	to murder
bunk	nonsense
carry a torch	to be hopelessly in love
cat's meow	superb, wonderful
cheaters	eyeglasses
crush	falling in love
dogs	human feet
drugstore cowboy	a fashionably dressed young man who hangs around public places trying to pick up girls
dumb dora	stupid girl
flapper	typical girl of the 1920s with bobbed hair, short skirt, and rolled-down stockings
flat tire	boring person
gate crasher	an uninvited guest
giggle water	alcohol
gyp	cheat
hep	up-to-date
high hat	snobbish
hooch	bootleg liquor
hoofer	chorus girl
kiddo	friendly form of address
kisser	lips
a line	insincere flattery
ossified	drunk
ritzy, swanky	elegant
real McCoy	genuine article
runaround	delaying action
scram	to leave quickly
Sheba	a young woman with sex appeal
sheik	a young man with sex appeal
speakeasy	a bar selling illegal liquor
spiffy	fashionable
struggle buggy	a car in which boys try to seduce girls
swell	marvellous
whoopee	a wild time

Things to do

Make up a conversation between two students using the slang of the twenties.

Make a list of current slang expressions that are used to express the same meanings.

Since crossword puzzles were a great fad of the twenties, try making some. Use a sheet of graph paper. The answers should all be slang words of the twenties. Include clues to help your class-mates solve the crosswords.

Silver Screen

Talking films were one of the greatest inventions of the twenties. But "talkies" did not arrive in Canada until 1927. For most of the decade, films were silent. They used subtitles on the screen and sound effects were provided by a piano or an orchestra.

The stars of the silent screen were idolized by the Canadian and American public alike. The gods and goddesses of Hollywood provided all the excitement that ordinary people lacked in their daily lives. Charlie Chaplin, affectionately called the "Little Tramp," needed no words to get across his hilarious comic rou-tines. Women swooned when they saw Rudolph Valentino in

Sound effects technician

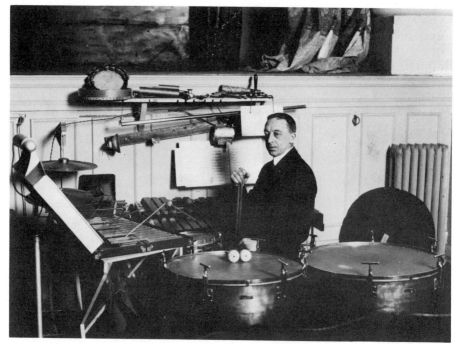

"America's Sweetheart," Mary Pickford

films. When Valentino died in 1926, police had to be called in to control the screaming mob that surrounded the chapel during his funeral. One American girl, pictures of Valentino clutched in her hand, shot herself. Two Japanese girls flung themselves into a volcano. The Italian leader Mussolini had to appeal to the grieving women of his country to stay calm.

The Canadian-born star, Mary Pickford, was often called "America's Sweetheart." Born in Toronto in 1893, she started on the stage at the age of five. She was paid $10 a day for her first film but at the height of her career was earning $10 000 a week.

As her popularity soared, Mary Pickford came to represent the luxury and wealth the film industry brought to its stars. When she retired from the screen, "America's Sweetheart" bought the rights to all of her old silent movies and refused to release them. Not until after her death in 1979 were her films rereleased.

The silent screen era ended abruptly in 1927. *The Jazz Singer*, starring Al Jolson, started talking films. Moviegoing became a way of life for most people. By the end of the decade there were more than nine hundred movie houses across Canada. Many of them were huge ornate palaces with carpeted aisles, sweeping staircases, and theatre organs used to entertain the audience at intermission. Movies were here to stay. Every kid wanted to spend Saturday afternoon at the show, and for many adults Hollywood movies were the most popular entertainment.

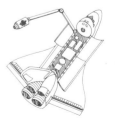

Sports

The twenties was Canada's golden age of sport. Hockey, football, and baseball were becoming professional. The real sports heroes of the decade were amateurs. They were often unknowns who came out of nowhere to grab the headlines and establish world records. Percy Williams is an outstanding example. This twenty-year-old sprinter, almost unknown in Canada, stunned onlookers at the 1928 Amsterdam Olympics. In both the 100- and 200-metre sprints he won a sensational double gold victory. Even competing athletes acknowledged him as "the greatest sprinter the world has ever seen."

Canada's most famous male athlete of the first half-century was Lionel Conacher. He piled up trophies and medals in wrestling, boxing, lacrosse, hockey, football, and baseball. One day in 1922 Conacher starred in championship games in two different sports. He hit a triple in the last inning to give Toronto Hillcrest the city baseball championship. Then he drove across town to play in the Ontairo Lacrosse Championship. In this game he scored four times. In football Conacher also excelled. In the 1922 Grey Cup game, he scored fifteen points leading the Toronto Argonauts to a 23–0 win over the Edmonton Eskimos.

Lionel Conacher

Edmonton Grads, 1935

The twenties was also a golden age of sport for women. Before World War I, the sports activities open to women were still very much in keeping with the traditional concept of femininity — croquet, skating, fencing, cycling, and lawn tennis. These were sports that could be performed gracefully without the kind of movement that caused sweating. By the 1920s, though, there was a greater social acceptability of body-contact sports. Women began to compete in a more rough and aggressive style. Many people still feared that competitive sports for women would lead to a loss of femininity.

In the early part of the twentieth century basketball became popular and was one of the first team sports played by women at a competitive level. The Edmonton Grads dominated the world of women's basketball for over twenty years. They were a team made up of students or graduates of McDougall Commercial High School in Edmonton. From 1915 to 1940 the team played 522 games and lost only 20. The Edmonton Grads represented Canada at four Olympics (1924–1936), and won twenty-seven consecutive Olympic games. Their conditioning and quick-passing teamwork made the Grads the undisputed world champions of women's basketball. Dr. James Naismith, the Canadian-born inventor of basketball, proclaimed the Edmonton Grads the greatest basketball team that ever stepped out on a floor.

Among individual Canadian female athletes, no one surpassed Fanny "Bobbie" Rosenfeld. She excelled in so many sports during her athletic career that she was called the "best woman athlete of the half-century." She was a star at basketball, hockey, softball, and tennis, but her greatest triumphs came in track and field. During the Amsterdam Olympics of 1928, Rosenfeld won a silver medal in the 100-metre dash and a gold medal in the women's 400-metre relay team. In the 800-metre race Rosenfeld settled for fifth place, rather than pass a younger, less experienced teammate.

Unfortunately, the golden age of women's sports did not last. By the mid–1930s many educators and medical doctors argued that girls and women were biologically unfit for athletics. Not until the 1960s did Canadian women regain the glory they won in the 1920s in a wide range of sports.

DEVELOPING SKILLS: COMMUNICATING HISTORY

Sometimes we think that the only way to communicate history is to write about it. However, historians have many ways to communicate or express the past.

A museum, for example, can mount an exhibit to explain and illustrate the building of the Canadian Pacific Railway. The curator, a historian who works in a museum, will collect photographs, models, costumes, artifacts, and primary source documents. The curator will display them so that the story unfolds before the eyes of the museum visitors.

Other historians use film as their medium. These historians film people reminiscing about what happened to them in the past and how world events affected their lives. Interviews with other historians are often included to give a scholar's perspective to the events.

Another creative way of communicating history is with a time capsule. A time capsule is often placed in the cornerstones of public buildings. The idea is that a future generation can open the time capsule and discover what was important to people from another generation. If you were going to make a time capsule, what would you put in it? Remember future generations are going to judge you by what is found there.

Class Project
A Decade in a Box
In a large cardboard box collect all the information you can find to show what life was like in the 1920s. Besides written work, try

to include some or all of the following: records, clothing, pictures, tapes of recorded interviews, drawings, models, charts and graphs. Organize the material so that it tells a complete story of life in Canada during the 1920s.

You could try out your time capsule on another class in your school. Later, in groups, you could make time capsules for each of the decades after the 1920s.

DIGGING DEEPER

1   Bring some records to class and listen to the music of the 1920s. Try to get someone to demonstrate the Charleston and other dances of the twenties.

2   In your opinion, who is the best male athlete in Canada today? Who is the best female athlete in Canada today? Give reasons for your opinions.

3   Research a Canadian woman athlete who has made a significant contribution to sport. Or, compare a female athlete of the 1920s with one who has distinguished herself today. What effects did the social and political climate of the times have on these athletes?

Ada Mackenzie – golf	Sandra Post – golf
Jean Wilson – speedskating	Sylvia Burka – speedskating
Gladys Robinson – speedskating	Laurie Graham – skiing
Myrtle Cook – track and field	Angella Issajenko – track and field
Florence Bell – track and field	Carling Bassett – tennis

4   Now, it's time to add more information to your matrix (see page 103). Trace the development of the same themes through this unit on Canada in the 1920s.

19
The Great Crash

I was always sick two Fridays of every school year, that is when I was in grades 10 and 11. The first Friday was in early October and the second was late in June.

Those two days were when the school had its big dances, the two of the year. Sure, I got asked. But I always had the flu, which translated means I didn't have any clothes. At school we wore a sort of black uniform, all the girls, so that's how I got by there, but at a dance, no way.

Kinda sad, isn't it? I might have met my one true love at one of those affairs.

What was it really like in the "Dirty Thirties"? Look at the pictures in this unit to get an idea of what the conditions were like.

What caused the Great Depression? Many people would answer this question by saying the stock market crash of 1929. However, the stock market crash was not the cause – it was only a symptom that the economy of North America was very sick. In order to understand the depression you have to understand how the stock market worked and what was happening in the 1920s.

Suppose you were living then. You and a group of friends want to form a new company to produce racoon coats (which were very fashionable). You will need to buy furs, rent a building, pay workers (furriers), hire a sales staff, and pay for advertising. You estimate that you will need $100 000 to start your company. How could you raise the money? You could use all your savings, or you could borrow the money from the bank, or you could raise money by selling stocks in your company. In this last case, you get people to invest in your company by buying stocks. If you sold 10 000 stocks at $10, you would have the $100 000 necessary to start your company. Each stock represents a piece of the business. The stockholder owns a share of the business and shares the company's successes and failures. To show his or her investment in the business, the stockholder is given a piece of paper called a stock certificate.

Most people would like to know how to make a fortune on the stock market. The answer is simple: buy plenty of stocks when their price is low and sell those stocks when their price is high. That sounds easy, but a great deal of knowledge, skill, and good luck are needed to make a fortune! Suppose that you would like to try. This is what you would do.

First, you would visit a stockbroker whose job it is to buy and sell stocks in a kind of marketplace known as the stock exchange. (Buying and selling stocks, and the place in which this is done, are both called the stock market.) The stockbroker will place your order and carry out the details of your transaction.

Let us suppose that you decide to buy some shares in a company called Canuck Racoon Coat Company. The stocks themselves represent a share in the ownership of that company. If there are 10 000 shares in the Canuck Racoon Coat Company and you own 100 of them, you own 1/100 of the company's shares.

People buy shares in companies in order to make money. Suppose you buy your 100 shares of Canuck Racoon Coat Company. You pay $25 per share. Your total investment is $2500. A few months later the value of the stocks has risen to $35 per share. This has happened because business has been booming and racoon coats have become a very popular item of clothing. At this point you sell your 100 stocks at $35 per share. You paid out $2500 but got back $3500. The difference of $1000 is called a profit or capital gain. In both buying and selling transactions you will have to pay your stockbroker a small fee for handling the business for you.

There is another way to make money from your stocks. Companies will usually divide some of the profits among the shareholders. These payments to shareholders are called dividends. Since you own 1/100 of the stocks in the Canuck Racoon Coat Company, you are entitled to receive 1/100 of the amount the company pays out in dividends.

The prices of stocks go up and down almost every day. There

Stock exchange

are many complicated reasons for this. One of the most important reasons is that if people wish to buy a certain stock, prices
will go up because they are willing to pay the price. If nobody
wants a particular stock, or if several people wish to sell it, the
price on the market will probably fall.

Explain in your own words the meaning of each of the following:

stocks	stock exchange	capital gain
stockbroker	investor	dividend

The Business Cycle

Economic conditions are generally subject to constant change.
There are good times when the economy is on the upswing, and
there are bad times when business declines. Economists who
chart the upswings and downswings of the economy over a
period of years call these ups and downs the "business cycle."
They identify four stages:

1 Prosperity;
2 Recession;
3 Depression;
4 Recovery.

The economy of North America in the 1920s is a good example of the prosperity stage in the business cycle. Prices and wages are high. Few people are unemployed. Business profits and production are high. When a recession sets in, business begins to slow down. Companies that have produced too many goods begin to realize they cannot sell everything they produce. Therefore, they begin to lay off some workers and cut back production. Unemployment rises. Workers who have been laid off have less money to spend. Others who still have jobs are more careful about how they spend or invest their money. Sales begin to fall. If the recession becomes very serious and widespread, it is known as a time of depression. Now many businesses are forced to lay off employees; some may go bankrupt. Unemployment reaches high levels. Eventually a shortage of consumer goods develops because of the cutbacks in production. To meet the demand businesses begin to increase production and to call back workers. Wage earners now have more money to spend and to put into the economy. The recovery stage of the business cycle commences. Eventually prosperity returns.

A RECESSION is when a neighbour has to tighten his belt. A DEPRESSION is when you have to tighten your own belt. And a PANIC is when you have no belt to tighten and your pants fall down.
T.C. Douglas,
first leader of the NDP

DEVELOPING SKILLS:
USING SIMULATION GAMES

What was Black Tuesday really like? How did the investors, stockbrokers, and company owners feel when the stock market crashed? How did they react? Historians need to understand the past, but to do so they must understand the forces that affected people in the past.

One way to gain insight into the past is through historical simulation games. In these games, you are faced with scenarios from the past. You must decide how you will act. The Stock Market Game will give you a chance to experience the thrills and the defeats of the stock market in the late 1920s.

The debriefing process is crucial to any simulation game. At each stage, stop and think about how you would feel if this was real life. What prompted you to make certain decisions?

You must always compare the simulation game with the historical situation. It doesn't matter if the game doesn't duplicate what happened in reality. What matters is that you gained insights into the complexity of events from the past.

The Stock Market Game
1   Pick three or four class members to be stockbrokers. The brokers set up their offices in the corners of the classroom. Brokers are given a supply of stock certificates and a stock record page.
2   The rest of the class are investors. Each investor makes up an expense sheet.
3   The purpose of the Stock Market Game is to gain experience in playing the stock market. Your aim is to make as much money as possible. You start with $5000 that has been left to you as an inheritance in your grandmother's will. You may invest any amount of money in one company or all three. For the purpose of the game, you cannot sell your stock during the first three cycles. The investor must carefully record each purchase on the expense sheet. The answers appear on page 449.

Cycle 1   Year 1925
Stocks for the following three companies are for sale:

Consolidated Mining and Smelting of Canada	at $50 a stock
Winnipeg Electric Light	at $30 a stock
International Nickel	at $25 a stock

Investors are given time to visit the stockbrokers and record their investments.

Cycle 2   Year 1927
Two years have passed. The economy of the country has been strong and the stocks have increased in value. Each investor calculates the profits made on these stocks if these stocks had been sold in 1927. Your teacher will tell you the amount of the increase.

Cycle 3   September 1929
Each investor calculates the profits made on these stocks.

Debriefing
Class discusses:
a) If this were real life, how would you feel?
b) What would investors do with their profits?
c) What would companies do with their profits?

Cycle 4   29 October 1929 – "Black Tuesday"
Each investor calculates the losses on these stocks.

THE BUSINESS CYCLE

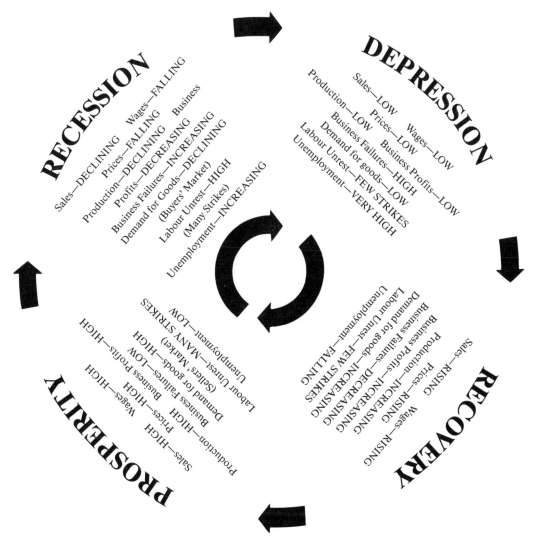

DEPRESSION

Sales—LOW
Prices—LOW   Wages—LOW
Production—LOW   Business Profits—LOW
Business Failures—HIGH
Demand for goods—LOW
Labour Unrest—FEW STRIKES
Unemployment—VERY HIGH

RECESSION

Sales—DECLINING   Wages—FALLING
Prices—FALLING   Business
Production—DECREASING
Profits—DECREASING
Business Failures—INCREASING
Demand for Goods—DECLINING
(Buyers' Market)
Labour Unrest—HIGH
(Many Strikes)
Unemployment—INCREASING

RECOVERY

Sales—RISING   Wages—RISING
Prices—INCREASING
Production—INCREASING
Business Profits—INCREASING
Business Failures—DECREASING
Demand for goods—INCREASING
Labour Unrest—FEW STRIKES
Unemployment—FALLING

PROSPERITY

Sales—HIGH   Wages—HIGH
Prices—HIGH   Business Profits—HIGH
Production—HIGH
Business Failures—LOW
Demand for goods—HIGH
(Sellers' Market)
Labour Unrest—MANY STRIKES
Unemployment—LOW

Investors should be given an opportunity to sell stocks to the teacher if they wish.

Debriefing
Class discusses:
a) How do you feel about your losses?
b) What would you do if this were real life?
c) How would your actions affect the economy of the country?
d) How would companies suffer?

Cycle 5   Year 1932
Investors who have held onto their stock must calculate their losses.

Debriefing
Class discusses:
a) What alternatives are open to investors?
b) Who would be buying stocks in 1932?
Teachers may, if they wish, develop new steps of stock prices to illustrate future upswings in the business cycle.

20
Causes of the Great Depression

The stock market crash of 1929 did not cause the depression. Rather, it was a symptom that the economy of North America was very, very sick. What had happened to the once strong and healthy North American economy? What were the causes of this sickness? What remedies could be prescribed to make it well again?

There seem to be as many explanations for the depression as there are experts to diagnose the illness. However, some of the major causes are as follows:

1 Over-Production and Over-Expansion

During the prosperous 1920s Canadian and American agriculture and industry reached high levels of production. Almost every industry was expanding. They spent large amounts of their profits adding to their factories or building new ones. Huge supplies of food, newsprint, minerals, and manufactured goods were being produced in Canada and simply stockpiled. Automobile centres such as Oshawa and Windsor produced 400 000 cars in 1930. To do this made little sense because Canadians already owned over a million cars and in the best year ever had purchased only 260 000. The Canadian market could absorb only so many goods. Even in the general prosperity of the 1920s many Canadians could still not afford to buy everything they wanted. As as result, large stocks of newsprint, radios, shirts, shoes, and cars began to pile up unsold in warehouses. Soon factory owners

Fruit store, circa 1930

began to panic and slowed down their production until some of these surplus goods could be sold. Workers were laid off. This meant that fewer and fewer families had money to spend on goods already produced. This in turn slowed down sales even more.

Industrialists seemed to have forgotten a basic lesson in economics: you should only produce as many items as you can sell. In the 1920s wages were simply not high enough for people to buy everything being turned out in the factories.

1 Why were Canadian families not spending their money?
2 Explain how over-production led to factory slowdowns.
3 Explain: "You should only produce as many items as you can sell."

2 Canada's Dependence on a Few Primary Products

Canada depended too much for its wealth on a few primary or basic products. These included wheat, fish, minerals, and pulp and paper. Canada's most important exports were these goods. They are known as staples. As long as there was a heavy demand in the world for these products, Canada would prosper. However, if there was a surplus of these goods on the world market, or if foreign countries stopped buying from Canada, our economy would be in serious trouble.

In the depression, certain areas of Canada, which depended largely on one primary product, found themselves in deep economic trouble. The Maritimes and the West were especially hard hit.

Secondary industries involve the processing or manufacturing of primary products. These would also suffer from any slowdown in production. A good example is wheat. In the late 1920s Canada faced growing competition from Argentina and Australia which were also wheat-exporting countries. The price of wheat on the world market began to fall. To add to the problem western farmers were faced with terrible droughts in the summers of 1929, 1931, and 1933–1937. Without adequate rainfall, no crops grew. With little income, farmers could not purchase machinery and manufactured goods from eastern Canada. Many could not afford to pay the mortgages on their farms. With no wheat to be shipped and no flour to be ground, railways and flour mills began to feel the pinch. The farmers' problems had caused a chain reaction in many parts of Canadian society.

1 Name examples of primary industries.

2 Name four industries that would also suffer if farmers could not sell their wheat or had no wheat to sell.

3 What would the economic consequences of a decline in the world sales of wheat be for Canada? What would the chain reaction be?

3   Canada's Dependence on the United States

The economy of Canada in the 1920s was closely linked with that of the United States. This is still true today. In those years we bought 65 percent of our imports from the Americans. Forty percent of our exports were sent to the USA. The Americans were  our most important trading partner. The USA has replaced Britain as the largest buyer of Canadian products and the largest supplier of investment funds for our industries. Even then we were in danger of what today is called a branch-plant economy. It was not surprising that when the American economy got sick, Canada also suffered. One comedian said, "When the United States sneezed, the rest of the world got pneumonia."

When the depression hit the United States, banks closed, industries collapsed, and people were out of work as factories shut down. No longer did Americans need our lumber, paper, wheat, and minerals. It was inevitable that Canada's economy would suffer too.

1 How much did Canada export to and import from the USA?

2 Why did a depression in the USA have such serious repercussions in Canada?

3   What do you think is meant by a branch-plant economy? Give examples.

4   High Tariffs Choked Off International Trade

In the 1920s European nations were recovering from a devastating war. They needed many of the surplus manufactured goods that the US and Canada produced. Unfortunately they were heavily in debt from the war and often could not afford to buy them.

At the same time, many countries adopted a policy known as protective tariffs. In order to protect their home industries from foreign competition, they placed high tariffs on foreign imports. Country X found that its goods were being kept out of country Y by high tariffs. Soon country X placed high tariffs on imports from country Y. Thus world trade began to slow down. Surplus goods in one country were kept out of another country that needed them. While high tariffs were used to protect home industries, they choked off international trade.

1   Why do countries put high tariffs on foreign goods? Who benefits from high tariffs? Who suffers?

2   Why was international trade important to Canada?

3   How did high tariffs between countries choke off international trade and contribute to the depression?

Drought near Swift Current, Saskatchewan

Tenants being evicted in Montreal

5   Too Much Credit Buying

All through the twenties Canadians were encouraged by adver-
tising to "buy now, pay later." A famous comedian, Will Rogers,
said that the way to solve the traffic problem was to remove from
highways all cars that hadn't been paid for. He meant that so
many cars were bought on credit that very few cars would actually remain on the road. Will Rogers was only joking but his
remark points up the fact that by 1929 credit buying was a well-
established custom. Why wait to buy a washing machine or a
phonograph or a tractor or a piano when you could have it now
with a small down payment?

Many families got themselves hopelessly into debt with credit
buying. The piano that cost $445 cash was purchased with $15
down and $12 a month for the next four or five years. It ended up
costing far more than it was worth. Sometimes by the time the
purchases were paid for, they were ready for the junk pile. One
radio comedian joked that he had said to his wife, "One more
payment and the furniture is ours." To this she replied, "Good,
then we can throw it out and get some new stuff!"

If the wage earner became sick or was laid off work it was often impossible to keep up the payments. As the depression worsened, many people lost everything. Their refrigerators, stoves, washing machines, cars, and even their homes were repossessed by their creditors (the people they owed money to).

1 How did too much credit buying lead to problems for many people during the depression?

2 Is it ever wiser to buy on credit rather than with cash? If so, when?

3 Why do many people prefer to pay cash while others use credit? Which way seems best to you?

6   *Too Much Credit Buying of Stocks*

For many people in the 1920s, the stock market seemed an easy way to get rich quickly. People in all walks of life gambled on the stock market. Rich business tycoons invested in shares but so did their chauffeurs and the typists in their offices. Feelings of confidence were at an all-time high. People expected that prosperity would last forever.

It was not even necessary to have a lot of money to play the stock market. You could buy stocks on credit just as you could a phonograph or a washing machine. The only thing needed was a small cash down payment, usually about 10 percent. The broker loaned you the rest of the money (at a high interest rate, of course!). But to buy $1000 worth of stock you needed only $100 cash. The idea was that as soon as your stocks went up in value you could sell them. Then you paid back your loan to your broker and pocketed the profits. This risky process was called "buying on margin."

Buying stocks on margin was not too expensive if stocks kept rising quickly in value. But what if your stocks didn't go up? Or, worse still, what if they went down? How would you pay back your loans? You would have to sell your stocks or risk financial ruin.

This is exactly what happened in October 1929. When the value of stocks started to drop, people panicked. They started to sell. Prices fell even lower as more and more stocks were dumped onto the market. The market was like a giant roller-coaster racing downhill. Nothing could stop it. In a few hours the value of most stocks nosedived by more than 50 percent. Shareholders lost millions. Big and small investors were wiped out in a few hours. Slowly it began to dawn on people that hard times were here. The Great Depression had begun.

1 How does a person gamble when playing the stock market?

2 Explain "buying on margin." Use an example to show that you understand how it works.

3   Why did investors panic in October 1929? As more and more investors tried to sell out, why did prices decline even more rapidly?

DEVELOPING SKILLS:
DISTINGUISHING BETWEEN FACTS AND OPINIONS

Whether you are reading a textbook or a newspaper, listening to a politician making a speech, or watching television, you must be able to distinguish between what is a fact and what is merely someone's opinion.

A fact is something that is known to be true. For example, western farmers were faced with terrible droughts in the summers of 1929, 1931, and 1933–1937. This can be investigated and found to be true.

An opinion is a firmly held belief that is not supported by actual proof. For example, someone states that the Great Depression was necessary after the free spending of the twenties. You can challenge her/his opinion. You can use facts to prove your point.

Sometimes people use words that signal that they are expressing an opinion. These "tip-off" words include "I think," "It seems to me," or "In my opinion." For example: "In my opinion, students watch far too much television" or "It seems to me that television is a very effective way of learning a lot of things."

The use of emotionally charged words may also be a clue that an opinion is about to be expressed. For example: "The government was cruel and stingy in its handouts to citizens suffering during the Great Depression." The emotional words are "stingy" and "cruel."

The big problem in distinguishing between fact and opinion comes when there are no "tip-off" words and when we don't know a lot about the topic under discussion. Say you read the statement "Farmers suffered more than any other group in society during the 1930s." Is it an opinion or a fact? It is important not to assume that it is a fact. Research the statement and see if it can be supported by evidence. Maybe you'll find evidence that suggests that single, unemployed men suffered the most during the depression.

Decide whether each of the following statements are facts or opinions.

1   The Great Depression had a devastating effect on most Canadians.

2   There was no unemployment insurance, no family allowance, and no government-run medical care in the 1930s.

3   Many governments adopted a policy known as protective tariffs.

4   When the value of stocks fell, people panicked.

5   The problem was that Canada relied too heavily on a few primary products.

6   Forty percent of our products were being sent to the United States.

7   This risky process was called "buying on margin."

8   Automobile centres such as Oshawa and Windsor produced 400 000 cars in 1930.

9   Canada's primary products included wheat, fish, minerals, and pulp and paper.

10   The market was like a giant roller coaster racing downhill; nothing could stop it.

DIGGING DEEPER

1   To help you understand the effects of the depression, identify a major industry in your area and assume it goes out of business. List all the secondary industries related to that industry. How will they be affected by the shutdown?

2   Invite a local stockbroker to visit your classroom. Ask questions about how the stock market works. You should ask her/him to explain the changes in regulations that would prevent the stock market from crashing today as it did in 1929.

3   This unit is full of new vocabulary about the stock market. In your notebook, make a dictionary of all the new words you encounter.

4   Write an article to accompany the following headline from the *Toronto Star*, 29 October 1929:

Stock prices crash early; slight rally later

5   Compare the economic condition of the late 1920s with those of today. Speculate about the possibility of a depression occurring again.

6   What could governments have done in the 1920s to prevent a depression?

21
What Was It Like?

In the memory of living Canadians, nothing like the Great Depression had ever happened before. To get an understanding of what social conditions were like in Canada in the 1930s, examine the material that follows. There are pictures, letters written to Prime Minister Bennett from suffering citizens, facts and figures, and memories collected through interviews with Canadians who remember those days.

Many unemployed men drifted from town to town across Canada looking for jobs. They rode 'free' on the railways by hiding in boxcars, perching on their roofs, or riding the rods underneath the trains. . . .

Mother Nature added to the problems of the West by turning off the tap. The resulting drought meant that large sections of the prairie topsoil just blew away during the 'Dirty Thirties.' Black blizzards of dust buried fences and drifted up to eaves of houses. In some places the dust drifts were so deep that highways had to be closed.

Railway crews used steam shovels to clear dust from the tracks near Grainger, Alberta.

Another disaster to hit the West was grasshopper plagues. The insects ate the crops as soon as they popped out of the ground. They even ate clothes hung out to dry on the line.

In the 1930s the Saskatchewan government paid children a penny for each gopher tail they turned in. It was an attempt to save the parched wheat from the hungry rodents.

There was no unemployment insurance, no family allowance, and no government medical care. The only

An unemployed person hitching a ride on a train

help available was government relief. Relief was emergency financial assistance to the unemployed to keep them from starving. There was no uniform system of relief across the country. The federal government gave large sums of money to local municipalities who administered the relief in their own way. The unemployed were never given cash, but only vouchers. The vouchers could be exchanged for food, rent, and other necessities.

Many penniless prairie families simply gave up in despair and abandoned their farms. The desperation and poverty can be seen on the faces of this family who are heading for the Peace River country. Between 1931 and 1937, 66 000 people left Saskatchewan, 34 000 left Manitoba, and 21 000 left Alberta.

Everybody who had a job really looked down his nose at the poor guy who didn't. I've never been able to understand this. I wouldn't say there was no compassion, but people seemed to take the attitude that if you didn't have a job you were just a bum.

"Pogey" was hobo slang for food, clothing, and shelter provided by public relief agencies.

A Manitoba judge, George Stubbs, observed of relief, 'It's not quite enough to live on, and a little too much to die on.'

Clearing track in Alberta

You asked me what a Bennett Buggy was? In the twenties, farmers bought automobiles, Chevs, Fords, Over-
lands, Reos, the Hupmobile, oh, . . . a lot that they don't
even make any more. Then came the crash and the
drought and nobody had any money for gasoline, let
alone repairs. . . . A car that wouldn't run.

Somebody got the idea of lifting out the engine and
taking out the windshield and sticking a tongue onto the
chassis . . . and that's where old Dobbin and Dolly got
back to work again. Two horsepower. Eight kilometres
an hour, but those oat burners got you there. Then somebody got the idea, the country was full of wits, to call
these contraptions Bennett Buggies. Poor old R.B. Bennett. All over Saskatchewan and Alberta there were
these carved up cars, named after him, and a constant
reminder that he'd been prime minister when the disaster struck.

Applying for relief was the most humiliating thing a
person had to do. When you were on relief, the fact was
clearly advertised to the world. Merchandise acquired by
voucher was seldom wrapped. Merchants did not feel
obliged to wrap shoe boxes or clothing when the customer was in no position to complain about it.

In Ontario, relief applicants had to turn in their liquor
permits before any aid was given. At that time citizens

Many families were hard-hit by the depression.

had to have a government permit to buy alcohol. Telephones had to be disconnected and the driver's licence handed in. This was done to guarantee that taxpayers' money was not used to finance any kind of luxury. Accepting a job or refusing to accept a job meant the immediate end of relief.

Bennett buggy

Soup kitchen line-up in Toronto

In 1932 the federal government began to finance a system of relief camps for single unemployed men. Many of the camps were in isolated areas of British Columbia. The men worked eight hours a day cutting brush, moving rocks, and building roads. In return they were fed and sheltered and paid 20¢ a day. The camps, however, became a source of great discontent. The wage of 20¢ a day was considered little better than slave labour. In June 1935 thousands of men, fed up with life in the BC relief camps, boarded freight trains bound for Ottawa to protest the government. This was known as the On-to-Ottawa Trek. The men got as far as Regina, where they were stopped by the Mounted Police.

Did you have a job during the depression?
– No, but my brothers in Kingston worked for 15¢ a day by driving tractors. I was on relief. They gave us prunes [to eat] and a pair of boots once a year. We got pants but no suits – just salvage, surplus clothes. I once asked Mayor Kaiser for food but he said no. That guy [the mayor] had butter on his table. Everyone else had fatty, lardy margarine. To get my relief, I killed rats in the dump on Gibb Street and dug sewers and ditches.

What was life like for you during the depression? Did your husband have a job?
– I remember my husband was very sick for the first few

A relief camp barracks

years of the depression. . . . He worked for a farmer and got $19 a month. We had to try to get by on it, but if his parents hadn't helped us, I don't know what we would have done. The doctor in Beaverton was really good and I remember he operated on my husband right on our kitchen table. He was really sick for a while there but the doctor had us pay him only $100. We owed him well over $500 but he told us he would wipe his books clean of what we owed him.

Can you think of ways you used to get extra money?
– We couldn't take in boarders because we couldn't afford to pay for food for them. I never drew a dime of welfare or relief and I'm darned proud of it. I was in World War I and I got a little pension.

Where did you get your clothes from?
– Mother made all the clothes for us from old clothes that had been given to us. I remember she knitted wool stockings because it was so cold. Mother's relatives would

send us old clothes and many of these had moth holes in them. I was embarrassed to wear the old clothes. It seemed mine were the worst of all the kids in the school.

How did you feel about the railroad riders?
A lot of them came to our place asking for food. We gave them meals but we made sure they washed first because they were all so dirty. We couldn't turn away these hobos since we had something to eat ourselves.

What was Christmas like?
— Mother and Papa always made sure we would get something for Christmas. Once they bought us a box of chocolates and that was a real treat. In our stockings we would get some apples, an orange, and some candies.

We couldn't afford to spend a lot on gifts. I remember giving a towel to my mother-in-law one Christmas. We gave little things like that.

What did you do for entertainment?
— There were parties held every second Saturday for those who didn't work. A great interest was shown in sports by everybody. Playing softball and flying kites were especially popular.
— We had a radio and went to the movies a few times. The kids would go swimming in the lake and creeks.
— There were plenty of house parties. Everybody from around town would get together and we all had a good time. The music was provided by anyone who could play an instrument.

How did your family make a living? What was life like for you during the depression?
— All during the twenties my father was a bricklayer in Toronto, but by mid-1930 he no longer had a job. . . . My parents figured that the only solution was to go and live on a farm where we could get enough to eat. As a result, my family sold our home in Toronto and moved to a farm near Ashburn, Ontario in the fall of 1930. There was an apple orchard and we raised various farm animals such as cows, chickens, and pigs. To earn money for our family, my parents travelled to Toronto in their old Durant [a make of car] and sold the farm goods there. We only had the car for a few years because it broke down and we could not afford to have it repaired. My parents went from house to house trying to sell apples and eggs. They did not make much money selling their farm produce

On-To-Ottawa Trek

because few people would buy, or could afford to buy, the goods.

— The reason people wouldn't admit poverty was because they were too proud. I remember people brought coal sacks uptown to get relief. It was very humiliating for people to be seen with these. Not everyone got relief though, because there wasn't enough to go around.

Passman Sask.
16 Oct. 1933

Dear Sir,

I am a girl thirteen years old and I have to go to school every day its very cold now already and I haven't got a coat to put on. My parents can't afford to buy me anything for this winter. I have to walk to school four and a half mile every morning and night and I'm awfully cold every day. Would you be so kind to sent me enough money to so that I could get one.

My name is
Edwina Abbott
[Reply: $5.00]

May 30/31

Mr. Bennette

Since you have been elected, work has been impossible
to get. We have decided that in a month from this date, if
thing's are the same, We'll skin you alive, the first
chance we get.

Sudbury Starving Unemployed

Craven, Alberta
Feb 11-1935

Dear Sir,

Please don't think Im crazy for writing you this letter,
but I've got three little children, and they are all in need
of shoes as well as underwear but shoe's are the most
neaded as two of them go to school and its cold, my husband has not had a crop for 8 years only enough for seed
and some food, and I don't know what to do. I hate to ask
for help. I never have before and we are staying off relief
if possible. What I wanted was $3.00 if I could possible
get it or even some old cloths to make over but if you
don't want to do this please don't mention it over radios
as every one knows me around here and I'm well liked, so
I beg of you not to mention my name. I've never asked
anyone around here for help or cloths as I know them to
well.

Yours Sincerly

Mrs. P.E. Bottle

[Reply: $5.00]

Ottawa
March the 4th 1932

Dear Sir,

I am just writing a few lines to you to see what can be
done for us young men of Canada. We are the growing
generation of Canada, but with no hopes of a future.
Please tell me why is it a single man always gets a refusal
when he looks for a job. A married man gets work, & if he
does not get work, he gets relief. Yesterday I got a
glimpse of a lot of the unemployed. It just made me feel
downhearted, to think there is no work for them, or in
the future, & also no work for myself. Last year I was out
of work three months. I received work with a local farm. I
was told in the fall I could have the job for the winter; I
was then a stable man. Now I am slacked off on account
of no snow this winter. Now I am wandering the streets
like a beggar, with no future ahead. There are lots of

single men in Ottawa, who would rather walk the streets, & starve, than work on a farm. That is a true statement. Myself I work wherever I can get work, & get a good name wherever I go. There are plenty of young men like myself, who are in the same plight. I say again whats to be done for us single men? do we have to starve? or do we have to go round with our faces full of shame, to beg at the doors of the well to do citizen. I suppose you will say the married men come first; I certainly agree with you there. But have you a word or two to cheer us single men up a bit? The married man got word he was going to get relief. That took the weight of worry off his mind quite a bit. Did the single man here anything, how he was going to pull through? Did you ever feel the pangs of hunger? My Idea is we shall all starve. I suppose you will say I cant help it, or I cant make things better. You have the power to make things better or worse. When you entered as Premier you promised a lot of things, you was going to do for the country. I am waiting patiently to see the results. Will look for my answer in the paper.

Yours Truly R.D. Ottawa

Murray Harbour, P.E.I.
March 24 1935

Premier Bennett:
Dear Sir:
I am writing you to see if their is any help I could get.

As I have a baby thirteen days old that only weighs One Pound and I have to keep it in Cotton Wool & Olive Oil, and I havent the money to buy it, the people bought it so far and fed me when I was in Bed. if their is any help I could get I would like to get it as soon as possible.

their is five of a family, Counting the baby.

their will be two votes for you next Election

Hoping too hear from you soon

Yours Truly.
Mrs. Jack O'Hannon
[Reply: $5.00]

Ardath, Sask.
Aug. 24/35

Dear Mr. Bennett,
I have heard mamma and daddy talk about you so much, and what a good man you are. I am a little boy eight years old and I'm in Grade III at school. I've wanted a little red wagon to hich my dog to for so many years, but daddy has no money. Please, Mr. Bennett would you send me

enuff money to buy my wagon. Thank you so much.
Your very good friend,
Horace Gardiner

Ardath, Sask.
Aug. 31/35
Dear Mr. Bennett,
Thanks very much for the money. I'm going to get the wagon. Mamma said I could.
Your friend,
Horace Gardiner
P.S. I am going to vote for you when I get to be a big boy.
Your friend,
Horace Gardiner

1   What sort of personal problems did people write about to Prime Minister Bennett? What could he do for them?
2   What were the special problems faced by the growing number of young single men? Was it right that married men got work or relief while single men did not? Why did the government give special preference to married men?
3   Why would a woman who wrote to Bennett beg him not to mention her name?
4   What help would be available today for a woman who gave birth to a one pound (450 grams) baby? What help was available to her in 1935? Do you think it was the duty of the government to help her? Why?

DEVELOPING SKILLS:
CONDUCTING AN INTERVIEW

An interview is a face-to-face meeting of people to talk over something special. Usually, one or both parties want to obtain information. When you go for an interview for a summer job, you want to know whether you want the job and the employer wants to know whether you are the right person for the job.

Journalists make their living by conducting interviews. Barry Broadfoot, a newspaper reporter and social historian, set out in 1971 to find out more about what life was like during the Great Depression. Armed with a tape recorder, background research, and good questions, he travelled across the country talking to people about their experiences during the depression. Broadfoot

Making lunch by the CN Railway tracks

talked mostly to "ordinary" people. He discovered how the collapse of the world economy affected them. In this chapter, you have already read some of the memories he collected. These memories are examples of primary source material on the Great Depression in Canada.

Conduct your own interviews with people who lived through the depression, and see if their experiences were similar to those you read about in this chapter. Share what you learned with your classmates.

The Great Depression

Interview people old enough to remember the depression. Take notes or tape record their impressions. Use the following questionnaire or make up one of your own. Share with your class what you discover in your interviews.

Suggestions for conducting good interviews:

1   Know what information you are after – have a definite reason for the interview.

2   Prepare well in advance by researching the topic to be talked about.

3   Write out your questions beforehand. The right question is the only way to get the right information.

4   Think of secondary or follow-up questions to get deeper explanations.

5   Write down as much of the information as you can in notes or take along a tape recorder.

6   Expand your notes as soon as possible after the interview.

Subject's name
Approximate age during the depression
Place of residence during this period

1   When someone mentions the depression, what kind of thoughts come into your mind?

2   Why was there a depression?

3   Did you have a job during the depression?

If YES	If NO
a) How much did you earn?	a) How did you survive?
b) Did you try to add to it in any way?	b) Were you in debt?
	c) How did you pay your rent?
c) What was your attitude toward the unemployed?	d) What help could you get on relief?
	e) Were you ever hungry?

4   What were the prices of goods that you remember?

5   What did you do for entertainment?
    What did teenagers do on Saturday nights?
    What was Christmas like during the depression?

6   What was your happiest experience of those years?
    What was your most unhappy experience?

7   How did you feel about the people running the government? Did you think they were doing all they could?

8   Could there be another depression? Why? Why not?

DIGGING DEEPER

1   Which regions of Canada were hardest hit by the depression? Suggest reasons why this was so.

2   Why were relief vouchers for food and rent given out during the depression instead of cash? Do you think vouchers were a good or bad idea? Why? We sometimes hear of people today

abusing the welfare system. Should vouchers rather than cash be given to welfare recipients today?

3 Imagine that your family's income dropped suddenly because the wage earner was unemployed. Make a list of the possessions you would sell in order to raise money. Rank these things in order from those you would be most willing to sell to those you would be least willing to sell.

4 Write a human-interest story based on a photograph in this unit.

5 Debate: Any able-bodied man who is unemployed and receiving relief should be required to work at some project, such as sweeping the streets, in order to earn his relief money.

6 During the depression many people in Canada suffered a great deal. The wealthy, however, noticed very few changes in the way they lived. Do some research to gather information on how the rich lived in Canada during the 1930s. Include facts on automobiles, holidays, clothing styles etc. Write an essay on "How the Other Half Lived."

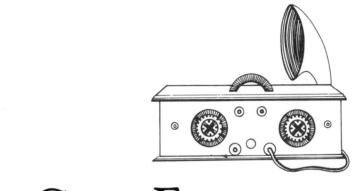

22
The Great Escape

Atop the Empire State Building, King Kong swats away at attacking planes just before they shoot him down. The screaming girl in his hairy paw is the Alberta-born leading lady, Fay Wray. When Miss Wray was first asked to play the role, she was told she would co-star with the tallest and darkest hero of Hollywood. Naturally she thought this would be the Hollywood heart-throb, Clark Gable. Instead, the hero turned out to be an enormous gorilla.

This was the golden age of Hollywood. For the price of a 25¢ ticket people could forget the dust storms and relief vouchers and enter the make-believe world of the Hollywood stars. The films, radio shows, songs, and magazines of those days provided a brief escape from reality. In the movies all the women were beautiful and all the men handsome. Crime did not pay and true love always triumphed in the end. Great film extravaganzas such as *Gone With the Wind* and Walt Disney's *Mickey Mouse* were popular box office attractions. Though all the films came from Hollywood, at least a dozen stars were Canadians. These included Beatrice Lillie, Marie Dressler, Norma Shearer, Deanna Durbin, Raymond Massey, and Walter Huston, who became famous international stars.

Of all the Hollywood child stars, none was loved more than Shirley Temple. She made her first film in 1934 at the age of four, and for the next four years was Hollywood's top box-office attraction. Her golden ringlets endeared her to millions as she sang and danced. Miss Temple's $300 000 yearly salary was boosted by the sale of Shirley Temple dolls, doll clothes, soaps, books, and ribbons. Many parents in the 1930s named their daughters after her and also did their daughters' hair in ringlets.

Shirley Temple dolls

The one possession every family tried to keep during the dark days of the depression was their radio. A radio provided a vital escape from the dreariness of ordinary life. In the 1930s the radio was the gathering spot in the home. Since these were the days before television broadcasting, families depended on the radio for home entertainment.

Like the movies, the most popular radio shows came from the United States. They included "Jack Benny," "George Burns and Gracie Allen," "The Lone Ranger," "The Inner Sanctum," and, of course, "Amos 'n' Andy."

At the height of its popularity in the early years of the depression, "Amos 'n' Andy" had a larger audience than any other program in the history of broadcasting. "Amos 'n' Andy" chronicled the comic misadventures of a pair of young black men who came north to Harlem, New York from rural Georgia to make a fortune in the taxicab business. Listening to the hilarious adventures of Amos 'n' Andy each evening amounted to a national craze in both the United States and Canada. Restaurants and bars had to put in radios so that their customers could listen to the program between 7:00 and 7:15 p.m., or else they would not have any customers. Incredible as it seems, some movie theatres stopped the film in mid-reel and at 7:00 p.m. wheeled in a radio and tuned

Freeman "Amos" Gosden and Charles "Andy" Correll are two white actors imitating Blacks

in "Amos 'n' Andy." Moviegoers would have stayed at home otherwise. Probably no one benefited more from the "Amos 'n' Andy" craze than their sponsors, the makers of Pepsodent toothpaste. In the depths of the depression, when many companies were going broke, Pepsodent saw its sales triple. Until this time most of the sponsors of network radio programs had been the manufacturers of radio sets. So, for better or worse, "Amos 'n' Andy" proved that sponsoring a popular radio show could lead to the sale of vast quantities of such goods as toothpaste, soaps, cigarettes, coffee, and laxatives.

Because Canadian airwaves were being filled with American radio shows, Prime Minister Bennett felt something had to be done. The Canadian Radio Broadcasting Commission (CBC) was started in 1933 to counteract American influence. Money was made available by the government to build more stations across the country and to improve the quality of Canadian broadcasting. In spite of the best efforts of the CBC, American programs were still more popular.

In 1939, the CBC covered the royal tour to Canada by the new king, George VI, and Queen Elizabeth. The first visit of a reigning monarch to Canada was carried by radio to even the most remote areas. The CBC was proving that it could be a powerful force in establishing a sense of national unity across Canada and counteracting the American influence.

Newspapers of the 1930s downplayed the harsh conditions of the depression because people became tired of reading bad news. Instead newspapers gave a great deal of space to human interest stories. One of the most spectacular was the birth of the Dionne quintuplets. Annette, Emilie, Yvonne, Cecile, and Marie, the world's first quintuplets to survive, were born to a poor Ontario family in 1934. Because the family was poor and already had several children, the Ontario government became the guardian of the quints. A special home was built for the girls, and nurses and teachers were provided for them. The Dionnes became a major tourist attraction, and millions of Canadians flocked to Callander, Ontario to look at the babies through a special one-way screen. The girls became an overnight sensation. Before long they were being used to sell many commercial products, including canned milk, syrup, dolls, breakfast foods, and soap.

Every fad that struck the United States was quickly copied in Canada. Card games such as bridge, begun in the United States, became Canadian favourites too. The game Monopoly started a craze because players could buy, sell, invest, borrow, and accumulate a fortune without risking a cent of real money.

The Dionne quintuplets

Throughout the 1930s daily life in Canada was growing more and more like daily life in the United States. People were so preoccupied worrying about money and trying to escape from the depression that there was not much concern about this situation. The influence of the United States on Canada through films, radio, magazines, and fads did not become an important political issue until the 1960s.

SOME RESULTS OF THE DEPRESSION

A famous author, Caroline Bird, has said that everybody who lived through the depression carried an invisible scar on their minds that would be there permanently. The depression would affect their thinking for the rest of their lives. What she meant is illustrated in the following comment of a person who was a teenager in the 1930s. "I would never again like to live through a depression. It makes a person want to cry remembering how horrible life was back then. My parents had to work so hard and they suffered a great deal. Me, I never buy a thing on credit. I always wait until I can afford to pay for everything in cash. We hang on to our money because in 1929 everyone was in the stock market and everybody lost. I want to have some money put away for a rainy day."

To such a person, the free spending and extravagance of her children and grandchildren seem unreasonable. She will never be able to get over the fear of having to face another depression.

At the same time, many survivors of the depression are determined that their children will be spared the hardships and poverty they lived through. Therefore, they tend to give their children luxuries they could never afford when they were young.

It was during the depression that the idea of the welfare state took root in Canada. This was the belief that society should support its citizens to prevent extreme economic hardships. Today parents receive family allowance cheques to help them raise their children. During the 1930s, this kind of monthly cheque would have seemed like a small fortune to many starving families. Today there is also unemployment insurance so that no one is allowed to starve because a job is not available. Senior citizens are provided with pensions. The ideas for the government helping its citizens originated during the depression.

DIGGING DEEPER

1   A major element of the entertainment of the 1930s was escapism. Define escapism. Why do you think people found it enjoyable during the depression?

2   Use an organizer to compare popular forms of entertainment today with the entertainment of the 1930s. How do you think people will rate this decade fifty years from now?

3   Debate: The government is expected to provide too many services for Canadians today. People should not expect the government to look after them from the cradle to the grave. People should care for themselves.

4   Debate: Kids today have got it too easy. If they had lived through the depression they would have known hard times but would be better for it.

5   The jobless rate in Canada flucuates from year to year and from region to region. Do some research to discover how many people are unemployed in Canada today. Compare that number with the jobless rate in Canada during the Great Depression.

What are the causes of unemployment? What region suffers the most? Is there a difference between the unemployment problem today and the one during the depression? Are there any cures for unemployment?

23
The Search for Solutions

When the stock market crashed in 1929, the prime minister of Canada was the Liberal, William Lyon Mackenzie King. King did not seem to know what to do about the depression other than to wait it out and hope things would get better. In 1930, King made the biggest political mistake of his entire career. Providing relief was the responsibility of the provinces and King, a Liberal, said that he would not give a "five-cent piece" to any province that did not have a Liberal government. In the election of 1930, those words kept coming back to haunt King. The voters refused to forget King's "five-cent piece" speech. The Liberals were voted out of office, and the Conservative party came into power.

The prime minister who replaced Mackenzie King was Richard Bedford Bennett. Bennett was a multimillionaire lawyer from Calgary. He was a stern, dignified, and very prosperous-looking gentleman.

During the election campaign Bennett had promised, "I will end unemployment or perish in the attempt." When he came to power, however, Bennett seemed to have no new ideas for handling any economic crisis. His policies were to give emergency funds to the provinces for relief. Military-style relief camps were set up for jobless single men in isolated parts of the country. The highest tariff in Canadian history was introduced to protect Canadian business from foreign competition. Unfortunately none of these acts had any great impact on the depression. These measures were like first-aid treatment and did not cure the depression. As times became more difficult, more and more people began to blame Bennett for their problems. Cars that could not run for lack

R.B. Bennett

of gas were hitched up to farm animals and called "Bennett buggies." The collections of shacks where the unemployed camped around cities were called "Bennett boroughs." "Bennett coffee" was a cheap substitute for coffee made from roasted wheat or barley. Newspapers were used as covers to keep warm on park benches. They were known as "Bennett blankets." A "Bennett barnyard" was an abandoned farm.

R.B. Bennett knew that the people of Canada were growing increasingly angry with the government. Finally, in 1935, just before an election, Bennett startled the nation by starting a program of radical reforms. The people called this "Bennett's New Deal." The program was copied to a large extent from a similar one introduced in the United States. In 1933 President Roosevelt had introduced a New Deal to end the depression. Roosevelt's idea was to use the government's resources to get the economy going. He reasoned that if people could afford things, more things would be manufactured and more workers would be employed who, in turn, would purchase more goods. Therefore, Roosevelt's New Deal gave farmers government money and began many large federal projects to increase employment for many people.

In 1935 Bennett decided to take action. He called for legislation to establish unemployment and social insurance, set minimum wages so workers could not be paid less than a specific wage, limit the hours of work, guarantee the fair treatment of employees, and control prices so that businesses could not make unfair profits.

Most people were startled by Bennett's radical new ideas. His political opponents suggested that the New Deal was nothing more than a plot to win votes in the forthcoming election.

They felt that Bennett had left his reforms too late to do any good. In the election of 1935, King and the Liberals swept back to power in a landslide victory.

NEW POLITICAL PARTIES

As the "Dirty Thirties" dragged on, more and more people became dissatisfied with the two main political parties – the Conservatives and the Liberals. The old parties seemed to have no new, fresh ideas for solving the country's economic troubles. Three new political parties were formed which promised to take more drastic action to eliminate the problems of the Great Depression.

The Co-operative Commonwealth Federation (CCF) was founded in Calgary in 1932. It held its first conference in Regina in 1933. It was formed by people who wanted to introduce economic reforms to end the human suffering caused by the Great Depression. The CCF supported the idea of a mixed economy (nationalized and private industries) and wanted Canadians to have pensions, health and welfare insurance, baby bonus, unemployment insurance, and compensation for injured workers. By 1961, the CCF had evolved into the New Democratic Party (NDP). The Liberals and the Conservatives have adopted their policies and now Canadians benefit from the original ideas of the CCF.

In 1935, the Social Credit party formed the government in Alberta. The premise for their party was that peoples' wages would always be less than the prices of goods and services, therefore, people wouldn't be able to afford to buy what was produced. To avoid this problem, "social credit," or money, would be distributed to people. However, once the party was elected, their economic theory gave way to conservative financial and social policies. The Social Credit party today bears little resemblance to its origins.

The Union Nationale party was founded in Quebec in 1935. It was a coalition party that began as a protest against the high unemployment and the severe economic hardship of the depression. Its members wanted social, economic, and political reform in Canada. In 1936, under Maurice Duplessis, the Union Nationale became the government of Quebec and governed until 1939.

However, political solutions did not end the depression. The Second World War ended the Great Depression. Many unemployed people joined the armed forces. Those who didn't serve in the army worked in factories producing war munitions.

DIGGING DEEPER

1   What could governments have done in the 1930s to reduce the horrible effects of poverty and unemployment?

2   Evaluate R.B. Bennett's effectiveness in solving the problems created by the depression.

3   The Great Depression was a turning point in Canadian history. Make a list of present government agencies and services that were not available for Canadians in 1930.

4   In the spring of 1935, thousands of men left relief camps in the West and started on a protest demonstration headed for Ottawa. Do some research on this On-to-Ottawa Trek. What were the demands of the protestors? Find out what happened when the marchers confronted the Regina police. What was the outcome of the trek?

5   Refer back to the matrix you started at the end of the second unit (page 103). You are now ready to add more information. Trace the development of the same themes through the 1930s.

24
The Rise of the
Nazi Dictator

On 4 August 1944, Nazi soldiers burst into an attic over a warehouse in Amsterdam. An informer had told them that eight Jews were hiding there. The Nazis found the Frank family and four other Jews. They had hidden in these cramped quarters for two years. While searching the attic, the sergeant picked up Mr. Frank's briefcase, and asked if there were any jewels in it. Mr. Frank said that it contained only papers. Disappointed, the Nazi threw the papers onto the floor. The little group that had spent twenty-five months in that attic was sent off to concentration camps.

However, there remained on the floor of the attic the diary of a thirteen-year-old girl, Anne Frank. All the time she and her family were in hiding, Anne had been describing the isolation and constant fear in which they lived. Though Anne died at the age of fifteen in a concentration camp, her diary was later discovered and published. It is the remarkable story of one young Jewish girl and her will to survive the Nazi persecutions. The following two passages from her diary tell part of Anne's ordeal:

20 June 1942
After May 1940 good times rapidly fled; first the war,
then the surrender of Holland, followed by the arrival of
the Germans which is when the suffering of us Jews
really began. Anti-Jewish decrees followed each other in
quick succession. Jews must wear a yellow star, Jews
must hand in their bicycles, Jews are banned from trains
and are forbidden to drive. Jews are only allowed to do

their shopping between 3 and 5 o'clock, and then only in shops that bear the placard 'Jewish shop'. Jews must be indoors by eight o'clock and cannot even sit in their own gardens after that hour. Jews are forbidden to enter theaters, cinemas, and other places of entertainment. Jews may not take part in public sports. Swimming baths, tennis courts, hockey fields and other sports grounds were also prohibited to them. Jews must go to Jewish school and many more restrictions of a similar kind.

9 October 1942
Our many Jewish friends are being taken away by the dozen. These people are treated by the Gestapo (Nazi secret police) without a shred of decency, being loaded into cattle trucks and sent to Westerbork, the big Jewish camp. Westerbork sounds terrible: only one washing cubicle for a hundred people and not nearly enough lavatories . . . It is impossible to escape; most of the people in the camp are branded by their shaved heads. . . . We assume that most of them are murdered. The English radio speaks of their being gassed.

Anne Frank was just one of the 6 million Jews who died in the horrible concentration camps of Nazi Germany. Another 24 million soldiers and civilians from all sides – Canadians, British, French, Russians, Dutch, Germans, Italians, Japanese, Americans, and others – bring the staggering loss to 30 million casualties in World War II. What caused the world to erupt into the second major conflict of this century?

CASE STUDY: GERMANY AFTER WORLD WAR I

Why did the German people turn to Hitler from 1918 to 1932?

Economic Problems: Inflation

Instead of taxing its people to finance World War I, Germany had borrowed the money. Thus it had burdened its citizens with a huge debt. To pay off this debt after the war, the German government simply printed more paper money. This was done even though the country's industry, agriculture, and commerce were not expanding because of the heavy reparations that had to be paid to the Allies. Instead of German wealth going back into the economy, it went to pay off the war debt. The rapid printing of marks (the basic unit of German currency) was not supported by real economic value, and this caused severe inflation.

3 Million Mark
(3 000 000 Mark)
zahlen wir gegen diesen Gutschein
dem Inhaber an unserer Kasse.
Die Einlösung dieses Scheines erfolgt von einem durch
die Tageszeitungen bekannt zu gebenden Tage ab.
Der Zeitpunkt, an dem dieser Schein seine Gültigkeit
verliert, wird in gleicher Weise bekannt gemacht.
HOECHST am Main, den 8. August 1923.
Farbwerke
vorm. Meister Lucius & Brüning

In the spring of 1922, about 300 marks could buy an American dollar. By early 1923, it took 50 000 marks to buy an American dollar! Soon Germans needed billions of marks to pay for a postage stamp. It took a shopping bag full of marks to get on a streetcar. Wages were often carried home in wheelbarrows full of almost worthless paper money. A lifetime's savings could become valueless in a matter of weeks. The bartering of goods became the accepted method of trading. Workers were paid daily and spent their pay as soon as possible lest its value should have fallen by the next day. As the paper money dropped in value, the government kept 300 paper mills working twenty-four hours a day to churn out more of the useless currency.

Advertisements from a Berlin paper for Schmidt's Delikatessen		
	1918 Prices	**1923 Prices**
Cabbage	2 marks per lb	6 million marks per lb
Dill Pickles	$1^1/_3$ marks per lb	$5^3/_4$ million marks per lb
Wieners	3 marks per lb	7 million marks per lb
	(1 kg. = 2.2 lbs.)	

1 Define inflation.
2 What was the major economic problem Germany faced after the war and why did it arise?
3 How did the German government attempt to solve the economic crisis?
4 Who would suffer the most from inflation? Why?
5 Who might benefit from the inflation? Why?

BALLOT BOX

Political Instability

After World War I Germany had more than a dozen major political parties. No party was strong enough to undertake the gigantic task of rebuilding a wartorn country. The main political parties fell into three general groups.

Communists	Social Democrats	National Socialists (Nazi)
Beliefs:		
Government should be run by the councils of workers. Industries and agriculture should be owned by the government rather than private individuals. The power of the military should be reduced. Workers should be powerful and protected.	Government should be run by elected representatives from all parties. A few key industries, such as railroads, should be owned by the government. The terms of the Treaty of Versailles, which limited the size of the army to 100 000 should be honoured. The Constitution must guarantee the rights of minority groups and workers.	Government should be run by the army and the wealthy. Industry should continue to be privately owned. The power of the military should be increased. Democratic government should be outlawed. The activities of Jews and foreigners should be severely restricted (since the Nazis believed that these two groups were responsible for Germany's economic problems).
Supporters often found among:		
Factory and agricultural workers, some intellectuals (teachers, professors), pacifists (those opposed to any form of fighting).	Some workers, professional people, Roman Catholics, some business people.	Army, unemployed, big business, farmers, aristocrats.

1 What were the positions of the major political parties in Germany toward:

a) the military?
b) industry?
c) who should run the government?

2 Which party would likely support the Treaty of Versailles?

3 Why would owners of big businesses and the very wealthy be willing to support the National Socialists and Hitler?

4 If you were a Jewish citizen living in Germany, which political party would you support? Why?

The Treaty of Versailles

The people of Germany were humiliated by the harsh terms of the Treaty of Versailles. They considered the new boundaries and reparation payments to be unjust. The war guilt clause was seen as a black stain on the honour of all Germans. On the morning of the signing of the Treaty of Versailles, the *Deutsche Zeitung* (German News) called for

VENGEANCE!
Today in Versailles the disgraceful Treaty is being signed. Do not forget it! The German people will, with unceasing labour, press forward to reconquer the place among the nations to which we are entitled! Then will come vengeance for the shame of 1919!

1 Review the main terms of the Treaty of Versailles listed in column A. Decide which of the groups or classes of people in column B would be opposed to each term. Why?

A		B
a) The French took rich prizes of German territory west of the Rhine – the Saar Valley with its coal fields and the provinces of Alsace and Lorraine. b) The German army was limited to 100 000. Germany could have no submarines, aircraft, or heavy artillery.	c) Germany was required to pay $5 billion in reparations. d) Germany's colonies were parcelled out to France, Britain, and Japan. e) Germany had to admit that it was totally to blame for all the losses and damages of the war (war guilt clause).	i) The military ii) Big business owners iii) The middle class iv) The working man v) The whole German people vi) The nationalists

2 To which of the groups in column B was Hitler appealing when he promised
   a) to rearm Germany?
   b) to get revenge on Germany's enemies?
   c) to cancel the Treaty of Versailles?
   d) to expand the army?
   e) to restore German honour?
   f) to win back by force all German territory?

Depression and Unemployment

In the United States in 1929 the stock market crashed, marking the beginning of a worldwide depression. The Americans could no longer afford to buy German-manufactured goods. American banks could no longer lend money to Germany to rebuild after World War I. Therefore, Germany had very little money and could not make their reparation payments. The shock waves of the depression hit Germany full force.

Germans who still had jobs saw their scanty wages fall steadily from month to month. Unemployed miners spent the winter in unheated rooms, sometimes breaking through fences at the mine to steal a few lumps of coal. In the woods around Berlin, families pitched tents or lived in packing crates when they couldn't afford to pay rents in the city. In the country, farmers stood with loaded rifles in a futile attempt to keep out the hordes of starving people who came out from the city to steal food for their families. After that people were reduced to welfare or begging in the streets.

News Item: Berlin 1932
Unemployment has now reached six million, half of Germany's labour force! People are deliberately seeking arrest in order to receive free food in prison.

To Germans who were bitter about inflation and economic troubles, Hitler and the Nazi party said:

> **Believe me, our misery will increase! The government itself is the biggest swindler and crook. People are starving on millions of marks! We will no longer submit! We want a dictatorship.**

1 Why would the American depression have an effect on the German economy?
2 What could Hitler and the Nazis promise the unemployed in order to win them over to the Nazi Party?
3 What did Hitler say was the cause of Germany's economic problems? What did Hitler promise to do about the situation?

STEPS TO THE WAR

During the years from 1918 to 1932, Adolf Hitler organized the Nazi party in Germany. Hitler promised the German people he would get back the land lost during World War I and restore Germany to world leadership. He preached to them that the pure German race, called Aryan, was the "master race" and deserved to rule the world. Hitler guaranteed to rid Germany of communists. He also blamed the Jewish people for Germany's defeat in World War I and for the economic hard times that followed. From the very beginning Hitler had been obsessed by hatred of the Jews (anti-Semitism). As early as the 1920s, when he wrote his book *Mein Kampf*, he was describing Jews as "deadly poison," "vermin," and "leering devils."

Hitler and the Nazi party gained control of the German parliament in 1933. Once in power, Hitler became a dictator, depending on force to keep control. Anyone who opposed him was rounded up by his secret police, the Gestapo and the SS (*schutzstafflen*), and thrown into prison or concentration camps. Jews were banned from all government jobs, broadcasting, teaching, working on newspapers, and in entertainment. By the Nuremberg Laws, Jews were not allowed to marry non-Jews. A Nazi campaign was begun to make life thoroughly miserable for the German Jews. Jews were banned from many shops and public buildings. Nazi bullies stood outside Jewish-owned stores and threatened customers who wanted to enter. By 1936 most Jews in Germany found it almost impossible to earn a living. Those who could escaped from Germany in that early period. Among those who left Germany was Albert Einstein, who worked on the atomic bomb.

Just before the war broke out, Hitler had begun a systematic rounding up of the Jews, placing them in concentration camps. When a German embassy official in Paris was shot by a young Jew in November 1938, a savage attack on German Jews followed. A huge fine was forced on the Jewish population. Seven thousand Jewish shops were looted, and 20 000 Jews arrested, many of whom were beaten savagely.

With Hitler in power, Germans were allowed to read and hear only what their leaders wanted them to know. Newspapers and radio were totally controlled by the Nazi party. Books containing ideas that did not please Hitler were burned in huge public bonfires. Teachers were required to be members of the Nazi party. Students were pressured to join the Hitler Youth Movement where they could learn Nazi ideas. Priests and clergy who dared to protest Hitler's methods were thrown in prison. Nazi Germany had become a totalitarian state where everything was controlled by the government.

Hitler had promised to make Germany a strong country. One of his first steps was to strengthen the army and the air force. A new German army was created under the slogan, "Today Germany. Tomorrow the world!" Weapons of war started to pour out of German factories. In a swiftly rearming Germany, the Nazi bullies were wiping out the last remnants of opposition to the new Nazi regime.

In Canada at this time, as almost everywhere, there was massive unemployment. In the United States and Britain millions were unemployed and on relief. In these countries there appeared to be no easy cure to the economic troubles. But in Germany, millions of people had now been persuaded that Hitler was the answer to all their problems. It meant the end of democracy in Germany and the advent of unthinking obedience to the dictator (the führer). Hitler had persuaded the Germans that their problems would be solved if they could get back the territories taken by the Treaty of Versailles.

The Nazi attempt to regain lost territories began in March 1938. Nazi soldiers crossed the frontier into Austria. Hitler argued that Austria should be a part of Germany because many Germans lived there, and all Germans deserved to live under the German state (the Reich). Hitler rode in triumph at the head of his army through the streets of Vienna, the capital of Austria. He found that through Nazi threats and troublemakers he could win victories without battles. Without firing a shot, Austria came into the German Reich. The other nations of the world did not attempt to stop Hitler from taking Austria because no one wanted to risk another world war.

Czechoslovakia was next on Hitler's list. Hitler demanded a piece of Czechoslovakia known as the Sudentenland. This territory was near the German border and contained a large number of German-speaking people. The brave Czechs were ready to fight Hitler, but France and Britain were not willing to help them. British Prime Minister Neville Chamberlain and Premier Daladier of France met with Hitler in Munich and agreed to allow Germany to have the Sudetenland. They believed this would save the world from war. The Czechs were not consulted. They felt furious about being sold out by their allies, but were helpless to resist. Though Chamberlain said the Munich agreement meant "peace in our time," many people disagreed. Winston Churchill, who was to follow Chamberlain as the British prime minister, called the agreement "appeasement," or giving in to the demands of a potential enemy. He argued that Hitler should be stopped now, at all costs.

Though Hitler had promised at Munich that he would make no

Adolf Hitler

new demands for territory, he soon broke that pledge. Six months later, in March 1939, Germany occupied all of Czechoslovakia. Then in August of the same year, Germany shocked the world by signing a non-aggression pact with the Soviet Union. The two long-time non-aggression enemies, Germany and Russia, promised not to fight each other and secretly agreed to divide Poland between them. Hitler was now free to plan his moves against France and Britain in the west since he no longer had to fear an attack from the Russians on the east.

Next Hitler demanded that the Polish Corridor, awarded to Poland by the Treaty of Versailles, be handed back to Germany. Poland refused. On 1 September 1939, the German army drove over the borders into Poland. The Poles were helpless to defend themselves against the German's new style of warfare, called *blitzkrieg* or "lightning warfare." *Blitzkrieg* demanded surprise, force, boldness, and close co-operation among the air force, tanks artillery, and infantry. In the *blitzkrieg* the German *Luftwaffe* (air force) bombed enemy aircraft on the ground, army barracks, headquarters, bridges, and railways. After the air attacks the Nazis raced ahead in tanks and armoured cars, moving deep into enemy territory. In the face of this concentrated attack the Poles could do nothing. The situation was now so dangerous that Britain and France realized they would now have to rush to the defence of Poland. There could be no more appeasement. Two days later, on 3 September 1939, first Britain and then France officially declared war on Germany.

DEVELOPING SKILLS:
PLACING INFORMATION ON MAPS

How powerful was Hitler? How far did his empire extend? One way to get an accurate picture of the power and dominance of Nazi Germany is through the use of maps. By placing information on a map, you can record and summarize historical events.

When you are creating a map, you must make sure that you have included sufficient and pertinent information. People should be able to use your map easily. When you're finished your map, exchange it with a classmate to see if your map is complete and useable.

Mapping Nazi Aggression 1938 – 1939
1 Start with an outline map of Europe. Mark the borders of Germany in 1938. Label the country and choose an appropriate colour or symbol to indicate Nazi control of the country.
2 What territory did Hitler seize in 1938? Label that country on the map and mark out its borders. Indicate that it is Nazi-controlled territory and the year of its occupation.
3 Indicate the territory gained by Nazi Germany by the Munich Agreement. What territory did Hitler seize in March 1939? Add this information to your map also.
4 Indicate the country seized by the armies of the Third Reich in September 1939.
5 Continue your map to show the extent of Nazi power by 1941. Show, with the use of arrows, the paths the Nazi army took as they overran the countries of Europe.

DIGGING DEEPER

1   In your notebook arrange the steps to the war in the order in which they happened.

Munich Agreement
Treaty of Versailles
Hitler demands Sudentenland
Hitler becomes leader of Germany
Germany invades Poland
Germany begins to rearm
Britain and France declare war on Germany
Hitler invades Austria
Germany signs pact with Russia

2   Decide whether the following are true or false:
   a) A dictator depends on force to stay in power.
   b) France and Britain gave in to Hitler at Munich because Germany had promised to pay reparations.
   c) Britain and France approved of Hitler's actions when he seized other countries.
   d) France and Britain declared war on Germany when Austria was taken over.
   e) In the Nazi state industrialists received generous contracts to produce weapons of war.

3   Discuss: Should force have been used by nations of the world to stop Germany when it invaded other countries?

25
The Dark Years

Black headlines on 3 September 1939 announced the grim news: "Britain and France at war with Germany!" Canadians were shocked, yet eager to do what they could to help Britain. However, in September 1939 Canada's entry into the war was not automatic, as it had been in 1914. Canada was no longer a colony bound to follow Britain into warfare. In the years following World War I, Canada had become an independent nation.

Prime Minister Mackenzie King quickly summoned the Canadian Parliament to discuss Canada's involvement in the war. On 9 September 1939 Parliament advised King George VI that Canada was declaring war on Germany. The next morning the message was received from London that the king had signed Canada's declaration of war. It was a momentous occasion – the first time that Canada had declared war on its own behalf. Though Canada was getting ready to fight, it had only about 10 000 soldiers in its armed forces. The Canadian army possessed only 14 tanks, 29 Bren guns, 23 antitank rifles, and 5 small mortar guns. The Canadian navy had exactly 10 operational vessels. It would be some time before Canada's armed forces reached an effective fighting size.

Within the first four weeks of action, Hitler's modern army had outnumbered and crushed the old-fashioned Polish defences. Next, the powerful German forces overran Denmark, Norway, Belgium, and the Netherlands. Hitler was free not to turn against France. For the second time in twenty-five years German troops poured across the French borders.

Thousands of British troops had rushed across the English Channel to help defend France. However, during the rapid German advance British forces became trapped and had to retreat to the seaport town of Dunkirk on the French coast. The British

Montrealers reacting to the war declaration

hastily collected a fleet of all available boats in order to get their soldiers back home again. Three hundred thousand soldiers were evacuated safely to Britain, but most of the heavy British war equipment had to be abandoned on the beaches of France. It was a terrible defeat for the Allies. France had fallen in six weeks and Paris was now occupied by the Nazis. A new French army known as the Free French, led by General Charles de Gaulle, was set up in England. The Free French army vowed to continue its fight against the Nazis.

Mussolini, the Italian dictator, at this moment decided to enter the war on the side of Germany. Almost all of Europe was in the hands of the Axis powers, Germany and Italy. There remained only the island of Britain. The *Luftwaffe* had several thousand bombers ready for heavy action. The German strategy was to knock out Britain by destroying its capital, London. The Germans hoped to paralyze the British government and demoralize the people by heavy bombing. Night after night wave upon wave of bombers attacked London and other important cities.

The Nazis called it a war of terror. It was designed to destroy the peoples' will to resist. Though thousands were killed, the British refused to give up. To the amazement of all, the greatly outnumbered Royal Air Force shot almost 3000 Nazi planes out of the skies in two months. Speaking of the Royal Air Force, Prime Minister Churchill said, "Never was so much owed by so many to so few." For more than a year the gallant pilots of the Royal Air Force defended Britain in what came to be known as the Battle of Britain. The Battle of Britain proved too costly for the Nazis in terms of pilots and aircraft. The Germans temporarily gave up the idea of trying to bomb Britain out of the war.

From 1939 to 1941 the United States remained neutral and was not directly involved in the fighting. After the fall of France, President Roosevelt urged his country to become a great producer of ammunition in order to help protect democracy. Finally in 1941, the Americans adopted a Lend-Lease policy. By this act, the Allies were not required to pay cash for war supplies from the United States. The reason for the American generosity was that the president considered the defence of Britain important to the security of the United States.

In June 1941 Hitler decided he could not defeat Britain from the air, so he turned eastward. He attacked his own ally, the Soviet

Troops being shipped overseas

RCAF pilots

Union. Hitler wanted to seize the natural resources of the USSR – grain, coal, iron, and oil. At first German armies scored tremendous successes in the USSR. In just three months they reached the outskirts of Moscow and Leningrad, the two most important Russian cities.

By now Hitler's ally in the Pacific, Japan, had become obsessed with the strategy and surprise of *blitzkrieg*. On 7 December 1941, Japanese planes came without warning and bombed the American naval base at Pearl Harbor, Hawaii. The attack, a complete surprise, left half the American fleet crippled or sunk. The next day the United States declared war on Japan. Three days later Germany and Italy, Japan's allies, also declared war on the United States. By 1942 the Japanese had engulfed all of the Philippines. A small Canadian force had been captured at Hong Kong, and the British colonies at Singapore, Malaya, Burma, and southeast Asia were controlled by the Japanese.

It seemed that victory for the Axis powers was close at hand. In Europe, Hitler's troops occupied almost every capital from Oslo in Norway to Athens in Greece. In the Pacific, Japan had a stranglehold on southeast Asia. It appeared just a matter of time before Japan and Germany took control of the remaining areas.

Hitler was now in a position to proclaim to his followers that the Nazi empire in Europe would last for a thousand years. The Germans, according to their führer, were destined to be the "master race" and all other people their slaves. The process of making people slaves had already begun in Germany. Nazi leaders were sentencing millions of Europeans, mostly Jewish, to slave labour and concentration camps.

Hitler had strengthened the defences of Nazi-controlled Europe until it was a fortress which it seemed no one could conquer. But soon the tide of war would begin to turn.

26
The Turn
of the Tide

By August 1942 the Allies had a plan. It was to send Canadian and British troops, restless for action, to test the German forces along the French coast at Dieppe. For some time the Soviets had been demanding that the Allies launch an invasion in the west. This would relieve some of the German pressure on the Russians in the east. The raid at Dieppe was planned to be a quick punch at the German stronghold. The Allies hoped to worry the Nazis, gather crucial information about their coastal defences, and then return safely to Britain. Dieppe would be a dress rehearsal for the full-scale Allied invasion of Europe, which would follow.

At 4:50 on the morning of 19 August 1942, 5000 Canadians began to land on the beaches at Dieppe. Boys from such places as Calgary, Saskatoon, Hamilton, Montreal, and Saint John eagerly sought action. However, the German forces were ready for the attack. By early afternoon nearly 900 of the Canadian troops were dead or dying, and over 1000 were wounded. Nineteen hundred prisoners of war were taken by the Germans, and only 2200 of those who landed that morning returned to Britain.

A French Canadian who fought with the Fusiliers Mont-Royal recalled his experience at Dieppe:

> . . . the wounded and dead lay scattered on the beach. Some of the wounded were trying to swim out to the boats [and] many were bleeding heavily, reddening the water around them. [Once ashore,]mortar bombs are bursting on the shingle and making little clouds which seem to

punctuate the deafening din . . . close to me badly muti-
lated bodies lie here and there. The wounded scream . . .
the blood flows from their wounds . . . For myself, I am
absolutely astounded to have reached the shelter of a
building. I was certain that my last hour had arrived.

In spite of the horrible loss of life at Dieppe, and though it appeared
to be a major disaster, important military lessons were learned.
When the decisive invasion of Europe finally came two years later,
the Allies remembered their Dieppe experience. This time fire
support by sea and air would be overwhelming, and a way would
be found to land large numbers of troops and equipment on the
open beaches of France.

In 1942, despite its great navy, the island of Britain was in
deadly danger. The highly industrialized island of 50 million
people could not live or fight without food and supplies from
outside. Britain depended on the food and war supplies being

Wounded Canadians at Dieppe

RATIONED
SUGAR ½ lb. a week PER PERSON
TEA ½ of the usual PURCHASE
COFFEE ¾ of the USUAL PURCHASE

Many goods were rationed during the war.

brought through the life line from North America. Everything depended upon the navy and its air division to make sure the precious cargoes got through safely.

This was not an easy task, for German U-boats lurked in the dark waters of the Atlantic Ocean. German U-boats (*Unterseebooten*) were deadly submarines able to pick off helpless merchant ships from the United States and Canada as they steamed toward British ports. Winston Churchill said later, "The only thing that ever really frightened me during the war was the U-boat peril." By day the U-boats hid submerged, and at night they surfaced. The merchant ships were sitting ducks for their attacks. Cargo vessels were being sunk at the rate of twenty a week, and the Germans were busy building eight U-boats for every one they lost. Fortunately, the Allies also improved their antisubmarine measures. The use of the convoy system, improvements in radar for underwater detection of submarines, and the protection of patrol aircraft helped drop the rate of Allied losses. By the end of the war nearly 800 German U-boats had been sunk.

In 1942 Canada was committed to a policy of "total war." Total war means the concentration of all industries, materials, and manpower upon the war effort. The war now affected everybody in Canada. Ration cards became necessary for buying gasoline, butter, sugar, meat, tea, and coffee. Since these goods were in short supply, the government limited the quantity a person could

buy. Without the ration coupon, a person could not obtain these products. Rubber tires, tubes, and antifreeze were very scarce. At the minimum, a family was limited to 545 ℓ of gasoline annually for its car. Many people could not take long trips in the summer. Butter, sugar, and meat were scarce and became luxury items. Silk stockings were scarce because the silk was needed for parachutes.

For most people, rationing caused little or no real hardship. Most people realized they were lucky not to be in Europe where the real war was being fought. People were encouraged not to hoard food, and to stretch their supplies as far as they would go. One woman recalled how the newspapers were always urging readers to do their bit for the war effort.

> **The newspapers, they were just propaganda sheets. My goodness, on the front pages, war, war, war, and in the insides, how to cook cheaper, how to do Victory Gardens, why we should have car pools, buy Victory Bonds and tell our friends they were traitors if they didn't load up on them too . . .**
>
> **You remember those Sunday sections, they were jammed with war stuff. How to cook cabbage, make cabbage rolls, and then drink the cabbage juice. Did they think we didn't know that stuff, like how to make a dollar do the price of ten? You'd think the idiots in their big offices in Toronto and Ottawa didn't know about the Depression we just went through – ten years of nothing.**

In many kitchens bacon fat and bones were saved to provide glycerine for explosives. People gave up buying new aluminum pots and pans and new stoves so that more airplanes could be built. Every child became a scrap gatherer. Scrap metal, rags, paper, rubber, foil, and wire coat hangers, anything that could be salvaged for the war effort was collected. Posters urged the whole family to help win the war.

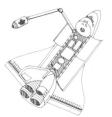

Before the war Canada was primarily a supplier of raw materials. In three years Canada had become a great industrial power. Now Canadian munitions factories turned out bombs, shells, and bullets for small arms. Shipyards worked full blast building cargo ships, trawlers, mine sweepers, small warships used in antisubmarine attacks, and landing craft. Shipbuilding became the second largest employer in the country. Aircraft manufacturers, such as DeHavilland, produced everything from training planes to fighting craft.

In 1942 the government decided to stop the production of civilian cars and turn over all automobile plants to the production of war vehicles. Now the plants produced trucks, jeeps, Bren gun carriers, and artillery tractors. It has been calculated that half of the vehicles used by the British in the North Africa campaign were stamped "Made in Canada." The Nazi general Rommel gave orders to his troops to try and capture Canadian-made jeeps because they did not get stuck in the sand as the German ones did. All kinds of military vehicles, tanks, radar equipment, and penicillin were now produced in large amounts in Canada for the war effort. Steel output doubled, while aluminum production increased by six times its original amount. Canadian farmers and fishermen provided astonishingly large amounts of wheat, flour, cheese, canned salmon, fish oil, bacon, ham, canned meat, and dried eggs for Britain and the Allies.

From eastern Canadian ports, particularly Halifax and Sydney in Nova Scotia, endless convoys of cargo set sail for Britain. Despite the heavy losses, the bulk of the much-needed supplies from Canada and the United States began to get through. With tanks and trucks and an adequate supply of food and ammunition, the Allies could face the Nazis on an equal basis. "There is no doubt now," said Winston Churchill, "of the eventual outcome." The tide had turned in the favour of the Allies. The almost unbroken series of retreats and defeats was over for the Allies. British and American soldiers were now on the offensive in the deserts of North Africa. American GIs (enlisted soldiers) advanced against the Japanese, island by island in the steaming jungles of the Pacific. Canadian, British, and American troops landed in Sicily and fought their way north into Italy. And on the Russian front, the most critical battle of all at Stalingrad approached a climax.

For over five months the Nazis had fought a savage battle to gain control over the city of Stalingrad in southern Russia. Stalingrad, now called Volgograd, was an important industrial city which controlled the rich oil fields of south Russia. The harsh Russian winter took its toll on the German troops. Hitler refused to allow a retreat. By January 1943, two vast Soviet armies had completely surrounded and trapped about 250 000 Germans. At least 100 000 Germans were killed and the remnants of the Nazi army surrendered to the Russians. An eyewitness described the plight of the beaten Germans:

Completely cut off, the men in field grey slouched on, invariably filthy and invariably louse-ridden, their weary shoulders sagging, from one defence position to another.

> The icy winds of those great white wastes which stretched forever beyond us to the east lashed a million crystals of razor-like snow into their unshaven faces . . . It lashed tears from the sunken eyes which, from over-fatigue, could scarce be kept open, it penetrated through all uniforms and rags to the very marrow of our bones.

Many said that the Soviet victory at Stalingrad was the turning point of the war. This was the farthest point of the Nazi advance into the USSR, and the greatest defeat Germany had yet suffered. The Soviets now started to push the Germans back toward Berlin.

Meanwhile, the systematic bombing of cities in Germany by the Allies had begun. At first the bombing was called precision bombing. Its aim was to destroy German industries, railways, highways, bridges, and oil refineries. However in 1942, Allied air chiefs decided to try to destroy the German fighting spirit by mercilessly pounding cities from the air. On the night of 30 May, a thousand bombers raided the city of Cologne. From 24 to 31 July, Hamburg was attacked eight times. Sixty percent of that city was destroyed by fire bombs and 80 000 civilians were killed. Later in the war, cities such as Dresden and Berlin were subjected to wave upon wave of British and American bombers.

D-Day – Day of Deliverance 1944

"OK, we'll go!" With these words General Eisenhower, commander-in-chief of Allied Forces, announced the beginning of the long-awaited invasion of Europe. Since the disastrous attempt at invasion at Dieppe, the Allies had been carefully planning. This time they would be ready. The Normandy beaches of northern France were selected as the sight of the invasion. Normandy was close to Britain and the invading army, supply ships, and reinforcements would have far to travel. A huge army gathered in the south of England. American troops numbering 1.25 million joined a similar number of British and Commonwealth troops. Four thousand landing craft, 700 war ships, and 11 000 planes were ready. Early in April 1944 Allied bombers destroyed rail lines and military trains in northern France. In May they bombed air fields and did serious damage to *Luftwaffe* bases.

The Germans guessed that an invasion was coming because of the troop buildup in Britain. Sixty Nazi divisions in northern France and the Netherlands were under the command of Field Marshall Rommel.

D-Day was fixed for 5 June 1944, but had to be postponed because of bad weather. The weather cleared briefly the next day,

Survivors of a bombing

and Eisenhower gave the order to go. At 2:00 a.m. on the sixth of
June, paratroopers were dropped to protect the landing forces.
Seventy-five minutes later, 2000 bombers began to pound the
German defences on the beaches. At 5:30 a.m. the air raids were
joined by the guns of the Allied warships. Then at precisely 6:30
a.m. the first waves of troops poured onto the beaches of France.
They faced underwater obstacles, land mines, barbed wire, and
heavy machine-gun fire from the Germans. But this time the
invaders kept coming. Within a week the Allies had 300 000
troops safely on shore. Within a month 1 million Allies had landed
with 200 000 military vehicles. Though the Nazis fought fero-
ciously, Hitler was now caught with war on two fronts, east and
west.

Before and after photos of a bombed German city

In August 1944 another Allied force invaded the southern part of France on the Riviera. These troops marched north to join those who landed at Normandy. Hitler struck back by unleashing his secret weapons, the flying bomb V–1 and the deadly, faster-than-sound rocket V–2, at war-weary Britain. These missiles were launched from Europe and aimed at British cities. Fortunately, as the Allied invading forces swept north through Belgium, they overran the rocket launching sites. As the Nazis retreated from Holland, they mercilessly flooded the low lands. As often happens in war, the innocent civilian population suffered the most – homes were destroyed and children suffered malnutrition. Until the Allies could bring in food supplies, some of the Dutch were reduced to eating tulip bulbs.

The troops were not the only ones fighting the war. Thousands of people in Europe joined in the fight against the Axis powers.

These civilians were known as the "underground." These bands of partisans, as they were known, struck at the Nazis in any way they could. They blew up railroads, factories, and bridges. They reported on Nazi troop movements and often helped to rescue Allied pilots shot down in German-occupied territory. Without the contribution and aid of these undercover agents, the liberation of Europe probably would have taken much longer.

As Allied armies pressed toward the Rhine River, Hitler called upon his soldiers to fight even more fiercely. He shouted that whoever gave up a centimetre of German territory while still alive was a traitor to the German people. In a last desperate move Hitler gathered his reserves and 3000 tanks. He hurled them against the Allies in western Europe. Eventually the Allies broke through. The German advance was halted and the retreat began. Hitler had lost 120 000 soldiers and 600 tanks.

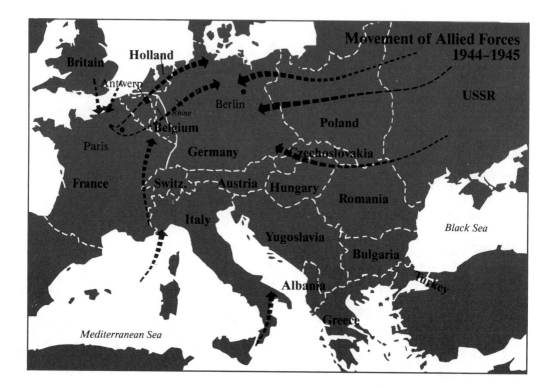

Meanwhile the Russians were swarming across Eastern Europe on their way to Berlin. Although everywhere the Germans resisted with skill and determination, they could not hold back the attack that was coming on all sides. By April 1945 the Russians were in the German capital of Berlin. Berliners fought heroically to defend their city, even using veterans and school boys to try and prevent the inevitable. But by now it was too late. The diary of a captured officer records the plight of Berlin in the last days:

> **27 April**
> Continuous attack throughout the night ... Telephone cables are shot to pieces. Physical conditions are indescribable. No rest, no relief. No regular food, hardly any bread. We get water from the tunnels and filter it ... Masses of damaged vehicles, half-smashed trailers of ambulances with the wounded still in them. Dead people everywhere, many of them frightfully cut up by tanks and trucks.

The end could not long be delayed. By 8 May 1945 fighting in Europe was all over.

Canadian soldiers surrounded by Dutch civilians

Since March 1945 Hitler had shut himself off from the truth. He had retreated into his bomb-proof bunker deep in the earth below the Chancellery building in Berlin. When Soviet troops were only a few blocks from the Chancellery, Hitler realized it was all over. He married his blond companion Eva Braun, and then dictated his last will and testament. In his will he again attacked the Jews and blamed the whole war upon them. He ordered the Germans to fight on and accused his generals of deserting him. Later the same day Hitler learned that the Italian dictator, Mussolini, had been captured and killed by partisans. Mussolini's body had been strung up by the heels in a public square in Milan. This convinced Hitler that he should not suffer the same fate. On 30 April 1945 Hitler shot himself. His bride took poison. According to the instructions he left, their bodies were carried out of the bunker, soaked in gasoline, and set on fire. For the next several hours their bodies burned until they were reduced to unrecognizable remains. One week later, Nazi Germany ceased to exist. VE Day, Victory in Europe Day, had arrived. The long struggle in Europe was over.

But Japan had still not been defeated. Japanese pilots were still flying suicide missions against Allied forces. These men were known as kamikaze pilots. They purposely crashed their planes onto the decks of Allied aircraft carriers and battleships. One pilot could kill many Allied sailors and pilots.

In July 1945, President Truman, who had become president upon Roosevelt's death in April, warned the Japanese to surrender or risk being totally destroyed. The Americans had a powerful new weapon — the atomic bomb. The Japanese refused to surrender regardless of the odds against them.

On 6 August 1945, an American bomber appeared in the sky

German refugees moving back through Canadian lines

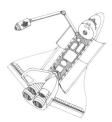

above Hiroshima. It carried a package about a metre long that would change the nature of war forever. The bomber was the *Enola Gay* and it carried an atomic bomb. In a few seconds, the city of Hiroshima was covered by a giant mushroom cloud of smoke and dust. A lightning-like flash covered the whole sky. Sixty percent of the city's developed area was destroyed by the blast and the resulting fires. Seventy-one thousand people were dead or missing, and 68 000 were injured. Nearly all buildings within 1 km of the blast had been flattened. An eyewitness described the blast:

> All around, I found dead and wounded. Some were bloated and scorched – such an awesome sight, their legs and bodies stripped of clothes and burned with a huge blister. All green vegetation, from grasses to trees, perished in that period.

Time Capsules/1945
courtesy Time-Life Books Inc.

Still the Japanese did not surrender. Three days later a second atomic bomb was dropped on the city of Nagasaki. Another 35 000 Japanese were killed and 60 000 were injured. Now the Japanese were ready to give up. On 10 August 1945, Japan surrendered to General Douglas MacArthur, the American commander in the Pacific. At last World War II was over.

The Nazi Death Camps

The Allies, mopping up in Europe in 1945, were horrified when they found the Nazi death camps. In these camps millions of the enemies of Nazism had been imprisoned and killed. Some were there because they were Jews and Hitler hated Jews. Others were political prisoners who had dared to speak out against the Nazis.

Dachau and Bergen-Belsen were typical of the camps in Germany. Here large numbers of Jews, communists, and Protestant and Roman Catholic clergy were imprisoned. All able-bodied men and women were put to work for the Nazi war effort. At least 5 million slaves were working in Germany by 1944. In some of the camps medical experiments were carried out on helpless human beings who were used as guinea pigs.

As European countries were occupied by the Nazis, the Jews in those lands were also sent to concentration camps. When Poland was invaded, sections of large cities, like Warsaw, were walled off and the Jews were forced to live in the ghetto. Rations in the Warsaw ghetto were reduced to starvation levels. For example, the following diet was provided:

> per person per month
> 2 kg flour   2 l of milk
> 185 g sugar   100 g of bread

Nutritionists have calculated that the average intake of calories was 170–230 calories per day in this ghetto. Normal intake of calories would be about 2000. In the Warsaw ghetto as many as twenty people lived in a room measuring 4 m by 6 m. There was little or no heat, despite the -25°C temperatures in the Warsaw winter of 1940. Epidemic typhus and dysentery spread unchecked. Bodies were left in the streets unburied. There were continuous raids, searches, and beatings by the Nazis. Jews were dying by the thousands, but not fast enough to please Hitler.

In long and secret talks with Himmler, the head of the German Gestapo, Hitler devised one of the most outrageous schemes in human history. He decided that every Jewish man, woman, and child would be transported to concentration camps and exterminated. This, he called the "final solution" to the "Jewish problem" in Europe.

At places like Auschwitz and Treblinka in Poland, millions of Jews were worked to death or sent straight to the gas chambers. At Auschwitz the victims were crowded into gas chambers that were disguised as showers. The shower rooms were sealed and Zyklon B gas was dropped into the chambers through a small opening in the ceiling. It took from three to fifteen minutes to kill all those confined within the chamber. The bodies were then removed by a special detachment of prisoners. Gold fillings from the teeth of the victims were yanked out, melted down, and made into gold bars. Other valuables such as watches, bracelets, and rings were also deposited by Himmler in secret bank vaults for future use. Then the corpses were placed in ovens for cremation. Six thousand could be gassed *in a day* at Auschwitz.

At other camps in Eastern Europe the victims were made to dig their own graves, and then were shot in the back by Gestapo sharpshooters.

Some of the most moving stories of bravery and heroism have come out of the death camps. At Auschwitz there was an eighteen-year-old girl, Rosa Robota. Rosa and many of her friends were forced to work for the Nazis in a gunpowder factory. They planned to steal enough gunpowder to blow up the crematorium and the gas chambers. Every day a dozen girls smuggled out small quantities of explosives hidden in the hems of their dresses. The explosives were buried around the camp until there was a sizeable stockpile.

On the afternoon of 7 October 1944, they successfully blew up Number 3 Crematorium. The Gestapo were enraged by this act of sabotage. An investigation was begun and Rosa and the girls were arrested. Every day Rosa was beaten, and after four days of torture the Nazis hanged her.

Hours before her death Rosa Robota managed to smuggle out a message from the death cell. It read, "Be strong and brave." The message helped give strength to others in Auschwitz who would become victims of Hitler's "final solution."

By the end of the war Hitler had destroyed over one-third of the Jews in Europe. It is estimated that 6 million humans among whom Anne Frank was one, were put to death. Their only crime was that they were not members of the "master race."

War in the Pacific Ocean Area

1941   Japanese attack American possessions at Pearl Harbor, Guam, Wake Island, Midway Island, and the Philippines.
Canada sends 2000 troops to defend Hong Kong.
Japanese bomb British bases at Hong Kong and Singapore.
Japanese destroy two British battleships — *Repulse* and *Prince of Wales*.
Japan threatens to invade Australia.

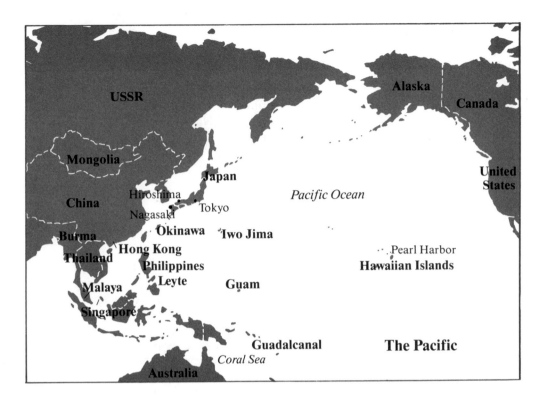

1942 US air-sea victories at the battle of the Coral Sea and Midway Island prove to be the turning point against the Japanese forces.

1943 Japanese threat removed from Australia.
The Allies are ready for a full-scale offensive. The United States is spending $9 million a month on the war effort.
British and other Allied forces fight jungle warfare against the Japanese in Burma.

1944 Invasion of the Philippines at Leyte Island under the command of General Douglas MacArthur of the United States. More soldiers go ashore at Leyte than land at Europe on D-Day.
American forces capture island after island from the Japanese—Guadalcanal, the Carolines, and the Marianas.
American bombing of Japan begins.

1945 After desperate fighting, American forces recapture the Philippine Islands.
Battle at Iwo Jima — 20 000 American casualties.
American and British troops capture the island of

Okinawa just 480 km from Japan.
British remove Japanese from Burma.
Atomic bomb dropped on Hiroshima.
Atomic bomb dropped on Nagasaki.
Japan asks for surrender, ending World War II.

DIGGING DEEPER

1   What is meant by the term "turning point of a war"? Where do you think the turning point came in World War II? Explain your reasons.

2   In World War II many reporters travelled with the Allied armies. You can research and write brief articles as on-the-spot reporters. Your articles can be organized into a class newspaper on the war years. Here are some events that you can investigate:

  a) the bombing of German cities;
  b) life as a crew member on a large bomber;
  c) living in a prisoner-of-war camp;
  d) the D-Day invasion;
  e) sailing with a convoy across the North Atlantic;
  f) life as an undercover agent behind enemy lines;
  g) what it was like when the German surrender was
       announced.

3   In the years since the dropping of the atomic bombs on Hiroshima and Nagasaki, many people have questioned the wisdom of President Truman's actions. Issue: Do you believe that the United States was justified in dropping the bombs on a largely civilian population? You are an advisor to President Truman. Use an issue-analysis organizer to outline what you consider to be the pros and cons of using the bombs on Japan.

4   Today there are atomic weapons hundres of times more powerful than the bombs dropped on Hiroshima and Nagasaki. The world knows that a war fought with atomic weapons could mean the end of all human life. Do you believe any nation would be justified in using atomic weapons today?

5   Some students might like to research the role played by American forces in the war in the Pacific. The topic could be presented under the headings:

  a) how the war began;   c) Japanese kamikaze
  b) the American campaign in   pilots;
       the Pacific;   d) the defeat of Japan.

27
The War on the Home Front

Conscription Again!

The conscription issue raised its ugly head again in World War II. This time Prime Minister Mackenzie King was determined not to let the question tear the country apart as it had during World War I. All the bitter feelings and hostility between the French and English over the conscription issue were in danger of flaring up once more.

At the beginning of the war Mackenzie King promised that conscription for overseas service would not be introduced. Determined to avoid the French-English split of 1917, the Liberals made this pledge to French Canada. However, as the war went on, the military situation began to deteriorate. Prime Minister King found himself in a corner. Many English-speaking Canadians began to call for compulsory military service. Britain had applied conscription from the start, and when the United States entered the war, they too introduced full conscription. Many Canadians whose relatives and friends were voluntarily fighting overseas resented the fact that other Canadians could escape wartime service. To meet public pressure, the government introduced compulsory military taining, but for home defence only.

By 1942 Mackenzie King realized that there was a strong pro-conscription feeling in most of the country. He decided to go to the nation with a plebiscite, which is a direct vote of all citizens on an issue of major national importance. Canadians were asked in the

Mackenzie King and Winston Churchill

plebiscite if they were in favour of releasing the government from its repeated pledges that it would not introduce conscription for overseas service. English Canada answered with an overwhelming 80 percent "Yes," but 72 percent of the province of Quebec said "No." English Canada was reassured by the vote. To satisfy Quebec, Mackenzie King emphasized that conscription was not yet necessary, and would only be used as a last resort. His famous statement about the policy was purposefully vague because it could be taken favourably by either side. King said, "Not necessarily conscription, but conscription if necessary."

In 1944 many citizens now said that conscription was necessary. The army was desperately short of troops. Soldiers who had been wounded two or three times were being sent back to the front lines to fight. Morale in the army was now collapsing. There were even threats that some officers would not serve unless conscription was introduced.

As a last resort King turned to Louis St. Laurent, the leading Cabinet minister from Quebec. King explained to St. Laurent the desperate situation in which the Liberal party found itself. There was real danger that King's government would collapse. With St. Laurent's co-operation, the prime minister announced a total of 16 000 draftees would be sent overseas, but no more for the time being. Only 13 000 of the draftees were sent overseas.

The motion to send 16 000 draftees overseas passed in the House of Commons by a majority vote of 143 to 70. Only one minister from Quebec, C.G. Power, resigned from the Cabinet. He protested that the government had broken its pledge to French Canada. There was some rioting in Quebec City and Montreal when the result of the vote was announced. However, the response in French Canada was not nearly as violent as it had been in 1917. Mackenzie King had won a victory for unity. Reasonable citizens in Quebec realized that King had tried hard to prevent conscription in order to keep the country together. King had done all he could to put off conscription as long as possible. He had paid attention to French-Canadian opinion. Although the French Canadians were unhappy about conscription, they gave Mackenzie King credit for doing his best.

Mackenzie King's conscription policy was probably one of his greatest political achievements. King had remembered and learned from the tragic experience of 1917. This time the conscription crisis did not tear apart the Liberal party nor did it succeed in dividing French and English Canada beyond repair.

Women Roll Up Their Sleeves for Victory

The Allies were committed to the idea of "total war." This meant using population and resources to the fullest extent. Both Canada and Britain brought women into the armed services early in the war. In 1941 the army created the Canadian Women's Army Corps. The air force formed the Canadian Women's Auxiliary Air Force, which later changed its name to the Royal Canadian Air Force (Women's Division). A short time later the Women's Royal Canadian Naval Service was created. By the end of the war, women in uniform numbered 50 000. Another 4500 women were in the medical services.

Overseas the women were not sent into front-line combat with the infantry and tanks. They did essential work, however, behind the lines in army headquarters. Although women did not fly planes or serve on ships, as radio operators they helped to guide back to base those who did. In regimental first-aid posts and in general hospitals in Europe and Britain, nurses and Red Cross workers treated the wounded and dying. Besides their nursing duties, they took time to read and write letters for the wounded and cheer up their patients.

A woman who served near the front recalled her wartime experiences:

> I was a Red Cross Corps worker so my job wasn't actually in surgery or a real nurse's job in the field, but we had to do all we could to help.

Tri-Service Monument in Winnipeg commemorates the involvement of Canadian women in World War II.

Some men were cheery, asking for a cigarette, joking. Some were in shock through loss of blood and just torn-up bodies ... and some of these were the ones who were dying. You got to know. They had this look about them, a whiteness, a look in their eyes. Some would die while you sat beside them. One did once, a young boy from Ontario, and he died as I was reading the last letter he got from his mother. He'd asked me to do it. He let out this kind of sigh and his head fell down a bit and then lifted up a bit and then fell down again and I knew he was gone. He had a lot of steel in his chest. I suppose he never had much of a chance.

It was a time when you could work twelve hours a day and another four if you wanted to, and you'd crawl into the tent just dead. The bombing didn't bother us. The shelling. Sometimes it sounded like thunder rolling across the lake, just like at home at the cottage, hour after hour, and it got to be part of you. If it was on, you didn't actually hear it, but when it stopped you did.

Similarly, women played a vital role in war industries at home. As in World War I, the war helped to prove that women could perform tasks as well as men. In 1939 there had only been 638 000 women in the work force in Canada. By 1944 there were 1 077 000. Traditionally only unmarried women worked, but now it became the patriotic thing for all women to help "fight Hitler at home."

Women in uniform

Overalls and the bandana became the symbol of service to Canada. Women by the thousands operated riveting machines in shipyards, welded parts in airplane factories, and worked on assembly lines in munitions plants. In rural areas they ran farms almost single-handedly while the men were away fighting. Jobs that had traditionally been done by men were now done effectively by women. These included work in lumber mills and as streetcar and bus drivers.

The government established the Women's Division of the National Selective Service under Fraudena Eaton. The task of the Women's Division was to recruit as many women as possible into vital wartime work. In ads in newspapers, in store windows, and in movie theatres women were urged to "back the boys up to bring them back." At first single women and childless married women were sought for employment. However, as more and more workers were needed, married women with children were encouraged to take full- or part-time jobs. In Ontario and Quebec the government established child-care facilities for women working in war industries. Married women were temporarily allowed to earn more money without their husbands having to pay higher income tax. Indeed salaries for women did rise significantly during this time. Women in the aircraft industry received an average weekly wage of $31, which was more than double what women earned before the war.

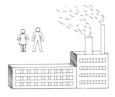

Women who could not serve in uniform or work in war industries still played a vital role as volunteers. They packed parcels for prisoners of war and knitted sweaters and socks for the fighting soldiers overseas. They worked in service clubs and canteens serving coffee and sandwiches to Canadians in uniform and Allied soldiers training in Canada.

Some people see the women's contribution to the labour force during World War II as a great breakthrough in expanding the traditional roles of women in Canadian society. But for many women the breakthrough was only temporary. Following the war, women often lost their jobs to returning servicemen. Also, the tax concessions to married women were removed and the government-sponsored day nurseries were discontinued. It seemed as if the government wanted married women to return to their homes and children or to the traditional female occupations such as teaching, nursing, and domestic services.

Government Control

As part of the commitment to "total war," the government assumed a great deal of control over the Canadian economy. The War Time Prices and Trades Board (WTPTB) froze prices, wages, and rents in order to keep down the cost of living. It drastically reduced the number of luxury goods that could be manufactured. Because wool was scarce, the WTPTB forbade the making of men's suits with vests, double-breasted jackets, cuffs, and pleats. Similarly, women's fashions were also influenced by the lack of material. The style became streamlined with tight, knee-length skirts, small hats, and close-fitting jackets.

To finance the war, the Canadian government increased direct taxes on individuals and corporations, and placed high sales taxes on luxury goods. Canadians were urged to buy Victory Bonds. To the credit of Canadians, of the $18 billion paid by Canada for the war effort, $12 billion was raised through the sale of Victory Bonds. Individual Canadians and corporations loaned money to the government which was to be repaid with interest after the war.

THE EFFECT OF WORLD WAR II ON CANADA

When war broke out in 1939, Canada was almost totally unprepared. Nevertheless, the country did its utmost to make a vital contribution to the war effort. By 1945, Canada emerged with an important place in world affairs.

In the first place, Canada made a major contribution of people, munitions, food supplies, and raw materials. In 1939 Canada's

Workers celebrate the building of their 100th tank.

three military services totalled just over 10 000 people. By 1945, 1 086 771 Canadians had worn a uniform, of whom 50 000 were women. Among these, fatal casualties numbered 22 964 for the army, 17 047 for the air force, and 1981 for the navy. In a nation of slightly over 11 million at the end of the war, these figures represent a great loss. Similarly, in terms of war production, Canadians worked miracles. Starting from almost nothing, Canadian plants turned out 800 000 motor vehicles, 16 000 aircraft, 900 000 rifles, 200 000 machine guns, 6500 tanks, over 400 cargo vessels, and nearly 500 escort vessels and mine sweepers.

Secondly, as in World War I, Canada's economy was strengthened by the war. In 1939, Canada still suffered the effects of the depression. Unemployment was widespread and the economy was just beginning to recover from the economic slump. By 1945 the Canadian economy was booming. The gross national production of goods tripled. Such materials as asbestos, aluminum, coal, manganese, chemicals, and paper, all contributed to the war and made Canada's industries expand rapidly. The production of key agricultural goods such as wheat, flour, bacon, ham, dried eggs, and canned meat and fish also underwent an economic boom.

Thirdly, the most striking consequence of the whole crisis was a new international status for Canada. Canada emerged from the war respected by the other nations of the world. At the same time, Canada seemed prepared to accept new responsibilities in maintaining worldwide peace. In a very real sense the war had assisted Canada in establishing its place as a "middle power" among nations.

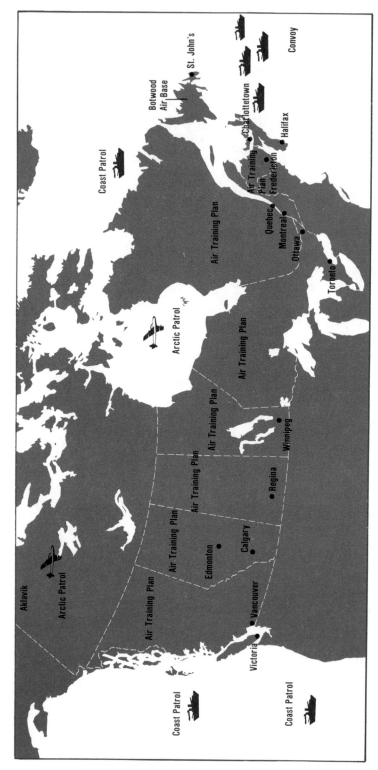

British Columbia

The products of BC's forests and rivers are turned to the war effort. The entire 1942 salmon catch was shipped to Britain. Pacific ports vie with Atlantic ports in shipbuilding.

The Pacific Coast Militia Rangers was formed when Japan entered the war. It is modelled after the Home Guard of Britain.

Prairies

The industrial resources of its towns and cities are working exclusively for the war effort. They are turning out guns, locomotives, uniforms etc.

Many world-famous pilots of the RAF and the RCAF have been trained in the Prairies.

Ontario

Ontario's car and farm-implement factories are manufacturing armoured vehicles, guns, and planes for the war effort. Many new plants have been created and are now producing planes, shells, explosives, and small arms.

Quebec

Quebec produces 75 percent of the asbestos used by the Allies. Aircraft, tanks, guns, shells, warships, and merchant vessels are produced in its industrial centres.

Fifty percent of Canada's newsprint is made in Quebec. It is a new source of strategic war metals and minerals.

Maritimes

Thirteen thousand vessels carrying 70 million metric tonnes of cargo have sailed from Canada's eastern ports to Britain. Ninety-nine percent of this tonnage has reached Britain.

Military Growth

Year		one unit = 4000 sailors
1939	◖	1800
1940	●●◖	14000
1941	●●●●◖	25 000
1942	●●●●●●●●◖	38 000
1943	●●●●●●●●●●●●●●●●◖	67 000

one unit = 50 warships

| 1939 | ◖ | 15 |
| 1943 | ●●●●●●●●●◖ | 500 |

one unit = 20 000 soldiers

1939	◖	4500
1942	●●●●●●●●●●●●●●●●●●●●◖	409 000
1943	●●●●●●●●●●●●●●●●●●●●●●◖	455 000

one unit = 10 000 pilots/crew

1939	◖	4000
1940	●●◖	22 500
1941	●●●●●●●◖	78 000
1942	●●●●●●●●●●●●◖	126 000
1943	●●●●●●●●●●●●●●●●●●●●	200 000

Women in Munitions

68 000	185 000	225 000
1941	1942	1943

Navy
1943
4000 women

Army Corps
1943
13 250 women

Air Force
1943
13 500 women

Increase in Output of Steel
Production
doubled

Prewar →

Increase in Output of Aluminum
Production
over six times

Prewar →

War Productions

1914–18	$1 002 672 413
1941	$1 200 000 000
1942	$2 600 000 000
1943	$3 700 000 000

The British Commonwealth Air Training Plan maintained 154 Flying Schools in Canada. Sixty percent of its graduates were Canadian.

The Canadian Red Cross Society
There were over 2 million members of the society. They sent 10 000 food parcels each week to prisoners of war.

Canada was manufacturing $1 billion in war materials and equipment for the United States. Canada was the fourth-largest producer of war supplies and equipment among the Allies.

DEVELOPING SKILLS:
UNDERSTANDING PROPAGANDA

Propaganda is the use of a publicity campaign to manipulate public opinion and attitudes. During World War II, both the Allies and the Axis powers used propaganda as part of their military strategy. It was often called psychological warfare. For the civilian population, propaganda was used to instill pride and confidence in their country, to inspire sacrifice, and to show the consequences of defeat. Propaganda also boosted military morale. It convinced soldiers that though they may have lost the battle the war was being won.

Nazi Germany's propaganda minister was Joseph Goebbels. His use of mass meetings, parades, and demonstrations to stir up support for the Nazi cause was unsurpassable. Adolf Hitler and Benito Mussolini were masters of propaganda. In their many public speeches, their great oratory skills convinced their citizens of the justness of the Axis cause.

The Allies also established a Psychological Warfare Division. In Canada, the Wartime Information Board was responsible for propaganda. The Wartime Information Board coloured the public's view of the war. It also started the first methodical use of public-opinion polls in Canada.

Propaganda generally appealed to peoples' emotions. Symbols, such as the flag, the family, the homeland, and the evil nature of the enemy, were used to influence the behaviour of people. It was believed that a picture was worth a thousand words. Therefore, posters were a popular form of propaganda. Film and radio were also used to spread the message.

Wartime propaganda was aimed at four main targets: enemies, Allies, neutrals, and the home front. When the enemy was the "target," propaganda emphasized eventual defeat. When aimed at the Allies, propaganda stressed unity, loyalty, and victory. For neutral countries, propaganda concentrated on the righteousness of their cause. On the home front, propaganda stressed the need for effort and sacrifice to attain victory.

A Thousand Words: The Propaganda War

Here are some examples of wartime propaganda. Examine the posters closely and answer the following quesitons.

1 Who is the intended target?
2 Who is the sender of the message?
3 What is the message of the poster?
4 What is the purpose of the poster?
5 How is the message relayed?
6 What is the effect of the poster?

In groups, try making propaganda posters. Here are some target suggestions.
- enemy — Nazi Germany or Japan
- Allies — Britain or France
- neutrals — the United States before 1941
- the home front — the conscription issue

DIGGING DEEPER

1   Is government propaganda necessary and important in wartime? Why? Is it important during peacetime? Why? What sorts of propaganda would you accept during peacetime?

2   During the Second World War many family farms and factories were run by Canadian women. What were the effects of the war effort on women's roles in society? What changes came about at the end of the war? Did these changes improve or hinder women's struggle for equality?

3   During the war the government established a day-care program for children whose mothers were working in war industries. How important do you think this program was in getting women involved in the war effort? Today there are over a half-million children under the age of six whose mothers work. What community services do you think should be offered to assist working mothers? Can society afford these services that allow women to work? Are these services seen as important priorities in your community?

4   Twice in the twentieth century the issue of conscription nearly tore the Canadian nation apart. Use an organizer to compare the two situations, and account for the different outcome of the 1944 crisis.

28
The Internment
of Japanese
Canadians

Shock and anger gripped the Canadian people when they heard the Japanese had attacked the American naval base at Pearl Harbor on 7 December 1941. That same night the Royal Canadian Mounted Police swept down on the Japanese community in British Columbia and began to make arrests. In the next few days thirty-eight "dangerous individuals" and "troublemakers" were rounded up. In the months that followed all Japanese nationals (people born in Japan but living in Canada) and Canadian citizens of Japanese descent were imprisoned under the Wartime Emergency Powers Act. They were taken from their homes, packed into trains, and usually sent to internment camps in the interior of British Columbia. The stronger men were assigned to work on road construction in northern British Columbia and Ontario. Others were used as farm labourers in the sugar beet fields of Alberta and Manitoba. Men who resisted were separated from their families and sent to a prisoner-of-war camp in Angler, Ontario.

It did not seem to matter to the Canadian government whether these people were born in Japan or Canada. In fact, more than 14 000 were second-generation Japanese born in this country. Another 3000 were naturalized Canadian citizens. There was no appreciation of the fact that 200 Japanese Canadians had fought in the Canadian army in World War I. Canada and Japan were at war, and all Japanese Canadians were considered to be potentially dangerous.

Japanese Canadians on their way to an internment camp

Most of the people of Japanese descent lived in British Columbia. Many owned small boats and fished for salmon along the British Columbia coast. Others worked in fish canneries or owned small plots of land where they grew fruit and vegetables for the Vancouver market. A few owned neighbourhood grocery stores or restaurants, or worked as domestic servants in the homes of the wealthy of Vancouver. Now their property was taken away and their businesses were ruined.

Discrimination was nothing new for the Japanese in Canada. The first known settler in Canada from Japan was Manzo Nagano. He is said to have stowed away on a British freighter docked at Nagasaki, not knowing where it was headed. When it stopped at New Westminster in May 1877, he jumped ship. Most of the early Japanese immigrants who followed Nagano to Canada came as labourers for the coal mines, lumber camps, and railways. Their intention was to make a fortune and return home. However, many ended up staying in Canada. Because there were few Japanese women to marry in Canada, marriages were arranged with women in Japan by using photographs. The women would later join husbands whom they had never seen. These women became known as "picture brides," and in 1913 some 300 to 400 women arrived through this kind of arrangement. Though many non-Japanese were shocked by this practice, it was consistent with Japanese custom. These marriages worked amazingly well because in Japan marriages were the joining of two families rather than just two individuals.

When they first arrived, Japanese immigrants in Canada were often praised for their hard work and eagerness. But their eventual success in farming and fishing alarmed and frightened many people in British Columbia. They were soon seen as tough competitors. Some citizens of British Columbia who felt their jobs might be threatened stirred up racist feelings against the Japanese. Racist feelings surfaced in Vancouver in 1907 when 5000 people attacked the Chinese and Japanese communities. Store windows were smashed and the crowd chanted "Down with the Japs" and "Keep Canada White." Japanese were excluded from higher-paying jobs in mining, denied the right to vote in British Columbia, and barred from the public service and professions.

It is probably not surprising that anti-Japanese feeling flared up again in British Columbia during the war. The shock of Pearl Harbor and the treatment of Canadian prisoners of war in Hong Kong turned Canadian public opinion against the Japanese Canadians. A Japanese-Canadian woman recalls how, on the day the war broke out, a man approached her on the street and spat in her face. Resentment was so bad that a Chinese woman wore a sign around her neck that said "I'm not a Jap, I'm Chinese."

Japanese in the fishing industry were the first group to be evacuated. Rumors that spread like wildfire suggested Canada

Japanese-Canadian fishing boats are confiscated.

would be attacked at any minute and that the Japanese were navy officers sent to spy on British Columbia waters. About 1200 fishing boats, that belonged to Japanese Canadians, were seized by the Canadian government and their owners sent to the interior of British Columbia. One person remembered:

> To this day I don't know what they thought about these fishing boats. They were our living. They were small boats made of wood. We had no radar, no radio, no echo sounder. Just tiny little vessels with their chuggy little motors and space for the fish we caught ... And they said we were charting the coast and waterways ... Why, we could go into Vancouver any time and buy British Admiralty charts of every single kilometre of the coast. But try and convince people that we were not spies, that we were not spying ... But oh no, no way. As far back as the late 1890s they had determined that they would kick the Japs off the water.

The RCMP was satisfied that the few Japanese who were possibly dangerous had already been arrested. The Canadian navy saw no problem now that the Japanese Canadians had been removed from the coast. The chief of the General Staff reported to the government, "I cannot see that they [Japanese Canadians] constitute the slightest menace to Canadian security." Still, politicians and British Columbia citizens were not satisfied. They continued to demand that all Japanese Canadians should be interned. In February 1942 the Canadian government decided to move all the Japanese Canadians away from the coast to inland centres. The government did this for two reasons: to prevent spying which could lead to an enemy invasion, and to protect Japanese Canadians from being harmed in anti-Japanese riots.

At first they were housed in the cow barns at Hastings Park in the Exhibition Grounds in Vancouver. Then most were sent by special trains to six ghost towns in the interior of British Columbia. They were allowed to take 68 kg of clothing, bedding, and cooking utensils for each adult. In towns such as New Denver, Slocan, ánd Greenwood, they were housed in crude frame huts. Two bedrooms and a kitchen had to be shared by two families. Until 1943 there was no electricity or running water. Living conditions were so bad that food packages from Japan were sent through the Red Cross to interned Canadians in British Columbia. In these remote communities they were kept under constant surveillance by the RCMP. Veterans of the First World War were also paid to watch over the settlement and report anything out of the ordinary. About 3650 Japanese Canadians were sent to work

An internment camp kitchen

A men's dining room in an internment camp

Checking the documents of Japanese Canadians

as farm labourers east of the Rocky Mountains. At Angler, Ontario the men were actually surrounded by barbed wire and guarded by veterans. Those considered to be the most dangerous were made to wear uniforms with red targets sewn on their backs.

When Japan surrendered, the Canadian government considered sending all Japanese Canadians back to Japan. This would have included many born in Canada who did not speak or understand any language except English. The deportation fortunately never took place because a number of Canadian citizens protested that this would be dishonourable and unfair to the Japanese Canadians. However, about 4000 decided to return to Japan in 1946.

Those who did remain in Canada did not have an easy time adjusting in the postwar years. Only a few went back to British Columbia. Instead they spread out across the country. Citizens of Japanese descent were finally given the right to vote federally in June 1948, and in British Columbia elections in 1949.

After the war, many of the Japanese Canadians were bitter when they found out that their land had been sold, often at a fraction of its value. They had been told that the government would hold their belongings in trust.

When we left we had to turn over our property to the Custodian of Enemy Property for safekeeping. Now that meant to us that when the war business was over we'd get our property back. Some just put everything in a bedroom and put a lock on the door and thought it would be safe. Some just left the stuff and people could walk in the take what they wanted. That happened. Oh yes. Often.

It was a terrible shock when we learned that this safekeeping business meant nothing, that all of our stuff had been sold at auction. There are people who were never told that they lost all their goods by confiscation because the Custodian just couldn't bother looking after it all. Others would get a cheque or a credit saying so much was due to them, but there were some people who got no money at all. Now that wasn't right. That safekeeping thing caused a lot of bitterness. People would say, 'That's all we had and now we've got nothing.' It made a lot of people pretty mad. First they take us from our homes and stick us in a dump, and now this.

One family's house sold for $50 at a government auction, and its contents for $8.50. One fishing boat sold for $150, a fraction of what it was worth. Most people felt that they received from the government between 5 percent and 10 percent of the real value of their property and possessions. In 1946 a Japanese Property Claims Commission was set up by the Canadian government. It was to review the claims of those who felt they had not been treated fairly for their confiscated property. Although in some cases additional money was made available, it never fully compensated for what had been lost.

DEVELOPING SKILLS:
IDENTIFYING AND CLARIFYING VALUES

A Child in a Prison Camp by Shizuye Takashima is the true story of a young Japanese-Canadian girl's experience in an internment camp during World War II. "Shichan," as she was known to her friends, has written of the three years during which she and her family were isolated in a camp. During the spring of 1944 she recorded a discussion her family had. They were trying to decide whether they should stay in Canada or go back to Japan.

Spring 1944
The war with Japan is getting very bad. I can feel my parents growing anxious. There is a lot of tension in the

camp; rumors of being moved again, of everyone having to return to Japan. Kazuo and his family leave for Japan. Many are angry they have left us. Some call them cowards, others call them brave! I only feel sad, for I liked Kazuo so much, so very much.

Father shouts at mother, "We return to Japan!" "But what are we going to do? You have your brothers and sisters there. I have no one. Besides, the children...." "Never mind the children," father answers. "They'll adjust. I'm tired of being treated as a spy, a prisoner. Do what you like; I'm returning!"

I can see Mrs. Kono looks confused. "My husband is talking of returning to Japan, too. I think it's the best thing. All our relatives are still there. We have nothing here." Yuki stares at her. "It's all right for you, Mrs. Kono, you were born there, but we weren't. I'm not going. That's all!" And she walks out of the house.

Mother gets very upset. I know she wants to cry. "I don't want to go to Japan, either," I say. "They're short of food and clothing there. They haven't enough for their own people. They won't want us back."

All of a sudden I hate that country for having started the war. I say aloud, "Damn Japs! Why don't they stop fighting?" Father glares. "What do you mean 'Japs'? You think you're not a Jap? If I hear you say that again I'll throttle you." I see anger and hatred in his eyes. I leave the room, go out of the house. I hear him say loudly to mother, "It's all your fault. You poison our children's minds by saying we're better off here."

And another argument starts. I am getting tired of it, and confused. I feel so helpless, and wish again I were older, than maybe I could go somewhere.... But I do not hate the people in Japan. I know Yuki doesn't hate them either, really. It's all so senseless. Really, maybe children should rule the world! Yuki tells me it is wrong for father, because of his anger at the wrong done towards him and us, to expect us to return to his country: "Sure, we're Japanese. But we think like Canadians. We won't be accepted in Japan if we go there."

A Child in Prison Camp
© 1971, Shizuye Takashima
published by Tundra Books of Montreal

1 What problems do Shichan's family face?
2 Describe what each member of the family would like to do.

3   Describe the behaviour of each member of the family. How does their behaviour relate back to their feelings about what is important to them?
4   Point out the ways in which the beliefs of mother, father, and Shichan are similar and different.
5   Suggest reasons why each person feels the way s/he does.
6   What other alternatives are available for the family?
7   Name some possible consequences for the family if they stay in Canada, or if they go back to Japan.
8   Pretend you are each of the people mentioned in the excerpt. What would you do about this situation?
9   Why did you decide on this course of action, and what might be some of the consequences you would have to face?
10   What do you think Shichan meant when she said, "Really maybe children should rule the world!"

DIGGING DEEPER

1   Should the internment of the Japanese Canadians have occurred? Why or why not? Who was responsible? What does this episode teach us about our Canadian society?
Do you think a minority group could be interned today? Why or why not?
Why were the Japanese Canadians interned and not the German Canadians?
Use an issue-analyis organizer to help you formulate an answer to these questions.
2   Role playing:
Role play a meeting in which the following people discuss whether the Japanese Canadians should be interned during World War II.

  a) Prime Minister Mackenzie King;
  b) Chief of the General Staff (General Stuart);
  c) a British Columbia politician;
  d) a Canadian-born leader of the Japanese community;
  e) a non-Japanese fisherman on the British Columbia coast;
  f) a representative of a British Columbia labour union;
  g) a lawyer interested in civil rights disputes;
  h) a person with a son in a Japanese prisoner-of-war camp;
  i) a citizen of British Columbia fearful of a Japanese attack on British Columbia.

3   Refer back to the matrix you started at the end of the second unit (page 103). You are now ready to add information for the time period 1939–1945. Trace the development of the same themes through World War II.

29
Plans for
Peace

On the decks of the giant US battleship *Missouri*, the Japanese formally surrendered to the American general, Douglas MacArthur. Eyewitnesses recalled the event. On the slate grey battleship, American admirals and generals, and British, Soviet, French, and Chinese military officials gathered for the signing ceremony. The Japanese foreign minister and the chief of the Imperial Staff were ushered on board. After a short speech by General MacArthur, they were led to a table and told to sign the Terms of Surrender. With expressionless faces, they put their signatures to a document that acknowledged the total defeat of Japan. General MacArthur then took a fountain pen from his pocket and placed his signature on behalf of the United States. MacArthur hesitated a moment, and then he stepped forward: "Let us pray that peace be now restored to the world, and that God will preserve it always."

Even before the war ended, the Allies started making plans for the peace that would follow the surrender of Germany and Japan. They agreed on the need for a new international organization to maintain peace and security after the war. The old League of Nations, formed to keep peace after World War I, had been a failure. Despite this failure, President Roosevelt of the United States, Prime Minister Churchill of Britain, and later General Secretary Stalin of the Soviet Union, were determined to set up an international organization where governments could settle differences that might otherwise lead to war. It was agreed that an international conference would be held at San Francisco in April 1945 to sign a formal charter or constitution.

Fifty nations took part in the San Francisco conference, including Canada. The preamble to the charter read: "We, the peoples of the United Nations, determined to save succeeding generations from the scourge of war, which twice in our lifetime has brought untold sorrow to mankind ... do hereby establish an international organization to be known as the United Nations." The member nations agreed to band together to remove any threat to world peace (collective security). They further promised to give economic, military, and political help to improve world conditions and to establish world peace and security. Canada believed in this idea of collective security. The two world wars had emphasized the need for nations to stand together against any kind of aggression (hostile, war-like acts). By signing the charter, Canada offered money and resources on the side of peace.

The United Nations has six major parts. The chart illustrates the organization: The General Assembly, Security Council, the Secretariat, Economic and Social Council, International Court of Justice, and the Trusteeship Council.

Canada's ambassador to the UN, Stephen Lewis

The General Assembly

The General Assembly is made up of all the member nations that belong to the United Nations. Each member pays a share of the cost of the United Nations, depending on its ability to pay. The General Assembly discusses and debates such problems as aid to developing countries and international use of the sea. It suggests ways of settling disputes that arise in various parts of the world. Each nation has one vote. If the General Assembly votes for UN action on a matter, it is turned over to the Security Council to be decided.

The Security Council

The real centre of power in the United Nations is the Security Council. It has the authority to take military or other action to maintain peace and security. Five nations are permanent members of the Security Council – the United States, the USSR, Britain, France, and the People's Republic of China. These powerful nations are known as the "Big Five." Ten non-permanent members are elected to the Security Council by the General Assembly for a term of two years. Canada has served four times, most recently in 1978.

The "Big Five" must approve all the major decisions of the Security Council. In other words, each of these five powers can veto or block Council decisions. When the UN Charter was drafted, these powerful nations demanded veto right. They argued that since they would have to provide most of the military security forces, they had the right to block any action they disliked. It was hoped that the veto power would seldom be used, but unfortunately this has not been the case. Many people think this veto power is a serious weakness in times of crisis.

The Secretariat

About 4000 workers from all parts of the world form the Secretariat or the working staff of the UN. It is headed by the Secretary-General who is nominated by the Security Council and elected by the General Assembly. S/he is the chief administrator and must co-ordinate the activities of the UN in all parts of the world.

The Economic and Social Council

The Economic and Social Council works for world peace by trying to eliminate the economic and social conditions that could cause war. In the days that immediately followed World War II this council concentrated on providing relief for war refugees. Later, it introduced programs to raise living standards and promote human rights. Many agencies set up by the Economic and Social Council carry out its goals. One of the most important agencies is the United Nations Educational, Scientific, and Cultural Organization (UNESCO). It has built schools, research facilities, and cultural centres in many of the underdeveloped areas of the world. Another is UNICEF, the United Nations International Children's Emergency Fund. Money collected on Hallowe'en is used to help children in war-ravaged countries and in places that have been struck by floods and other natural disasters. The World Health Organization (WHO) is concerned with problems of world health and medical research.

The International Court of Justice

This court was set up to settle disputes between nations in a peaceful manner. Unfortunately no member can be compelled to attend. However, the court does rule on cases in which the member nations have agreed to abide by its decision.

The Trusteeship Council

The Trusteeship Council was set up to take care of those colonies taken from the defeated countries of both world wars. Many of these colonies were in Africa. The goal of the council is to administer the trusteeships until they can become independent. At present only one trust territory remains: the Pacific Islands once owned by Japan.

It was hoped in 1945 that the United Nations Organization would be able to avoid the problems experienced by the League of Nations. President Roosevelt was determined that this time the United States would join the world organization. The USA was now the greatest power in the world and led the way in supporting the UN. The permanent headquarters of the United Nations was built in New York City. American participation, as well as that of the USSR, made the UN much stronger than the old League had been. The UN was further strengthened by the fact that it had the power to use military force if necessary. The League of Nations never had such a provision.

In the League, unanimous approval was required of all members before action could be taken. The UN is stronger because its Security Council may act if a majority (including each of the "Big Five") approves an action.

The other great strength of the United Nations was that it recognized that world peace depended on more than taking

THE UNITED NATIONS SYSTEM

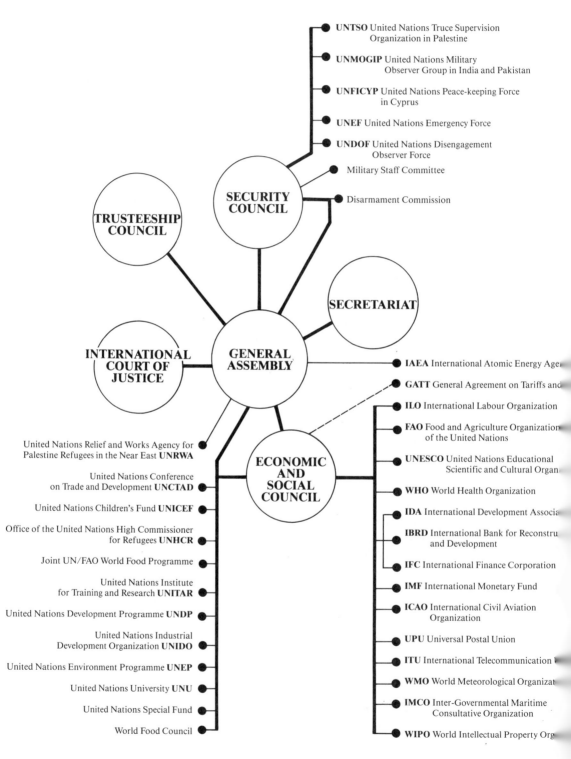

UNTSO United Nations Truce Supervision Organization in Palestine

UNMOGIP United Nations Military Observer Group in India and Pakistan

UNFICYP United Nations Peace-keeping Force in Cyprus

UNEF United Nations Emergency Force

UNDOF United Nations Disengagement Observer Force

Military Staff Committee

Disarmament Commission

SECURITY COUNCIL

TRUSTEESHIP COUNCIL

SECRETARIAT

INTERNATIONAL COURT OF JUSTICE

GENERAL ASSEMBLY

IAEA International Atomic Energy Age

GATT General Agreement on Tariffs and

ILO International Labour Organization

FAO Food and Agriculture Organization of the United Nations

UNESCO United Nations Educational Scientific and Cultural Organ

WHO World Health Organization

IDA International Development Associa

IBRD International Bank for Reconstru and Development

IFC International Finance Corporation

IMF International Monetary Fund

ICAO International Civil Aviation Organization

UPU Universal Postal Union

ITU International Telecommunication

WMO World Meteorological Organizat

IMCO Inter-Governmental Maritime Consultative Organization

WIPO World Intellectual Property Org

ECONOMIC AND SOCIAL COUNCIL

United Nations Relief and Works Agency for Palestine Refugees in the Near East **UNRWA**

United Nations Conference on Trade and Development **UNCTAD**

United Nations Children's Fund **UNICEF**

Office of the United Nations High Commissioner for Refugees **UNHCR**

Joint UN/FAO World Food Programme

United Nations Institute for Training and Research **UNITAR**

United Nations Development Programme **UNDP**

United Nations Industrial Development Organization **UNIDO**

United Nations Environment Programme **UNEP**

United Nations University **UNU**

United Nations Special Fund

World Food Council

united action against aggression. For this reason the Economic and Social Council, with its many agencies, set out to attack the problems that could lead to war: poverty, disease, energy needs, food and water shortage, pollution, and unemployment.

DIGGING DEEPER

1   Select one of the agencies of the United Nations (such as UNESCO, UNICEF, and WHO). Do some research to find out what work the agency does. You may wish to write to the Information Division of the United Nations, New York City, for particular details. Present a short report to your class where you describe the agency's functions and evaluate its achievements.

2   In the left-hand column are five weaknesses of the League of Nations. In the right-hand column describe the features of the United Nations that try to correct the weaknesses of the League.

3   Some people have said that the Economic and Social Council of the United Nations has done more for world peace than the Security Council. Do some research on the work of the Economic and Social Council in order to explain what they mean. Do you agree with this opinion? Why or why not? Why is the Security Council often unable to take action when conflicts break out between nations?

4   Refer back to the matrix you started at the end of the second unit. Add information for the time period 1939–1945. Trace the development of the same themes through this unit on World War II.

30
Canada in the Postwar World

On the night of 5 September 1945 an international drama began to unfold in Ottawa. Igor Gouzenko was a young clerk in the Soviet embassy in Ottawa. He decided to defect and live permanently in Canada. He smuggled 109 top-secret documents out of the embassy under his shirt. His idea was to turn the secrets over to authorities in return for a new start in life in Canada.

For thirty-six hours no one would take Gouzenko seriously. A member of Prime Minister King's staff even suggested that he return to the Soviet embassy and replace the documents! By this time Gouzenko was desperate. The theft had been discovered and Soviet embassy officials had broken into Gouzenko's apartment. Fortunately, a neighbour called the Ottawa police. They arrived just as Gouzenko was being hustled away by the Soviets. Finally the RCMP were convinced that Gouzenko was telling the truth.

Igor Gouzenko

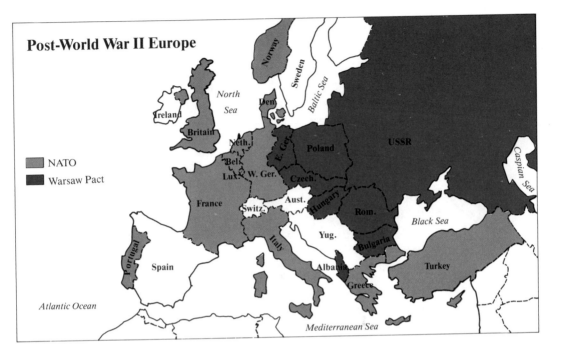

Post-World War II Europe

NATO

Warsaw Pact

Norway

Sweden

Baltic Sea

North Sea

Den

Ireland

Britain

Neth.

E. Ger.

Poland

USSR

Caspian Sea

Bel.

Lux.

W. Ger.

Czech.

France

Switz.

Aust.

Hungary

Rom.

Black Sea

Italy

Yug.

Bulgaria

Portugal

Spain

Albania

Turkey

Greece

Atlantic Ocean

Mediterranean Sea

The documents Igor Gouzenko turned over contained shocking information. They revealed that a massive spy ring was operating in North America out of the Soviet embassy in Ottawa. From the files provided by Gouzenko, the police were able to discover several top agents working in Canada, the United States, and Britain. In Canada the agents included two colonels, a navy officer, a squadron leader, a member of Parliament, and clerks in government offices. In the United States and Britain the trail led to the arrest of scientists who had worked on the first atomic bomb. Since the United States was the only nation that had the atomic bomb, the USSR was desperate to have atomic information.

Canadians were shocked by the news. They were most astounded that the USSR, a former wartime ally, was spying on its friends. But nations that are allies during a war often quarrel when the war is over. They become rivals for the control of the nations they have defeated. This was certainly true after the end of World War II. Both the United States and the USSR came out of the war as superpowers, stronger than any of the other nations. They could be expected to compete to establish influence over defeated countries. The huge Soviet army poured into Eastern Europe. By the end of the war, the USSR had engulfed 22 million people. Since 1939, they had increased their territory by almost 500 square km. Germany, Czechoslovakia, and Poland had been forced to give land to the USSR at the peace conference. The USSR was the leading communist nation and seemed determined to spread communism into the countries of eastern Europe it had taken over from Germany. The United States worried that the spread of communism would mean strict government control over the lives of people in eastern Europe. In Britain, Winston Churchill said that the Russians were stretching an "iron curtain" of secrecy around eastern Europe. A vastly enlarged USSR was surrounded by Iron Curtain countries who took their orders from Moscow. This was the beginning of the "Cold War."

The term "Cold War" originally meant that the two superpowers would try to defeat each other by any means short of actual fighting. It would be a "cold," not a "hot" war. The Cold War has, however, included several armed conflicts. But there has never been an actual declaration of war between the United States and the USSR.

The first open clash in the Cold War was in 1947. It was caused by events in Greece and Turkey. In Greece political confusion followed World War II. Greek communists were struggling with supporters of the Greek king for control of the government. The USSR was helping the Greek communists. At the same time Stalin was trying to seize oil-rich lands on the Black Sea in Turkey.

President Harry Truman announced that the United States would help Greece and Turkey and any other nation threatened by communism. The United States would follow a policy of "containment." They would try to "contain" or stop the spread of communism anywhere in the world. This policy became known as the Truman Doctrine. With American military and economic help, Greece and Turkey were both able to resist communist pressures at this time.

There were, however, serious problems in other parts of Europe as well. Much of Europe lay in ruins after World War II. The United States was determined to help rebuild Europe and stop the influence of the USSR.

The American secretary of State, George C. Marshall, announced the European Recovery Plan, or the Marshall Plan, as it is now known. This was a huge self-help program of American economic aid for Europe. Vast amounts of machinery, raw materials, food, and building supplies were sent to help Europe recover from the war. Canada was already giving aid to Europe, but welcomed the opportunity to assist in the Marshall Plan. In the first year (1948), Canada shipped $706 million in goods to war-torn countries. During the five years of the plan, $13.5 billion of supplies were given to sixteen European nations by the United States and Canada. As western Europe recovered and became

Louis St. Laurent (second from right) at a NATO meeting, 1952

more prosperous, the possibility of a communist takeover faded.

The war had given a tremendous boost to the Canadian economy. Our great natural wealth meant that we were one of the few nations who could help the war-shattered world. There was a marked change in Canada's foreign policy following World War II. A country's foreign policy is the way it handles its relations with other countries. It is designed to achieve certain national goals such as trade, friendship, defence, commerce, and immigration. Following the war there seemed to be a new willingness for Canada to play an active part in great events on the world scene. Prime Minister King was determined that Canada would play an important part in the postwar world. Obviously Canada could not influence international politics as much as the great powers – the United States, the USSR, Britain, France, and China. But neither was Canada a small, weak, or unimportant country. Because of Canada's natural resources, military might, size, and political stability, Canadians looked at their country as a "middle power." King established a foreign policy to help make Canada a middle power.

Canada's foreign policy from 1945–1959 was based on four major areas of concern:

1   support of the North Atlantic Treaty Organization for defence;
2   support of the United Nations to promote world peace;
3   co-operation with the United States in continental defence;
4   co-operation within a strong Commonwealth.

Canada and NATO

The year 1948 was a crucial one in the Cold War. The USSR was continuing to expand, first by trying to take control of the city of Berlin, and then by moving their troops into position to seize Czechoslovakia. The United States, Canada, and other Western powers viewed this expansion with alarm. They decided to take joint action to defend themselves.

On 4 April 1949 the North Atlantic Treaty Organization (NATO) was formed. Twelve nations signed the treaty. They were Belgium, Britain, Canada, Denmark, France, Iceland, Italy, Luxembourg, Netherlands, Norway, Portugal, and the United States. (By 1955 these countries had been joined by Greece, Turkey, and West Germany.)

Canada's Prime Minister St. Laurent, who followed Mackenzie King, was an early supporter of a defence alliance. St. Laurent realized that the weakness of the United Nations was that it had no permanent armed force of its own. The UN was not able to defend Canada against a possible Soviet threat. St. Laurent said in the House of Commons, "We are fully aware ... of the inadequacy of the United Nations at the present moment to provide the nations of the world with the security which they require." Canada's contribution to NATO has cost hundreds of millions of dollars in armed forces and military equipment.

The NATO alliance committed its members to collective security. This meant a kind of safety in numbers. All members banded together and promised to defend each other in the event of an attack. An attack on one member was considered an attack against all. Thus it was hoped that the combined strength of the NATO alliance would discourage the USSR from taking any hostile action against NATO members.

The USSR responded in 1955 to the creation of NATO by forming its own military alliance, the Warsaw Pact. Its members were the USSR, Albania, Bulgaria, Czechoslovakia, East Germany, Hungary, Poland, and Romania. Thus in 1955 Europe was again divided into two hostile camps – NATO and the Warsaw Pact.

Support of the United Nations

Canada was one of the original signers of the Charter of the United Nations. It was dedicated to supporting UN activities. When war broke out in Korea in 1950, Canada showed it was willing to help the United Nations keep peace in the world.

The Korean War was the first real test of the UN's peacekeeping ability. The Koreans had been an independent people for centuries. They had been taken over by Japan in the early 1900s. When

Korea was liberated at the end of World War II, the Soviet army occupied the northern half of the country. A communist government was established there. American troops occupied the southern half. The 38°N parallel was the border. The United Nations had been trying to reunite the Koreas with no success.

In June 1950 a powerful North Korean army invaded South Korea. It seemed likely that the heavily armed North Koreans would take over the entire country.

The matter was brought to an emergency meeting of the Security Council of the United Nations. At that moment the Soviet delegate was refusing to attend (boycotting) the Security Council. The USSR was, therefore, not able to exercise its veto power. The Security Council agreed to take action. It ordered North Korea to withdraw its forces. It called on members to send military forces to Korea. General Douglas MacArthur was appointed to command these UN troops. Most troops were from the United States, but other nations, including Canada, did contribute to the peacekeeping effort. Canada sent one infantry brigade, three naval destroyers, and an air transport squadron, about 8000 soldiers in all. (Four hundred and six Canadians were killed in the Korean War, and over one thousand were wounded.) Canada had shown the world that it was prepared to play a responsible role as a middle power.

Princess Patricia's Light Infantry

The Korean War ended in 1953 with a truce. Both sides agreed to stop fighting. The United Nations' action had saved South Korea. However, the war did not succeed in uniting the two Koreas. Both sides were back to a line approximately where they had started in 1950.

In 1956 a situation arose which could easily have developed into a major war between the superpowers. Egypt's head of state, Colonel Nasser, decided to take over the Suez Canal. The canal was a vital trade route in the Middle East. Ships could travel from the Mediterranean Sea to the Red Sea and Indian Ocean through the Suez Canal. The Egyptian action greatly alarmed Israel, Britain, and France. These nations retaliated by attacking Egypt. The USSR threatened to send missiles for use by Egypt. The United States warned that it would step in if the USSR intervened. A very dangerous chain reaction was building up.

Frantic activity took place at the United Nations. Members desperately looked for a way to reduce the tension. Lester B. Pearson was at that time Canadian Secretary of State of External Affairs. Pearson persuaded the General Assembly to order all foreign troops out of Egypt. Then he convinced the UN to set up a United Nations Emergency Force (UNEF). This would be an international police force. It would be positioned between the rival armies.

The UNEF was Pearson's brainchild. Its members were to be drawn from middle powers who had no personal interest in the dispute. The force would not fight unless attacked. Instead, it would observe, investigate, mediate, and report back to the UN General Assembly. The force would be composed of 6000 soldiers. One thousand were Canadians. Major-General E.L.M. Burns of Canada would command the UN force.

In the days that followed, Egypt, Israel, Britain, and France obeyed the ceasefire. The UNEF succeeded in bringing peace to the Middle East. Much credit for this success must be given to Lester Pearson. For this achievement, Pearson was awarded the Nobel Peace Prize in 1957. It was a great honour for him and for Canada.

In his Nobel address, Pearson referred to the relationship of peace and people, "In the end, the whole problem always returns to people ... to one person and his own individual response to the challenge that confronts him."

Co-operation with the United States in Defence

By the mid-1950s, both the United States and the USSR had developed guided missiles that could carry nuclear warheads capable of wiping out a large city. One ten-megaton hydrogen

Lester B. Pearson (left) receiving the Nobel Peace Prize, December 1957

bomb was at least forty times more powerful than the atomic bomb dropped on Hiroshima. Lying directly between the USSR and the United States, Canada was located in an important position. Missiles fired from the USSR at the United States could reach their target in a matter of hours. Since the USSR's missiles would probably be fired across the North Pole, a means of early detection would have to be found. Suddenly the Canadian Arctic became of immense strategic importance.

The permanent Joint Board of Defence was reorganized. Three chains of radar stations were built to detect an air invasion of North America. The Pinetree Radar System was built along the Canadian-American border. Along the 55°N parallel was the Mid-Canada Line, and the Distant Early Warning Line (DEW) was situated along the Arctic coastline. Ships and aircraft provided radar surveillance on both the Atlantic and Pacific coasts.

This co-operation between Canada and the United States was further increased in 1958. The North American Air Defence Command (NORAD) was set up. NORAD brought the air defence of the two countries into a fully-integrated joint command. The commander is an American, the deputy-commander is a Canadian. Deep within the Cheyenne Mountain in Colorado the operation centre for NORAD was constructed. If there was a nuclear attack by the USSR, the defence of North America would be directed from NORAD headquarters. From here nuclear missiles could be fired in retaliation against the USSR. It was hoped that the NORAD defences would keep the USSR from ever striking North America.

Co-operation within a Strong Commonwealth

The Commonwealth of Nations grew out of the old British Empire. Many of Britain's former colonies, like Canada, were gaining their independence. However, they chose to stay together in a voluntary organization of independent states known as the Commonwealth. All the member nations acknowledged the British monarch as head of the Commonwealth, though not necessarily the head of state of all member countries. Some countries, like Canada, kept the monarch as the head of the government. Others established their own monarchs or became republics with no monarchs. Countries of many different languages, religions, races, and cultures share membership in the Commonwealth.

Canadians have one of the highest standards of living of all the Commonwealth countries. Therefore Canada has done a great deal to give economic aid to all parts of the Commonwealth. In 1950 the Colombo Plan was set up by India, Pakistan, Ceylon, Australia, New Zealand, and Britain. The organization was later joined by Canada, the United States, Japan, and a number of countries in Southeast Asia. Its purpose was to give technical and financial help to developing countries in Asia.

It was hoped that through the Colombo Plan living standards throughout Asia would be improved. Canada has been a major supporter of the plan. In the first year $25 million was pledged for factories and equipment. A nuclear power generating plant was given to India, a cement factory to Pakistan, and aid in irrigation and transportation systems was given to several countries. Under the plan Canadian universities, governments, and industries have educated students from developing countries. Thousands of young people have studied medicine, forestry, education, agriculture, and administration. By 1973 Canada had contributed $2 billion to the Colombo Plan.

DIGGING DEEPER

1   Following is a list of terms used in this chapter:

middle power	superpower
Truman Doctrine	foreign policy
Cold War	Colombo Plan
Marshall Plan	Warsaw Pact

Use each term correctly in a sentence to show you understand its meaning.

2   What were the goals of the Truman Doctrine and the Marshall Plan? How successful were these policies?

3   Germany was defeated and heavily damaged at the end of World War II. Was the United States wise to help rebuild Germany and make it an ally? Explain your point of view.

4   Why was the Korean War called an international police action? Did its outcome strengthen or weaken the security of the world? Explain your answer.

5   To broaden your understanding of Canada's role as a peace-keeper, individual students or groups can investigate one or more of the operations in which Canada played a part. Research could be summarized in an organizer form under the headings:

- causes;
- Canada's role;
- Canada's impact during the crisis;
- significance for Canada.

6   Canada is a member of both the United Nations and NATO. What are the arguments for and against our memberhips in these organizations?

7   Discuss how Canada's foreign policy between 1945 and 1959 might have affected the attitudes of people in other countries to Canadians.

8   Are there any advantages in having the United States responsible for Canada's defence? What are the disadvantages?

9   Do some research on the Commonwealth:

- On a world map, mark the location of the Commonwealth countries.
- Why was it founded?
- Which nations have joined since it was founded and why?
- Which nations have left since it was founded and why?
- What does the Commonwealth do today?
- What advantages and disadvantages are there for Canada in being a member of the Commonwealth?

10   Debate: Canada should help the poor people in our own country instead of sending foreign aid to faraway countries.

31
Confident Canada: Growing and Prospering

NEW CANADIANS

In 1945, refugee camps in Europe were filled with hundreds of thousands of people. Many had seen their homes destroyed and their families separated. Many had survived the Nazi concentration camps. Thousands saw their homelands now being taken over by the Soviets, and refused to live under communist rule.

Even after the war ended, shortages and hardships remained a way of life in Europe. Families lived among the ruins of bombed-out buildings. A few lumps of coal, a bar of soap, or a small package of coffee were considered luxuries. It was almost impossible to obtain any kind of meat, and desperately needed medicines were in very short supply.

At the United Nations the refugees were known as "displaced persons." In Canada they were often referred to intolerantly as DPs. Gradually, though, Canada began to open its doors to welcome an increasing number of displaced persons. All through the 1930s and early 1940s Canada's immigration policy had been very restrictive. That is, Canada had only been accepting people from white Commonwealth countries. When only 7576 immigrants came to Canada in 1942, it marked the lowest number to arrive since 1860. Now that the war was over, Canada began to return to an open door policy. For one thing, Canada needed trained people for postwar development. But the policy was also changed for humanitarian reasons. The suffering of so many thousands in Europe could not be allowed to continue. In the year 1948, 50 000 refugees immigrated to Canada. Immigration played an important role in the expansion of Canada's population after the war. Starting slowly with war brides and displaced persons, the flow built up in the decade of the 1950s. In 1957 it reached 282 164 people, the highest total since 1913.

The first to arrive in Canada were the war brides with their children. This is not too surprising, considering that one in five Canadian soldiers who went overseas as bachelors came home married. In late 1944, the first of 40 000 war brides began arriving in this country. Twenty thousand children were brought along with them.

The Canadian Wives' Bureau was set up in London, England to prepare the war brides for their new life in Canada. Charlotte Whitton, at that time a social worker, wrote a brochure which was given to all war brides overseas. It was full of practical information for women about living in Canada. It included such items as tips on how to order from the mail-order catalogue and the sleeping arrangements on Canadian trains. The Red Cross and the YWCA also did their part to help the war brides settle in. But all the help in the world could not prepare some of them for what they found upon arriving in Canada. Many Canadian men had exaggerated how well-off they were at home. Many a war bride arrived expecting to find the modern home she had been promised. Instead she

British war brides arriving in Canada

found herself alone on an isolated farm with no conveniences. Other women had to live with in-laws who were complete strangers until their husbands returned home from Europe. A few of the war brides were so homesick and discouraged that they went back to their own country. However, most stayed, adjusted, and took up their new lives in Canada.

Two war brides remember their first impressions of Canada.

> I really hadn't the slightest idea what to expect when I arrived in Quebec. We stayed three months in St. Jean and then moved to Drummondville where we settled. Of course, I'd known that my husband was a French-speaking Canadian, but it was quite a shock to find that his relatives spoke no English at all. Although his family was a bit put out that he'd married une Anglaise (and a Protestant one at that), they were very good to me.

> My husband and I had two great days in Saskatoon when I arrived. We'd never had a real honeymoon in England, and those two days were all we could afford. Then we took the train to his home town, Birsay, Saskatchewan. At that time it was an all-day trip to cover the 160 kilometres. What a welcome awaited us at Birsay station. I felt like the Queen of England! All the people of the village and surrounding farm area were there to welcome me. I met my in-laws, two lovely people who still had their York-shire accents.

In the two decades after World War II, more than 2.5 million people came to Canada as immigrants. Although about one-fifth went on to settle in other countries, the majority stayed and lived in Canada. The largest group came from Great Britain, followed by Italy, the United States, Germany, Greece, Portugal, Poland, and the Netherlands.

Both of these last two groups had strong wartime connections with Canada. The Polish army had fought alongside the Canadians in northwest Europe and Italy. Polish fliers had trained in Canada, and after the war, many Polish refugees decided to make Canada their home. Doctors, lawyers, engineers, and highly trained technical people were among the Polish immigrants. Many took jobs as dishwashers and janitors, and worked very hard in order to get established in Canada.

The Dutch also had a soft spot in their hearts for Canada. Canadians had helped to liberate Holland from the Nazis. Crown Princess Juliana of the Netherlands had lived in Ottawa during the war. A room in the Ottawa Civic Hospital had been declared

Dutch territory so that her third daughter could be born on "Dutch soil." After the war 30 000 Dutch people – mostly farmers – began to arrive in Canada. For years Holland expressed its gratitude to Canada with an annual gift of tulip bulbs which bloom in the springtime in the parks of Ottawa.

There was one very important difference between the immigrants of Laurier's time and those who came after World War II. Most of the latter settled in urban centres in central Canada or British Columbia. At the opening of the century, immigrants had settled largely in rural areas. Ontario received about 50 percent of the mid-century immigrants, Quebec 25 percent, British Columbia 10 percent, and the combined prairie provinces about 12 percent. Only 3 percent settled in the Atlantic region. The typical immigrant of the early 1900s had been a farmer or a labourer. The immigrant of the late 1940s and early 1950s was usually a skilled worker or a professional person.

A NEW PRIME MINISTER: LOUIS ST. LAURENT 1948 – 1957

Mackenzie King had led Canada through the Second World War. In fact he had been prime minister longer than anyone in the Commonwealth. He had been leader of the Liberal party since 1919, when he had been chosen to succeed Sir Wilfrid Laurier. But by now he was tired and sick, and in 1948 King gave up the leadership of the party. When he retired, a long era in Canadian politics ended.

The following are some assessments of Mackenzie King. Which would you agree with and why? Which do you disagree with and why?

> "Very few people it would seem had loved King; not many even liked him; but vast numbers had voted for him."
> "He has been hated and adored. My own guess is that historians will not be able to deny him the elements of great statesmanship."
> "He left Canada a more independent community than he had found it."
> "His zeal for national unity . . . helped to prevent an explosion that would have made things much worse."
> "He had some unpleasant characteristics."
> "King was at his best when the political storms were at their worst."
> "He genuinely believed he was doing good things for the people and for the nation."

Louis St. Laurent was the second French-Canadian prime minister in Canadian history. He had been a prominent corporation lawyer in Quebec City who had come to Ottawa and entered politics out of a wartime sense of duty. He was fluently bilingual. His popularity in Quebec had greatly helped Prime Minister King and the Liberals to carry that province during the conscription crisis in 1944. During the federal election campaign of 1949, St. Laurent spent so much time patting the heads of small children and kissing babies that a reporter had nicknamed him "Uncle Louis." The nickname stuck with St. Laurent and conveyed the image of a kindly, elderly gentleman.

A New Province: Newfoundland Joins Confederation

On 1 April 1949, Newfoundland, including Labrador, became Canada's tenth province. It is said that some people on that island hung black flags out the window and wore black armbands in protest. Others gathered in community halls to celebrate becoming Canadians.

Newfoundlanders had flatly rejected Confederation in 1867, preferring to keep up their historic ties with Britain. Sir John A. Macdonald was disappointed when Newfoundland rejected Confederation. He had once remarked, "The Dominion cannot be considered complete without Newfoundland. It has the key to our front door."

Since 1855 Newfoundland had been self-governing. The world-wide depression of the 1930s, however, had hit the island very hard. The government went broke and had to accept British administration and assistance. After World War II, Joseph R. Smallwood began to urge fellow Newfoundlanders that it was time to join Canada. Smallwood, a former organizer of a fishermen's union, publisher, and radio personality, became the driving force for Confederation. It was a tough fight. The anti-Confederationists warned that it would mean the end of Newfoundland. Confederation would bring economic ruin. The Roman Catholic Church feared that Confederation would mean the end of Roman Catholic education. But Joey Smallwood held out the promise of the baby bonus. Newfoundland families were large families. A family of nine or ten was not considered overly large. The promise of a monthly allowance from the Canadian government for each child seemed like a fortune to most Newfoundlanders. Indeed in 1949 conditions for most people were poor by any standard. There was a shortage of schools, hospitals, roads, and jobs. If Newfoundlanders believed Joey Smallwood, all they would have to do would be to join Canada and then sit back and wait for the cheques to arrive!

Joey Smallwood

Are You in This List?

To All Mothers: Confederation would mean that never again would there be a hungry child in Newfoundland. If you have children under the age of 16, you will receive every month a cash allowance for every child you have or may have.

To All War Veterans: Canada treats her Veterans better than any other country in the world. She has just increased their War Pensions 25 percent. Under Confederation you will be better treated than under any other form of government.

To All Wage-Workers: All wage-workers will be protected by Unemployment Insurance. Newfoundland, under Confederation, will be opened up and developed. Your country will be prosperous. Your condition will be better.

To All Over 65: You would have something to look forward to at the age of 70. The Old Age Pension of $30 a month for yourself, and $30 a month for your wife ($60 a month between you) will protect you against need in your old age.

To All Railroaders: You will become employees of the biggest railway in the world, the C.N.R. You will have security and stability as C.N.R. employees. Your wages and working conditions will be the same as on the C.N.R. Under any other government you face sure and certain wage-cuts and lay-offs. You, your wives and sons and daughters and other relatives should flock out on June 3 and vote for Confederation.

To All Building Workers: Under Confederation Newfoundland will share fully in the Canadian Government Housing Plan, under which cities and towns are financed to build houses. 1000 new homes will be built in St. John's under this Plan.

To All Light Keepers: You will become employees of the Government of Canada. Your wages and working conditions will be greatly improved. You will be treated just the same as the light-keepers in the 5 Canadian light-houses already in Newfoundland.

To All Postal-Telegraph Workers: You will all become employees of the Government of Canada, at higher salaries and much better working conditions.

To All Customs Officials: You will become employees of the Government of Canada, at better salaries and much better working conditions.

To All Gander Workers: You who are now employed by the Newfoundland Government will become employees of the Government of Canada. The Department of Transport of the Government of Canada will operate Gander. They will not try to make Gander pay by cutting you down and trying to make you pay the costs of operating the Airport. Everybody on Gander will be better off under Confederation.

To All Fishermen: The cost of living will come down. The cost of producing fish will come down. The Government of Canada will stand back of our fisheries. The Fish Prices Support Board of Canada, backed by Canada's millions, will protect the price of your fish.

To All Newfoundlanders: The cost of living will come down. The 120 000 children in our country will live better. The 10 000 Senior Citizens of our country will be protected in their old age. Newfoundland will be linked up with a strong, rich British nation. Newfoundland will go ahead with Canada.

The Confederate, May 31, 1948

In a direct public vote on the issue (referendum), Newfoundlanders voted by a narrow majority – 52 percent to 48 percent – to join Canada. Smallwood was appointed the province's premier. By the terms of union, Newfoundland received the same financial benefits as other provinces as well as special assistance because of its unstable economy and low standard of public services. The federal government took over the island's public debt and the operation of the Newfoundland Railway.

NEW PROSPERITY

A tall pillar of flame and smoke shot up into the Alberta winter sky. The crowd of oil workers, geologists, and officials let out a whoop and a cheer. It was 13 February 1947, and the fabulous Leduc Number 1 oil well near Edmonton had just come in. That day a new stage in Alberta's oil and gas boom began.

Oil company crews had been exploring for oil intensively in the West since 1913. But until the Leduc strike about 90 percent of

Drilling for oil on the Prairies

Canada's total output was coming from the Turner Valley near Calgary and Norman Wells in the Northwest Territories. By 1947 Turner Valley production was falling off by about 10 percent a year. Thus, when Leduc Number 1 started pumping, oil hysteria swept the country again. Almost overnight sleepy little towns near Edmonton became boom towns. Soon more than 1200 wells were steadily producing in the Leduc area.

In a sense Leduc marked the beginning of the postwar economic boom in Canada. However oil was just one of the natural resources that led to the dynamic growth of Canada's economy after 1945.

In every area of economic activity new production records were set. At no time before had Canada experienced such tremendous expansion. When the Ungava Peninsula in northern Quebec became the centre of high-grade iron ore mining operations, tent cities sprang up overnight in the bush. A great aluminum smelter

was built at Kitimat far up the British Columbia coast. Construction began on a railway to Great Slave Lake to assist the development of mining resources in the Northwest Territories. Uranium from northern Saskatchewan, and from Elliot Lake and near Bancroft in Ontario went into the production of new American nuclear weapons. Britain and the United States contracted to buy as much uranium as Canada could produce. Potash development in Saskatchewan did much to improve the economy of that province in the 1950s and 1960s. The construction of refineries, processing plants, and the world's longest oil and gas pipeline added to the prosperity of Canada.

During the postwar economic expansion in Canada new resources began to take the place of the old ones. For a long time wheat had been Canada's leading export. Now wheat stood in third place in Canada's trading list. Newsprint and lumber moved into first place. Next came resources that were unknown or reasonably unimportant exports before World War II – uranium, natural gas, oil, iron ore, and chemical products. With the development of these new resources Canada's economy became much more diversified.

Exports and Imports (1958)	
Major Exports from Canada	**Major Imports to Canada**
newsprint	machinery and parts (non-farm)
lumber, timber	automobile parts
wheat	petroleum
wood pulp	electrical equipment
aluminum	automobiles
uranium	engines and boilers
nickel	tractors and parts
copper	iron and steel products
iron ore	aircraft and parts
asbestos	other farm machinery, tools, and parts
farm machinery and tools	cotton fabrics
barley	paper products
beef cattle	coal

Canada's oldest and strongest trade links have always been with its partners in the North Atlantic community – the United States

and Britain. Before World War II, Canada's exports went mostly to Britain and other parts of the world, and Canada's imports came mostly from the United States. During the war Canada's trade with Europe declined because of the U-boat menace. At the same time close trading relationships grew up between Canada and the United States.

In the postwar years the American economic boom made the United States the fastest-growing market for goods in the world. Canada's geographic relation to the United States made it possible to take advantage of this large market. Besides, Canada had most of the resources the United States needed and wanted. The trade friendship between these two countries was further strengthened by the tremendous flow of American capital into Canada. The money came in to help with the large-scale development of Canada's natural resources. Technical know-how was also borrowed from the Americans. The fact that Canadians share many of the same tastes as Americans also improved trade on both sides of the border. In the postwar years the United States became Canada's chief customer.

Canada's Trade Partners (1958)		
exports to (in millions of dollars)		imports from (in millions of dollars)
$1326.5	Britain and Western Europe	$823.5
2808.1	United States	3460.1

Canada and the United States were now each other's best customers. Most Canadians thought this was a good thing. Huge American markets for Canadian goods meant more jobs for Canadians and a high standard of living. Heavy American investment in Canada was helping to develop our resources and finance major industrial projects. However, some informed Canadians warned that American domination of the Canadian economy was a serious threat. There was a real danger that some major industries such as oil, minerals, and paper could some day be completely owned by the Americans. These Canadians were also alarmed by the growing trade imbalance: Canada was importing more goods from the United States than it was exporting across the border. As early as 1957 a Royal Commission on Canada's economic prospects, headed by Walter Gordon, warned of the danger of too much foreign ownership in the Canadian economy. It strongly advised the Canadian government to make policy decisions about this important issue.

Hydro-electric station near Cornwall, Ontario

More than any other project of the 1950s, the construction of the St. Lawrence Seaway illustrates Canada's spectacular industrial growth. For years Canadian and American officials had talked of improving the inland waterway route of the St. Lawrence River and the Great Lakes. This would allow ocean-going ships to travel as far as the western end of Lake Superior. It would also be possible to harness the rapids of the St. Lawrence River for hydro-electric power. Both Ontario and New York State desperately needed the extra power that this project could produce.

Although the joint plan had been discussed thoroughly, the Americans continued to hesitate. American railroads were afraid they would lose business if ocean vessels could stream directly to cities such as Detroit and Chicago. In 1951 Canada decided to go ahead with the construction of the St. Lawrence Seaway on its own. Only at the last minute did the Americans decide to join in. The United States probably realized that once built, the Seaway would be entirely within Canadian territory and control, unless the project was a joint agreement. So the Americans decided to join in.

The planning and design of the Seaway, and most of the construction, was carried out by Canadians. The control dam required by the power project flooded a large area between Cornwall and Iroquois in Ontario. Entire communities had to be removed and new homes were built for 6500 people. Sixty-five

Opening of St. Lawrence Seaway

kilometres of the CNR were rerouted and Highway 2 was reloca-
ted. The St. Lawrence Seaway was officially opened 26 June 1959
by Queen Elizabeth II for Canada and President Eisenhower for
the United States. This project is an outstanding example of the
strong commercial ties that bind the Canadian and American
economies.

New Steps to Independence

Under the Liberals, Canada took further steps toward becoming a
completely independent nation. The Supreme Court of Canada
was set up in 1949. Nine justices of the Supreme Court became
the final court of appeal for Canadians. No longer would Canadians be allowed to appeal the decisions of their court cases to the
Privy Council in Britain.

In 1952 Vincent Massey became the first Canadian-born governor general of Canada. This prominent Canadian had played an
important part in producing the 1951 Massey Report. The report
had pointed out the danger of the growing American influence on
Canada's culture. Radio, films, books, television, art, music, and
even sports in Canada were all in danger of being swamped by the
American influence. Massey pointed out that one solution would
be to set up an organization called the Canada Council to promote

the Canadian arts. This was done in 1957, and Canada Council money still helps to encourage and support artists, scholars, musicians, and writers. In his years as governor general, 1952 to 1959, Vincent Massey visited all areas of Canada. He wanted to give Canadians a sense of pride in their country and a sense of national identity.

As the election of 1957 approached, the Liberal government seemed old and tired. The prime minister himself, Louis St. Laurent, was seventy-five years old. The Liberals had been in power since 1935 and seemed to have lost touch with the people. To many it seemed that the government no longer listened to the people of Canada.

A wild and bitter debate which broke out in Parliament in 1956 showed just how bad things had gotten. The Liberals had decided to finance the building of a trans-Canada pipeline, which in itself was a good idea. The pipeline would carry natural gas from its source in Alberta to markets in Ontario, Quebec, and the United States. In Parliament the opposition wanted to ask questions. Why was the government loaning $118 million to a pipeline company that was 83 percent American-owned? How much of the natural gas would end up in the United States? Was the Trans-Canada Pipeline Company getting too generous a deal from the Canadian taxpayer?

C.D. Howe, the cabinet minister in charge of the pipeline, was impatient to get construction started. He did not want to sit around the House of Commons debating the issue. The government forced the bill through Parliament using closure. This is a special rule limiting the amount of time that a bill may be discussed in Parliament. The opposition raised a storm of protest, but the bill was passed by the Liberal majority. Forcing the pipeline bill through Parliament hurt the St. Laurent government. Now John G. Diefenbaker, leader of the Conservatives, had a major issue on which to fight the next election. Diefenbaker claimed that by using closure, the Liberals had trampled on the rights of Parliament. He thundered that this was one more example of the American takeover of the Canadian economy. Above all, Diefenbaker argued that the Liberals had been in power too long and had lost touch with people's feelings. In the election of June 1957, 112 Conservatives were elected to 105 Liberals. John Diefenbaker became prime minister. In another election the following year, there was a Conservative landslide in Canada. The Conservative party won the largest majority of any party since Confederation (Conservatives 208; Liberals 49; CCF 8). For the first time since the days of John A. Macdonald, the Conservatives won a large number of seats in Quebec (50 of 75).

DIGGING DEEPER

1 Imagine you are a war bride and you have just arrived in Canada to join your Canadian husband. Write a letter to your family in Britain. Include in your letter how you feel and some of your first impressions of Canada.

2 Make a two-column chart. In the left-hand column, make a list of the factors that were pushing people out of Europe after World War II. In the right-hand column, list the factors that were pulling people to Canada at this time.

3 a) Research the reasons why Newfoundland rejected Confederation in 1867.

   b) List the factors you think were important in persuading Newfoundlanders to vote for joining Confederation in 1949.

4 In 1949 the people of Newfoundland voted in a referendum to join Canada. How many other provinces joined Confederation in this way? Why do you think the referendum was important in Newfoundland's case?

5 How did Canada's trade pattern change after World War II? Explain the factors that account for this.

32
The New Vision of Canada

Early one morning in 1909 a fourteen-year-old newsboy talked to Sir Wilfrid Laurier. The boy resolved then and there that one day he too would be prime minister. By 1958 John George Diefenbaker had reached his goal. He was the prime minister of Canada and leader of the party with the greatest majority in Parliament in history.

The road to political power had not been easy for John Diefenbaker. He was born in rural Ontario near Owen Sound, but his family settled on a homestead in northern Saskatchewan in 1903. One summer he was a travelling book salesman and slept "in almost every haystack in Saskatchewan." In 1919 he graduated with a law degree from the University of Saskatchewan and became a prairie lawyer. Over and over in his early career Diefenbaker suffered defeat. Among these defeats was the time he did not get elected mayor of Prince Albert. Four times he was defeated in provincial and federal elections before he won a seat in the House of Commons in 1940. And twice he was rejected by his Conservative party for the leadership before they turned to him in 1956.

Diefenbaker was the first prime minister of Canada of neither British nor French background. He was intensely proud of his German background and was conscious that he represented a large number of Canadians who were neither British nor French. He brought into politics the sort of people who had not been there before: a Chinese member of Parliament, a Ukrainian minister of Labour, and a Native senator. For the first time a woman, Ellen Fairclough, was named to the federal Cabinet. Fairclough's

Prime Minister John Diefenbaker and US President Dwight D. Eisenhower

appointment as secretary of State represented a breakthrough in public service for all women.

Diefenbaker was also proud of his family's days as homesteaders in the West. He saw himself as the champion of the common person. Indeed he had the tremendous ability to appeal to ordinary Canadians and win their devotion. Long experience as a criminal lawyer had made him a dynamic and persuasive speaker. On stage or before television cameras he revealed a kind of political charisma. This meant that by the strength of his personality and his spellbinding oratory, he was able to stir up many Canadians and win their support.

The following excerpts are from a speech by John Diefenbaker in which he presented his "vision" of what Canada could become. This speech was made on 12 February 1958.

Ladies and gentlemen, we started in the last few months, since 10 June, to carry out our promises, and I can tell you this, that as long as I am Prime Minister of this country, the welfare of the average Canadian will not be forgotten.

This national development policy will create a new sense of national purpose and national destiny. One Canada. One Canada, wherein Canadians will have preserved to them the control of their own economic and political destiny. Sir John A. Macdonald gave his life to this party. He opened the West. He saw Canada from East to West. I see a New Canada — a Canada of the North.

We will open that northland for development by improving transportation and communication and by the development of power, by the building of access roads. We will make an inventory of our hydro-electric potential.

Canadians, realize your opportunities! This is only the beginning. The future program for the next five to seven years under a Progressive Conservative Government is one that is calculated to give young Canadians, motivated by a desire to serve, a lift in the heart, faith in Canada's future, faith in its destiny.

This is the message I give to you my fellow Canadians, not one of defeatism. Jobs! Jobs for hundreds of thousands of Canadian people. A new vision! A new hope! A new soul for Canada . . .

To the young men and women of this nation I say, Canada is within your hands. Adventure. Adventure to the nation's utmost bounds, to strive, to seek, to find, and not to yield. The policies that will be placed before the people of Canada in this campaign will be ones that will ensure that today and this century will belong to Canada. The destination is one Canada. To that end I dedicate this party.

1   Why would Diefenbaker feel he was following in the footsteps of John A. Macdonald?

2   Pick out the elements in the speech that would appeal to the "average Canadian." Explain your answer.

Over the next four years the Diefenbaker government produced some impressive legislation. Much of it was concerned with working toward the vision of Canada outlined by Diefenbaker. Money was poured into badly needed housing. A great irrigation and power project was begun on the South Saskatchewan River. Federal money helped construct the Trans-Canada Highway linking all the provinces. Many kilometres of "roads to resources" were built in the North. In the field of radio and television, the government set up the Board of Broadcast Governors to supervise the quality of broadcasting. Native people were given voting rights equal to those of all other Canadians.

Perhaps of all the programs, the one that gave Diefenbaker the greatest sense of accomplishment was the Canadian Bill of Rights. Citizens of many countries had their rights guaranteed by their constitution. In Canada these rights had been upheld by custom and tradition rather than by law. Now in 1960 an act of

Parliament was passed granting Canadians the traditional freedoms:

- Freedom of speech (right to state an opinion without being afraid of government or law).
- Freedom of assembly and association (right to hold meetings, parades, and join clubs).
- Freedom of religion (right to worship as you please).
- Freedom of the press (right to publish opinions without fear of the government or law).
- Right of the individual to equality before the law (right to a fair trial, legal council, and protection against being unfairly imprisoned).

One of the greatest successes of the Diefenbaker government was a series of massive wheat deals. Tremendous wheat surpluses had piled up on the prairies in the 1950s. Granaries, port terminals, and prairie grain elevators were jammed with wheat which farmers were unable to sell. Diefenbaker understood the desperate economic situation of the farmers. He succeeded in arranging huge wheat sales to the People's Republic of China and other communist nations. A backlog of 19.9 million t of wheat were exported and Diefenbaker won the unending political support of prairie farmers.

In spite of these successes, Diefenbaker's appeal to Canadians began to fade. In 1959 both Canada and the United States went through an economic slowdown. By 1962 unemployment figures in Canada had climbed higher than in any year since the Great Depression.

That same year the Conservative government devalued the Canadian dollar to 92.5¢ of American currency. The purpose of this move was to discourage foreign imports, to stimulate Canadian exports by making them cheaper to buy, to encourage foreigners travelling in Canada, and to discourage Canadians from travelling in other countries. However, the government's action was unpopular. The people tended to blame the government for the country's economic problems.

Although he had had tremendous backing in Quebec in 1958, Diefenbaker did not seem to understand the needs of that province. Few members of Parliament from Quebec were given important Cabinet positions. In 1959, however, Diefenbaker did appoint General Georges Vanier, a French Canadian, as governor general. Even this step did not stop Quebec enthusiasm for the Conservative government from fading.

Difficulties with the United States over the defence of North America also were problems for the Diefenbaker government. In

1958 Canada signed an agreement with the United States setting up the North American Air Defence Command. Canada and the United States were to share air forces and air defence systems. Despite the agreement, the Diefenbaker government refused to accept nuclear warheads for the Bomarc B, a surface-to-air missile. Diefenbaker felt that arming the Bomarcs with nuclear warheads would set back the hopes for nuclear disarmament in the world. His opponents argued that the Bomarc without nuclear warheads was useless. The government's indecision over the question of nuclear weapons added to growing criticism of Diefenbaker. The Cabinet itself split over the issue, and three ministers (including the minister of Defence) resigned while several others decided to retire from federal positions. The Conservative party, which a few years before had won the largest victory in history, was a shambles.

The early 1960s saw the revival of two smaller political parties. The first of these was the CCF. In the election of 1945 the CCF party won twenty-eight seats. By 1958 their number in the House of Commons had dropped to eight. In 1961 a convention was held by the CCF and the Canadian Labour Congress to found a new party. It would be called the New Democratic Party. It was hoped that the party would gain support from farmers, the educated middle class, and labour. The colourful and energetic premier of Saskatchewan, T.C. "Tommy" Douglas, agreed to be leader.

The New Democratic Party stood for such things as full employment, free education, Canadian control of the economy, public

Tommy Douglas, first leader of the NDP

ownership of important natural resources, and a national medical insurance plan.

Almost from the beginning the NDP showed greater signs of success than the CCF. In 1962, nineteen NDP members were elected to the House of Commons. Support was drawn mainly from industrial and mining regions of Ontario and British Columbia.

The Social Credit Party also went through a reorganization period in 1961. A new national leader, Robert Thompson, was chosen. Social Credit had been in power in the provincial governments of Alberta since 1935 and British Columbia since 1952. However, in the federal election of 1958, it had won no seats. To everyone's surprise, Social Credit did very well in the election of 1962. The party had one main campaign argument. It was that the country's economic difficulties were the result of the heavy national debt that had developed with the Conservative government. Twenty-six members were elected from Quebec, and four from western Canada. The Quebec wing of the party was led by a fiery car dealer from Rouyn, Quebec, Réal Caouette. Social Credit success in Quebec was probably the result of dissatisfaction many Quebeckers felt with both Liberals *and* Conservatives. In 1963 Caouette and most of the Quebec wing broke away from the party to form the Ralliement des Créditistes (Social Credit Rally). When they did this, Social Credit lost any hope of being a truly national

Bomarc missile

party. The Ralliement des Créditistes is based solely in Quebec.

In the election of 1963, the Liberal party was able to attack Conservative mismanagement of the economy. They also criticized the government's indecision on defence policy and Canada's worsening relationship with the United States. On 8 April 1963 the Canadian public decided. The Conservatives were defeated and the Liberal party formed the government in Canada.

Lester "Mike" Pearson, the new prime minister, was a sharp contrast to Diefenbaker. Pearson had become leader of the Liberal party when Louis St. Laurent retired in 1958. When Pearson was only seventeen he had enlisted in the army to fight in the First World War. At the time he was transferred to the Royal Flying Corps, an officer said to him, "Lester is not a very belligerent name for a man who wants to be a fighter pilot. We'll call you Mike." The name stuck. After the war "Mike" Pearson taught at the University of Toronto, and then joined the Department of External Affairs. Pearson enjoyed a successful diplomatic career, which included being Canada's ambassador to the United States. He had also been active in the United Nations from its beginning, and had been President of its General Assembly in 1952–1953. He had gained international respect for helping create the UN Emergency Force in the Suez crisis of 1956. For his contribution to world peace, he received the Nobel Prize for peace in 1957. Unlike Diefenbaker, Pearson was soft-spoken and never really seemed at home in the give-and-take of the House of Commons debates.

During the time Pearson was prime minister, his government pushed forward reforms in many fields. A medical insurance plan and a Canada pension plan were set up. The Company of Young Canadians was set up to help Native people and the urban and rural poor. The Company sent Canadian volunteers to help people help themselves and gain self-respect.

Two important steps were taken in the field of defence. The nuclear warheads that the Diefenbaker government could not decide on were installed on Canadian missiles in 1963. Also, the Liberal government made the three branches of the Canadian armed forces into one joint command. By joining the army, navy, and air force, the government hoped to improve Canada's peace-keeping capacity and create a more effective fighting force.

In 1963 the Pearson government set up a Royal Commission on Bilingualism and Biculturalism (Bi and Bi Commission). It was to examine the relations between French and English Canadians and to consider Quebec's role in Confederation. For some time French Canadians had been complaining that they did not feel like equal partners in Confederation. The Commission studied the issue for several years. It concluded that Canada was passing through its greatest crisis. Among the major recommendations of the Bi and Bi Commission were the following:

i) Canada should be officially declared bilingual by making French and English the official languages of the federal Parliament and courts;

ii) New Brunswick and Ontario should officially declare themselves bilingual provinces;

iii) provinces where the minority group is more than 10 percent
should provide government services in both English and
French;

iv) the region of Ottawa-Hull should be made a national capital
area and should be officially bilingual;

v) students in all provinces should be given a chance to study
both official languages;

vi) more French Canadians should be employed in the federal
government;

vii) in Quebec, French should be the main language of work,
government, and business.

By 1970 many of the major recommendations of the commission
had been carried out.

Partly to please Quebec, the Liberals decided to adopt a new
Canadian flag. It would replace the Canadian Red Ensign with its
Union Jack in the upper corner and the Canadian Coat of Arms
diagonally opposite it. The ensign was disliked by many French
Canadians because of its close association with Britain. Many
non–French-Canadian citizens also thought it was time for Canada to have its own distinctive flag. The design of the new flag
submitted to Parliament by the Liberals purposely avoided British and French symbols — the Union Jack and the fleur-de-lis.
Instead, there were three red maple leaves sprouting from a single
stem on a white background. At each end of the flag were vertical
blue bars. The colours red, white, and blue were the only historical
connection. The flags of both Britain and France contain these
three colours.

In Parliament, John Diefenbaker led the opposition to "Pearson's Pennant." Diefenbaker, proud of Canada's British connections, wished to keep the Red Ensign. He was not alone. Many
veterans who had fought bravely under the Red Ensign in two
world wars did not want to see it replaced.

Months of controversy followed. Finally an all-party parliamentary committee recommended a new design. It was a single red
maple leaf on a white background with red borders at each end.
Diefenbaker and some of the opposition hoped to delay the passing of the flag bill. Their plan was to filibuster. Filibustering
means talking on endlessly until the plan has to be dropped so the
government can go on with other business. For thirty-three days
opposition members stated and restated their reasons for reject-
ing the new flag. Neither side would give in. Finally the Liberal
government ended the debate by using closure. At 2:30 in the
morning of 15 December 1964 Canada's new red maple leaf flag

was officially passed. It was a scene full of emotion. As the vote was announced (163 for, 78 against) the MPs rose to their feet to sing "O Canada" and "God Save the Queen."

Certainly the happiest feature of Pearson's term as prime minister was the celebration of Canada's centennial year 1967. Canada marked the one-hundredth birthday of Confederation with many ceremonies and celebrations throughout the year. The biggest celebration was the International Exposition, "Expo 67," held at Montreal. During the summer of 1967 Pearson was host to a steady stream of state visitors, including Queen Elizabeth II and Prince Philip.

As centennial year drew to a close, Pearson announced his decision to retire as leader of the Liberal party. In the final speech to his party, he mentioned those achievements of which he was most proud. They included the introduction of the new flag and centennial year. But Pearson went on to stress the need for national unity: "We who believe in our country must work with a passionate intensity to see that Quebec separatism doesn't happen; that the Canadian dream does not end but is realized in a Canadian destiny worthy of those who have brought us so far in our first century."

DIGGING DEEPER

1 Why do governments in Canada change hands? List as many reasons as you can. Why did Canadian electors reject the Diefenbaker government in 1963? What brought the Liberals to power in 1963?

2 Lester Pearson held at least six major jobs in his lifetime: wartime pilot, university professor, ambassador, politician, secretary of state for external affairs, and prime minister. What skills do you think Pearson must have had to have held each of these jobs?

3 Why are symbols, such as a flag, important to a country? Why would some groups of people be strongly opposed to a new flag?
Try to think of some other symbols that represent Canada.
What are the symbols of the province in which you live? Does your school or community have special symbols? How do you feel when you see these symbols used?

4 The Bi and Bi Commission challenged both English and French to make serious changes in their attitudes in order to make Confederation work.
Read the quote from the Royal Commission carefully. Make a chart in your notebook in two columns labelled "What the English should do" and "What the French should do." Summarize in

your own words the recommendations to both cultural groups.

> From evidence so far accumulated, it appears to us that English-speaking Canadians as a whole must come to recognize the existence of a vigorous French-speaking society within Canada, and to find out more about the aspirations, frustrations, and achievements of French-speaking Canadians, in Quebec and outside it. They must come to understand what it means to be a member of a minority, or of a smaller partner people, and to be ready to give that minority assurances which are unnecessary for a majority. More than a century ago, Sir John A. Macdonald wrote to an English-speaking friend: 'Treat them as a nation and they will act as a free people generally do – generously. Call them a faction and they become factious.' They have to face the fact that, if Canada is to continue to exist, there must be a true partnership, and that the partnership must be worked out as between equals. They must be prepared to discuss in a forthright, open-minded way the practical implications of such a partnership.

> On the same evidence, it seems to us that French-speaking Canadians for their part must be ready to respond positively if there are to be truly significant developments towards a better partnership. It would be necessary for French-speaking Quebeckers to restrain their present tendency to concentrate so intensely on their own affairs and to look so largely inward. Problems affecting all Canada are their problems too. They would need to beware of the kind of thinking that puts 'la nation' above all other considerations and values. They too, like the English-speaking, should forget the conquest and any psychological effects they think it left. They would have to avoid blaming English-speaking Canadians for shortcomings which are their own and at times, to remember that English-speaking Canadians have their feelings too. They, as well as the English-speaking, must remember that, if a partnership works, each party must give as well as get.

Bi and Bi Royal Commission

5   Refer to the matrix you started at the end of the second unit (page 103). Trace the development of the same themes through the postwar period.

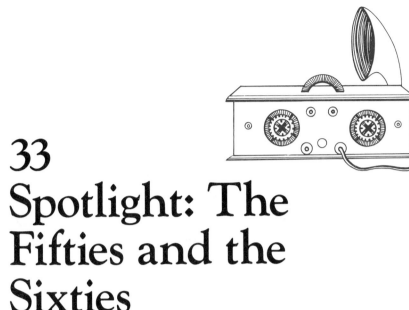

33
Spotlight: The Fifties and the Sixties

SPUTNIK

The space age began in 1957. In October 1957 the USSR launched the first satellite into space. The world was astonished! People were no longer confined to the earth's surface – and space captured everyone's imagination. The success of *Sputnik I* was followed a month later with *Sputnik II*, which carried a dog into orbit. The United States launched the *Vanguard I* in 1958. The space race was on!

In 1961, the Soviet Yuri Gagarin was the first person to travel in space. He was closely followed by two Americans, Alan B. Shepard Jr. in a suborbital flight, and John Glenn, who circled the earth three times in the *Friendship 7* capsule.

In 1969 the world watched in awe as Neil Armstrong, followed by Edwin Aldrin, walked on the moon's surface. This was certainly one of the most impressive space accomplishments since the first Sputnik was launched in 1957. Since then men and women have made long flights in orbiting satellites to explore the secrets of our solar system. Craft, without crews, have also explored the planets of Mars, Venus, and Jupiter to try to increase our knowledge of the universe.

SUBURBS AND URBANIZATION

New growth of Canadian cities was a result of the postwar expansion. More industrial jobs in cities, and the conveniences of city

In a realm all its own... Cadillac

living made Canada's rural population fall from 38 percent in 1951 to 26 percent in 1966. By the mid-1960s Montreal was still the largest urban centre, although Toronto was growing fast. Vancouver remained in third position, but Ottawa was challenging Winnipeg for fourth place.

Almost overnight suburbs mushroomed all around the cities. Developers began to build planned communities using the neighbourhood plazas or schools as their focus. The spread of suburbs led to fads in home design and decorating. Every house had a picture window and, if possible, an attached garage or carport. Inside, white woodwork was popular and the living room featured three walls painted one colour, and the fourth covered with wallpaper.

In the garage was the car that made suburban living possible in the first place. During the 1950s, Canadians bought 3 541 381 passenger cars. Each year's model seemed to grow longer, lower, and wider. North Americans believed that "bigger was better," so enormous V-8 engines, two-tone colours, and power steering were added. Outlandish tail fins became the fad of the 1957 and 1958 models.

HULA HOOP

In the 1950s there was no fad quite like hula-hooping. The idea was supposed to have come from Australia where bamboo hoops were used. North American hoops were made of plastic. Hula-hoop manufacturers made $45 million from the fad in one year. An impressive record was set by ten-year-old Pamela Brown of Brantford, Ontario when she twirled a hoop for 3 hours and 5 minutes, an estimated 15 938 twirls.

ROCK 'N' ROLL AND ELVIS

It all began in 1954 when Elvis Presley wrote and recorded a couple of nice lively tunes for his mother's birthday. The recording engineer liked what he heard, and called Elvis back in a couple of months to cut a single called "That's All Right, Mama." A Memphis disc jockey started to give it some air play on the radio, and orders poured in. It seemed that Elvis had something special. Elvis was not sure what it was, but later remarked, "I don't want it ever to end."

Many teenagers considered Elvis Presley the "King of Rock 'n' Roll." They screamed and shouted when he sang "Love Me Tender," "Hound Dog," or "Heartbeak Hotel" in concert, or saw him in such movies as *Blue Hawaii* and *Kid Galahad*.

When he died at his estate, Graceland in August 1977, thousands of fans paid their respects to the "King" who had given rock 'n' roll its style two decades before.

Elvis Presley

Beatles

BEATLES

In 1964 teenagers discovered the Beatles. To the shock of adults, young people copied shaggy Beatle haircuts, bought Beatle buttons, watches, wigs, dolls, and wallets, and repeated Beatle lyrics, such as "She loves you, yeah, yeah, yeah," over and over again. Sociologists called "Beatlemania" a form of protest against the adult world. They said it could not last. The experts were wrong. The boys from Liverpool, England were recognized as making the most important advances in popular music in our era. The 1960s belonged to the Beatles. The 1950s was the era of the solo singer, but with the popularity of the Beatles, the 1960s saw the growth of musical groups.

STRATFORD

During the 1950s Canadians began to get serious about setting up a distinctive Canadian theatre. In the sleepy little town of Stratford, Ontario, Tom Patterson had an idea. He persuaded Tyrone Guthrie, a famous director, to produce a Shakespearian festival at Stratford. In a circus tent beside the Avon River, the Stratford Shakespearian Festival held its first season in 1953. Year after year the crowds continued to come until the Festival Theatre was eventually constructed.

Toronto Dance Theatre

Stratford's success became an inspiration for theatres across the country. Drama lovers built the Neptune Theatre in Halifax, the Manitoba Theatre Centre in Winnipeg, Theatre New Brunswick in Fredericton, and similar theatres in many other centres across Canada.

Thanks to Stratford and these others, Canadian actors and actresses have become internationally known. These include Kate Reid, Jessica Tandy, Lorne Greene, Margot Kidder, William Shatner, Kate Nelligan, Christopher Plummer, Donald Sutherland, Don Harron, and Gordon Pinsent. Though some of these performers went to the United States or Europe to establish their reputation, many did get their start in Canadian theatres such as Stratford.

BALLET

In 1951 a twenty-nine-year-old ballerina named Celia Franca founded the National Ballet of Canada. Celia and Betty Oliphant travelled more than 8000 km across Canada in search of talent.

Three hundred auditions were held in schools and public halls. From these, twenty-eight dancers were chosen. The company could only afford to pay the dancers $25 per week, and $5 more for performances. But they opened their company that year to rave reviews in Toronto and Montreal. Then they went on tour throughout southern Ontario. Because of the drive of Celia Franca and others like her, ballet has won an important place in the hearts of Canadians.

Similar companies sprang up around the same time. These include the Royal Winnipeg Ballet and Les Grands Ballets Canadiens in Montreal.

TELEVISION

Can you imagine what it was like not to have television? Did you realize TV did not become widespread in Canada until the 1950s? People living along the American border were able to pick up American programs before that. However, it was not until 1952 that the CBC introduced its television service. Even then stations were few and far between, and television was not available in the less populated regions of Canada until years later. The screens were small, everything was in black and white, and the pictures were often lost in a snowstorm of dots. But television caught on quickly. By 1954 Canadians owned more than a million television sets.

By the end of the 1950s, television had completely revolutionized Canadian life. Eating habits changed when families bought TV tables so they could eat their meals in front of the set. Children were watching so much television that homework suffered. Children's viewing habits became an urgent topic at hundreds of parent-teacher association meetings. Conversation ceased when guests who didn't own a set dropped in. They were motioned to sit down and be quiet. Family life itself underwent great changes because of television. Families that used to go to church on Sunday evening, or play games or visit relatives, suddenly found themselves watching the "Ed Sullivan Show."

Among the favourite Canadian shows and entertainers were comedians Wayne and Shuster, Tommy Hunter on "Country Hoedown," "Front Page Challenge," and "Hockey Night in Canada."

LITERATURE

The fifties and sixties saw the emergence of several important Canadian novelists and poets. Among them were Mordecai Richler, Hugh MacLennan, Irving Layton, Robertson Davies, Leonard Cohen, and Margaret Laurence.

Gabrielle Roy

Gabrielle Roy was born into a French-Canadian family in St. Boniface, Manitoba, the youngest of eleven children. She loved to write short stories in French and her mother encouraged her to do so, even though the situation of a French-Canadian writer in Manitoba seemed hopeless at that time.

In two of her novels, *The Street of Riches* and *The Road Past Altamont*, she recounted her childhood experiences in rural Manitoba. One of her best-known works, *The Tin Flute*, describes the poverty and pride of the people of the St. Henri district of Montreal. This novel was chosen by the Literary Guild of America in 1947 as the book of the month.

Gabrielle Roy lived in Quebec City where she felt at home among fellow French-speaking Canadians. She commented on the issue of Quebec separatism, saying, "My great hope would be that Quebec would realize itself as a fully distinct part of Canada, and stay Canadian, bringing to Canada a part of its riches."

Gabrielle Roy won France's most prestigious literature prize, the Prix Goncourt. In Canada, she won the Governor General's Award for literature three times. Gabrielle Roy died in 1983 in Quebec City.

Hugh Garner

Hugh Garner's family moved to Canada from England when he was six years old. They settled in Toronto's Cabbagetown district, a poor and run-down part of the city.

Garner dropped out of school in grade 10 and held a variety of low-paying jobs after that. When the depression hit, Garner, like thousands of young men, set off across Canada and the United States on the freights. Later he wrote about those days, telling "the stories of ordinary people, living ordinary lives, happy or sad about everyday things of life."

Many of his short stories have been adapted for television. They are hard-hitting and often show the seamy side of life. But Garner was one of the first Canadian writers to show that the urban poor were good subjects for fiction.

DEVELOPING SKILLS:
BRAINSTORMING TECHNIQUES

At some time, you probably have been stumped by a problem. What to buy your mother for her birthday? Often the best way to solve this problem is to ask a few different people for suggestions. This technique can work for solving more complex problems too.

Brainstorming is a technique whereby a group of people discuss a particular problem and try to find the best solution. It is helpful and often time-saving as one person's idea might trigger an even better idea from someone else. Brainstorming makes your task easier, more fun, and usually better and more creative solutions are suggested.

Here are some guidelines to follow that will make your brainstorming session successful.

1   Choose someone in your group to record all the ideas.

2   Write down as many ideas as you can. Remember that quantity helps to produce quality.

3   Your ideas can range from the serious to the wacky. It's up to you!

4   All answers are acceptable. Don't reject any ideas until you're finished.

5   Get everyone in the group involved.

6   Combine or improve upon ideas.

7   Don't give up when there is a lull. There is usually a break between the obvious solutions and the less obvious ones.

8   When you have finished brainstorming, evaluate and categorize all your solutions. Determine if any ideas are missing. Decide which idea is the best and why.

Brainstorm a "Fabulous Fifties" Day

Discuss why certain decades in the twentieth century have names such as the "Roaring Twenties," the "Dirty Thirties," and the "Fabulous Fifties." Are these decade labels appropriate?

Brainstorm everything you already know about the fifties that make it fabulous: fads, fashions, movies, plays, dances, television, hairstyles, jargon, cult figures, and humour.

Classify the information you have brainstormed. In small groups, choose topics of interest to you and do some further research on the "Fabulous Fifties."

Present your research using the format – A "Fabulous Fifties" Day. You might invite people who lived during the 1950s to see and hear your presentations. Ask them to share some of their experiences about growing up in or living through that decade.

DIGGING DEEPER

1   You are now ready to add information about the 1950s and 1960s to your matrix from the second unit. Trace the development of the same themes through this unit.

34
The Asbestos Strike

The province of Quebec had the largest asbestos plant in the world. Asbestos is a fibrous material that neither burns nor conducts heat. This makes it very valuable to many industries. Forty percent of the world's supply of asbestos came from Quebec. Almost all of it was exported to the United States.

In February 1949 over 2000 workers of the American-owned Johns-Manville plant in Asbestos, Quebec, went on strike for higher wages. Their major demand was a 15¢ per hour wage increase. This would bring them up to $1.00 per hour. They were also asking for an increase in paid holidays to nine per year, and double-time for work on Sunday. In addition, they were worried about getting asbestos dust cleaned up in the mills and the town. The dust was dangerous to their health. At the beginning of the strike the townspeople joked that when the miners stopped working, they had accidentally hit on the best way to get rid of the dust.

The Union Nationale government of Quebec under Premier Maurice Duplessis had always been strongly opposed to labour unions. Unions in Quebec were tolerated only if they remained weak and if the workers were opposed to strikes. It was Duplessis's view that the employer offered jobs to the people of the community and workers should be grateful for the employment provided by the companies. In Quebec a union could be outlawed if it had any communists among its leaders. Since Duplessis had the final say on who was a communist, this law could be used against any union of which he disapproved.

Asbestos workers leaving the factory

The Quebec premier declared the Asbestos strike illegal and sent in the Quebec provincial police. Duplessis accused the strike leaders of being saboteurs, that is, people seeking to cause trouble. The workers complained of police brutality and unfairness to the strikers. The strike continued.

As the strike dragged on into May, it grew more ugly. Johns-Manville had begun to use strikebreakers. Some were old employees and some were new ones brought in from outlying towns and villages. So the company was still producing asbestos, but at a much reduced level. Through all of this, Duplessis continued to support the anti-union American company. A letter from the chairman of the Johns-Manville Company to Premier Duplessis thanked him for

> ... the firm support which you and your government have given us in seconding our efforts to maintain ourselves in an adequate position. It was a great comfort for me this morning to be able to assure our board of directors of your constant support, as well as the protection which continues to be accorded to our properties and our strikebreakers and others working in the plant.

In the meantime, the strikers' families suffered hunger and real need. They were especially annoyed when they found out that the strikebreakers had been given a 10¢ per hour wage increase. To the men who had gone on strike demanding only 5¢ per hour more than that, it seemed like a real slap in the face. Tensions erupted. The strikers set up barriers and roadblocks on routes leading into the town, smashed windows of strikebreakers' homes, and threatened non-striking workers. And at one of the demonstrations some visiting journalists were even arrested. Among them was Pierre Elliott Trudeau.

On a day known as "bloody Thursday" the strikers tried to interrupt factory production by stopping strikebreakers on their way into the plant and by picketing company property. When the strikers stopped a car with four police officers in plain clothes, one of the police officers fired two revolver shots. With that the crowd went wild. The police were hauled from the car, kicked, and beaten into unconsciousness. The strikers were now in complete control of the town.

Early the next morning 400 provincial police went into the town to restore order. This time the role of strikers and police was reversed. Heavily armed with shotguns, sten guns, revolvers, tear gas, and billies, the blue-and-brown clad officers finally restored order. Two hundred strikers were arrested. Several miners were savagely beaten – a reporter for *Time* magazine described this as "sickening." Gradually peace returned to the town of Asbestos, but great bitterness remained. Most of all it was directed against the provincial police. Jean Marchand, strike leader, released a signed statement to the press. In it he compared the behaviour of the provincial police with "Hitler's elite troops."

The strike dragged on for another two months until a settlement was reached. The workers went back with a 10¢ per hour increase in wages and two more paid holidays. But at least a hundred miners remained out of work because the strikebreakers had been kept on by the company. The workers had gained very little.

One of the most significant aspects of the Asbestos strike was that the Roman Catholic church had publicly opposed the government of Quebec. The Catholic church had supported the workers, raised money to feed their families, and acted as a mediator between the company and the strikers.

The Asbestos strike marked the beginning of rapid social changes that were coming in the province of Quebec. During the late 1940s and early 1950s, Quebec was shaken by a series of long, bitter, and often violent strikes. Quebec was starting to emerge into a modern industrial province. The labour unions were begin-

Maurice Duplessis (third from left) at a ribbon-cutting ceremony

ning to challenge the rigid rule of the Duplessis government. Rapid changes in Quebec's society and economy were soon to follow.

The Asbestos strike attracted the attention and changed the thinking of several young Quebec thinkers. Among those who took part in the strike were several men who would soon make names for themselves. Jean Marchand, the union leader, would go on to a federal Cabinet post. The reporter who covered the story for the newspaper *Le Devoir*, Gérard Pelletier, would become a Cabinet minister and the Canadian ambassador to France. Pierre Elliott Trudeau, who had been present during part of the 142-day strike, later edited a book of essays and articles about it. Eventually, of course, he would become prime minister of Canada. They were among many other Quebec thinkers sympathetic to the strike who became leaders of Quebec and Canada in the 1960s. The strike was a turning point in their lives.

KNOWING THE TERMS

Company union
All the workers of a local company join to improve their working conditions. The office clerks, drivers, and plant workers of a local dairy would be an example of a company union.

Collective bargaining
Representatives of the workers and the employer meet together to discuss their problems. They try to reach an agreement on such items as wages, hours, and conditions of work.

Strike
Employees refuse to work until the employer reaches an agreement with them on disputed matters, usually wages and conditions of work.

Lockout
The employer refuses to allow the employees to work until a settlement is reached.

Blacklist
Union leaders and troublemakers are not rehired after the strike. Also, other companies in the same industry will not hire them.

Strikebreaker
A person who refuses to honour the picket line and works during the strike. Sometimes s/he is already employed by the company. However, the company will often hire new people to work.

DEVELOPING SKILLS:
ROLE PLAYING

Role playing helps to make the past come alive. You can travel back in time and become embroiled in the events and problems of the past. Role playing is like being an actor or actress in a movie or television show. To prepare for the role you must imagine what it would have been like to live in that time and at that place. Try to put yourself in the place of your character. What would life be like in those circumstances? What choices would you have to make?

Steps in role playing
1   You will be assigned a role to play. You should identify with your character. Make sure you have knowledge of the situation so that you can act out a solution. You should participate and co-operate actively.
2   In groups, go to a quiet place to plan and prepare your roles. You may find it helpful to reread the chapter to find out how your characters would act. You might need to do a little research to learn more about the forces that affected your character.
3   Act out your situation. When your group has finished you should be able to reach a decision about the event in the past.
4   Hold a class discussion about your role-playing experience. Were the characters realistic? How did you feel in your role? Why did you feel that way? What did you discover about your character? What new insights about the past did you gain from role

playing? What solutions did you find? How did your solutions differ from those taken in the past?

Role play
Set up an imaginary commission to investigate the Asbestos strike. More than half the class should play the role of strikers. Others may play the role of owners and managers of Johns-Manville. A few students may take the role of judges. The role cards and questions for each group to work on follow.

Strikers
You are the workers and you have gone on strike to force the company to meet your demands. The cost of living has risen but your wages have remained the same. You are fighting to get the asbestos dust cleaned up in the plant and the town.

With these things in mind, consider the following questions and try to develop the attitudes and opinions of the strikers.
1   As a worker why do you think you went on strike?
2   Are your reasons justified? Why?
3   Find out all you can about the disease asbestosis.
4   Who are your leaders and supporters?
5   What are the demands of the workers?
6   Why does management oppose you?
7   Do you think management has the right to bring in strike-breakers? Why?
8   Do you think violence is justified in trying to win your case?

Owners
You are the bosses, the owners, and the managers of the factories. The workers at your plant in Quebec have gone on strike, causing you to lose money and profits. With these things in mind, answer the following questions and try to develop the opinions that you think management would have.
1   As an owner, why do you think the workers went on strike?
2   Were the workers justified?
3   Why do you oppose the strike?
4   Should people have the right to strike? Why or why not?
5   Should management have the right to bring in strike-breakers? Explain your answer.
6   What role do you think the police should play in the strike?
7   If the strikers give up, will you allow them back to work without punishing them?

Judges
You are the judges in this case. Try to find out exactly what happened and try to make a decision about who was right. In this

strike there has been violence and property loss. Two groups in society with different attitudes and opinions are in conflict. Listen to both sides and ask questions. Keep order so that all sides of the controversy may be heard in court. Do not hesitate to tell people to let someone else speak, if necessary. If workers or bosses are merely sitting there, try to get their opinions. You may direct questions to individuals if you wish. Make up some questions in advance to ask both sides.

DIGGING DEEPER

1   View the film *Mon Oncle Antoine* (1971, NFB). It is an interesting portrayal of life in a Quebec asbestos town. Watch the film and try to visualize the conditions of the miners in the 1940s. Find out what changes have taken place since then (hours of work, wages, conditions of work, benefits).

35 The Quiet Revolution in Quebec

In order to understand what happened in Quebec after World War II, you must have some understanding of the relations between the French and English in Canada. Use the following quiz to check your own knowledge of early Canadian history. As you discuss your answers with your class, you will be learning some facts about French Canada. Any events in the early history you are not sure about should be checked out in library books or other texts and reviewed.

1 The capital city of Quebec is a) Montreal
   b) Sherbrooke c) Quebec City.
2 Outside of Quebec the largest portion of French Canadians live in a) Prince Edward Island
   b) Alberta c) New Brunswick.
3 The first French-Canadian prime minister was
   a) Sir Wilfrid Laurier b) Louis St. Laurent
   c) Arthur Meighen.
4 The percentage of the population of Ontario that is French Canadian is about a) 2 percent b) 10 percent c) 30 percent.
5 The early French settlers in North America treated the Native people a) as friends b) with neglect
   c) with persecution.

6   Canada is a bilingual country. What percentage of Canadians can carry on a conversation in both French and English?   a) 6 percent   b) 13 percent   c) 47 percent.

7   In the history of Canada since its discovery by Cartier in 1535, the French have controlled Canada a) for much less time than the British   b) for a little less time than the British   c) for about the same amount of time as the British.

8   Ever since the battle of the Plains of Abraham, French Canadians have felt   a) like conquered people   b) second-class citizens   c) both of the above d) none of the above.

9   After an uprising in 1837 in Quebec, Lord Durham recommended that   a) the French should be assimilated by the British   b) the French should all be sent back to France   c) the French in Quebec should be allowed to set up their own country.

10   Which French-Canadian Father of Confederation most helped to persuade his people to believe in a united country?   a) Antoine A. Dorion   b) George Etienne Cartier   c) Etienne P. Taché.

11   Confederation was a compromise worked out to a) put down the French Canadians once and for all b) prevent French Canadians from joining the United States   c) make Quebec a full and equal partner with the other provinces.

12   In the eyes of Quebec Louis Riel was a hero. In English Canada he was seen as a traitor. This was because   a) Riel led the Métis in a struggle against English settlement on the Prairies   b) Riel was a French-speaking Roman Catholic   c) Riel was a symbol of the division between French and English Canada   d) all of the above reasons.

Maurice Duplessis, premier of Quebec from 1936 to 1939 and 1944 to 1959, ruled Quebec with an iron hand. Duplessis was called le Chef, the Chief. His government was a one-man rule. It was generous and dedicated, but it could also be harsh and dictatorial. Opponents called the age of Duplessis "la grande noirceur," which means the great darkness. Certainly Quebec's resources were developed under Duplessis, mostly with American money. But development in Quebec was often done in a corrupt manner. For almost every bridge, road, or hospital built, Duplessis expected something in return. He demanded political favours, campaign funds, or votes. And he got them.

Some characteristics of Maurice Duplessis are described by Pierre Laporte:

> At Shawinigan Duplessis once declared that if the voters re-elected a member of the Opposition, a bridge needed for the heavy local traffic would not be built. They were warned. And when they elected a Liberal Opposition member anyway, the bridge was not built while Duplessis was alive.
>
> In Verchères County, Duplessis said during a political meeting in 1952: 'I warned you not to elect a Liberal candidate. You did not listen to me. Unfortunately your riding did not receive any of the grants that could have made it a happier place in which to live. I hope you have now learned your lesson and that you will vote against the Liberals this time.'
>
> Until 1956 the secondary roads of the Verchères County remained in a lamentable condition. A priest had to ride a tractor for over 8 km to reach the parish church of St. Anatole. A physician was unable to get to a patient because the roads were impassable. So it was no surprise when the farmers of this riding declared, on the eve of the 1956 election: 'We have elected a Liberal in 1944, 1948, and 1952. This time we are going to vote for new roads.'

Although Duplessis was creating a new industrialized Quebec, he emphasized the old ways of thinking. Quebec society was largely closed to outside influences. The Roman Catholic church and the old French-Canadian ties to the land were emphasized in order to keep Quebec separate from the rest of Canada.

In September 1959, while visiting northern Quebec, Maurice Duplessis had a stroke and died. The age of Duplessis was over. One-man government began to crumble away. Pressures for change were suddenly let loose in Quebec. Reforms began almost immediately. But the real change came when the new Liberal government under Jean Lesage was elected in 1960. It was the beginning of the Quiet Revolution.

THE QUIET REVOLUTION

Lesage gathered around him an impressive team of cabinet ministers which included René Lévesque as minister of Natural Resources. The Quiet Revolution of the Liberals promised to do two things. One was to improve the economic and social standards of the people of Quebec. The other was to win greater recognition for all the French in Canada.

One of the first programs of the Liberals was for the government to take over control of hydro-electric power companies. This also included the building of the Manicouagan Power Dam, one of the largest in the world. French-Canadian engineers from all parts of Canada and the world returned to Quebec to work on the project. The phrase used was "on est capable" or "we can do it!"

Another slogan of the Quiet Revolution was "maîtres chez nous," meaning "masters in our own house." The government began to replace programs that the church had previously run. These included hospital insurance, pension schemes, and the beginnings of medicare. To do this the Quebec Liberals had to struggle with Ottawa for a larger share of the tax dollar.

One of the most sweeping reforms was the modernization of the entire school system. In the past the schools of Quebec had been run by the church. Most of the teachers were priests, nuns, or brothers. They provided a good education, but not in business and technology which was what Quebec now needed. Lesage wanted a government-run school system that would equip modern Quebec with brains in engineering, science, business, and commerce.

Robert Charlebois, popular Quebec folksinger

The new freedom of expression in Quebec gave rise to a flood of books, plays, and music about the French culture in Quebec. In the theatre Gratien Gélinas became one of the most popular contemporary playwrights. The 1960s saw a tremendous output of Quebec movies. French-Canadian filmmakers have always been far more successful than English-Canadian filmmakers. New directors like Claude Jutra began to emphasize in their films themes drawn from Quebec life. Of all the artists, the singers of Quebec in the 1960s used political themes and messages the most. The song "Mon Pays" by Gilles Vigneault won an international award at the Brussels Music Festival in 1965. This song describes Vigneault's tender feelings toward his "country" – Quebec – and his French-Canadian heritage.

But all was not well in the province of Quebec. Things were going badly between the French and the English. There was almost no real personal contact between the two founding cultures of Canada. Hugh MacLennan wrote about the "two solitudes," – the English and French in Quebec and Canada who seemed to live parallel but completely separate lives.

The Royal Commission on Bilingualism and Biculturalism showed that the "two solitudes" were not always equal. The study showed a breakdown of average male wages in Quebec by ethnic group. At the top of the economic ladder were the Quebeckers of British origin. Their average annual wage in 1960 was $4940. Average wages then declined through a number of other ethnic groups: Scandinavian, Jewish, German, Polish, and Asian. All of these other groups were largely English-speaking. Then, almost at the bottom of the economic scale, were the French-Canadian Quebeckers. Their average annual wage was $3185.

Another complaint was that most of the top jobs in the province of Quebec were held by English-speaking persons. Although the French greatly outnumbered the workers of British origin in Quebec, twice as many British as French held high paying, high-status professional and managerial jobs. Thus the French, 80 percent of Quebec's total population, were among the least favoured in their own province.

The Commission report warned that Canada was going through the worst crisis of its history. Unless there was a new and equal partnership between the founding cultures of Canada, a breakup was likely to result.

Some Quebeckers suggested that the only solution to Quebec's problems was separatism. Separatism is the desire of a province to break away from the Canadian union. The separatists, as they were called, demanded immediate independence for Quebec. They said that as long as Quebec was associated with the rest of

Canada, French Canadians would never be treated as equals.

The idea of separatism was not new in Quebec. Often in troubled times between the English and French, someone raised the possibility of Quebec leaving Confederation. This occurred when Louis Riel was hanged, and again when the Canadian government introduced conscription in 1917. During the Quiet Revolution of the 1960s, a small but influential group in Quebec began to talk seriously again about separation.

One of the early separatist groups of the 1960s was the Rassemblement pour l'Indépendance Nationale (RIN). One of its founders, Dr. Marcel Chaput, wrote a book, called *Why I am a Separatist*, that shocked English Canada. In it he described the way a French Canadian is made to feel inferior every day of his life.

- The French Canadian's country is the whole of Canada, but he is accepted only in Quebec.
- The French Canadian is told that he belongs to the great French civilization, but at the same time he hears someone speak of "those damned Frenchmen."
- The French Canadian is forced to be bilingual; the others are unilingual.
- The French Canadian hears nothing but praise at school and elsewhere for the beauty of the French language; he is obliged to learn English.
- The French Canadian is told that Canada is a country which united two cultures; he has difficulty getting service in west Montreal [English-speaking areas] if he uses French.
- The French Canadian enters the French university only to study from American text-books.
- The French Canadian is told all about national unity, but he is ordered: "Stay in your province."
- The French Canadian hears people insist that Canada is an independent country; every day he sees another country's queen on his coins and on his stamps.

THE FLQ

The Front de Libération du Québec (FLQ), founded in 1963, was a smaller but more radical group of separatists. The FLQ had no leader, but was a collection of separate cells or groups of young people. Their idea was to use terrorism as a weapon to achieve independence for Quebec. A number of bombs were exploded, mostly in Montreal, and at least one person was killed.

Another separatist group, the ALQ (l'Armée de Libération du Québec), became even more violent. They robbed banks to get

A mailbox bomb explodes in Montreal

money and raided arms depots of the Canadian Armed Forces for
ammunition. They set bombs in letter boxes in the English-
speaking districts of Montreal and attacked army barracks. A
favourite slogan of many of the separatist groups was "Québec
Libre" – "Free Quebec."

Between 1963 and 1970, it is estimated that there was a terrorist bombing somewhere in the province once every ten days.
Terrorism did not result in the independence of Quebec, as hoped
for by the FLQ and other separatists. However, it did help alert
many English Canadians to the grave problems in the heart of
Canadian Confederation.

Many French-Canadian nationalists in Quebec were not separatists. They believed that separatism had no future. The answer
lay in a strong federalism in which French Canadians could play a
full role in a genuinely bicultural Canada. You will recall that
Canadian federalism is a system of government in which several
provinces are brought together under one central government,
though the provinces have their own provincial and local governments. Three prominent Quebeckers who believed in federalism,
and thought it could be made to work in Quebec, went to Ottawa in
1965 as Liberal members of the Canadian Parliament. They were
Pierre Trudeau, Jean Marchand, and Gérard Pelletier, sometimes
referred to as the "Three Wise Men" from Quebec.

In the Quebec provincial election of 1966, the people again turned to the Union Nationale under Daniel Johnson. Johnson was elected premier on the slogan "Equality or Independence." He warned Ottawa that Confederation had only a few years left to change or breakup. Unless Quebec was given "special status" in Confederation, it would have to separate and go its own way as a separate nation. This demand for "special status" included control over economics, social welfare, and housing, and sufficient tax powers to carry out these responsibilities. Quebec also wanted to be able to deal directly with foreign governments in matters of culture and education. This last demand especially was rejected by Ottawa, which claimed complete control in international affairs.

QUÉBEC LIBRE!

The conflict between Ottawa and Quebec was dramatized in August 1967 by a visit of the president of France, General De Gaulle. De Gaulle came to Canada at the invitation of the Quebec government to inspect the magnificent site of Expo '67. He sailed up the St. Lawrence River on board a French missile cruiser, *Colbert*, and was given an enthusiastic welcome when he landed at Quebec City. From there he travelled to Montreal in an open car. All along the route, which was lined with Quebec and French flags, De Gaulle was cheered by the crowds. Canada's flag was nowhere to be seen.

At a reception held by the city of Montreal, President De Gaulle appeared on a balcony to address a wildly cheering throng, many of whom were separatists. He told the people that he felt that day as he had on the day France was liberated from the Nazis in 1944. He ended his speech with the resounding cry, "*Vive le Québec libre!*" ("Long live free Quebec"). "*Québec libre*" had been the well-known slogan of separatists and terrorists since 1963. De Gaulle seemed to be giving his enthusiastic support to the separatists in their struggle for the liberation of Quebec.

Canadians watching De Gaulle on television were stunned by his comparison of their government with the Nazis. Prime Minister Pearson was outraged by De Gaulle's intereference in Canadian affairs. Pearson issued a sharp statement to the press, labelling as "unacceptable" De Gaulle's encouragement to "the small minority of our population whose aim it is to destroy Canada." The prime minister went on to say that "The people of Canada are free. Every province in Canada is free. Canadians do not need to be liberated. Indeed, many thousands of Canadians gave their lives in two world wars in the liberation of France."

Bombing on Montreal street

General De Gaulle cancelled the rest of his trip and returned immediately to France. Until De Gaulle's retirement in 1969, relations between France and Canada continued to be tense because of this affair.

Meanwhile protests, demonstrations, and violence continued in Quebec. René Lévesque had already left the Liberal party and started the Movement for Sovereignty Association. In 1968, with part of the RIN, he formed the Parti Québécois (PQ). Lévesque always opposed terrorism and insisted on democratic and moderate means for achieving independence. While the independence movement was growing in Quebec, Pierre Trudeau had taken over as leader of the Liberals and prime minister when Pearson resigned in 1968.

On the eve of the election, 24 June 1968, the St. Jean Baptiste parade was held in Montreal. Prime Minister Trudeau stood on the platform with the special guests. In the crowd were some radical separatists determined to demonstrate against Trudeau. The parade turned into a riot. People began throwing bottles and rocks. Most of the guests on the platform dashed inside for safety, but Trudeau remained on the platform. The people of Canada, watching on television, saw their prime minister standing firm

THE NEW KING CHARLES: DE GAULLE CONTEMPLATES A DISTANT CORNER OF THE GRAND DESIGN

against the radical separatists. The next day, headlines, such as "Trudeau defies separatists," appeared in newspapers across the country as Canadians went to the polls. They clinched an already assured victory. Trudeau won a resounding majority in the election. It was a vote of confidence from English Canada and much of moderate Quebec.

In April 1970 the Liberals also won a victory in the provincial election in Quebec. They had a new leader, Robert Bourassa. After a decade of turbulence and change, Bourassa appeared to represent stability for the province. However, as we shall see, the Bourassa years were far from quiet in Quebec.

DIGGING DEEPER

1 Place the following events in French-English relations in chronological order, from earliest to the most recent:

- Manitoba Schools Question
- Confederation
- the execution of Louis Riel
- conscription crisis of World War I

- the Plains of Abraham conquest
- rebellion in Lower Canada
- exploration of the interior of North America by Radisson and
  Groseilliers
- Lord Durham's report

2   Review the contributions to Canada by early French-speaking
individuals:
- Mother Marie de l'Incarnation
- General Montcalm
- Samuel de Champlain
- Louis-Joseph Papineau
- George Etienne Cartier

3   Duplessis often said, "There wouldn't be employees without
employers." What does this statement mean? How did his actions
during the Asbestos strike illustrate this belief?

4   One Canadian historian believes that the Quiet Revolution did
not begin quietly in 1967. He says it began violently in 1949 in the
little mining town of Asbestos. Do you agree or disagree with his
viewpoint? Justify your opinion.

5   If you were a French Canadian living in Quebec in the 1960s,
would you have joined the separatist movement? Why or why not?

6   In your opinion, what were the most important achievements
in this period of the history of Quebec?

36
Life Begins at One Hundred

CANADA BEGINS ITS SECOND CENTURY

At 11.50 p.m. the lights of Parliament Hill flickered off. In a few minutes it would be 1 July 1967. A crowd of 50 000 people on the lawns of the Parliament Buildings held sparklers aloft to light up the night sky. Suddenly the sky blazed with red, white, blue, and green fireworks. Then at midnight the carillon chimed "O Canada" and the huge throng joined in singing. As the anthem ended, there followed an outburst of cheering, clapping, and horn honking such as Ottawa had not heard in a hundred years. Many of the party-goers broke open champagne and stayed to dance in the streets until the sun dawned on the first day of Canada's second century.

The capital's welcome of Canada's one-hundredth birthday was repeated all across the country. Canada broke into a frenzy of Dominion Day parades, picnics, and pageants. Church bells pealed joyously and were answered by hundred-gun salutes. In Edmonton, Alberta Premier Manning cut the first slice of a giant, eight-tier birthday cake for thousands of party-goers. At schooner races in Halifax, 20 000 people ate bowls of fish chowder in the Halifax Public Gardens. The crews of eight voyageur canoes, who were racing from Alberta to Montreal, stopped to celebrate with 30 000 Winnipegers at a regatta on the Assiniboine River. Students at Kimberley, British Columbia sewed together 60 bedsheets to make a 610-m maple leaf flag. And St. Paul's, Alberta, a Centennial-mad town, built a UFO landing pad to welcome any little green visitors to the Centennial celebrations.

1867 | 1967

Expo '67, Montreal

There was scarcely a city, town, or village in the country without a new Centennial park, library, or concert hall to dedicate. In Prince Edward Island, Premier Campbell led a ceremony of rededication to Confederation. It was here in Charlottetown in 1864 that the Fathers had first met to discuss union. In nineteen cities and towns, great-grandchildren of the Fathers of Confederation solemnly laid wreaths at the gravesides of their famous relatives.

Most people would agree that the crowning achievement of the Centennial celebrations was the world's fair known as Expo '67 at Montreal. The purpose of the Centennial was to show Canadians and the world an unforgettable picture of our land and its people.

As Canada headed into its second century, all three of the major political parties chose new leaders. The first to be chosen was the Conservative, Robert Lorne Stanfield. At a Conservative party convention in 1967 a bitter debate raged. The Conservatives decided to replace John Diefenbaker as leader with Stanfield. The new party leader had been the respected premier of Nova Scotia. In 1968, the Liberal party met to find a replacement for Lester Pearson, who had chosen to retire. Eight candidates were in the running for the leadership, but the party chose Pierre Elliott Trudeau, a bachelor and a former university professor from Montreal. Three years later, in 1971, David Lewis was chosen to replace T.C. Douglas when he stepped down from the leadership of the New Democratic Party. Thus the three major parties had new national leaders to deal with the changing issues facing Canada as it headed into its second century.

Indeed the whole world was undergoing many social changes in the late 1960s. In both North America and Europe, young people in particular were questioning society's values and points of view. Many decided that the way to challenge society was to protest. There were antiwar demonstrations demanding that the United States remove its forces from the war in Vietnam. Minority groups such as blacks and Native people marched to protest the unfair conditions under which their people lived. There were sit-ins in the universities as the students demanded more say in the running of the schools. In Canada there were outbreaks of violence as separatists attempted to draw attention to the problems of the French minority. Another group rebelled by dropping out of society. They became "hippies." Outwardly they rejected many of society's values. They wore their hair long and dressed exotically. Experiments with drugs and communal living were common.

Citizens protesting Canadian involvement in the arms race

Trudeaumania

TRUDEAUMANIA

It was in this atmosphere of change and rebellion that Pierre
Trudeau became prime minister. To many Canadians Trudeau
seemed to be the man of the hour. For one thing he was a French-
speaking Quebecker. He understood Quebec and would be able to
please that province. He was youthful, casual, and informal. He
appealed to young people partly because he drove fast sports cars
and had been photographed doing jack-knife dives into swimming pools and riding a camel. As minister of justice, Trudeau had
convinced people he was cool under pressure, logical, and schol-
arly. Above all, on television he showed wit and confidence. His
charisma on television and at huge political rallies proved to be a
real vote-getter.

Trudeau adopted a whole new campaign style. He arrived in
many cities by jet, and then descended into a suburban shopping
centre parking lot by helicopter. From there he mingled with the

crowd, shaking hands and accepting kisses from admirers. Trudeau made some general remarks to the crowd about building the "just society." Hecklers were put down easily with quick-witted replies. He ended by challenging Canadians to take a chance on the future and vote for the Liberals. Smiling for the cameras, he then tossed the flower from his buttonhole to the crowd. In a few minutes he reentered the helicopter and was whisked away to his next rally. He seemed to be willing to meet the people and discuss the issues with them in plain talk. The crowds loved him. The press called it "Trudeaumania."

Next to Trudeau, Robert Stanfield appeared steady, but dull. He was particularly uneasy in front of news cameras. Once he complained that every time he left the House of Commons, "You walk out and they shove a bunch of microphones in your face. In thirty seconds you are expected to produce a profound and intelligent answer to an extremely complicated national issue." Stanfield's answers were thoughtful and honest, but his slow manner of speaking made him seem indecisive and weak. It was not surprising when Trudeau was elected in 1968, and again in 1972 and 1974, but with reduced majorities.

DIGGING DEEPER

1   In what ways were the 1960s years of rebellion and change?
2   Why were Canadian voters attracted to Pierre Trudeau in 1968? Ask someone who remembers the election of 1968 what s/he can recall of Trudeaumania.
3   Campaign styles are more important than campaign issues. Discuss this statement with respect to Trudeaumania in 1968. Is this statement true of political leaders today? Justify your answer.
4   Refer to the matrix you started at the end of the second unit (page 103). Trace the development of the same themes through the 1950s and 1960s.

37
Canada in a Changing World

As Canada entered its second century, Prime Minister Trudeau called for a complete review of Canada's foreign policy. The energetic prime minister believed it was a good time to examine Canada's relations with other countries of the world. Expo had focussed the world's attention on Canada. Now Canada was going to focus its attention on the role it should play in the world.

Beginning in 1968, interested Canadians from all walks of life were invited to take part in what was called the Trudeau Review. Politicians, journalists, professors, business leaders, financial experts, and church and labour leaders offered opinions and advice. The eventual result was the publication in 1970 of six booklets titled *Foreign Policy for Canadians*. They were to be the blueprint for Canada's foreign policy in the 1970s and beyond.

Canadians were informed that Canada now had six basic national goals:
1 to help the Canadian economy grow stronger;
2 to keep Canada independent;
3 to work for peace and security;
4 to promote fairness and equality for everyone;
5 to improve living conditions for all people;
6 to protect our natural environment (conservation).

What were the reasons for the Trudeau Review? For one thing, the major nations of Western Europe had now recovered from the effects of World War II. Canada's importance in defending Europe was now far less crucial than it had been in the two decades following the war. Britain was moving closer to its European neighbours for trading purposes. Canada recognized that this could mean becoming totally dependent upon the United States for trade and defence. Japan and China were reemerging as great powers and many new nations in Africa were becoming independent.

At the same time, many thoughtful Canadians were beginning to worry about increasing American control over all aspects of Canadian life. Many were also critical of the American involvement in the war in Vietnam. They thought the Americans should withdraw their troops from Vietnam in the interest of world peace. For all these reasons, it seemed like a good time for Canada to take a hard look at its foreign policy.

The Trudeau Review decided there were three possible paths the government could follow:

1 it could leave foreign policy as it was in the past, or,
2 it could seek to be tied even more closely with the United States, or,
3 it could seek to develop trade and friendly relations with other countries in order to reduce Canada's dependence on the United States.

This last path, later called The Third Option, was the policy the Trudeau government decided to pursue.

CANADA AND EUROPE

Canada's friendship with Europe seemed very natural considering the vast number of Canadians who were British, French, or other European descent. Many recent immigrants also came from Europe, and they maintained strong ties with their country of origin.

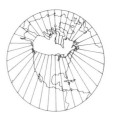

In 1975 Britain joined the European Economic Community (the European Common Market). The Common Market is a group of Western European nations who trade freely with each other without tariffs. Canadians worried because Britain, as a Common Market member, would no longer be able to offer low tariffs to Commonwealth nations. Yet it was vital that Canada should trade more with Europe in order to reduce our dependence on the United States.

Prime Minister Trudeau's frequent trips abroad were part of an effort to develop closer ties with the Common Market. He wanted to promote the sale of Canadian technology, especially nuclear-power plants. He also wanted to attract more European investment to Canada. In July 1976, an important step was taken. Canada and the EEC signed an Agreement for Commercial and Economic Co-operation. The agreement promised to increase

trade, investment opportunities, and a sharing of scientific and technological information between Canada and the Common Market countries. Swedish and French car manufacturers established branch plants in Nova Scotia and Quebec. Money from several European nations was being invested in Canadian real estate and industry.

Prime Minister Trudeau also visited the USSR. Since Canada geographically lies between the two superpowers, Trudeau wanted to build up ties of friendship with the USSR. He also realized that the USSR had great experience in northern development. This could be useful to Canada in developing the Arctic. Furthermore, Canada wished to trade with the USSR and its Eastern European allies. In April 1973 a $200 million sale of wheat and barley was made to the USSR. Another sign of increasing good will between Canada and the USSR had been an agreement signed two years earlier to exchange scientific, technical, and cultural information. The hockey games that followed between Team Canada and the USSR were examples of the increasing openness between the two countries.

CANADA AND THE PACIFIC

In its search for new trading partners, Canada began to look more seriously at the nations of the Pacific. Trudeau pointed out that Canada should take advantage of its ringside seat on the Pacific.

The first contact established by the government was with the People's Republic of China. Though the communists had taken over the mainland of China in 1949, the communist government had not been recognized by Canada and the United States. By 1970 Canada and China had exchanged ambassadors and Canada had supported China's admission to the United Nations. It took another two years before the United States recognized Red China. Trudeau paid an official state visit to China in 1973 and at that time China placed a huge order for 5 million t of Canadian wheat over a three-year period.

An important trading relationship had also been built up with Japan, now Canada's third most important trading partner. In 1976 the two countries had signed an agreement to increase their trade – particularly in coal. The Japanese have since invested money in Canadian industries and the development of our natural resources.

As part of the new directions of foreign policy in the Pacific, Canada has continued to build strong trading links with Australia, New Zealand, and other Commonwealth countries in that region. The government has encouraged universities to set up

Asian study programs and our immigration policy has been changed to allow more Asians into Canada.

A ceasefire agreement was signed by the United States, North Vietnam, and South Vietnam in 1973. Canada agreed to serve on the International Commission of Control and Supervision/ICCS set up to observe the Vietnam peace settlement. It soon became obvious that the ceasefire would not work. One Canadian was killed and several others were held prisoner. Therefore, the Trudeau government decided to withdraw Canada from ICCS duty in July 1973.

After the fall of Saigon (now Ho Chi Minh City) in 1975, many Vietnamese fled their homeland. In late 1978, tens of thousands of Vietnamese left their country for political and economic reasons. They arrived on the shores of nearby countries in broken-down, overcrowded boats. Most of them had endured nightmarish journeys on the high seas. Worldwide attention was drawn to the "boat people."

In 1979, Canada announced a program of private sponsorship to aid the refugees. The government agreed to allow into the country the same number brought in by individual Canadians or groups. Church groups and private citizens responded with compassion and sponsored over 32 000 people from wartorn southeast Asia. However, many people are still living in refugee camps in southeast Asia.

CANADA AND THE REST OF THE WORLD

The foreign policy review also suggested that Canada strengthen its ties with Latin America. Trudeau visited Mexico, Cuba, and Venezuela in 1976. Our trade with Latin America increased from $1099 million in 1970 to $3418 million in 1976. Canada also gave an increasing amount of development funds to a number of Latin American countries. When a revolution took place in Chile in 1973, Canada admitted hundreds of refugees.

Canada's major concern in the Middle East was to bring about a lasting peace to the Arab-Israeli conflict. In 1973 we agreed to return to the Middle East in a peacekeeping role. One thousand and fifty Canadian military specialists became part of the United Nations Emergency Force maintaining the ceasefire by providing supplies, transportation, and communication. After our withdrawal from the ICCS in Vietnam, this action reassured other countries that Canada was not abandoning its peacekeeping efforts.

Since the 1950s, many colonies in Africa have emerged as independent nations. Canada provided large amounts of money, food, and technical aid to these developing nations. This help was given to both Commonwealth and French-speaking African states.

CANADA AND THE UNITED NATIONS

The Trudeau foreign policy review recommended that Canada work hard to support the United Nations and make it an effective organization for international co-operation. However, the review expressed a growing feeling of disappointment over the UNs lack of power to keep peace in the world. It suggested that Canada try to shift the UN emphasis from peacekeeping to social and economic development. Canada contributed heavily, and has continued to do so, to all those UN organizations that are striving to help poor nations and are working for disarmament and human rights. Canada contributed the ninth largest share of the regular annual budget to the United Nations. In the 1970s Canada served on major UN peacekeeping missions in Cyprus, the Middle East, and Kashmir.

The issue of China's membership in the United Nations brought Canada into conflict with some other UN members, especially the United States. Since 1966, Canada had said that it was becoming increasingly more important that the People's Republic of China (communist China) be represented at the UN. At the time, the UN only recognized the former government of China which was established on the island of Taiwan. In 1971, Canada provided leadership in getting China admitted to the UN and expelling the representatives from Taiwan.

On 1 January 1977, Canada began a two-year term on the UN Security Council. This was the fourth time we had filled one of the non-permanent seats on the Council since the UN was established.

CANADA, THE COMMONWEALTH, AND THE FRENCH-SPEAKING COMMUNITY

Canada continued to value belonging to the "family" of nations that makes up the Commonwealth, with the queen as head of the family. The Commonwealth family is spread throughout the world and is made up of forty-eight countries. As one of the strongest members of the Commonwealth family, Canada continued to help the smaller and weaker members with generous financial aid. Canada found that the Commonwealth provided a good framework for peaceful working out of disagreements among family members. The heads of government in the member nations met every two years, and more than fifty conferences were

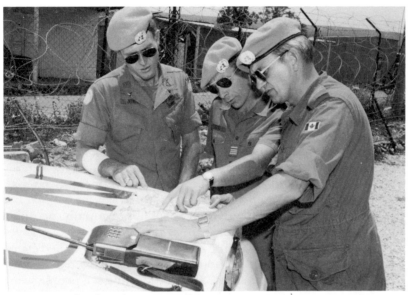

UN peacekeeping force in southern Lebanon

organized annually under Commonwealth sponsorship. In 1978 Canada was host to the 11th Commonwealth Games in Edmonton, Alberta, and the 12th Congress of Commonwealth Universities.

Since almost one-third of all Canadians are French-speaking, the federal government sought to strengthen ties with the French-speaking community of the world. These were the countries that are entirely or partially French-speaking, and were known as La Francophonie. Membership involved participating in educational, cultural, and sports activities organized by the various countries. A portion of Canada's foreign aid was directed toward the French-speaking developing nations.

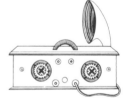

CANADA'S FOREIGN AID TO DEVELOPING COUNTRIES

In Canada a typical Sunday dinner may be a roast of beef, but in much of the world Sunday dinner is no more than a bowl of rice. In the 1970s there was an estimated 4.2 billion people on the earth, and more than 2.5 billion of them were starving. By the year 2000 those starving people could double in number. The average Canadian may say, "I know what hunger is. It's the gnawing feeling you get between meals." But that is not the kind of hunger that billions of people experience. Hunger – real starvation – bloats the stomach, caves in the cheeks, and strips the flesh from the rib cage. And when it is prolonged, it ends in lingering death.

Consider these facts:

- The average income of people living in underdeveloped countries was less than what the average Canadian family received from the government in family allowance payments.
- Mali had one doctor for every 38 821 people; Canada had one doctor for every 593.
- Canada gave 1 million t of wheat annually to the world's hungry in 1974–1977. That amount would have provided the starving with one slice of bread every five days.
- The UN estimated that in Africa and the Far East 25 to 30 percent of the population suffered from malnutrition.
- Bangladesh had one hospital bed for every 9896 people; Canada had one for every 110.
- North Americans spent over $3 billion annually on their pets. This is enough to feed the hungry for a year.
- In Asia, Africa, and Latin America, people went to bed every night wondering if they had enough food for the next day to keep alive. In the United States and Canada thousands of people went to bed every night wondering if they had enough will power to stay on their low-calorie diet.

Most of the starving billions are found in the underdeveloped countries, or what have come to be called Third World countries. Nations are often grouped into three or more categories depending on their wealth and social condition.

The First World includes the advanced industrial nations. They have strong economies, are usually wealthy, and have democratic governments. The United States leads this group. Japan, West Germany, Britain, Canada, Australia, New Zealand, France, and most other western European nations also qualify.

The Second World is a term used for the communist countries. These would include the USSR, the People's Republic of China, Hungary, East Germany, Czechoslovakia, Poland, and other east European communist countries. Generally the Second World is wealthy, but not as rich as the First World.

The Third World is made up of all the rest of the countries. Nations that are only beginning to develop their trade and industries belong in this group. So do those nations that claim to be politically non-aligned, that is, independent of both the First and Second Worlds. Many of these countries depend on just one crop or one mineral. Many are also faced with exploding population growth. It is estimated that they have over 200 000 new mouths to feed every day.

In the Third World there are so many sharp contrasts between countries that some experts now insist that there are really five

Country	Map No	Country	Map No	Country	Map No
Antigua & Barbuda	7	Kenya	29	Seychelles	31
Australia	39	Kiribati	47	Sierra Leone	18
Bahamas	3	Lesotho	21	Singapore	37
Bangladesh	35	Malawi	26	Solomon Islands	41
Barbados	10	Malaysia	36	Sri Lanka	33
Belize	4	Maldives	32	Swaziland	22
Botswana	23	Malta	16	Tanzania	27
Canada	2	Mauritius	30	Tonga	44
Cyprus	15	Nauru	48	Trinidad & Tobago	13
Dominica	8	New Zealand	40	Tuvalu	46
Fiji	43	Nigeria	20	Uganda	28
The Gambia	17	Papua New Guinea	38	United Kingdom	1
Ghana	19	St. Kitts & Nevis		Vanuatu	42
Grenada	12	(St. Christopher)	6	Western Samoa	45
Guyana	14	St. Lucia	9	Zambia	25
India	34	St. Vincent	11	Zimbabwe	24
Jamaica	5				

worlds. Arab countries such as Saudi Arabia and Kuwait, which are enormously wealthy from oil resources, might properly be called Third World. The new category Fourth World would more properly include countries that have some raw materials and some industrial potential. Such countries need outside help to get their economies going. Peru, the Arab Republic of Egypt, and Liberia could be called Fourth World countries. Those countries that exist in desperate poverty may be referred to as the Fifth World. Most have per capita incomes of less than $100 per year and few resources of any kind. They are barely able to feed themselves. Bangladesh, Chad, Nepal, and Afghanistan are said to be in this category. The new categories of Fourth and Fifth World may help us to see the wide diversity of conditions in countries traditionally referred to as Third World.

How could Canada help Third, Fourth, and Fifth World countries? The goal of Canada's foreign aid program was, and is, to do something to reduce the gap between Canada's wealth and the poverty of Bangladesh and countries like it.

In the past it was often thought that development aid to these countries would automatically help all of the poor people in them. This simply did not happen. Foreign aid supplied by rich nations usually found its way to the small wealthy class (large landowners, government officials, business people) in the Third World countries. Little of it got into the hands of the poor for whom it was really intended. In some African nations foreign aid was used by the white minority for military purposes to keep down the black majority. In other Third World countries the money was spent on glamour projects such as stadiums, swimming pools, and convention centres. Recognizing these problems, Canada's foreign aid policies have been reviewed and a new strategy for international development has been adopted.

The Canadian International Development Agency (CIDA) was created in 1968 to co-ordinate all Canadian aid from government and non-government (churches and charities) programs. Among the most important points in our assistance program from 1975 to 1980 were the following:

- Canada would continue and even increase its programs of development assistance.
- Canada would concentrate the bulk of its aid on countries where the per capita income is less than $375 a year.
- Canada would place its major emphasis on helping countries to improve food production and distribution, rural development, education and training, public health, shelter, and energy. As an example, in Senegal, West Africa, fishing was a vital source of food and employment. Three-quarters of the fishermen used dugout canoes. Canada provided outboard motors, helped build and equip workshops for their maintenance, and set up a system for selling the fish caught. From 1970 to 1975, the number of motorized boats rose from 2000 to 4800, and the fish caught nearly doubled. The help from Canada went directly to the fishermen, and the whole country benefited as a result.

- Canada would continue to provide emergency food, aid, and disaster relief to stricken areas of the world.
- About two-thirds of Canada's aid would be direct (bilateral) aid, going from the Canadian government to the government of the Third World country. The rest would be distributed through multilateral programs – given to international agencies such as the World Bank, OXFAM, and UNESCO.
- Canada would strive to raise its foreign aid to reach the United Nations target of 0.7 percent of Canada's Gross National Product (GNP). GNP is the value of all goods and services produced by the economy of a country in a year.
- Canada would make interest-free loans to developing countries. In the past these loans had been made with the condition that the developing countries buy goods made in Canada. This was known as tied-aid. In the future Canada would gradually remove the tied-aid restrictions on loans to developing countries.

GETTING ALONG IN THE GLOBAL VILLAGE

The Engineers of Malawi

In Malawi, a Commonwealth country in southeast Africa, CIDA is involved in a water-scheme project that is drawing international recognition. Water is being piped by gravity from mountain streams to taps in villages. For the first time clean water is available to rural people within 1 km of their home. The goal of the project is to have clean water and adequate sanitation for all the people of Malawi by 1990.

The program's success is based on community participation. The government provides the expertise and the piping and the villagers do the rest. The villages choose people who, with a little training, become the system's engineers. They construct and maintain the system. The system is technically uncomplicated and designed to last a hundred years.

CIDA has completed four water projects that serve over 150 000 people at a cost of $1.5 million. Malawi has contributed about one-third of the funds.

River Blindness in West Africa

Canadians know that black flies are pests. But in the tropical conditions of west Africa, there is a black fly whose bite can lead to blindness, commonly called river blindness. When the fly bites, a parasite enters the human blood system. The flies can deliver a thousand bites in a day. The disease leaves one in six villagers blind.

Three UN agencies and the World Bank started to combat the disease in 1974. The first phase of the program was spraying the breeding sites along the 18 000 km of rivers and forests to kill the larvae. The aerial-spraying work is contracted to Viking Helicopters of St. Clet, Quebec. The flying project is worth $7.6 million to the company. The government of Canada has contributed $5 million to the program since 1974.

Canada is also active in the second phase of the program, a chemotherapy program that is trying to find a cure for river blindness. The Canadian contribution for 1984 was $1.35 million.

Women at Work: Bangladesh

Every year, tropical monsoons drench the land with rain and cause the numerous rivers of Bangladesh to overflow. During the monsoon season, the earthen roads used to disappear under the flood waters and become impassable.

Today, however, fifteen-member work crews of rural women reinforce the roads and smooth out the deep ruts and potholes. They use simple hand tools to do their work. The advantages of the program are:

- It provides a steady income for the most disadvantaged women in the country.
- A 96 000 km road system is being developed which will assist rural people to get supplies and ship their produce to market.
- The roads will reduce the social isolation of rural farms and villages.

This almost year-round maintenance program has been developed with the help of CIDA. Canada's contribution to the program in 1984–1985 was $6.45 million.

CANADA AND DEFENCE: NATO AND NORAD

In the late 1960s Canada began to have second thoughts about its role in the defence of Europe. Even before the results of the Trudeau Review were published, the government took steps to change Canada's role in NATO. Canada withdrew 50 percent of its ground troops from European bases. Canadian forces left in NATO would no longer use nuclear weapons. Canada's defence budget for NATO would be frozen at $1.8 billion per year until 1972, one of the lowest budgets of any NATO member. Funds would not be available to replace military equipment that was old-fashioned and out-of-date. The government obviously felt that the role of

A CIDA project in India

Canada's armed forces should be concentrated on North American defence and the Arctic.

Canada's changing NATO role obviously upset several of our NATO allies. The West Germans in particular made it very clear that if Canada wished to have trading links with Europe, it must help maintain the NATO defences in Europe. As a consequence, between 1975 and 1977, there was almost a total about face in Canadian defence policy. Canada bought 128 Leopard 1 tanks from West Germany and 18 Aurora long-range patrol aircraft to guard north Atlantic shipping lanes. Canada bought anti-armour and anti-aircraft missiles. It began a selection process to find new attack aircraft. In addition the government decided to raise the defence budget by 12 percent per year for five years. Canada was showing its allies and trading partners that it was returning to a serious commitment to NATO.

Changes in defence policy took place in Canada's role in NORAD. In 1972 the Trudeau government began to dismantle the two nuclear-armed Bomarc missile bases in Ontario and Quebec. The Canadian government felt that the threat of war between the United States and the USSR had definitely decreased. Some critics of NORAD even urged that we abandon NORAD completely. They argued that the United States would never allow a foreign power to attack Canada. Other critics of NORAD complained that the United States often acted without consulting Canada anyway.

An example of this occurred in 1973 when American President Richard Nixon placed American forces on worldwide alert. This took place during the Arab-Israeli war. Canadian forces with NORAD were automatically involved. However, the Canadian minister of National Defence was not officially informed until eight hours after the president had declared the alert.

In 1975 the Canadian government strongly reaffirmed its commitment to NORAD. The top two defence priorities were pinpointed as:

1 the surveillance and protection of Canadian territory and coastlines;
2 the defence of North America in co-operation with US forces.

DEVELOPING SKILLS:
MAKING ORAL PRESENTATIONS

A Model to Follow

1 Introduction
Before you start your presentation, you must decide on the theme or purpose of your presentation. What are you going to tell your audience? What are you going to prove?

2 Content
Be sure your research is accurate. Know your facts well enough so that you can teach your audience. Your presentation will be much more interesting if you put all your ideas in your own words. Another trick to make it interesting is to maintain eye contact with your audience. To do this you must know your presentation well enough so that you won't have to read your notes.

3 Examples
Your audience will enjoy your presentation a lot more if you use examples to prove your points.

4 Organization
A very important part of your presentation is organization. Your audience will have trouble understanding your presentation if there is no order to it. It will be helpful if you write down a plan to follow. A good way to organize your material is by arranging it in categories.
   a) select the main idea;
   b) select material to support the main idea;
   c) arrange the material in a logical sequence.

5 Summary
Sum up clearly what you have been saying. Emphasize your position again. Give your audience something to think about by raising a new question.

You are a Canadian government official making a presentation to a community about Canada's role in a changing world. Research a topic, and then make an oral presentation on Canada's role in:
- Foreign policy in Europe
- Foreign policy in the Pacific
- United Nations
- La Francophonie
- Commonwealth
- CIDA
- NATO
- NORAD

DIGGING DEEPER

1 Examine the six basic national goals of Trudeau's foreign policy. Rank them in order of importance from most to least important. Be prepared to defend your ranking with valid reasons.

2 Canada gave $1.309 billion in direct country to country aid in 1986. Another $1.9 billion was spent multilaterally through the United Nations and other international organizations. However, a parliamentary committee on international affairs has recommended a basic change in Canadian foreign aid programs.

The committee thinks foreign aid should be tied directly to the human rights record of recipient countries. Any country violating human rights should be declared ineligible to receive Canadian funds. Some countries, such as the US, already use this method.

What would the advantages and disadvantages be to withholding Canadian foreign aid from countries with poor human rights records?

3 Use a comparison organizer to summarize Canada's roles in these fields in the 1970s.
- Peacekeeping
- Defence
- Trade
- Foreign aid

4 Compare Canada's foreign policy goals from 1945 to 1970 with those from 1971 to 1984. How could you explain any change in these goals?

38 Quebec in Crisis

5 October 1970
8:15 a.m.

The doorbell rang in the luxurious home of the senior British trade commissioner in Montreal, James R. Cross. Two men carrying a gift-wrapped package told the servant who opened the door that they wanted to deliver it to Mr. Cross. Admitted to the house, they pulled a rifle from the package, seized Cross, and took him away.

11:30 a.m.

Ransom demands from the kidnappers were received at a radio station. They identified themselves as members of the FLQ (Front de Libération du Québec) and asked for the release of twenty-three "political prisoners" being held in jail for bombings and terrorist activities. They also demanded transportation for the kidnappers to Cuba or Algeria, $500 000 in gold bars, and the publication of the FLQ Manifesto (statement of beliefs). The government had forty-eight hours to comply or Cross would be killed.

8 October

The FLQ Manifesto was read over the radio and television network of Radio Canada. The manifesto called the people of Quebec to revolution, and ended with the words,

> Long live free Quebec! Long live our comrades who are political prisoners! Long live the Quebec revolution! Long live the FLQ.

The other demands of the kidnappers were refused by the government.

10 October
Quebec Labour Minister Pierre Laporte was in his front yard tossing a football with his nephew and some other young people. A blue Chevrolet stopped in front of his house and four men with machine guns shoved Laporte into the back seat. The car sped away. The No. 2 man in the Quebec government had been kidnapped. The Quebec government now began to take the crisis seriously. Premier Bourassa took refuge in Montreal's Queen Elizabeth Hotel surrounded by armed guards. The kidnappers of Laporte identified themselves as a second cell of the FLQ.

12 October
In Ottawa federal troops took up positions around government buildings and provided escorts for important government politicians.

14 October
A group of sixteen prominent Quebeckers, including René Lévesque and Claude Ryan, issued a statement. They blamed the federal government for creating an atmosphere of "military rigidity." They argued that Quebec be allowed to work out the crisis on its own, and that the two hostages be exchanged for the political prisoners in jail.

Meanwhile in Toronto, Premier John Robarts of Ontario said there should be no compromise with the terrorists.

15 October
Mass meetings of university students in Montreal expressed sympathy with the FLQ and shouted slogans of revolution. The Quebec premier asked Ottawa for troops to back up the Montreal and provincial police forces working around the clock to track down the terrorists. Troops of the Royal 22nd Regiment moved into the streets of Montreal to guard public buildings. One thousand paratroopers from Canadian Forces Base Edmonton were flown to the base at St. Hubert just outside Montreal. Armored personnel carriers and soldiers with rifles and submachine guns took up posts in the streets of Montreal.

16 October, 4:00 a.m.
Prime Minister Trudeau, on the advice of the Quebec government, proclaimed the War Measures Act. It was the first time the act had been used in peacetime. Regulations under the act outlawed the FLQ and allowed police anywhere in Canada to detain people without charge for up to twenty-one days and without trial for up to ninety days. Now the police

Claude Ryan

and military could arrest people just on suspicion of belonging to the FLQ. Asked by a reporter how far the government
would go, Trudeau replied, "Just watch me."

In pre-dawn raids the police rounded up, among others,
fifty members of the Parti Québécois. A total of 465 were
eventually arrested. Gerald Godin, later to become a PQ
member of the Quebec National Assembly, recalled how the
police smashed down his front door in the middle of the
night. "I got up to investigate, I thought it might be firemen
next door, and there were these policemen standing around,"
he said. "I asked them what they were doing there and they
said they had come to arrest us." Godin asked them to
produce a search warrant, but "one gave a little half-smile
and told me to turn on the televison. I turned it on and there
was the announcement that during the night the government had passed these extreme measures." Godin was held
for seven days.

The reaction of the Canadian press to the introduction of
the War Measures Act was cautious approval.

18 October
In the early hours of the morning the body of Pierre Laporte
was found in the trunk of the same car used to kidnap him.
Amazingly the car was parked near the armed forces base at
St. Hubert. Laporte had been choked to death with the reli-
gious chain he wore around his neck.

Canadians waited tensely, wondering what would happen next.

27 October
Barbara Cross went on television to plead with the kidnappers for her husband's life.

15 November
A CTV program,"W5,"announced the results of a poll in which 87 percent indicated they were in favour of the introduction of the War Measures Act. Less than 6 percent opposed the introduction of this legislation.

4 December
Police surrounded a house in suburban Montreal where James Cross had been held for fifty-nine days. After hours of bargaining, a black Chrysler carrying Cross, the armed kidnappers, and their lawyer drove to the Expo '67 site. The kidnappers surrendered Cross and their arms to a Cuban diplomat. In exchange, the kidnappers were then whisked away to Dorval Airport and flown to Cuba.

Canadian Armed Forces entering Montreal during the FLQ Crisis

Pierre Laporte's body was found in this car trunk.

28 December

Three FLQ members accused of kidnapping and assassinating Laporte crawled out of a tunnel hidden under a farmhouse south of Montreal. They surrendered to the police and where charged with the murder of Pierre Laporte. The FLQ Crisis was over.

The FLQ Crisis in October 1970 ended seven years of violence in Quebec. But it did not end the turmoil or the differences between French and English. Most Quebeckers supported the steps taken by the Ottawa government at the time. However, the idea of Canadian soldiers having to keep peace in Quebec was disturbing to most Canadians. In time the feeling grew that Ottawa had overreacted. Too many questions remained unanswered. Was there really the danger of an "apprehended insurrection" in Quebec as Trudeau claimed? Were the rumours true that there was a widespread conspiracy about to take over the government of Quebec? If the trouble was in Quebec, why did the government take away the basic civil rights of every Canadian? These questions have never been properly answered by the Canadian government. Thus, much bitterness lingers for the hundreds of people arrested for nothing more than their nationalistic beliefs.

Let us listen in to the conversation of two women discussing the FLQ Crisis and the War Measures Act. One is Solange Chaput Rolland from Quebec and the other is Gertrude Laing from Alberta. Their conversation was recorded in 1972 in their book *Face to Face*.

SOLANGE: It is so difficult to explain how we felt when the army was here. The army in Quebec, for whatever reason, is a peculiar symbol. I felt reassured, and at the same time, I hated the army in Quebec. It was the Redcoats again! I know that what I am saying will make our readers jump, but to me, *"l'armée au Quebec, c'est l'occupation!"* (the army in Quebec means occupation). I know we *asked* the soldiers to come, because at that time we really thought that a lot of people needed to be protected. But while I was physically reassured, at the same time I was psychologically hurt. *L'armée est au Quebec! Le Quebec est occupé!* (The army is in Quebec! Quebec is occupied!)

GERTRUDE: I think I would have felt the same way if they had come to Alberta to protect me from my fellow-Albertans.

SOLANGE: ... To me, the army was a symbol of English Canada.

GERTRUDE: To me, it represents simply a force that I don't want. I realize that there are times when it is necessary, like taking medicine when you're ill, but I'm sure that psychologically I would have had the same reactions as you.

SOLANGE: You know ... the Patriotes and the revolt of 1837 are very much alive today in Quebec. We seem to be re-living history. Some of the FLQ militants in jail are beginning to sound like heroes for some of our youth. I have even heard that there are classrooms in Quebec where huge posters of Paul Rose, who is accused of the murder of Pierre Laporte, hang on the walls. This is the part which I despise. But to come back to the army, I must say something. The army came once because the government of Quebec asked for protection for some of its citizens. Now there are a number of people in Quebec, and I think I am one of them, who believe that if tomorrow we were to vote massively for the independence of Quebec, the Canadian Government, backed by nine other provinces, would send the army back, not to keep us in Confederation because they want us, but so as not to disrupt the Canadian Confederation.

GERTRUDE: Some Canadians have said quite openly that they would "send in the troops", but I wonder if they would if the time ever came.

SOLANGE: At the time that Prime Minister Trudeau proclaimed the War Measures Act, did he appear in the eyes of the whole country as the leader that the people had voted into power to put Quebec in its place?

GERTRUDE: If you are thinking that this was the logical result of the election to office of the man who many people expected would "put Quebec in its place", I would say No.

SOLANGE: I say Yes, Yes, Yes!

GERTRUDE: I don't think this was the feeling of most Canadians. On the other hand, if you mean that at that moment he became the true leader of the country, at any rate of English-speaking Canada (and I think to a large extent French-speaking Canada too), the leader who took the action that most of the people approved of, that most of the world approved of, then I would say Yes. I think he gained enormous prestige even in the eyes of Canadians who up to that point had not been convinced of his leadership. I have to say, however, that personally I found it hard to accept his action; I felt that we didn't need this extreme measure, although certainly I was in no better position than anyone else to know that. I was also very much afraid of the long-term political consequences.

SOLANGE: When the War Measures Act was proclaimed, I was in Winnipeg, and I was awakened that morning with words that still haunt me: "Ottawa has declared war on Quebec!" You can imagine how I felt! For about ten minutes I really believed this, until by listening to the news, I began to understand that Premier Bourassa had asked the troops to come to Quebec.

There is no doubt that the War Measures Act was a very drastic act. We still don't possess all the facts surrounding the FLQ crisis, but we certainly know now that there was not an armed guerilla uprising planned, that there was not an "apprehended rebellion", that only thirty-two guns were found, and so on. I believe that our government over-reacted, but I think I would have done the same thing if I had been in their shoes. What I cannot accept is that the government has neither given us the facts, nor admitted that it over-reacted. As a result, we live in a very uncertain atmosphere. If the government was sure that there was a possibility of open rebellion, they were right to take the steps they did. But since there is nothing to confirm this opinion, are we to suppose that we will once again be occupied if another crisis arises in Quebec?

1 To what event in the past was Solange referring when she said "It was the Redcoats again!"?
2 What do you think Solange meant when she said she was "psychologically hurt" by seeing the army in Quebec? Can you explain why she may have felt this way?
3 Solange compared the FLQ uprising with the rebellion of 1837. Point out similarities and differences in the two uprisings.
4 Do you think the Canadian government would be justified in sending the army into Quebec to keep it in Confederation? Explain your answer.
5 Explain how the FLQ Crisis caused Trudeau to gain "enormous prestige" in the country.
6 Gertrude feared the long-term political consequences of the crisis. Suggest what they might be.
7 How would a Quebecker feel on hearing the words "Ottawa has declared war on Quebec!"? Why?
8 In what respects did Solange feel the War Measures Act was too drastic? What were her fears for the future? Do you believe her fears were justified? Why?

One of the top priorities of the Trudeau government was to improve the position of French Canadians within Confederation. Even before the FLQ Crisis the government had taken steps to give greater recognition to the French language. In 1969 the Official Languages Act was passed. It declared:

The English and French languages are the official languages of Canada for all purposes of the Parliament and Government of Canada and possess and enjoy equality of status and equal rights and privileges as to their use in all the institutions of the Parliament and Government of Canada.

In other words the act guaranteed that both French and English Canadians could deal with the federal government in their own language. The government also pledged to provide more jobs in the federal government for French-speaking citizens. Until that time only 14 percent of the top government jobs were held by the French, even though they made up 25 percent of the population.

The government also tried to encourage regional economic development by providing huge sums of money for this purpose. Of course the money was available for all poor regions of Canada. However, it was hoped that the federal funds for Quebec would help raise the economic level of French Canadians.

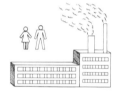

In addition, the Trudeau government showed a willingness to try to find ways of revising the Constitution. Not only Quebec, but several provinces as well had criticisms of the Constitution. Trudeau wanted to revise the Constitution in such a way that it would guarantee increasing equality for French and English Canadians. In that way Quebec would not need any special status within Confederation.

Although the FLQ Crisis had seemed to end the radical separatist movement in Quebec, moderate separatists continued to grow in number. By 1968 they had formed their own political party, the Parti Québécois, dedicated to Quebec independence. The leader of the PQ was René Lévesque, who had been one of the stars of the Lesage administration. He had left the Liberal party in 1967, and within a year the PQ had been formed and had 20 000 supporters.

René Lévesque was born in an isolated village in the Gaspé Peninsula. Because he grew up in the countryside and in a family that was not wealthy, he had always felt very close to the common people of Quebec. It is said that young René learned to read by sitting on his father's lap and listening to great French literature being read. During World War II he left his studies at Laval University to become a war correspondent in Europe. When he returned to Quebec he became a television journalist, explaining the events

René Lévesque

of the world to the people of Quebec. The popularity of his show earned him a wide audience in his province. In 1960 Lévesque entered provincial politics and was elected to the Assembly as a Liberal. He was one of the moving forces of the Quiet Revolution. Almost single-handedly he brought about the nationalization of Quebec hydro-electricity. He was reelected in 1962 and 1966.

By 1968 Lévesque and the Parti Québécois were convinced that Quebec should become an independent state. Only by independence could Quebeckers become their own masters with absolute control over their own affairs. Otherwise Quebec would be completely assimilated by the English or completely torn apart by the radical separatists. But separatism for Lévesque did not mean revolution. He hated "all forms of violence whose only result can be to divide and weaken even further the small nation of Quebec."

Most political observers in 1968 did not think the PQ had much chance of challenging the two leading parties – the Liberals and the Union Nationale. But they did not take into consideration the undercurrents running through the province of Quebec. The PQ zoomed off from a standing start, and by November 1976, eight years after it was founded, it would become the provincial government of Quebec.

In the meantime, the Liberals under Robert Bourassa came to power in Quebec. Since the Bourassa government strongly opposed the separatist movement, most Canadians breathed a sigh of relief. The Bourassa government began to build the huge

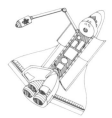

James Bay Hydro-electric Project. The premier called it the "project of the century." Because it would flood and destroy large areas of Quebec traditionally held by Native people, it was strongly opposed by many Native people's organizations. It was also fought by environmental groups because it would block several of the greatest rivers of the province. Unlike the hydro project of the 1960s, which had been built by French Canadians, the construction and finance of the James Bay Project was by Americans as they would get most of the power.

Similarly, in order to provide jobs for Quebec, the government turned over an enormous block of the province's forests to a giant American corporation. Many people in Quebec criticized these moves. It seemed to be the same kind of concessions that Duplessis gave to the Americans in the 1940s and 1950s in order to attract American investment dollars into Quebec.

The Quebec government, like that of some other provinces, urged that federal powers be weakened and provincial powers strengthened in some areas. Quebec was especially interested in getting increased provincial control over communications and immigration. Prime Minister Trudeau was prepared to discuss the constitutional changes necessary to satisfy some of Quebec's demands. In June 1971 Trudeau and the provincial premiers met at Victoria, British Columbia to discuss increasing the provincial powers in the Constitution. A compromise was reached that seemed to satisfy the provinces and the federal government. However, at the last moment Quebec decided to reject the new Constitution. Bourassa said that it did not provide sufficient authority to the province in the field of social security. As a result of Quebec's rejection of the Victoria agreement, the attempt to revise the British North American Act was set aside.

The government of Quebec was intensely concerned about the use of the French language in Quebec and the increasing number of non-French immigrants coming to Quebec. The French language, they believed, was the most important way they could keep alive the French culture. Yet an increasing number of immigrants from Europe coming to Quebec preferred to educate their children in English. Immigrants no doubt believed that if their children spoke English, they could move anywhere in North America and feel at home. In order to guarantee the French language top place in Quebec, the government introduced Bill 22. This bill proclaimed French as the official language of Quebec. It also ruled that children of immigrant families must attend French schools rather than English. The legislation was widely criticized by non-French Quebeckers and especially by immigrants who had recently come to the province of Quebec.

The Bourassa government was reelected in 1973 with a strong majority. But the Parti Québécois increased its support and managed to win 31 percent of the votes in the province. During the next three years, Bourassa's government was marred by several scandals and charges of corruption. It seemed unable to do anything about rising prices and increasing unemployment. The province was rocked by one strike after another in the public service: police, hydro workers, teachers, hospital employees, and fire fighters. As the Bourassa government appeared to be failing, more and more Quebeckers turned to what seemed to be the only attractive alternative – René Lévesque and the Parti Québécois. Many Quebeckers voted for the PQ not because they were in favour of separatism but because Lévesque promised them clean, competent government.

DIGGING DEEPER

1   What democratic rights of Canadians were lost when the War Measures Act was enforced in 1970?
2   Did the Canadian government overreact when it introduced the War Measures Act? Why?
3   Is this type of law ever justifiable in peacetime? Explain your answer.
4   Suggest other ways in which the government might have handled the threat in Quebec without taking away the civil liberties of all Canadians.
5   What effects would the FLQ Crisis have on each of the following? Explain your answers.
    a) separatism in Quebec;
    b) the English minority in Quebec;
    c) Prime Minister Trudeau;
    d) people living in other parts of Canada;
    e) the Liberal party in Quebec;
    f) foreign diplomats and business people living in Quebec.
6   Take a stand: Social protest sometimes involves violence. The FLQ Crisis was an example of this. Do you think violence is ever justified in drawing attention to a group's goals. Explain your reasons.

39
Quebec Under
the Separatists

15 NOVEMBER 1976

For days the public opinion polls had been saying that René Lévesque and the Parti Québécois could win the provincial election. In English Canada nobody wanted to believe that the separatists could ever come to power in Quebec. Even the most dedicated PQ members had their doubts. They knew their party would gain in strength, but they held out very little hope of actually winning the election. Then the first election results began to pour in. It looked like the Parti Québécois was going to sweep the province.

The huge crowd that had gathered in the Paul Sauvé Arena in Montreal could scarcely contain its excitement. Over and over they chanted the slogan "Quebec to the Quebeckers." Eventually their leader, René Lévesque, arrived and made his way to the platform. By this time the arena was packed to the rafters. When he stepped up to the microphone to speak, the crowd broke into a frenzy of cheering. It was a full five minutes before they allowed him to speak. The Parti Québécois had driven the Liberals from office, winning 68 of the 106 seats in Quebec. For the first time in their history, Quebeckers had elected a government dedicated to the establishment of an independent Quebec. In an emotional speech, Lévesque urged his supporters to keep a reasonable, friendly attitude toward Canada. Then he put forward the challenge, "Now we have to build this country of Quebec."

The Parti Québécois victory in Quebec sent shock waves across Canada. As the Task Force on Canadian Unity described it:

PQ supporters meet René Lévesque

That election victory was the culmination of a long historical process; it was also the beginning of a new era in the life of our country. There had been other occasions in Canadian history when provincial governments were elected in opposition to Confederation, but never before had the goal of provincial independence been sought with the firmness of purpose displayed by the leaders of the Parti Québécois. For the first time since it was created in 1867, the Canadian political union faced the genuine possibility that one of its largest provinces might leave.

For many Quebeckers, however, "15 November 1976 announced the hour of freedom." Others said, "Quebec is awake now. . . . We have stood up and we shall not sit down again for quite a while." A well-known historian from Quebec warned English-speaking Canadians "to realize the former Canada they were used to exists no more because the old Quebec itself is dead and buried." The triumphant slogan "Frogs have teeth" was chalked on walls all over Montreal.

A French-speaking person in Montreal expressed it this way:

My dear English-speaking countrymen. You are actually kept ignorant of what goes on in Quebec by the news media. A good example of this is that on 15 November you were so ignorant of what was going on in Quebec that you were astonished and almost in a state of collapse after the victory of the Parti Québécois. You never thought that this was possible because you don't know what goes on in Quebec.

Shortly after the Quebec election, Prime Minister Trudeau described the situation to the Canadian people:

> Quebeckers, like citizens of other provinces, are proud. They seek personal fulfilment in a free and independent way. The central question is whether this growth of freedom and independence is best assured by Canada, or by Quebec alone. Canadians must think about this brutal question now. Not only think about solving it in words, but by deeds, and through their attitudes . . . The country will only remain united – it should only remain united – if its citizens want to live together in one civil society.

The Quebec that the Parti Québécois took over in November 1976 contained about 4.5 million French Canadians and just over 1 million English-speaking Canadians. That 4.5 million was equal to the population of six provinces put together – Newfoundland, Prince Edward Island, Nova Scotia, New Brunswick, Manitoba, and Saskatchewan. Another 1.5 million French-speaking people lived in other parts of Canada. But 6 million French-speaking people were less than 3 percent of the English-speaking population of North America. The fact that so small a French minority survived and flourished in North America has been called in Quebec "the miracle of survival."

Small cities and towns of Quebec like Granby, St. Jean, or Chicoutimi looked typically North American, but there was a difference. About 99 percent of the people in those places lived in French. French was taken for granted as being perfectly normal. There were no great conflicts between the English and French here. The few English students in the area were bused to English schools.

However, Montreal presented a much different case. It was here that the two cultures, English and French Canadian, often faced each other and clashed. In the city itself there were 1.2 million Francophones and 800 000 of English origin. It was a sixty–forty split that made Montreal a lively and enriching place. Until the mid-1970s visitors could come to Montreal, and, apart from some French signs or voices, not realize they were in the second largest French-speaking city in the world. In the eyes of many French Montrealers, that was an insult long endured. The Parti Québécois was determined to make the atmosphere of Montreal more French.

Most of Quebec's English-speaking citizens lived in Montreal. It was said that it was possible and common for English Montrealers to have no real contact with French Montrealers. The English lived

Montreal, old and new

in separate neighbourhoods, went to different schools, and attended the English university, McGill. To complicate the problem, most of the immigrants who settled in Montreal chose to join the English-speaking community. They wanted to send their children to English schools because English was the language of North America. And so in the largest city of the province a gulf existed between the two language groups.

Another cause of grievance was that many Québécois believed all the English in the province were rich. They imagined that all the English lived in luxurious mansions in well-off neighbourhoods like Westmount. A popular French Canadian song spoke of "les anglais dans les chateaux sur la montagne" (the English in the castles on the mountain). The French, by comparison, lived at the bottom of the hill in poorer districts of Montreal, such as St. Henri.

This picture of Quebec society was not completely true. There were French who lived in splendid homes in places like Laval-sur-le-lac, and there were English who were far from being rich living in places like Point-St. Charles. However, there was an element of truth in this economic grievance. Figures produced in 1970 showed that the average salary for English Canadians in Quebec was $7900. French Quebeckers were at the bottom of the scale, with an average of $6000. The gap between French and English salaries had narrowed by 23 percent since 1960. That trend continued during the 1970s, but the gap still existed and the Parti Québécois was determined to do something about the reality of the richer English and the poorer French.

Closely connected to this was the old economic grievance that the bosses were English and the workers were French. If you were French and you wanted to get ahead economically in Quebec, you had to be able to speak English. If you were English, you could be successful in business without knowing a word of French. Again the 1970 average income figures proved that there was a certain amount of truth to this charge. English-speaking Montrealers who did not speak French were at the top of the income scale at $7250. French Montrealers who were not fluent in English were at the bottom of the scale with an average of $5100. In second place were the bilingual Anglophones, and in third place were bilingual Francophones.

In 1972 the Gendron Commission carried out a massive inquiry into all aspects of language use in Quebec. It showed that English was the language of top jobs and promotion in Quebec business. For example, in the Royal Bank of Canada, based in Montreal, only five of its top eighty-five management jobs were held by French Canadians. The government has made a serious effort since then to increase the use of French in private industry to make sure that more French Canadians are given management positions.

An incident occurred in 1976 that illustrated the deep divisions in Quebec over the two official languages. The federal government decided to introduce bilingualism in air and ground communications in all Quebec airports. Up to that time air traffic controllers used French only at five small provincial airports. English-speaking pilots across Canada went on strike protesting the new policy. They argued that English is the universal language of the International Civil Aviation Organization (ICAO). For safety's sake, they argued, English should be used. Many Canadians supported the English-speaking pilots' point of view. On the other hand, French-speaking pilots maintained that the ICAO approves the use of English as well as the language generally used at the airport.

For nine days English-speaking pilots refused to fly and Canada's air service was paralyzed. The federal government appointed a commission to report on whether the two languages could be used safely in flight communications. But the damage had been done. French Canadians took the strike as a personal and public insult. Once again their language seemed to be under attack by

English Canadians. The commission later reported, after months of study, that flying into bilingual airports in Quebec was no more dangerous than flying into other airports. But the report came out too late. Because of that incident, many French-Canadian Quebeckers gave up on Confederation. As René Lévesque himself admitted, this incident helped win tens of thousands of votes for the Parti Québécois.

The PQ took steps to do something about the language issue by passing the controversial Bill 101. This bill went even further than Bourassa's language legislation, Bill 22. French was confirmed as the only official language of the province. No business could display a sign in a language other than French. French was made the language of business and commerce. Doctors and nurses lost jobs in hospitals because they could not speak French fluently.

Probably the most controversial section of the bill concerned the language of education. Immigrants and all future immigrants to Quebec would not be allowed to send their children to English-speaking state schools. This was particularly resented. It meant

Protesting Bill 101

that immigrants from the United States, Britain, and all parts of Europe coming into Quebec would be forced to educate their children in French. English-language schools would be allowed to continue in Quebec. They would be limited to children already enrolled in the English school system or to children having at least one parent who received his or her elementary education in an English school in Quebec.

> Update on Bill 101
> Alliance Quebec, an English-rights group, challenged Bill 101 in the courts.
> 1979   The Supreme Court ruled citizens had the right to use either French or English in the courts and legislature of Quebec.
> 1982   Quebec court ruled that the limiting of English schooling in the province was unconstitutional.
> 1984   The Supreme Court upheld the Quebec court ruling that the limiting of English schooling was unconstitutional.

Anglophones in Quebec were dismayed with the new language charter. Some businesses announced that they were having difficulty in getting employees with school-aged children to accept transfers to their Montreal offices. Under Bill 101, families of English-Canadian business people transferred temporarily to Quebec would be compelled to send their children to French schools. The Task Force on Unity commented on this issue as follows:

> We firmly believe that the children of all Canadian citizens who move to another province should continue to have access to educational services in the language, be it French or English, in which they would have obtained them in their former province of residence. It seems to us to be only just and fair that every French and English person have access to essential health and social services in his or her principal language wherever numbers warrant; the same applies to an accused person in criminal trials. To our mind, these are the basic rights which each province should accord its English or French-speaking minority.

The PQ leaders explained that they were protecting their language and culture just as the Canadian government was taking steps to protect Canada from being swamped by the American culture. Those businesses that left the province were accused by the PQ of practising economic blackmail.

The Parti Québécois stressed the importance of gaining independence for Quebec. But despite their election victory in 1976, polls showed that only a small minority of Quebeckers wanted full independence from Canada. Most people seemed to draw back from asking for a complete break. Perhaps they feared that they would be swamped economically, culturally, and politically if they had to share the North American continent with the United States and Canada. Opinion surveys throughout the 1970s consistently showed that less than 20 percent of Quebeckers favoured independence. However, as many as 84 percent said they wanted some kind of change.

Lévesque was not able to move far ahead of public opinion. For one thing, he promised that his government would hold a referendum before making any move toward independence. He said he would abide by the results of the referendum even if independence was rejected. Lévesque told the Canadian Jewish Congress:

Whatever is going to happen is going to happen as democratically as we have acted the last ten years . . . We will do our best to win that referendum. But if we lose, it goes without saying that we'll respect that decision.

Some other senior PQ members later disagreed with the premier. They have said that referendums would continue to be held until an affirmative vote was achieved.

In the years and months leading up to the referendum, heated debate took place on the issue in all parts of Canada. There seemed to be three main options for Quebec. They were:

1 complete independence;
2 sovereignty association with Canada;
3 a renewed federalism.

AN INDEPENDENT QUEBEC NATION

The Quebec nationalists wanted an independent or sovereign state that would have full control over its territory and the people. It would make its own laws, set its own taxes, and determine its own economic, social, and cultural policies. As a sovereign state it would set up its own foreign policy and would enter into its own treaties with other sovereign nations. If necessary it would raise an army to defend itself and police to enforce its laws.

Independence for Quebec would not be a simple affair. Hundreds of problems would come up over sharing and ownership. They would include territory, finance, economics, powers, and division of assets. But before these could be solved, there would be constitutional problems to iron out. *Could Quebec legally leave Canada? Would Canadians have to agree to Quebec separation?*

One of Canada's top authorities on the Canadian Constitution was Senator Eugene Forsey. Forsey claimed that no province had the legal right to secede from Canada. The British North America Act would have to be changed by the British Parliament. Forsey believed that Parliament in Britain would not do this until it was absolutely sure that the government of Canada and all the provinces of Canada had a chance to be consulted.

Senator Forsey suggested that no Canadian government would even begin to negotiate independence for Quebec until it had held its own vote (referendum) in that province. Ottawa might even refuse to negotiate until it had submitted the whole question to all Canadians in a general election. Suppose the Quebec and Canadian governments managed to agree on the details of separation – even then the Canadian government might decide to submit the agreement for approval to the whole Canadian nation.

Many English-speaking Canadians argued that Quebec could not leave Confederation without consulting the rest of Canada. Premier Davis of Ontario presented a viewpoint along this line. He stated, "It is utterly unrealistic to argue that for Quebeckers the only issue is the determination of their own future. No such fundamental decision can be taken without profoundly affecting us all."

Many Quebeckers believed that the people of Quebec had the right to determine their own destiny. They recalled how Newfoundland came into Confederation in 1949. The people of Newfoundland decided in a referendum that they wished to join Canada. No national referendum was held in the rest of Canada. If the people of a region can decide to *enter* Confederation, the people of Quebec should be allowed by a referendum to vote to *leave* Confederation.

A break between Canada and Quebec might not be without violence. A few Anglophones in Montreal indicated that they were ready to call on the Canadian Armed Forces or even volunteers to defend their right to be part of Canada. *If civil war broke out in Quebec, would English-speaking people in Canada be prepared to go to the defence of the English minority in Quebec?*

If Quebec became an independent nation, where would its boundaries be located? Would an agreement be made to provide a land link connecting Atlantic Canada and the rest of the country? Who would control the St. Lawrence Seaway which is jointly owned with the United States? Then there was the matter of what would be done with northern Quebec. In 1912 the federal govern-

Protesters in Quebec

ment gave Ungava, which was part of the Northwest Territories, to Quebec. Canada would probably demand that this territory be given back. Similarly in 1927 Britain's highest court, the Privy Council, awarded Labrador to Newfoundland. Newfoundland had already indicated that it was determined to hold on to its mainland territory. Quebec outside Confederation would have to accept very different boundaries than it had in 1980. It could be limited to the boundaries that Lower Canada had when it joined Confederation in 1867. This would exclude the site of the James Bay Power Project, as well as vast mineral and forest resources.

SOVEREIGNTY ASSOCIATION WITH CANADA

Lévesque said he wanted a Quebec that was independent or sovereign, but closely joined to Canada in a kind of common market. Quebec would have its own citizenship and immigration laws,

which Lévesque regarded as essential to preserve the French culture. However, Quebec and Canada would have a common trade policy with the same tariffs and rules, and possibly the same currency. Lévesque called this sovereignty association. Lévesque outlined this idea to a group of prominent American bankers at the Economic Club in New York.

> **This new partnership could take the form, essentially, of a common market based on a customs union, permitting free passage of persons, goods, and capital, as in the countries of Western Europe. Additionally, if the desire is mutual, we are ready to go further, as far as monetary union (use of the same currency).**

However, not everyone in the PQ agreed with Lévesque's idea of sovereignty association. Some provincial premiers said if Quebec became independent, they did not necessarily want an economic union with it. Premier Blakeney of Saskatchewan said:

> **If Quebec decided to separate, we would have to ask ourselves what advantages there would be in maintaining links with a Quebec which is unwilling to continue supporting a federal government, but which would continue to benefit from our tariff structure. I cannot imagine very many in Saskatchewan being interested in such a proposition.**

The federal government issued a series of reports written by a team of economists. The reports concluded that sovereignty association would not be profitable for the rest of Canada. They also warned that Quebec was much more dependent on the rest of Canada for its manufactured goods than the rest of Canada was on Quebec. The Ottawa experts said that the separation of Quebec would cause economic hardships for all the provinces. But the impact on Quebec would be particularly severe. Quebec was heavily dependent on sales to the rest of Canada, and therefore hundreds of thousands of jobs in Quebec could be at stake.

Lévesque has dismissed this as federal propaganda. He believed that the provinces of Canada would negotiate with an independent Quebec because it would be in their own interests to do so. Experts on Lévesque's team maintain that it would cost Canada dearly if its provinces did not have an economic association with Quebec. "Just for instance," says Lévesque, "at least 100 000 jobs in Ontario depended immediately on the Quebec market."

Aside from how Quebec and the rest of Canada could weather the split up of the country, a number of other issues would have to be solved.

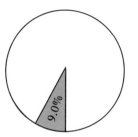

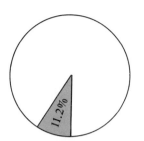

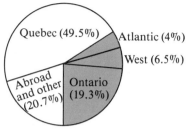

From the Atlantic region
to Quebec

From Ontario to Quebec

From Quebec to the rest
of Canada (29.8%)

Shipments of manufactured goods, 1974

*How would the assets and debts of the federal government be
divided between an independent Quebec and the rest of Canada?* The Parti Québécois suggested that assets should be divided
on the basis of population and personal income. Quebec's share
should be about 27 percent. However, one Quebec minister
warned that Quebec would not pay any share of Canada's war
debts or debts to build special projects in other provinces.

Dividing up the assets of the Canadian National Railways and
Air Canada, for example, would be extremely complicated. Settling Quebec's share of the St. Lawrence Seaway or federal proper-
ties in Canada or overseas would involve long and bitter
negotiations.

How would the currency issue be resolved? Would Quebec
have its own currency? Or, would it be possible, as Lévesque had
suggested, for Quebec and Canada to have a joint currency and a
central bank. This question was of critical importance. Until it
was decided, the value of the Canadian dollar would be uncertain
in the eyes of the world.

Then there were questions about labour. *Would Quebeckers be
allowed to come into Canada to work?* What would happen to the
employees of large Canadian companies whose head offices were
in Montreal? Would they be permitted to work in Quebec?

These were just some of the questions that would have to be
worked out if the sovereignty association option between Canada
and Quebec was chosen.

A CHANGED FEDERAL SYSTEM OF GOVERNMENT

Even people in Quebec opposed to separation said that things
could not remain as they were. An organization called the Positive
Action Committee was formed in Quebec to fight separatism. The
committee warned Canadians outside Quebec that change must

come and come fast if Canada was not only to survive, but to flourish.

Quebec was not alone in wanting to change the relationship of the provinces to the federal government. Many English-speaking Canadians were also critical of the way the political system had been working. According to the Task Force on Canadian Unity,

Although the BNA Act has served Canada well for 111 years, in a variety of changing circumstances unforeseen by the Fathers of Confederation, and although there have been numerous slight adjustments over the years, there is a growing gap between the structure created in 1867, and the social, economic, and political realities of the vastly different Canada of 1979. *We believe therefore that there should be a new Canadian constitution to meet the aspirations and future needs of all the people of Canada.*

Canadian provinces other than Quebec also wanted more political powers for themselves. The western provinces were demanding more control over their natural resources. Alberta wanted to set its own price for Alberta oil, not Ottawa. Ontario and Atlantic Canada likewise had complaints. Ontario talked about wanting to control cable television. It wanted to be able to put up trade barriers on goods from other provinces that competed with Ontario products. Atlantic Canada insisted that oil found off its coasts belonged to the provinces and not to all of Canada. Atlantic Canada thought it deserved more say in transportation decisions affecting its ports and railways.

There were moves underway to give Canada a new constitution and replace the BNA Act of 1867. If a new Canadian constitution could be worked out, it was thought it might still be possible to persuade Quebec to remain part of Canada. The new constitution would have to recognize the partnership between the French and the English in the history of Canada and the distinctiveness of Quebec. It would also have to give much greater power to all the provinces to run their own affairs. It would be a way of preserving Canada as a nation that would include Quebec. At the same time, it was a way of satisfying the various groups within the country.

When the PQs announced the referendum date, Joe Clark and the Conservatives were in power in Ottawa. However, by the date of the referendum Trudeau and his experienced Quebec members were back in office. Instead of facing a weak Anglophone defence from Ottawa, the PQ encountered an aggressive, well-oiled political machine. Jean Chrétien, minister of Justice, lead the federal "non" campaign. The federal Liberals probably helped tip the balance in favour of the "non" vote.

DIGGING DEEPER

1 a) Suppose your family had moved to Quebec in 1978 because your mother or father was transferred there. Your parents have lived all their lives in Ontario and do not speak French. Under Bill 101 would your younger sister be allowed to start kindergarten in an English-speaking school? Explain your answer. How do you think your parents would feel about this?

   b) A French-speaking family from Quebec has just been transferred into your community. Are French schools available for the children? Find out what education, health, and court facilities are available in your community for the French-speaking minority.

2 Explain why many immigrants to Quebec preferred to send their children to English schools.

3 Why is a person's language important? Why did the province of Quebec feel it was necessary to protect the French language?

4 Pretend you are one of the following people. Explain the reasons why you would or would not have supported the PQ in the election of 1976.

   a) manager of an American branch plant based in Montreal
   b) a recent Italian immigrant with school-age children
   c) an English-speaking Quebecker
   d) a middle-class French-speaking businesswoman
   e) a French-speaking university student
   f) a person held for eight days by the police during the FLQ Crisis

5 Summarize the three main options for Quebec before the referendum in a comparison organizer. Some headings are:

- What powers Quebec might have
- What would be the impact on Quebec
- What would be the impact on the rest of Canada
- What would be the difficulties of implementation
- Who would support the option

6 Three language groups live in harmony in Switzerland. Do some research to explain the Swiss success. Compare Switzerland's political, geographic, and language situation with Canada's.

40
Non, merci!

It was the evening of 14 May 1980. Prime Minister Trudeau stood before ten thousand wildly cheering supporters in Montreal's Paul Sauvé Arena and made a solemn commitment.

There were just six days remaining in the referendum campaign. The Parti Québécois government was seeking a mandate from voters to negotiate sovereignty association for Quebec. Trudeau's words that night were credited with swinging many undecided voters against the separatist option.

"I am making a solemn commitment," said Trudeau, "that after a 'non' vote, we are going to set into motion the mechanism of constitutional renewal. We will not stop until it has been achieved."

"Now I address myself solemnly to Canadians in other provinces," Trudeau continued. He pointed toward the seventy-three Quebec members of Parliament surrounding him on the platform. "We in Quebec are putting our heads on the block. When we tell Quebeckers to vote 'non', we are telling you that we will not accept that a 'non' be interpreted by you as an indication that everything is fine, that everything can remain the way it was before. We want changes made. We are putting our seats at stake to obtain these changes!"

The Trudeau pledge was the prelude to the patriation of our Constitution.

The referendum campaign was intense. Premier Lévesque and the PQ desperately wanted the vote to be a resounding "oui." The referendum was a critical test for the PQ government. The PQs had been elected on a separatist platform. The main purpose of

their party was to gain a form of independence for Quebec. A "oui" vote would be an enormous boost for the independence movement and a grave setback for national unity. The federal government and the provincial Liberals, under Claude Ryan, were urging the people of Quebec to vote "non." A resounding "non" vote would derail the issue of independence — at least for the time being.

The "oui" and "non" sides placed ads in newspapers, in magazines, on television, and radio. Quebeckers were bombarded with propaganda and had to work their way through a lot of literature to reach a decision. They had to decide if sovereignty association would benefit Quebec or not. What would be the losses, especially the economic ones?

This chart was part of the PQ referendum literature. They were attempting to prove the decline in influence of French Canada in the House of Commons.

Un Canada de Plus en Plus Anglais

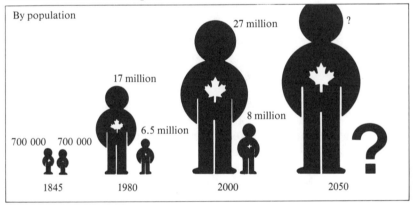

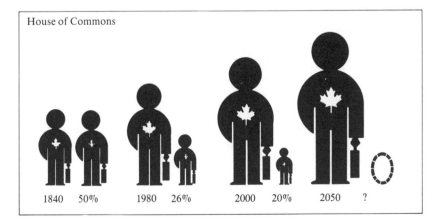

However, every time Lévesque argued that there was no place for Quebeckers in Ottawa, the federal government countered by pointing to Marc Lalonde, Jean Chrétien, Monique Begin, André Ouellet, Jeanne Sauvé, and Pierre Trudeau. These people occupied high political offices in Canada. It was obvious in Canada that the French were indeed powerful.

The "oui" and "non" forces held massive rallies. At one of these rallies, Lise Payette, a PQ Cabinet minister, made a speech that may have lost the battle for the Parti Québécois. She accused all women who would vote against sovereignty association of being "Yvettes." Yvette was the little girl in a Quebec primary school reader. In the stories, Yvette always stayed home to cook and sew while her brother had exciting adventures. To many women, Payette was suggesting that women who opposed sovereignty association were submissive and incapable of thinking for themselves.

Many women in Quebec were outraged by Payette's careless remark. Within a week of Payette's speech, they had organized an "Yvette" movement and staged a mass rally with 15 000 "Yvettes." One of the speakers said, "We are mothers who have inherited this great country from our ancestors. We intend to hand it on to our grandchildren intact."

A large majority of women voted "non" in the referendum. Afterward one PQ organizer said, "The 'Yvettes' killed us."

The referendum question was deliberately vague. It didn't ask if Quebeckers wanted to separate from Canada. The referendum merely asked whether voters would authorize the Quebec government to begin negotiations with the federal government on sovereignty association.

Here is the text of the question:

The Government of Quebec has made public its proposal to negotiate a new agreement with the rest of Canada, based on the equality of nations; this agreement would enable Quebec to acquire the exclusive power to make its laws, administer its taxes, and establish relations abroad – in other words, sovereignty – , and at the same time, to maintain with Canada an economic association including a common currency; any change in political status resulting from these negotiations will be submitted to the people through a referendum; on these terms, do you agree to give the Government of Quebec the mandate to negotiate the proposed agreement between Quebec and Canada?

The question may have been vague, but the results were not. Sixty percent voted "non." However, it was English-speaking Quebeckers and citizens whose first language was neither French nor English who swayed the vote. French-speaking Quebeckers accepted the concept of sovereignty association. A record 82 percent of the people voted. The vote broke down as follows:

Results of sovereignty-association referendum 20 May 1980		
	Oui	Non
	(percentage)	
French-speaking Quebeckers	60	40
English-speaking Quebeckers	9	91
Non-French- or English-speaking Quebeckers	16	84

BRINGING HOME THE CONSTITUTION

Trudeau's speech of 14 May had not been an empty political promise, but a sincere commitment to a new Canada. He was determined that Canada would have a new federal system of government.

For years there had been an on-going discussion about revising the BNA Act. Trudeau believed there had been enough talk. Now was the time to act. Less than one month after the referendum, Trudeau organized a first ministers conference to draft an agenda for summer-long constitutional negotiations. However, the premiers could not agree on how to revise the Constitution. Trudeau was frustrated by their inability to reach a decision. He went on national television to tell Canadians that the federal government would act on its own, or unilaterally, to bring home the Canadian Constitution.

In early November 1981, Trudeau made one last attempt to involve the provincial premiers in the patriation process. For four days, the prime minister, the ten provincial premiers, and an army of officials debated the issue at the National Conference Centre in Ottawa. They were trying to devise a plan that would make it possible to amend the Constitution in Canada. They also wanted to include a Charter of Rights and Freedoms to protect all Canadians. It was a stormy session. Eight premiers were firmly opposed. Trudeau's only allies were William Davis of Ontario and Richard Hatfield of New Brunswick.

At the last possible moment, a deal was hammered out. Nine of the ten provinces and Ottawa reached an agreement. However, Quebec refused to sign the accord. Lévesque stalked out of the meeting saying that Quebec had been betrayed. He complained that the deal confirmed what he had always suspected, that "Quebec is alone."

Three main points were included in the accord:
1 The power to amend the Constitution would be brought home from Britain;
2 Changes to the Constitution could be made if the federal government and seven provinces (representing 50 percent of the population) agreed;
3 A Charter of Rights and Freedoms would be added to the Constitution.

The MPs Agree: Bring It Home!

The public galleries were jammed. People had been lining up for hours in the hope of getting a seat at the historic event. It was 2 December 1981, and the MPs were about to vote on the patriation package. To a roaring chorus of "O Canada," the federal MPs voted 246 to 24 in favour of bringing the Constitution home to Canada. One MP had left his hospital bed in order to vote. Liberal MPs were all wearing red carnations in their lapels. One MP said, "The flowers reflect the blossoming of a new country, the blooming of a new Canada." It was a proud and joyful moment.

But, in the province of Quebec, the PQ government ordered the Quebec flag to be flown at half mast to signify the "insult done to Quebeckers by English Canada."

The Constitution Comes Home

A Canadian delegation went to London, England to ask the British Parliament for approval to change the BNA Act. In 1867, the

Fathers of Confederation had not included a formula for changing the BNA Act in Canada. It was a British act, so every time a change was required, Canadians had to ask the British Parilament to make changes.

On 8 March 1982, the British House of Commons debated and passed the Canada Act. It was 115 years to the day since the BNA Act had become law. Now, at last, Canada's status as a fully independent nation was recognized.

On Parliament Hill, at 11:37 a.m. on 17 April 1982, Queen Elizabeth II, with Pierre Trudeau by her side, gave royal assent to the Canada Act. The carillon in the Peace Tower pealed "O Canada" as citizens celebrated the coming home of our Constitution.

THE PARTI QUEBECOIS AFTER THE REFERENDUM

One province – Quebec – did not consider the constitutional issue to be resolved. Although they had been defeated in the referendum issue, the PQs were returned to power in the 1981 election. Their victory was due to their good economic performance, which had seen the creation of 6500 jobs in Quebec between 1977 and 1980. They also promised to leave the issue of sovereignty association alone.

However, the PQ did not leave all "French" issues alone. In September 1982, they amended Bill 101. The amendment required all businesses and stores in the province to have their signs in French only or risk fines up to $1000.

This amendment was unpopular with the Anglophone population of Quebec, and with many Francophones as well. Five merchants, charged with having bilingual signs, decided to fight the amendment to Bill 101 in the courts. They were backed by an organization called Alliance Quebec.

Almost three years later, in January 1985, the Quebec Superior Court ruled that French-only business signs were a violation of Quebec's human rights charter.

This decision came at a low point for the PQ. In late 1984, Lévesque had announced that the PQ would not make sovereignty association an issue in the next provincial election. This angered many hard-core separatists in his party and in his Cabinet. Many Cabinet ministers, most notably his minister of Finance, Jacques Parizeau, resigned. In 1985, Lévesque left politics, and he was replaced as leader of the PQ by Pierre Marc Johnson. Johnson lost the next provincial election, and the Liberals, under leader Robert Bourassa, returned to power.

The Parti Québécois was floundering. Without sovereignty association as their platform, they were indistinguishable from

René Lévesque conceding defeat on sovereignty-association referendum.

the other political parties in Quebec which had also adopted a brand of Quebec nationalism.

In November 1987, Johnson resigned as party leader. The hardliners were glad to see him go. They wanted a leader who would reflect their goals of independence for Quebec.

The Quiet Revolution had brought Quebec into the twentieth century. Now, Quebeckers were struggling to come to terms with their role in Confederation.

MEECH LAKE ACCORD

It would take a new government and five years before Quebec signed the Constitution. In 1987, Prime Minister Brian Mulroney accomplished a great feat. He persuaded all the first ministers, who were meeting at Meech Lake, to hammer out a new constitutional agreement. This agreement satisfied every province. Important changes were proposed so that, as Mulroney put it, "we could welcome Quebec back into the Canadian family."

When the details of the Meech Lake Accord were made public, former prime minister Trudeau broke a three-year political silence to denounce the agreement. Trudeau argued that the proposal gave far too much power to the provinces, particularly Quebec. He warned that, in his opinion, it would result in a powerless federal government.

During meetings in June 1987, the constitutional amendments were finalized. The major changes to the 1982 Constitution were:

1 Quebec was to be recognized as a "distinct society" within Canada;
2 Provinces would be allowed to opt out of any new national programs and still receive money from Ottawa for their own programs;
3 Provinces would be given a say in the appointment of Supreme Court justices and senators;
4 Future changes to federal institutions, or granting provincial status to territories would require agreement by Ottawa and all the provinces.

Both Ottawa and the ten provincial legislatures must ratify the accord. According to the 1982 Constitution, this must be done within three years.

THE CONSTITUTION AND NATIVE RIGHTS

The 1982 Constitution guaranteed the "aboriginal rights" of the Native people. Between 1982 and 1987 Native groups lobbied diligently to have self-government for Native people entrenched, or firmly established, in the Constitution. They sought control of land, schools, and social services so that Native people could make their own decisions about the economic and cultural future. Meetings were held on several occasions to try and resolve the issue.

In April 1987, another round of talks ended in failure. The premiers of British Columbia, Alberta, Saskatchewan, and Newfoundland were unwilling to entrench the concept of self-government for hundreds of Native groups until the details of each self-government agreement could be spelled out. Without their support, the amendment could not pass as the consent of the federal government and seven provinces representing 50 percent of the population is necessary for a constitutional amendment.

Native leaders were bitterly disappointed. Some of them talked about having the courts settle the issue of their constitutional rights or appealing to the United Nations for assistance. No immediate plans were made for any future talks.

DIGGING DEEPER

1 Explain what these key words in the referendum question mean.

>   sovereignty
>   economic association
>   mandate to negotiate

2 Suggest some reasons why Lévesque and the Parti Québécois would have drafted such a vague referendum question.

3 Explain the role played by the federal Liberals and the "Yvettes" in the "non" campaign.

4 Why did Quebec separatism rise in the first place? Why did it decline? Following the referendum, do you think the idea of separatism has been derailed in Quebec? Why or why not?

5 Read this comment by Mulroney on the Meech Lake Accord of 1987.

Because Quebec was not a signatory to the Constitution there were two Canadas emerging when this government took office – those Canadians who had accepted the Constitution and those who had been left out. Now there is one Canada, strong and united.

Explain what the prime minister meant. Why would most Quebeckers agree with Mulroney's statement?

6   The following quote is Pierre Trudeau's comment on the 1987 Constitutional Accord.

Those Canadians who fought for a single Canada, bilingual and multicultural, can say good bye to their dream. We are, henceforth, to have two Canadas, each defined in terms of its language. And because the accord states that "Quebec constitutes within Canada a distinct society" and that "the role of the legislature and government is to preserve and promote this distinct identity," it is easy to predict what future awaits anglophones living in provinces where they are fewer in number than Canadians of Ukrainian or German origin.

What did Trudeau predict would happen to Anglophones living in Quebec? What did he think would happen to Francophones living in other provinces? Was he correct? Why?

7   Make a timeline of the events that have happened to the Constitution from June 1987 until now.

8   This political cartoon appeared in the *Toronto Star* on 4 June 1987. What is the cartoonist's point of view?

41
The Beaver and the Elephant: Canadian-American Relations

"Living next door to the United States," said Prime Minister Trudeau, "is like sleeping in the same bed as an elephant. No matter how friendly and even-tempered is the beast, one is affected by every twitch and grunt." If the elephant rolls over in its sleep, the Canadian "beaver" must be ready to jump. Nine times out of ten the elephant and beaver get along very well together. Once in a while, however, the elephant gets a little grumpy, or the beaver feels threatened. When this happens these oddly matched neighbours sit down and talk together about their problems. In many ways the comparison made by Trudeau was a good one. The United States is certainly a giant – the richest and most powerful nation in the world. It has ten times our population and economic production. As a military power the United States greatly overshadows Canada.

The American superpower is Canada's nearest neighbour. In fact Canada shares a border with only one foreign power, the United States. Almost 70 percent of our trade is with the United States and more than 70 percent of foreign investment in Canada is made by Americans. Of course the United States is Canada's most important military ally through our defence agreements.

As Canada entered its second century, many people became increasingly alarmed over the amount of control the American "elephant" had on our lives. Our economy, our foreign policy, and our culture were each affected by the twitches and grunts of the United States.

CANADIAN INDENTITY?

THE AMERICAN INFLUENCE ON THE CANADIAN ECONOMY

As a young country Canada welcomed foreign investment. First it was British money that got the wheels of industry started in Canada. Gradually more and more American money poured into Canada to keep the wheels turning. Throughout the 1950s and early 1960s, most Canadians thought foreign investment was of great and unquestionable benefit. But by the early 1970s, Canadians discovered just how much of their economy was owned by foreign investors, especially Americans. Several government studies at this time made Canadians more aware of the seriousness of the situation (The Watkins Report of 1968, the Wahn Report of

1970, and the Gray Report of 1971). Many Canadians became concerned about how much control the Americans did have over our economy. It was felt by some that if this trend continued Canada would reach a point of no return. These people were known as economic nationalists. They believed that Canada could not go on selling its resources and industries to foreigners without eventually losing political independence as well. They wanted the economy run by Canadians for Canadians. Otherwise not only the economy, but also Canada's cultural identity, would become completely dominated by the United States.

On the other hand, a large number of Canadians favoured American investment in Canada. They pointed out that the Americans were willing to invest their money in businesses in Canada when many Canadians were not prepared to take the risk. The high standard of living many Canadians enjoyed was one of the benefits of having American investment in our economy. Those who favoured American investment often lived in Atlantic Canada and the West. They were prepared to welcome even more American investment into Canada.

As facts about American investment in Canada became known, Canadians debated the pros and cons of foreign investment in our country. Newspapers conducted polls to find out how Canadians felt about American investment in Canada. People who believed that American investment was a good thing for Canada felt that it:

1   created thousands of jobs for Canadians;
2   provided money to help develop Canadian resources and industries when Canadians were unwilling to take the risk to do it;
3   helped raise the standard of living in Canada to almost the same high level as the United States;
4   brought advanced technical knowledge and machinery into Canada;
5   American-owned companies paid taxes to the Canadian government;
6   gave business to Canadian-owned companies;
7   profited Canadians who bought shares in American-owned businesses;
8   provided Canadians with a greater variety and the highest quality of manufactured goods;
9   made for friendly relations between Canada and the United States.

People who believed that American investment was a bad thing for Canada, such as the economic nationalists, felt that it:

1   led to American takeover of Canadian economy (Canadians should have control over their own economy);
2   made profits leave the country and go to the United States;
3   meant top jobs often go to Americans;
4   took Canada's natural resources out of the country for processing. Canada had to buy back the resources as expensive manufactured goods.
5   made us more "American" in our tastes and production methods;
6   discouraged technological advances in Canada (it was easier to borrow technological advances from the Americans);
7   caused key decisions about expanding or shutting down a plant to be made outside the country;
8   sometimes restricted the trade of Canadian branch plants with countries considered unacceptable by the United States (an example was Cuba);
9   brought American-based unions into Canada.
   Which argument makes the most sense to you? Why?

Case Study: The Denison Mines Case

In 1970 much of Canada's uranium was controlled by foreign-owned companies. Canada possessed some of the richest uranium fields in the world. Denison Mines Limited of Toronto controlled about 40 percent of the known reserves of uranium in Canada. The rest of Canada's uranium was owned by foreign companies. It became known in 1970 that Stephen B. Roman planned to sell his stocks in Denison Mines to an American firm, the Continental Oil Company of Delaware. This sale would have left less than 10 percent of Canada's uranium resources in Canadian hands. Therefore the Canadian government took action to block the sale. Trudeau surprised the business community by announcing that uranium was too important a resource to be controlled by foreigners. The government took further steps to limit foreign ownership of the uranium industry to 33 percent or less. At least two-thirds of the shares of the uranium companies must be owned by Canadians.

Roman was amazed and upset by the government action. He claimed that he needed the money from the Denison Mines sale for his other investments. He said that the government was discriminating against him while allowing foreign interests to control other Canadian resources. He even tried to sue the prime minister and the minister of Energy for damages in the amount of $104 million. The Ontario Supreme Court, however, dismissed Roman's case, saying that the government was acting in the "best interests of Canada."

The economic nationalists were happy with the Denison Mines decision. They said it showed what the government could do about foreign ownership. However, the government did not continue this policy of strong action. Foreigners continued to buy Canadian industries as well as land and resources.

FOREIGN INVESTMENT IN THE CANADIAN ECONOMY

Economic nationalism flourished during the Trudeau era. The Liberal government introduced many new policies and laws that would limit foreign investment in the Canadian economy. These initiatives decreased foreign ownership from 36 percent to 26 percent between 1970 and 1981.

1   Foreign Investment Review Agency (1974)

This agency was established to screen foreign investment entering Canada. Any takeover of a Canadian company or the starting of a foreign-owned business first had to be approved by the Foreign Investment Review Agency (FIRA). The government emphasized that FIRA was not trying to block or discourage foreign investment. Its purpose was to ensure that foreign investment would have significant benefits for Canada and Canadian citizens. FIRA examined such questions as:

- Will it (takeover or company) provide jobs for Canadians?
- Will there be additional exports?
- Will it improve production and industrial efficiency?
- Will Canadians be involved as shareholders or managers?
- Will it promote technological development?
- Will it use Canadian parts and services?
- Will it increase product variety?
- Will this investment be a good thing for Canada?

From May 1974 to August 1982, approximately 3865 investment applications were examined. Of these, 293 were rejected and 3572 were considered beneficial to Canada.

FIRA was resented by Americans and some Canadian business leaders who believed in economic expansion. Provincial governments were worried that FIRA might cut off the flow of much-needed money for resource industries. Therefore, the provinces pressed Ottawa to give them input into the review of potential foreign investors.

2   Canada Development Corporation (1972)

As early as 1963, Walter Gordon, finance minister in the Pearson government, had suggested setting up the Canada Development Corporation (CDC). It was almost ten years before the idea was carried out. The aim of the CDC was to help develop and maintain strong companies that are controlled and managed by Canadians.

The CDC was given $250 million by the Canadian government to invest in Canadian companies. It also raised money by selling shares to the Canadian people. Sixty-five percent of the CDC is owned by the government and the remaining 35 percent is owned by Canadian investors. The CDC has invested in private Canadian companies that deal in petrochemicals, mining, gas pipelines, and pharmaceutical products. In 1980, the CDC was worth $3 billion.

3   Special Laws

The federal and provincial governments passed specific laws regarding foreign ownership of certain important industries. For example, no more than 25 percent of Canadian banks could be owned by non-Canadians. Only companies with at least 8 percent Canadian ownership could be granted television or radio broadcasting licences. Direct government participation in rail and air transportation, nuclear energy, and Arctic oil and gas exploration was another way of maintaining Canadian control in important economic areas. The government of Saskatchewan took steps to buy back American-owned potash mines in the province. Potash is used in fertilizer, and one of the world's largest deposits of potash is in Saskatchewan. Since 1976 the government-owned Potash Corporation of Saskatchewan (PCS) has bought 34 percent of the potash industry in Saskatchewan. In 1971 in Ontario the government granted the book publishers, McClelland and Stewart Limited, a million dollar loan in order to keep the business Canadian-owned. This was done to keep one of the two remaining large Canadian publishing companies under Canadian control.

4   Special Income Tax Deductions

To encourage investment in Canadian-owned industries, citizens were allowed to make an income tax deduction on profits earned in these companies.

THE ENERGY CRISIS

In the summer of 1979 many American states faced severe gasoline shortages. Signs saying "Out of Gas" became a common sight in many service stations. Where there was a supply of gasoline, strict rationing had to be enforced. Lineups at the gas pumps often stretched for blocks as weary motorists waited to buy their $5 limit. Travellers were sometimes stranded on American highways and some trucking companies could not operate their vehicles because of lack of fuel.

Until the early 1970s, Canada and the United States had taken all forms of energy (oil, gas, electricity, coal) very much for granted. North Americans were the greatest energy consumers in the world, and both Canada and the United States were major energy producers. But in 1973 the Organization of Petroleum Exporting Countries (OPEC) began to limit the export of oil and increase its price. Forbidding foreign ships to enter or to leave a port is called an embargo. At the height of this Arab oil embargo, Canada was shipping 1.3 billion barrels of oil daily to the United States. During this crisis, the Canadian government reexamined its reserves. Canadians were shocked to find out that Canada was not the oil-rich nation we thought it was.

Experts predicted that Canadian oil supplies would not be adequate to meet future home needs. In 1975 the Canadian government established a crown oil company – Petro Canada. Petro Canada profits, made from the sale of gasoline to Canadian consumers, were pumped back into exploration for oil and gas for future generations. The government felt that a Canadian-owned petroleum industry would allow the huge petroleum profits to stay in Canada.

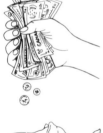

People called continentalists on both sides of the border argued that Canadian energy resources should be shared with the United States. Since Canada and the United States make up North America, they believed the riches of the continent should be shared. Continentalists also believed in free trade. That is, all goods, including energy, should travel freely over the border without being taxed.

The Liberal government, however, held a different point of view. At the risk of upsetting our American neighbours, the government decided to phase out our oil exports. The export level of oil to the United States was therefore reduced as of January 1975 to 800 000 barrels a day. In 1976 the allowable amount was set at 460 000 barrels daily, and in 1977 it was reduced to 260 000 barrels a day. Americans at first found it hard to adjust to this policy. They were accustomed to importing Canadian oil at low prices. They found it difficult to understand and accept Canada's export policies. Canada was of course ready to help the United States with energy in times of emergency. During the severe winter of 1976–1977, Canada approved additional exports of oil and gas to the United States on an emergency basis.

An example of co-operation between Canada and United States in energy resource sharing was the northern gas pipeline agreement of 1977.

After weeks of tough negotiations, Canada and the United States have agreed on a gas pipeline route to bring Arctic natural gas to southern markets in the United

States and Canada. Both the National Energy Board in Canada and President Carter in the United States have agreed on the pipeline route beginning at Prudhoe Bay in Alaska. The privately-financed pipeline will wind through Alaska, parts of the Yukon, British Columbia, and Alberta. It will then make its way into the lower forty-eight states. There is the possibility that eventually a spur line (the Demster line) will be built through Dawson to connect to the main pipeline. The Demster line will carry Canadian natural gas from the Mackenzie River delta area. The United States will pay up to a hundred per cent of the cost of the spur line. The builders (Foothills Pipe Lines Limited) will pay property tax to the Yukon of $30 million maximum annually for the life of the pipeline. This tax will pay for any environmental damage done to the land or the livelihood of the native peoples by the construction of the pipeline. Construction will start in the early 1980s. The project will cost around $10 billion.

THE NATIONAL ENERGY POLICY

By 1980 the Canadian "beaver" was feeling threatened again by the energy crisis. The federal government, under the Liberals, introduced the National Energy Policy (NEP), and this made the American "elephant" grumpy. The Americans feared they would be hurt economically by NEP.

The goals of NEP were:

1 To bring about 50 percent Canadian ownership of the Canadian oil and gas industry by 1990.
The oil crisis of the 1970s had awakened Canadians. They suddenly realized that most of the Canadian oil and gas industry was foreign owned. Seventeen of Canada's top twenty-five oil companies were foreign owned, mostly by Americans. These companies accounted for 72 percent of Canadian oil and gas sales. The federal government wanted to get this strategic industry back into the hands of Canadians. Their answer was Petro Canada which would purchase foreign-owned oil and gas firms at a fair market price. In 1981, Petro Canada bought Petrofina and in 1982 it purchased BP Canada.

2 To make Canada self-sufficient in energy by 1990.
Oil production would be increased until it was no longer necessary for Canada to buy oil from anybody else. At the same time, oil consumption would be reduced by the development of alternate sources of energy.

" HOWDY NEIGHBOR — YA'LL SPARE A CUP OF ENERGY ? "

3   To have a made-in-Canada oil price.

The government did not want Canadians to be at the mercy of fluctuating world oil prices. Oil prices had risen from $3 a barrel in 1973 to over $40 a barrel in 1980. The federal government wanted the price Canadians paid for oil to be below the price charged by the OPEC.

Details of the NEP incensed many Americans. The US-controlled multinationals argued that the new high taxes imposed on them made it unprofitable to continue oil exploration. They retaliated by pulling many of their drilling rigs out of Canada. The drop in oil and gas exploration increased unemployment in the Canadian West.

The American ambassador to Canada openly attacked NEP. He felt that non-Canadian oil companies were being discriminated against. He charged that incentives given to Canadian-owned firms decreased the value of American-owned branch plants.

To many Americans, NEP was the latest and most anti-American initiative introduced by the Canadian government. FIRA, CDC, and now NEP were seen as unfriendly actions to take against a neighbour and ally.

DIGGING DEEPER

1   Compare FIRA and NEP in an organizer. Criteria for comparison could include:

- aims
- methods
- similarities
- differences
- successes
- failures
- supporters
- opponents

2   The issue of Canada's relationship with the United States has been an important theme in Canadian history. Prepare a timeline outlining the relationship. On your timeline, note the periods when Canadian-American relations were a critical issue in Canadian history. Indicate on the timeline when Canadian-American relations were friendly and when they were strained.

3   Research the Auto Pact. Find out why the pact was seen as necessary and how it was meant to work. Who benefits most from the pact? Why?

In 1977 a special government study made some serious criticisms of the Auto Pact. Discover what these criticisms were. Where do the major political parties stand on this issue?

4   Some people have suggested that as a way of strengthening the Canadian economy, individuals and governments should buy Canadian products whenever possible. How would a "Buy Canadian" policy benefit the country? Examine your own buying pattern over the last year. When faced with the choice of a Canadian-made or foreign-made product, which did you buy?

Plan a "Buy Canadian" project to make the whole school aware of what you have discovered.

5   Discuss Trudeau's comment that living next door to the United States is like sleeping with an elephant. Do you think this is an accurate description of the two countries and their relationship? Why?

42
Canadian-American Relations in Mulroney's Canada

MULRONEY: THE BOY FROM BAIE-COMEAU

In 1984, after a walk in an Ottawa snowstorm, Pierre Trudeau decided to resign from public office and return to private life in Montreal. At the Liberal party convention, delegates elected John Turner to be the leader of the Liberals. As the Liberals were in office, he also became the prime minister of Canada. Turner had been a minister of Finance in Trudeau's Cabinet in the 1970s, but had resigned to return to a Bay Street law firm.

The Conservative party had also changed its leader. Many Conservatives blamed Joe Clark's ineptitude for the defeat in the House of Commons and for their ability to win only one seat in Quebec in the last election. Brian Mulroney, a bilingual Quebecker from Baie-Comeau, won the leadership of the Conservative party in a bitterly contested leadership convention.

After only a few months in office, John Turner called a general election for 4 September 1984. Thus, the stage was set for Canadians to choose between two new leaders.

The key to the Conservative election strategy was to win a large number of seats in Quebec. With ninety-five seats at stake, Quebec held the key to an election victory for the Conservatives. For the first time in the history of the Progressive Conservative party, it looked like they might stand a chance in Quebec. It had a bilingual, Roman Catholic, native-born Quebecker as its leader.

The history of the Conservative party in Quebec is erratic. Sir John A. Macdonald had a strong French-English coalition in Quebec, but it disappeared in 1885 when he signed Louis Riel's death warrant. Then, Quebec gave its support to a native Quebecker and Liberal, Wilfrid Laurier. Briefly, in 1958, Diefenbaker and the Conservatives had swept to power in the province, but this did not last for long. French-Canadian ministers held only minor portfolios and exercised little power or influence in the Diefenbaker government. Diefenbaker's policy of "hyphenated Canadianism" seemed to mean assimilation by the English majority. Quebec support for the Conservatives plummeted to 14 seats in 1962 and to only 8 seats in 1963.

From 1963 to 1984, the Liberals controlled Quebec federally. This support was bolstered by another native-born Quebecker, Pierre Trudeau. The challenge facing Mulroney was to establish the Conservative party in his own province.

Television debates played an important role in the election campaign of 1984. One of the debates was organized by the National Action Committee on the Status of Women. It forced the party leaders to focus on issues of grave concern to Canadian women, such as equal pay for work of equal value. In another of the debates, held in French, Mulroney's clear stand on language rights convinced Quebeckers that Mulroney was one of them and Turner was not.

Prime Minister Brian Mulroney

On election day, Canadians expressed their preference for the Conservatives in resounding terms. They gave an overwhelming majority of 211 seats to the Conservatives, the largest electoral victory in Canadian history. In Quebec, Mulroney's Conservatives surpassed the Diefenbaker sweep of 1958 by winning 58 seats. Now there was a government in power in Ottawa with elected representatives from all parts of the country. The Liberal party, which had dominated the national political scene for so long, was left in tatters. The Liberals barely survived nationally. They won only 40 seats. The New Democratic Party, led by Ed Broadbent, won 30 seats.

The Progressive Conservative government's first goal after assuming power in 1984 was to establish better relations with the United States. Americans had not always reacted favourably to Canadian policy decisions.

THE DEFENCE OF A CONTINENT

Star Wars

Canada's defence policy is dominated by a fact of geography – we share the North American continent with a superpower. Canadians and Americans co-operate in the defence of the two nations. But, the superior American military might has meant that the United States plays a dominant role. In 1957, Canadians and Americans formed the North American Air Defence Agreement (NORAD) which integrates the air forces of the two nations. Although there have been some problems with NORAD, most notably during the Cuban Missile Crisis and the Vietnam War, in general it has worked well. Our defence relationship with the US has even extended to letting Americans test unarmed cruise missiles in northern Alberta.

However, the joint defence of North America took on new dimensions when President Reagan announced the Strategic Defence Initiative (SDI), more commonly known as Star Wars. Reagan proposed to spend billions of dollars on an inter-continental ballistic missile system (ICBM). SDI was a highly sophisticated defence system to protect the United States against an enemy nuclear attack. Star Wars was a defence shield against nuclear weapons.

The Mulroney government was troubled about the course of action to take. Should Canada participate in Star Wars research? Would a refusal affect the friendly relations the government was trying so hard to develop? Would participation in Star Wars create jobs in Canada? Would our membership in the North American

Aerospace Defence Command (formerly NORAD) commit us to participate in SDI?

The issue was resolved when the US government said they did not expect Canada to participate officially in Star Wars research. However, they were pleased when Mulroney promised that no barriers would be put in the way of private Canadian companies who wanted to bid on SDI contracts.

The Polar Sea

In 1985, the US Coast Guard icebraker, the *Polar Sea*, crossed the Arctic waters of the Northwest Passage. It sailed through the passage from Greenland to the Beaufort Sea and Alaska. Its mission was unspecified research for the United States Navy.

Canada claimed the Northwest Passage as internal waters. Any nation wishing to sail through this passage needed to have Canadian permission. However, the United States simply informed Canada that they would sail through these waters. Ottawa took no action about the intrusion onto Canadian territory.

Both governments were surprised by the public outcry in Canada. Even if most Canadians live in a thin, heavily populated strip along the US border, the North has a special place in their hearts and their minds. Canadians saw the *Polar Sea* incident as a challenge to our sovereignty over the Arctic waters. The Mulroney government responded to public pressure and began to talk about building a polar icebreaker, stepping up patrol flights in the Far North, and drawing new boundary maps that would define Canada's sovereignty in the area more clearly.

At a 1987 summit meeting between Mulroney and Reagan, the Americans offered to make a concession of Canada's claim to Arctic sovereignty. The Americans would uphold Canada's ownership of the Northwest Passage against all nations except the United States. That meant American ships and aircraft would be free to roam through Canada's Northwest Passsage at will.

Acid Rain

Another problem between the neighbours was the increasing concern over acid rain. Acid rain is caused by emissions of sulphur dioxide from factories, refineries, and other industrial plants. Acid rain destroys our environment by killing the fish in our lakes and rivers and killing our forests. Acid rain can also harm our health. The toxic chemicals associated with acid rain can contaminate our drinking water and can work their way into our food chain.

Canadians treasure our natural landscape, captured in the renowned paintings of the Group of Seven. Now they are watching in horror as these same lakes and forests die from acid rain. In 1985, the annual emission of sulphur dioxide in Canada was 4.8 million t, however, in the United States it was 24 million t. Some of the acid rain that falls in Canada is produced by our industries. But, more than half comes from the industrial smokestacks of the northeastern and midwestern United States.

Neither the Liberals nor Conservatives have had much success in persuading the Americans to do anything about acid rain. In 1982, Canada proposed a 50 percent reduction in sulphur emissions. The proposed reductions would protect many ecosystems. However, nothing concrete has emerged from this proposal. The Reagan Administration was unwilling to antaganize "big business" interests by demanding expensive pollution controls. American companies threatened to close their factories if they were forced to install pollution controls. The American government bowed under this threat.

The American government did not promise to take any steps to reduce sulphur dioxide emissions. This poison would continue to pour over our border killing our environment. Their only promise was to do more research on acid rain. The Canadian government appeared unable or unwilling to jeopardize American friendship over this environmental issue.

FREE TRADE: AN IDEA WHOSE TIME HAS COME?

Under a variety of names, free trade with the United States has been talked about for more than a century.

1854 British Reciprocity Treaty with the United States is thought to have brought economic benefits to Upper and Lower Canada.

1865 US cancels Reciprocity Treaty. This helps to push the British North American colonies toward Confederation.

1911 Election fought on reciprocity issue. Laurier's Liberal government negotiates a reciprocity agreement on natural products. The Conservatives and "big business," who fear the market would be flooded with cheaper American goods, defeat the Liberals. Reciprocity is seen as a threat to economic and political sovereignty.

1935 Canada and the United States sign a trade treaty that reduced tariffs on a large number of items.

1947 The King Liberal government secretly negotiates a massive trade agreement with the United States. However, King changes his mind at the last minute and cancels the deal.

1965 The Auto Pact allows free trade in automobiles and parts between Canada and the US. It guarantees an increased number of jobs in the auto industry in Canada.

1985 Brian Mulroney announces, in the House of Commons, that Canada will try to negotiate a free-trade agreement with the United States.

FREE TRADE WITH THE UNITED STATES

In September 1985, Mulroney took a large step toward improving relations with the United States. He proposed solidifying the trade and economic links between the two countries in a binding form. He wanted free trade between Canada and the United States. Mulroney wanted to negotiate "the broadest possible package of mutually beneficial reductions in tariff and non-tariff barriers between the two countries." It was a gamble, but it could offer enormous benefits. Free trade was certain to be one of the great issues of the mid-1980s. It would also be one of the major issues in the success or failure of Mulroney's Conservative government.

By mid–1987, the battle lines in Canada were clearly drawn over whether we should enter any kind of free-trade deal with the United States. On one side, were groups and individuals who favoured the deal. They included most of Canada's large and small businesses, the Canadian Chamber of Commerce, financial institutions, most of the provincial premiers, the Royal Commission of Economic Union and Development Prospects for Canada, and the Canadian Consumers' Association. The forces against free trade consisted of nationalists, pensioners, unions, churches, womens' groups, and ordinary citizens. What were the positions of both sides?

Free trade
- Trade is vital
- America is our best cus-
  tomer
- To deal with US protection-
  ism
- More productivity
- More jobs
- More benefits for consumers
- Free trade works elsewhere
- More foreign investment

No free trade
- Free trade benefits only "big
  business"
- Free trade would swamp the
  Canadian marketplace
- Loss of jobs
- Lost investment
- Threat to social programs
- Threat to Canadian culture
- Threat to political sover-
  eignty

Support for free trade by region February 1986				
	Atlantic Canada	Quebec	Ontario	West
		(percentage)		
Agree	57	53	45	65
Disagree	26	34	45	25
No opinion	17	13	10	10

The Eleventh-Hour Agreement

January 1988 was the deadline for a free-trade deal between the
United States and Canada. To meet this date, a draft proposal had
to be ready by 3 October 1987. With the two chief negotiators,
Simon Reisman of Canada and Peter Murphy of the United States,
so far apart on so many issues, many people thought the deal
would never be ready. If the deal was not worked out by that time,
the US Congress would not have the necessary sixty working days
to suggest changes or amendments.

Just thirteen days before the deadline, Reisman walked out of
the negotiations. He said the talks were dead as it was impossible
to work out a deal. This dramatic, grandstanding move shocked
the Americans. They urged Canada to reopen negotiations.

Trade Minister Pat Carney, Finance Minister Michael Wilson,
and the prime minister's chief of staff were sent to Washington for
frantic last-minute negotiations. Minutes before the midnight
deadline, it was announced that Canada and the United States
had reached an agreement-in-principle.

WILL THIS BRAIN, REMAIN...?

Some of the major points of the deal were:

- **Elimination of tariffs** The two countries would eliminate tariffs starting 1 January 1989.
- **Dispute-settlement mechanism** A five-member panel, with at least two members from each nation, would be established. The panel would discuss any issues causing trade problems between Canada and the US.
- **US investment in Canada** Canada relinquished the right to screen, prevent, or impose any restrictions on US investment in Canada. American investors would no longer be required to protect Canadian jobs or to conduct research in Canada.
- **Energy** The United States has unlimited access to Canadian oil, gas, and electricity. Some experts predict that an American decline in production of oil and gas will raise American dependence on foreign petroleum from 30 percent to between 50 to 60 percent in the 1990s.

    Americans may need Canada's energy sources to keep their industries producing. Even if Canada starts to run out of energy resources, we must provide America with a proportional amount of what is available.
- **Agriculture** All tariffs on agricultural products and processed foods would be eliminated over a ten-year period.

As soon as the continental trade deal was announced, the debate in Canada began. Provincial leaders in Quebec, Saskatchewan, Alberta, and British Columbia were quick to give their support. The agreement opened the door for Quebec to make huge sales of hydro-electric power to the northeastern United States. Western producers of oil and gas and hogs and cattle welcomed the chance to sell their products freely on the American market.

Provincial premiers in Manitoba, Ontario, and Prince Edward Island voiced opposition to the deal. The premier of Manitoba, Howard Pawley, believed the deal would permit greater foreign ownership of Canadian resources. Among the potential losers in Ontario were the grape growers and wine makers, the music-recording industry, food processing plants, and the auto parts industry.

Since the Canada-US Auto Pact was signed in 1965, US manufacturers had to have 60 percent of their parts and labour produced by Canadians. If this criterion was not met, they could not ship their cars to Canada duty free. The new provisions would allow cars to enter the country duty free with only 50 percent Canadian parts and labour.

Prime Minister Mulroney promised public hearings and an open debate in Parliament on the free-trade proposal. Canadians faced months of discussion about free trade.

In many ways the debate was similar to the one that occurred over Reciprocity in 1911. It is true that the politicians have changed their coats – in 1911 the Liberals were advocating free trade and the Conservatives were opposing it – but the arguments have remained virtually the same. In the 1980s, people who believed in free trade saw it as the key to Canadian economic prosperity. Finance Minister Michael Wilson called free-trade opponents "weak" and "dominated by fear." In 1911, Laurier had attacked his critics saying their views "were based on self-interest and fear for the future of the country."

The 1911 reciprocity opponents warned of possible American takeover. They advised that Canada should have "no truck or trade with the Yankees." In 1987, Liberal leader John Turner warned that the country was being "sold down river" as a result of free trade. Ed Broadbent, leader of the NDP, claimed that he "feared for the future of the nation" if this agreement came into place.

Laurier's campaign for free trade was hurt when important Americans fed the fear some Canadians had of the deal. One prominent American politician talked about the day when the American flag would fly over all of North America including the North Pole.

Canadian free-trade negotiator Simon Reisman and his US counterpart Peter Murphy

In the 1987 debate, US Trade Representative Clayton Yeutter told Congress that Americans gave very little and gained a lot from the deal. Also, President Reagan predicted that there would be an economic boom after the free-trade deal similar to the boom produced by the union of the Thirteen Colonies. Reagan called the free-trade deal a "new economic constitution for North America."

Critics of free trade seized upon these comments. To them, they were proof that free trade would be dangerous for Canadian economic and political independence. Turner warned Canadians that Reagan was really saying "The Canadian economy is being taken over by the American economy."

There are important differences in the Reciprocity debate of 1911 and the free-trade debate in the 1980s. When Canadians rejected reciprocity in 1911, they knew they could rely on the British Empire for trade. After all, for most of our history, Canada did far more trade with Britain than with the United States. But, in 1988, times and conditions have changed. Canadians have almost three times as much trade with the US as with the rest of the world combined. The British have developed strong economic ties with the European Economic Community. Britain is no longer interested or able to take Canada freely into its market.

Some experts warn that no trade deal may be worse than this deal. They believe that if either Parliament or the US Congress rejects the deal, a trade war between the two countries would follow. With protectionism being so strong in America, the US will probably erect higher and higher trade barriers and Canada would retaliate.

Laurier once predicted that the twentieth century would be the century of Canada and Canadian development. In 1911, some people believed that Canada would never live up to Laurier's prediction because reciprocity failed. In 1987, Mulroney hoped that Canada would use the free-trade agreement to reach its full economic potential.

DEVELOPING SKILLS:
SAMPLING PUBLIC OPINION

An opinion survey is an excellent way to discover what the public thinks about a local or national issue or personality. The popularity of governments is often polled. Sometimes the government will use this information to decide when to call an election or how to proceed on a sensitive issue, such as capital punishment or free trade. Polls only indicate what people feel at the exact time they are asked the question. Questions sometimes lead people to give an answer that does not truly reflect their feelings on an issue. Polls are supposed to be accurate to within four percentage points either way. So, if the sample is large enough, the poll will be fairly accurate.

Here are the steps to follow in planning and writing an opinion survey.

1   Decide what kind of information you want to collect. Suppose you want to discover whether Canadians agree or disagree with free trade with the United States.

2   Decide who your target audience will be and how large a group you would like to survey.

3   When you prepare your questions make sure
   • They will give you the answers you're searching for.
   • The wording is clear, precise, and simple.
   • They are arranged in a logical order.
   • They are worded so they do not offend anyone (bias, race, religion, or sex).

4   Decide whether to ask open or closed questions. Most opinion surveys use closed questions as they are the simplest and easiest to analyse. A closed question gives the survey participants the answers and asks them to choose one. An example of a closed question is:

Should Canada seek a free-trade agreement with the United States?

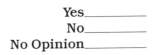

The third option (don't care, don't know, or no opinion) will make your survey more accurate. If only presented with two options, participants might choose one of them even though they really don't have an opinion. If the vast majority of respondents express no opinion, you will know that the question is not an issue. You can then eliminate it from your survey.

5   Make sure there are no problems with your survey. Ask several friends or classmates to answer the questions. Are the questions too long and complicated? Is the survey too long?

6   Prepare your final draft. Pay special attention to its overall appearance. It should be typed neatly and well-spaced on the page. Directions should be clear.

7   Conduct your opinion survey.

8   Tabulate your answers. Transfer the information from all the answer sheets onto a single work sheet, called a tally sheet. Double check your results. Accuracy is essential.

9 Prepare tables and graphs to present your information in a form that is easy to analyse.

You can also display your information in a bar graph or a pie graph.

A series of public-opinion surveys were carried out on the issue of free trade between 1984 and 1986. The results are shown here. As a class, update this information by conducting a similar opinion poll. You may wish to ask probing questions about the free-trade issue (e.g. loss of jobs, US political takeover of Canada).

	For	Free trade Against	Uncertain
		(percentage)	
April 1984	78	17	5
June 1985	65	30	5
November 1985	58	31	11
February 1986	54	35	11
June 1986	52	36	12

Pat Carney

Prime Minister Brian Mulroney chose Trade Minister Pat Carney to oversee the free-trade negotiations with the United States. This made Carney the most important woman in the Cabinet and one of the most powerful Cabinet ministers in the Mulroney government.

Pat Carney has had a remarkable career. She was the first woman business columnist for a large Vancouver newspaper. After she left journalism, Carney started her own successful consulting business in Yellowknife. She was first elected to the House of Commons in 1980. Carney was the first female Conservative elected to Parliament from British Columbia.

Pat Carney caused her first stir in Ottawa when she refused to take her seat in the House of Commons. As a single parent with a fourteen-year-old son she wanted to use the free airline pass granted to MPs spouses for her son. The rules would not permit this alteration. However, her boycott of the House prompted a changing of the rules.

Carney has often been attacked by the opposition for her role in negotiations. As minister of Energy, Mines, and Resources, the opposition believed she favoured big oil companies over the provinces. She came under attack again when the Americans increased the tariff on "shakes and shingles." The opposition believed she was soft on the US.

Pat Carney has proved herself to be a tough, able politician by defending her policies in the House of Commons. Some people see Pat Carney as a future prime minister of Canada.

DIGGING DEEPER

1   Use an organizer to compare the viewpoints of each political party on free trade. Your research should focus on the ninety-day review period between 4 October 1987 and 3 January 1988.

2   Imagine you are a member of a Canada-US committee studying the affects of acid rain on the environment. What recommendations would you make to your government?

3   Nuclear weapons are a major issue of the late twentieth century. Do you support the development of nuclear weapons? Do you think SDI is a valuable system? Why?

43
Developing Our Canadian Identity

How does the United States affect your life? To what extent is your lifestyle influenced by patterns that have been "made in the USA"? Do you resent this influence, or do you welcome it? Make a profile of your tastes and attitudes by answering the following questions. The results will help to show you how much the United States influences your life. What do you think the results will show?

Favourite movie of the last year

Favourite actress

Favourite actor

Two favourite television programs

Favourite television news program

TV channel watched most often

Radio station listened to most often

Favourite musical group

Favourite female singer

Favourite male singer

Two favourite magazines

Make of family car

Favourite professional hockey team

Favourite female athlete

Favourite male athlete

Most admired political figure, living or dead

Most admired woman

Most admired man

City in North America you would most like to visit

Place you spent your last vacation

Favourite breakfast cereal

Favourite brand of jeans

Favourite professional football team

Analyse your responses to the questionnaire.

a) Go through your answers and sort out which are American and which are Canadian.
b) How "American" is your lifestyle? How do you feel about this? Why?

c) What answers revealed you to be "Canadian"? Suggest possible reasons for this.

d) How "Americanized" do you think Canadian life is? Suggest reasons for this.

e) Do you think the results of your questionnaire will be different ten years from now? Why?

Culture consists of everything that we believe, do, and make. It includes all the ideas, religious beliefs, and knowledge that has been gained through time. It involves everything we create and pass on to future generations. It contains all the things we have made – our technology, buildings, cities, poems, and games. In other words, our culture includes art, music, religion, language, work, play – everything that makes one group of people different from another.

In a Canadian high-school literature class, a student was asked to identify Margaret Laurence and Earle Birney, two of Canada's most popular writers. The student replied, "Never heard of them. They must be Canadian." This remark tells us a lot about Canada's culture. Nowhere else in the world is the culture of one country so dominated by another as is Canada's by that of the United States.

Consider the following facts that illustrate the American cultural influence on Canada. Three out of every four books and magazines bought in Canada are foreign (mostly American). Only 4 percent of the records sold in Canada have Canadian content. Ninety-seven percent of screen time across the country is booked for American and a sprinkling of other foreign films. Three out of every four hours of television watched by Canadians are taken up with American programs.

Now consider the American domination of one aspect of your life – television. Research scientists have estimated that in your first eighteen years you will have watched 20 000 hours of television. This means that before you graduate from high school, you will have spent many more hours in front of television sets than you have spent in the classroom. If you are typical of Canadians, 15 000 of those hours will be spent watching American programs. To put it another way, for almost three hours of each and every day of your life, you have been exposed to American culture and American values.

Many Canadians argue that they prefer American shows. Of course, with a population ten times the size of Canada, American producers can afford to spend much more money on television production. Their programs are often slicker and, therefore, more appealing to the audiences. However, American television can have a tremendous impact on our lives. If we spend most of our time watching American shows, it follows that we will learn more about American society and become more like Americans. Canadians might begin to look on our society as if it were American. American values might become our values. Canadian society might gradually be taken over by the United States. Culturally we could cease to exist as a separate nation.

Canadian nationalists have worried about the effect of American television on Canadian life. The government has already taken steps to tackle the problem. In 1968 the Canadian Radio-Television and Telecommunications Commission (CRTC) was set up to supervise radio and television broadcasting in Canada. This government agency issued broadcasting licences to Canadian-owned companies. It made sure that 60 percent of prime-time television (6:30–11:00 p.m.) and 30 percent of AM radio were Canadian in content. Commercials were limited to twelve minutes per hour. Cable television was seen as a major cause of

Top TV shows: English   A typical winter week, 1986.

Show	Audience (in millions)
COSBY SHOW	Foreign
FAMILY TIES	Foreign
WALT DISNEY	Foreign
DALLAS	Foreign
CHEERS	Foreign
NIGHT COURT	Foreign
HIGHWAY TO HEAVEN	Foreign
MISS TEEN CANADA	Canadian
NEWHART	Foreign
KATE & ALLIE	Foreign
A TEAM	Foreign
MIAMI VICE	Foreign
CBC NATIONAL NEWS	Canadian
FRAGGLE ROCK	Canadian
REMINGTON STEELE	Foreign
CBC JOURNAL	Canadian
HOCKEY NIGHT IN CANADA	Canadian
BEACHCOMBERS	Canadian
TOMMY HUNTER	Canadian
PETER USTINOV'S RUSSIA	Canadian

Audience (in millions)

Canadian programs   Foreign programs

Source: Vital Links, Canadian Cultural Industries, April 1987

Top TV shows: French   A typical winter week, 1986

Show	
PEAU DE BANANE	
LA BONNE AVENTURE	
POIVRE ET SEL	
EPOPÉE ROCK	
ENTRE CHIEN ET LOUP	
MONTRÉAL EN DIRECT	
L'ÂME SOEUR	
LES DESSOUS D'HOLLYWOOD	
LE CRIME D'OVIDE PLOUFFE	
LES DEUX FONT LA PARE	
L'OR DU TEMPS	
SAMEDI DE RIRE	
RSVP	
PAUL, MARIE ET LES ENFANTS	
POP EXPRESS	
LE PARC DES BRAVES	
DALLAS	
MAGNUM PI	
CHACUN CHEZ-SOI	
M. LE MINISTRE	

Audience (in millions)

■ Canadian programs   ▨ Foreign programs

American domination. When cable television moved into an area, people were able to watch more American shows. The number of people watching Canadian shows went down. Since $50 million was being spent by Canadian companies advertising on US border stations, in 1976 the Canadian government took action. They passed a law that stopped Canadian advertisers from deducting from their income tax the cost of advertising on American television.

The electronic media probably had more impact on Canadians that any other form of Americn influence. Radio and television flooded Canada with American programs and advertising. The CRTC was the government's attempt to increase the amount of Canadian content in the media.

WHAT IS THE CANADIAN NATIONAL IDENTITY?

Foreigners often have trouble distinguishing Canadians from Americans. Yet Canadians travelling overseas do not like to be mistaken for Americans. They usually wear a maple leaf symbol on their jacket or backpack to identify themselves as Canadians. *What makes Canadians different from Americans? What is the Canadian national identity?*

Suppose your school was twinned with a school in a newly independent nation in Africa. Your principal has asked your class to put together some sort of presentation about Canada that could be sent to the African school. The audio-visual presentation should describe for the Africans what Canada and Canadians are like. You should try to make clear to the Africans how Canadians differ from Americans. You should show some elements of the Canadian national identity. The following comments will help you put together your presentation on the Canadian identity.

The Land One of the strongest feelings uniting Canadians is the land itself. The vastness and grandeur of the landscape is distinctively Canadian. Although more than half of the population live in cities of over 100 000, the land is still an inescapable influence. Even the city dweller does not have far to travel to get back to the open and rugged beauty of the land.

Tom Thomson and the Group of Seven were the first artists to express in their paintings the Canadian feeling for the land. Their art expressed what many Canadians felt – a sense of belonging to the rugged northern environment we call Canada.

Take a look at the coins and paper currency of Canada and the United States. The Americans have on their money pictures of national heroes, monuments, or symbols of power and authority, such as the eagle with bolts of lightning in its talons. Canadians, on the other hand, picture the land – prairies, mountains, rivers, schooners, moose, beavers, and loons.

Regional Differences Canada is a large country, one of the world's largest, but nature has subdivided it into many regions. Each of these regions retains certain unique features and claims strong loyalties from those who live there. Regional differences are often visible. Westerners and Maritimers complain about the people in prosperous central Canada. Central Canada ignores these comments, except to come back with an occasional joke about "Newfies" or Westerners. People in northern Ontario mutter about "Hogtown" (Toronto) in the south – unless of course they have already moved there themselves. Maritimers sometimes feel forgotten; Westerners think they are ignored by Ottawa. There are English Canadians who grumble that the country is being run by the French, and there are French Canadians who gripe that business is dominated by the English.

The People The most distinctive feature of Canadian society is that it is the joining together of French and English. The two official languages and cultures of the founding nations have con-

David Crombie, secretary of State, presents citizenship papers to a new Canadian.

tinued to survive side-by-side. The American humourist Henry Morgan lived for a while in Canada. The biggest difference he noticed between Canada and the United States was the bilingual characteristic. "I have been here for almost ten weeks now and the only difference I've found is that when you pick up a jar that says 'peanut butter' the other side says 'beurre d'arachides.' " Many people think it is this official bilingual and bicultural quality of Canada that will save it from being swallowed up by the United States. They feel that French-Canadian culture makes Canada unique and helps protect the Canadian identity from American influence.

Because two official languages already existed in Canada, more recent immigrants have kept many aspects of their cultural heritage. Government policy has encouraged them to keep customs brought from their homelands. We sometimes call this the Canadian "mosaic." A mosaic is made by placing small pieces of tile or glass in mortar. Canadian society is a mosaic because people from different lands contribute a variety and richness to the whole country, but remain distinct. In Canada the many languages and

Expo '86, Vancouver

cultures do not weaken the Canadian identity, but in fact make it strong and unique. Support is growing among English-speaking Canadians for bilingualism. A 1986 poll showed that a majority of English-speaking people supported bilingualism.

Canadians not Americans In many parts of the world people do not distinguish Canadians from Americans. Yet most Canadians resent being called Americans. Canadians and Americans look much the same and dress similarly. Most of us speak the same language, though the accent might be different. The differences between us are not always evident, but they exist. A recent survey of Canadians and Americans suggested that Canadians are more trusting, less sexist, more optimistic, and happier than Americans.

There is the touch of anti-Americanism in our Canadian identity. Canadians worry about American economic control and cultural influence. This feeling goes way back in the history of our country. In the late 1700s, after the American Revolution, many settlers came from the United States to the Maritimes and Ontario. They were known as the United Empire Loyalists because they wished to stay loyal to Britain. They did not want to be Americans. When the Americans briefly invaded Canada during the War of 1812, both English and French fought together to keep their land free of American economic and political control. At the time of Confederation, the Fathers looked closely at the American model of government and decided it was not for Canada. The founders of modern Canada decided in 1867 to keep the British system of government. Unlike the United States, Canada kept the British monarch as head of the new country. It was a deliberate decision that showed the rest of the world that we were not Americans.

Ben Johnson, the world's fastest human, was one of many Canadians who carried the Olympic torch toward Calgary for the 1988 Olympic Games

Sports Sport is the popular form of entertainment that best demonstrates the Canadian spirit. In Canada the most popular sport is hockey. Even the smallest community will build a hockey arena and support a hockey team. The 1987 Canada Cup hockey series illustrated this hockey enthusiasm. In the closing minutes of the last game against the Soviet Union, Canada scored the winning goal and won the Canada Cup. English Canadians, French Canadians and Canadians of all other backgrounds rushed into the streets cheering and shouting, "We beat them!". Bruce Kidd, a former outstanding Canadian world-class runner, has written, "If the CPR held the country together during the early years of Confederation, certainly 'Hockey Night in Canada' has done so in recent years."

Performing Arts (music, dance, drama) The music of Canada has always been part of its identity. The early folksongs were those of the *habitants* and *voyageurs*. In songs they described the routine of the fishermen, the backbreaking toil of the railway builders, and the loneliness of the pioneer settlers. Recently singers such as Gordon Lightfoot and Tom Connors have continued to tell the story of Canada in song. The building of the railroad was the theme of Lightfoot's "Canadian Railroad Trilogy." "The Wreck of the Edmond Fitzgerald" dealt with the loss of a lake freighter on Lake Superior. Stompin' Tom Connors was official Ambasssador of Good Will for Prince Edward Island during its centennial in 1973. Connors sings about the people, places, and things of Canada, such as "Black Donnelly's Massacre," "Bud the Spud," and "Sudbury Saturday Night."

Music has always helped keep alive the distinctive culture of French Canada. Popular singers in Quebec do not simply translate American songs, but write lyrics and compose music that

emphasize the French-Canadian way of life. Gilles Vigneault, in his song "Mon Pays" writes about his feelings for his province. Pauline Julien, and Robert Charlebois each express a strong French-Canadian identity in their music.

Popular singers and groups are also making Canada known elsewhere. Anne Murray, Joni Mitchell, Paul Anka, René Simard, Bryan Adams, Corey Hart, Honeymoon Suite, Glass Tiger, Murray McLaughlin, and The Nylons are well-recognized artists on both sides of the border. Classical performers such as the late Glenn Gould and André Gagnon, Maureen Forrester and Jon Vickers, the Canadian Brass Quintet, and symphony orchestras from several major Canadian cities have won international respect for Canada.

Since World War II more Canadians than ever before have been exposed to theatre in English and French. The theatre scene in Toronto has become one of the most dynamic in North America. New theatre companies such as the Tarragon and Passe Muraille have introduced important Canadian plays to Canadian audiences. Among them have been *1837: The Farmer's Revolt*, a dramatization of the Mackenzie rebellion; *Ten Lost Years*, a picture of life in Canada during the depression; and *Billy Bishop Goes to War*, the story of one of Canada's World War I heroes.

Michel Tremblay has written several plays about the lives of poor French people in Montreal. David Freeman has written about the handicapped in Canadian society. Diane Dupuy is the founder and director of the Famous People Players. This is a

Margaret Laurence, Canadian novelist

troupe composed mainly of mentally handicapped adults. Their touring puppet show won critical acclaim during 1986 on Broadway.

Literary and Visual Arts (literature, painting, sculpture, architecture) Any list of literary and visual artists is bound to leave out more than it includes. Many of our writers and artists have won international recognition for their work.

A unique theme that runs through Canadian literature is "survival." Canadian writers have been fascinated by the idea of people trying to survive in the Canadian environment. Hugh MacLennan and Gabrielle Roy have traced our English and French roots in their novels. Antonine Maillet, an Acadian writer in New Brunswick, has written a moving play about an Acadian charwoman entitled *La Sagounine*. W.O. Mitchell has spoken for the West while Thomas Raddall has spoken for the East. Mordecai Richler has given us Montreal through the eyes of Duddy Kravitz and John Marlyn has portrayed what it was like to be an immigrant growing up in Winnipeg. Pierre Berton has told the tales of the CPR and the Gold Rush days of the Klondike. Modern poets Leonard Cohen, Irving Layton, Raymond Souster, Margaret Atwood, and Earle Birney, to name a few, have given us a picture of Canada in poetic images.

Canadian artists have attracted national and international attention. From French Canada the names include Paul-Emile Borduas and Jean-Paul Riopelle. In English Canada some of the more influential painters include Jack Bush, Harold Towne, Alex Colville, Ken Danby, Robert Bateman, and William Kurelek.

Perhaps no group has contributed more to the Canadian identity than the Native artisans. The Inuit in particular have

Inuit artist at work

portrayed everyday life among their people with soapstone carvings of seal hunts and family scenes.

French-Canadian film makers have continued to thrive, probably because they do not have to compete with English-speaking films from Hollywood. Films made in Quebec have promoted French culture, and have won important Canadian and international awards. Claude Jutra has won attention for his films *Kamouraska* and *Mon Oncle Antoine*. In 1975 Michel Brault's film *Les Ordres* won an important award at the Cannes Film Festival. The following year, *J.A. Martin, Photographe* won the award for the best Canadian film. In 1986, *The Decline of the American Empire* won critical and public acclaim.

The English commercial film industry and the National Film Board have produced some important Canadian films. These include *Goin' Down the Road*, the story of two Maritimers trying to establish themselves in Toronto; *The Battle of Crowfoot*, about an early Blackfoot chief; and *Why Shoot the Teacher*, a story of a teacher in a one-room school in the prairies of the 1930s. In 1985, Sandy Wilson's film, *My American Cousin* won many film awards.

Changing Roles for the Family and Women   In the earlier years of this century, most Canadians lived in "extended" families. That meant that parents and children lived with grandparents, or close to relatives. Aunts, uncles, cousins, and grandparents were usually close by and everyone worked together to make life easier. But times changed. More people moved into cities in search of work and a better living standard. Relatives were gradually left behind. The extended family was replaced by the nuclear family because of changes in society.

In the nuclear family there may be two parents or one. Mothers frequently work outside the home and assist with the financial support of the family. Fathers sometimes take responsibility for raising the children and doing a share of the housework. Noticeable changes have been occurring in the family unit.

The role of women has also changed in Canadian life. Women in Canada today do not struggle for the right to vote or for the freedom to work. Today's struggle is to bring about a change in attitudes and greater opportunities for women to be involved in the mainstream of Canadian society.

For example, according to *Women in the Labour Force, 1975* from 1964 to 1975, the number of Canadian women working increased by 68 percent. Women now make up over 54 percent of the labour force, and more than 10 percent of families are headed by a single parent.

Although the majority of the labour force is female, they tend to face a lot of job discrimination. Women tend to cluster in typically female jobs. For example, based on 1981 census information 97.5 percent of nurses were female, but only 5.5 percent of doctors and surgeons were female. In the financial industry an estimated 93 percent of tellers and cashiers were women, but only 25 percent of people in financial management positions and 1 percent in senior positions were women.

However, this is slowly changing as more and more women enroll in post-secondary and graduate programs. In 1982–1983, women made up 50 percent of the total university enrolments. In 1970–1971, women only made up 37 percent of the student body. Now they have the knowledge and the skills to reach higher positions.

Wage disparity exists in the work force. Frequently women are not paid equal salaries for work of equal value. There has been a $6000 to $17 000 salary gap between men and women doctors.

DIGGING DEEPER

1   What was the most popular television show for French viewers in 1986? What was the most popular show for English viewers in 1986? Where did each show originate? What foreign show is popular with both French- and English-language viewers? Suggest some reasons for the two patterns. What do these findings suggest about the preservation of a truly distinctive Canadian identity?

2   Keep a record of the television viewing habits of your class for a week. What percentage of your viewing was American television? How did your statistics compare with the accompanying graphs?

3   Do you think CRTC Canadian content rules in broadcasting are fair? Explain your answer.

4   What impact does American culture have on other countries? Why is the Canadian experience unique?

5   It has been said that Canadians dislike being mistaken for Americans, but will defend Americans to the British. Why do Canadians work so hard trying to show the rest of the world we are not Americans? Why would Canadians defend Americans to other countries of the world?

6   Do you feel that French Canada helps to protect the Canadian identity from American influence? How?

7   Refer back to the matrix you started at the end of the second unit of study. Now add information for Contemporary Canada. Trace the development of the same themes through this unit.

44
Wrapping It Up

WHAT WOULD LAURIER THINK?

If the ghost of Sir Wilfrid Laurier were to return to Canada today, how do you think he would react? What changes would he notice? What would he think of present-day Canada?

Consider these famous remarks that Laurier made in his lifetime:

> The best and most effective way to maintain friendship with our American neighbours is to be absolutely independent of them.

> My object is to consolidate Confederation and to bring our people, long separated from each other, gradually to become a nation. This is the supreme issue. Everything else is subordinate to that idea.

> The nineteenth century was the century of the United States, the twentieth century will be the century of Canada.

To what extent do you think Laurier was correct when he predicted that the twentieth century would belong to Canada? Would Laurier be happy with the present state of French-English relations in Canada? What would be his opinion of Canadian-American relations today?

DIGGING DEEPER

1 Slogans are brief, catchy phrases that get people excited about an idea. They are important because people use them as rallying cries for all sorts of things, from fighting wars to winning votes for a political party. Here is a list of slogans. Match each slogan with the idea, event, or person that it refers to. After you have done the

matching, choose three of the slogans and discuss what they mean.

Slogans

1	Iron Curtain	a)	Prime Minister Chamber-
2	No truck or trade with the		lain
	Yankees	b)	General De Gaulle
3	The Just Society	c)	Clifford Sifton
4	Maîtres chez nous	d)	Pierre Trudeau
5	Peace in our time	e)	W.L. Mackenzie King
6	The last best west	f)	The Quiet Revolution
7	Vive le Québec libre	g)	The election of 1911
8	Conscription if necessary	h)	Winston Churchill
	but not necessarily		
	conscription		

2 Now that you have discussed these slogans, make a collection of others. Bumper stickers are one place to look. Discuss the collection in class. Which slogans are used most frequently? Classify the collection according to which ones have to do with politics, social problems, and religion.

3 Think back across the Canadian history you have read in this book.

a) Which decade in this century would you most like to live through? Why?

b) What do you think of the times you are living in now?

c) Do you think that this decade will be remembered as one of the most important in Canadian history?

4 Imagine you had the chance to put ten objects into a time capsule to be opened by Canadians in the year 2500 A.D. What would you place in it to show people of the future what life is like today?

5 What do you think Canada will be like in the year 2000? Write a short essay describing your ideas.

6 This text was published in 1988. Prepare a timeline of major events in Canadian history since then. You may decide to use a long roll of paper and put it on the bulletin board of your class-room. Include political, social and economic events as well as any that illustrate the major themes of this book.

7 Styles of art change from one period to another. Make a collec-tion of Canadian art in different periods of this century. Write a short report describing these styles.

8 Make a fashion history of Canada. Collect pictures of clothing styles from Canada's past. Mount the pictures on large sheets of paper and write a short essay to explain the changes and what they reveal about Canadian lifestyles.

9 In groups of five, prepare pantomimes which illustrate dramatic events in Canadian history. Let the rest of the class identify the event being dramatized.

10 Some historians have pointed out that Canada has struggled since its beginning to form a nation independent from the United States. This struggle has continually involved some kind of American challenge and a Canadian response to that challenge. In the period 1860-1880 the Americans seemed to be threatening a political takeover of Canada. This challenge certainly helped to hasten Confederation and our birth as a nation. It also encouraged the building of the CPR and the settlement of the West.

From 1920-1940 there came the American cultural challenge. The influence of the American media was having a growing effect on Canadian styles, sports, and entertainment. From 1950 to the present a strong economic challenge has been felt in Canada.

Do you agree with the "challenge and response" theory? What do you think was the Canadian response to the American cultural and economic challenges?

11 Discuss the truth of the following comment by Wilfrid Laurier: "Compromise created this nation, nothing but compromise will hold it together." Think of as many examples from our history as you can in which compromises have played a part in keeping Canada together.

STOCK MARKET GAME (Answers)

	Cycle 2	Cycle 3	Cycle 4	Cycle 5
Consolidated Mining and Smelting of Canada	$274.00	$575.00	$235.00	$9.50
Winnipeg Electric Light	$85.00	$110.00	$25.00	$2.00
International Nickel	$52.00	$72.50	$29.00	$4.50

Acknowledgements

338 *Duplessis* by Conrad Black. Used by permission of the Canadian Publishers, McClelland and Stewart, Toronto; 147 Henri Bourassa; 269–270 *Six War Years*, copyright © 1974 by Barry Broadfoot; 163, 213, 285 *Ten Lost Years*, copyright © 1973 by Barry Broadfoot; 282 *Years of Sorrow, Years of Shame*, copyright © 1977 by Barry Broadfoot. Reprinted by permission of Doubleday, a division of Bantam, Doubleday, Dell Publishing Group, Inc.; 349 *Why Am I A Separatist* by Marcel Chaput. Reprinted by permission of McGraw-Hill Ryerson Limited; 379–381 *Face to Face* by Solange Chaput-Rolland and Gertrude Laing. Used by permission; 387 *Canada: A Modern Study* by Ramsay Cook, John Saywell, and John Ricker, © 1963 by Irwin Publishing Inc. Permission granted by the publishers; 260 *Hitler and Germany* by B.J. Elliot. Used by permission of Longmans, London; 235–236 *Anne Frank's Diary* Used by permission of Valentine, Mitchell & Co. Ltd., London; 306 *The War Brides* by Joyce Hibbert © 1978 by Peter Martin Associates. Used by permission of Irwin Publishing Inc.; 346 *The True Face of Duplessis* by Pierre Laporte © 1960. Used by permission of Harvest House, Montreal; 142 *The Great War and Canadian Society: an oral history* by Daphne Read. Used by permission of New Hogtown Press, Toronto; 262 Time Capsules/1945, courtesy Time-Life Books Inc.; 393 *Calgary Herald* (UPI), 14 May 1977; 101 *The Kingston Daily Standard*, 20 September 1911. Used by permission of The Whig-Standard; 122 *The Winnipeg Tribune*.

Every effort has been made to trace the original source of material and photographs contained in this book. Where the attempt has been unsuccessful, the publisher would be pleased to hear from the copyright holders to rectify any omission.

Photo Credits

CFP Canadian Forces Photo; CTA City of Toronto Archives; GAI Glenbow-Alberta Institute; MTLB Metropolitan Toronto Library Board; OFL Ontario Federation of Labour; PAC Public Archives of Canada; PAM Provincial Archives of Manitoba; VPL Vancouver Public Library.

4 Toronto Transit Commission, Scarborough Board of Education/ Dennis Broughton; 5 Canada Post Corporation; 12 Office of the Governor General of Canada; 13 Department of the Secretary of State of Canada/Victor Pilon; 16 SSC Photocentre/683905; 18 Office of the Minister of Communications; 23 House of Commons; 29 Ontario Ministry of Housing; 30, 31 Elections Canada; 38 Royal Canadian Mounted Police; 55 Ontario Hydro; 58, 61 PAC; 68 Greenpeace; 71 Wawatay News/Grant Luloff; 77, 78 CTA James Collection; 80 PAC/C14090; 81 PAC/PA10401, CTA James Collection; 88 PAC/C28727; 98 PAC/L1054; 99 PAM; 107, 110, 111 private collection; 113 Royal Canadian Military Institute; 119 PAC/PA1456; 125 Imperial War Museum, London, England; 128 Ontario Archives Toronto/S15042; 130 PAC/PA1654; 132 PAC/PA2614; 133 PAC; 139 Saskatchewan Archives Board/RB8132; 140 CTA; 141 CTA/858; 143 PAC/PA364; 144 Public Archives of PEI/2320–67–9; 146 CTA/736; 148 PAC/C6859; 151 PAC/117663; 157 PAC, PAC, National Museum of Canada, Art Gallery of Ontario; 159 *Regina Leader Post*; 160 The United Church of Canada Archives, Toronto; 166 MTLB; 167 Archives of Ontario; 169 CTA; 173 CTA; 175 MTLB; 176 CTA James Collection/8054; 178 CTA/42; 181 Archives of Ontario; 182 CTA/643; 183 City of Edmonton Archives/EA10–1996; 187 CTA.1902; 188 MTLB; 190 GAI/ND31504; 191 CTA/969B; 192 CTA James Collection/8200; 193 Provincial Archives of Alberta/BI2636/2; 198 CTA/144; 204 CTA/339; 206 Agriculture Canada; 207 PAC/C30811; 212 GAI/NC6–12955b; 213 GAI/A771–3; 214 GAI/ND3–6742, GAI/NA2434–1; 215 CTA; 216 PAC/PA35133; 218 CTA; 222 VPL; 226, 227 MTLB; 228 Archives of Ontario/S801; 232 Archives of Ontario/S4420; 237 MTLB; 243 PAC/C11452; 247 PAC, *The Gazette*, Montréal; 248, 249, 252 CFP; 253 PAC, *The Gazette*, Montréal; 257 Ullstein Bilderdienst, Berlin; 258, 259 CFP; 261 PAC, 262 CFP; 268 CTA James Collection/1390; 270 University of Winnipeg, *The Winnipeg Free Press*; 271 VPL; 273 CP Archives; 277 MTLB, MTLB, PAC/C90883, Library of Congress, Washington, DC; 280 PAC/C46350; 281 VPL; 283 PAC/C24452, VPL; 284 PAC/C47387; 289 Permanent Mission of Canada to the United Nations; 294 PAC/PA129625, *Montréal Star*; 297 MTLB; 299 PAC/PA133333; 301 PAC/PA114544; 305 PAC; 311 Imperial Oil Ltd./3246; 314 Ontario Hydro; 315 Ontario Hydro/D2248; 319 MTLB; 322 PAC/C15160; 324 *The Winnipeg Free Press*; 325 PAC/C36219; 330 MTLB; 331 PAC/C35680; 332 MTLB; 333 "Eagles Assist The Ascension" by Dennis Highway, Toronto Dance Theatre, Andrew Oxenham; 338 PAC/C57897; 340 PAC/C53641 *The Gazette*; 347 MTLB; 350 PAC/PA113485; 352 PAC/PA113484; 353 *Maclean's*; 356 PAC; 357 MTLB; 358 Reprinted with permission, *The Toronto Star*; 365 CFP/WO Vic Johnson; 370 CIDA; 376 MTLB; 377 PAC/PA113488; 378 PAC/PA114389; 383, 387 Canapress; 389 Canadian Government Travel Bureau/S2622; 391 Canapress; 395 MTLB; 406 Canapress; 407, 409, 411, 418 Reprinted with permission, *The Toronto Star*; 421 Department of the Secretary of State of Canada; 424 Ontario Ministry of the Environment, Acid Precipitation Branch; 427 Canadian Alliance for Trade and Job Opportunities; 428 Reprinted with permission, *The Toronto Star*; 429 Canapress; 438 Victor C. Last; 439 Department of the Secretary of State of Canada; 440, 441 Canapress; 442 MTLB; 443 Challé Design Consultants Inc.

Index

Turner, John, 420, 430

Union Nationale, 233
Unions, 340–41
United Nations (UN), 289–93, 298–300,
    364–65
        Emergency Force (UNEF), 300, 364
Urbanization, 82, 329–30

Vanier, Georges, 12, 321
Versailles, Treaty of, 159–61
Vimy Ridge, 124

War Brides, 305–06
War Measures Act, 375–76, 380–81
Warsaw Pact, 298
Wartime Elections Act, 58–9
Wilson, Cairine, 184
Women
        changing roles, 141–44, 184, 444
        discrimination in workplace, 54–5
        in government, 16, 18–9, 65, 421
        in sports, 193
        inequality, 83
        "Persons" case, 183–84
        right to vote, 57–9
        role in World War I, 141–44
        role in World War II, 269–72
        status of women, 421
        suffragists, 143–44

Women's Christian Temperance Union
    (WCTU), 57, 83
World War I
        background, 107–12
        casualties, 122, 145, 150–51
        conscription, 145–50
        cost to Canada, 151–53
        declaration of war, 112
        last hundred days, 126
        peace treaties, 159–161
        total war, 138, 253–55, 272
        unrestricted submarine warfare, 134
        war at sea, 132–34
        war in the air, 128–31
        Western Front, 120–21
World War II
        Canada declares war, 246
        causes, 236–40
        D-Day, 256–57
        Dieppe invasion, 251–52
        effects on Canada, 272–75
        last days of Berlin, 260–61
        total war, 253–55, 269, 272
        turning point, 251–56
        underground, 259
        war in the Pacific, 264–66

Ypres, 121–22